# FINANCE FROM
# KAISER TO FÜHRER

**Recent Titles in**
**Contributions to the Study of World History**

# FINANCE FROM KAISER TO FÜHRER

## Budget Politics in Germany, 1912–1934

C. Edmund Clingan

Contributions to the Study of World History, Number 79

GREENWOOD PRESS
Westport, Connecticut • London

**Library of Congress Cataloging-in-Publication Data**

Clingan, C. Edmund.
    Finance from Kaiser to Führer : budget politics in Germany, 1912–1934 /
    C. Edmund Clingan.
       p. cm.—(Contributions to the study of world history, ISSN 0885–9159 ; no. 79.)
    Includes bibliographical references and index.
    ISBN 0–313–31184–6 (alk. paper)
       1. Budget—Germany—History—20th century.  2. Finance,
  Public—Germany—History—20th century.  I. Title.  II. Series.
HJ2108.C585   2001
336.43′09041—dc21        00–034137

British Library Cataloguing in Publication Data is available.

Library of Congress Catalog Card Number: 00–034137
ISBN: 0–313–31184–6
ISSN: 0885–9159

First published in 2001

Greenwood Press, 88 Post Road West, Westport, CT 06881
An imprint of Greenwood Publishing Group, Inc.
www.greenwood.com

Printed in the United States of America

The paper used in this book complies with the
Permanent Paper Standard issued by the National
Information Standards Organization (Z39.48–1984).

10 9 8 7 6 5 4 3 2 1

# Contents

# Figures and Tables

## FIGURES

## TABLES

# Acknowledgments

In this work, there have been so much help and so many suggestions that one runs the risk of leaving out many people who have helped to shape this shape. I shall nevertheless try my best.

My first debt of thanks must go to my parents, JoAnn McNamara and Eldon Clingan. Not only did they provide me with generous financial assistance, but they also aided my spirit at times when I thought this work might not be concluded. My mother read through the entire manuscript and provided direction where my thoughts seemed to be wandering. These are debts I can never truly repay.

At the University of Wisconsin-Madison, Professor Theodore Hamerow directed my work and gave me strong guidance throughout my career as a graduate student. Without his constant advice and motivation, there seems little doubt that I would have faltered at some point. This fine scholar upholds the tradition of Ranke, Meinecke, and Holborn. Professors James Donnelly and Stanley Payne also read an early version of this text and, like Professor Hamerow, have continued to be good friends and advisers.

The staff of the Memorial Library in Madison, the Chester Fritz Library of the University of North Dakota, and the New York Public Library provided great assistance. I am particularly grateful to Edward Duesterhoeft of the Microforms Center in Madison, who displayed great humor and patience in allowing me to read and copy pages from many newspapers.

I received a grant from the Fulbright Commission to conduct research in Germany during 1988-89. The Office of Research and Program Development of the University of North Dakota provided a grant that allowed me to travel to Germany in 1996 to conduct additional research. My special thanks to Ken Dawes and Shirley Griffin from that office.

Many people gave me practical and intellectual aid. I would like to give particular thanks to James Albisetti, Albert Berger, Richard Beringer, John M. Blewer, Karl Dietrich Bracher, Gregory Eghigian, Gerald Feldman, Mark Gingerich, Norman Goda, Hal Hansen, Michael L. Hughes, Larry Eugene Jones, Jacob Judd, Richard Kehrberg, Stephen Leist, Donald McKale, William C. McNeil, David A. Meier, Hans Pohl, Pamela Riney-Kehrberg, Paul Roach, Daniel Rogers, Barbara Welter, Henry Wend, and Andrew Whiteside.

I used the Friedrich Ebert Stiftung in Bonn as my first research headquarters and am very grateful to the Social Democratic Party, particularly Frau Meister. The able staff at the Federal Archives in Koblenz and Potsdam helped immeasurably. Frau Meiburg served as my liaison and generously helped me to track down files of the Finance Ministry vital to this project. I also spent considerable time at the Political Archive of the Foreign Office in Bonn and deeply appreciated all the aid that the staff under Frau Dr. Marie Keipert, the director of the archive, gave me. The people at the Historical City Archives in Köln offered their full cooperation with the Nachlass of Chancellor William Marx, which was very helpful. Dr. Buchstab of the Archiv für Christliche Demokratie, Konrad-Adenauer-Stiftung, allowed me to look at the collected writings of Adam Stegerwald, which have been compiled there. The Geheime Preußische Staatsarchiv in Berlin-Dahlem did a superb job for me under the difficult conditions of trying to reassemble the Prussian archives. The Institut für Zeitgeschichte in Munich allowed me to look at the papers of Lutz Graf Schwerin von Krosigk.

My special thanks go to my editor at Greenwood, Heather Ruland Staines, and the rest of the staff that has worked hard to make this book readable and presentable.

Once again, I thank all the people here and apologize to any who were inadvertently omitted. Any errors of fact or style are, of course, my own.

# Abbreviations

| | |
|---|---|
| *ADAP* | *Akten zur deutschen auswärtigen Politik* |
| ADGB | General German League of Unions (Socialist) |
| BAK | Bundesarchiv, Koblenz |
| BAP | Bundesarchiv, Potsdam |
| BIS | Bank for International Settlements |
| BVP | Bavarian People's party |
| CDU | Christian Democratic Union |
| *DBFP* | *Documents on British Foreign Policy* |
| DDP | German Democratic party |
| DNVP | German National People's party |
| DVP | German People's party |
| GM | Gold Mark |
| FY | Fiscal Year |
| IfZ | Institut für Zeitgeschichte, Munich |
| KPD | Communist party of Germany |
| M | Mark |
| NL | Nachlass (Papers) |
| NLP | National Liberal party |
| NNP | Net National Product |
| NSDAP | National Socialist German Workers party (Nazi) |
| PA | Political Archives, Foreign Office, Bonn |
| PrStA | Prussian State Archives, Berlin-Dahlem |
| RdI | National Federation of German Industry |
| RM | Reichsmark |
| SPD | Social Democratic party of Germany |
| *VdR* | *Verhandlungen des deutsches Reichstags* |

# Introduction

On June 14, 1934, the government of Adolf Hitler announced that it was suspending payment on all foreign debts, including bonds from happier times. In 1924 the Reichstag had passed the Dawes Plan, which featured a loan from American bankers. The Dawes Plan had marked a key point in the stabilization of the Weimar Republic because it settled a longstanding international crisis, and its passage began the stable period when many members of the German National People's Party (DNVP) grudgingly supported the Republic. Another set of bonds dated from the 1930 Young Plan. The state of Prussia had taken two other loans in 1926 and 1927 to pay for infrastructure improvements such as streets and canals. The two countries holding most of these bonds, the United States and Great Britain, made face-saving agreements that delayed repayment until 1945. Under a 1953 treaty, the Federal Republic of Germany would pay the principal while the interest would accumulate until Germany was united. In the postwar years, negotiation settled most of the outstanding debts of the German Reich, but the Dawes, Young, and Prussian loans remained in limbo.[1]

In 1945 the issue of how the Nazis paid for their war seemed fairly clear to the Allies. They indicted Hjalmar Schacht, the President of the Reichsbank. "Through Schacht's financial genius, monetary measures were devised to restore Germany to full production; and through the control of

---

1. Ron Chernow, *The House of Morgan: An American Banking Dynasty and the Rise of Modern Finance* (New York, 1990), pp. 395-396. John Weitz, *Hitler's Banker: Hjalmar Horace Greeley Schacht* (Boston, 1997), p. 162. Preußische Geheime Staatsarchiv (PrStA), Berlin-Dahlem, Rep. 151, Prussian Finance Ministry, 1074/4. *New York Times*, January 6, 1995. Harold James, *The German Slump: Politics and Economics 1924-1936* (Oxford, 1986), p. 407.

imports and exports, which he devised under his new plan of 1934, German production was channeled in accordance with the requirements of the German war machine."[2] Since Schacht's credit system was not in the official budget, it allowed for secret rearmament, which could explain why the war caught the Allies off guard. As the trial progressed, it became clear to some that Schacht was not in control of the system, much less the grand architect. The tribunal acquitted him. Who was responsible? Hitler, Hermann Göring, and other Nazi leaders did not have the fundamental knowledge or experience of economics and budgeting to create such a delicate system. Some blamed the underwriters of New York. American Congressman Alvin O'Konski charged that

The international do-gooders who wanted business above all else saw to it that Germany got enough money from us to make herself strong enough to start a second world war. . . . As early as 1923 the international do-gooders in America . . . started to rebuild Germany's war machine. Instead of murderers in World War I the international do-gooders now started to tell us how wonderful the German people really were. . . . So in 1923 [*sic*] the international do-gooders in America got through the Dawes Plan and the United States of America gave Germany a $200,000,000 loan plus a breathing spell of four years in which reparation payments for Germany's damage in World War I were reduced 40% . . . . Who made Hitler? Nobody but America's international do-gooders gave Hitler the money to make the weapons that killed our boys.[3]

I am approaching this issue not from the direction of World War II but from that of the Weimar Republic. My early research concerned the creation of a policy of deficit spending under Finance Minister Peter Reinhold in 1926, how that system worked, and how it fell apart at the end of 1927. That work is the heart of this book. I noticed during my research that several men involved in creating deficit policy resurfaced in 1932 with the government of Franz von Papen and continued into the Nazi period, including Lutz Schwerin von Krosigk, Reich Finance Minister from 1932 to 1945, and Johannes Popitz, Prussian Finance Minister from 1932 to 1944. Neither of these men were members of the Nazi party when they joined the Cabinet. I wondered if it was possible that Krosigk and Popitz had learned key lessons on deficit financing in the mid-1920s and applied them to the budgets of the 1930s.

I was interested in far more than just the technicalities of budget making. Reinhold had not come out of a vacuum. What lessons came from the prewar period and the hyperinflation? Could the state of the budgets and the manner of their passage indicate the stability or instability of the political system? I traced budget politics back to the late imperial era before I could find

---

2. Office of the United States Chief on Counsel for Prosecution of Axis Criminality, *Nazi Conspiracy and Aggression* (Washington, DC, 1946), vol. I, pp. 350-351.

3. *Congressional Record*, 79th Congress, 1st Session, p. A3694.

another time of budget stability, and this led me to the idea of the "twelve-year crisis," with monetary, fiscal, domestic, and international factors interacting with one another. I was also deeply interested in the intersection of money and politics. Who financed these deficits? What influence did those creditors wield? I had done considerable research on the negotiation and passage of the Dawes Plan, which was the keystone of international finance of the 1920s. To what degree was it fair to say that American loans financed the deficits of Weimar's "golden years"?

Finally, I wanted to explore the issue of corporatism. Charles Maier made a deep impression on me with his argument that the passage of the Dawes Plan created a corporatist system in Germany. In the twentieth century it seems that corporatism in a variety of forms has competed with liberal democracy. Leaders of institutional groups, notably large corporations and labor unions, wield power instead of the winners of elections. Only the permanent expert members of the civil service represent the "government." Popular influence is entirely indirect. Individuals who are not part of a corporate pressure group lose their voice. In theory, everyone should fit into some group, but in practice this does not work. I grew up in New York City in the 1970s, when a corporatist model was imposed over government with some success and remarkably little protest. To what degree was the electoral appeal of the Nazis an anticorporatist rebellion? If that were true, then the crisis at the end of the 1920s was of quite a different nature than the crisis of the early 1920s. The middle years of Weimar were not a brief breathing space, but a period of genuine stability. If Weimar stabilized itself successfully, there is no reason to think that it could not have continued, whatever the resentments of the peace treaty, the Inflation, and the revaluation.

A complete political, economic, and financial history of the Weimar Republic would amount to thousands of pages. Several fine books have been written on aspects or parts of this time. Fritz Fischer discussed the interplay among fiscal policy and international and domestic problems in *War of Illusions* but ends with the outbreak of the war. Gerald Feldman has covered the period from before the war to 1924 in extensive detail. Harold James and Theodore Balderston looked at fiscal policy, monetary policy, and German trade from the mid-1920s to the mid-1930s. Maier compared Germany, Italy, and France from the end of the war to about 1925. William C. McNeil traced the path of international finance in the middle and late 1920s. To cover the period from 1912 to 1934 may seem like hubris, but I will stick to a few limited themes.

First, Germany gradually nationalized fiscal policy. Before World War I, the Reich had remarkably little taxing and spending power as it transferred most tax revenue to the individual states. Attempts to introduce a national income tax proved fruitless. In the 1920s, the Reich increased its tax authority and left ever less for the states. It stressed international problems, especially reparation, as excuses to force austerity on the states. The states turned to long-term foreign loans to relieve the pressure, but these became unavailable after

1927.    During the Depression, Chancellor Heinrich Brüning reduced the
spending authority of the states even more.    By 1934, Adolf Hitler had
eliminated the autonomy of the states entirely and made them units of the nation-
state.

Second, the Germans gradually learned how to control deficit spending.
The   Kaiserreich ran only modest deficits and mostly paid for the war until
1916.   After that time, the budget got completely out of control, and no one had
the expertise to structure the debt properly and make the necessary payments.
The result was the hyperinflation that destroyed the German Mark.   For two
years, the government feared to run any deficit, but beginning in 1926 with
Finance Minister Peter Reinhold, deficits again became part of the landscape.
Although the capital market in Germany was very weak, the Reich, states, and
cities ran deficits supported in part by foreign loans.   By the end of the 1920s,
those loans had dried up and the Germans had to start figuring out new ways to
handle deficit spending.   An attempt at austerity by Brüning was a catastrophe
that led to the rise of Hitler and the appointment of experts such as Krosigk and
Popitz who had learned during their years in Reinhold's Finance Ministry to
handle deficits of considerable size.

Third, Germany from 1912 to 1934 did not face just one continuous
crisis with many facets.   German history in the early twentieth century has
usually been divided according to the political regime: the empire of Wilhelm
II, the Weimar Republic, and the Nazi Third Reich.   Because of this, analysts
miss many trends and continuities while ascribing breaks to the political change.
In the last several years, Gerald Feldman has found continuity by terming the
period 1914 to 1924 as "the Great Disorder."   Stuart Robson took a different
tack, dating the crisis to the Battle of Verdun and calling the period to 1923 "the
German Time of Troubles."[4]   Breaking the barrier of 1918 has the useful result
of showing that Germany was not beset by one crisis after another in an
unbroken chain from 1914 to 1933.   I propose to characterize this era with two
separate crises: a crisis that began with the electoral victory of the Social
Democrats in 1912 and ended with the passage of the Dawes Plan in 1924, and
a second very different crisis that broke out several years later and ended with
the triumph of fascism.   The first crisis had four distinct aspects: a domestic
political crisis, an international crisis marked by World War I and its aftermath,
a monetary crisis as Germany tried to cope with the recent introduction of paper
money and the ensuing loss of confidence, and a financial crisis with worsening
budget problems before, during, and after the war.   Each of these four crises
interacted with one another in a variety of ways.   The social and economic

---

4. Stuart Robson, "1918 and All That: Reassessing the Periodization of Recent
German History," in Larry Eugene Jones and James Retallack, eds., *Elections, Mass
Politics, and Social Change in Modern Germany: New Perspectives* (Cambridge, 1992),
pp. 331-344.

modernization process had stretched the political system to the breaking point. One may apply Jürgen Habermas' idea of the public sphere to nineteenth-century Germany: a place where elites debated policy as representatives of the entire public while private interests took care of many public needs. After the turn of the century, this became increasingly unworkable. Germany's international situation declined while it had trouble securing more loans from creditors. Problems in the money supply led to the effective legalization in 1909 of paper money. The Social Democrats (SPD) broke through in 1912 and the government could no longer exclude them. The debates over the budget, which had been relatively harmonious since the government's victory in the Prussian constitutional crisis of the 1860s, now became acrimonious. The 1912, 1913, and 1914 debates were long and bitter and made worse by supplementary military requests. The empire had long seen the Reichstag refuse government proposals, but now the parliament began to make its own policy. The crisis of the war led directly into the problems of the postwar period, but the old system was not dead yet. Politicians who had grown up in the days of the empire continued to pursue an elite form of politics. The middle-class parties in particular--the Democratic Party (DDP), the Catholic Center, the People's Party (DVP), and the German Nationalist People's Party (DNVP)--tried to carry on politics in the old style for a time without organizing on the local level.

In its death throes, the public sphere system could not provide answers to the pressing problems: Germany was an international pariah, deeply in debt, and beset by inflation. The government tried one stopgap solution after another until the final calamity of 1923: the invasion of the Ruhr, the attempt at passive resistance, and the hyperinflation. This calamity was solved by the currency stabilization of 1923, the tax decrees of 1923-24, and the passage of the Dawes Plan, which ended both the international crisis of reparation and the domestic political crisis by starting to reconcile the German Nationalists to the Republic.

Only with the utter death of the old regime was the path clear for organized interests--veterans' groups, farmers' groups, big businesses, and labor unions--to take the lead in dominating the system. The middle-class parties still had not organized themselves autonomously but fell increasingly under the influence of these interest groups. The turning point came with the passage of the Dawes Plan. It offered a bridge back to the global community by providing economic stabilization and pointing the way for debt settlement. The moderate parties all rallied around it, but pressure from the industrial groups won final passage. In an extraordinary move, the Nationalists allowed free voting, and half of their members gave the Dawes Plan the votes sufficient to pass.

Maier's landmark work *Recasting Bourgeois Europe* compared postwar stabilization in France, Italy, and Germany. In his view, the war had legitimized labor. Support grew for corporatism in which state power would dissolve in favor of local works councils and "industrial self-governments."[5] Conservatives wanted to centralize class transactions while technocrats labored for efficiency. The passage of the Dawes Plan now pointed to a system of "societal corporatism" in which representatives from business and labor would work together in a system growing from the basis of civil society. The stabilization of the mid-1920s brought a conservative corporate system to Germany with both big business and big labor wielding great influence.

Yet this corporatist compromise did not hold in Germany. In the wake of the Dawes Plan, a conservative government took power, led by Hans Luther and Otto von Schlieben. This government seemed determined to revive its old prewar alliance with iron and rye interests by passing stiff tariffs and running an austere fiscal policy. As part of a new financial compromise, it reduced the share of the budget going to states and cities, marking another step in the nationalization of fiscal policy. The coalition fell apart at the end of 1925. Despite pleas from agricultural interests, the DNVP bolted the coalition over the Treaties of Locarno, and Germany was in a deep recession. While Italian fascists embraced the corporatist model, German fascists gained great electoral mileage by attacking both business and labor. Michael Hughes emphasized the voters' anger at the Nationalists for breaking their campaign promise of 100% revaluation of debts and life insurance policies. Voters deserted the DNVP in droves.[6] Many in the Nationalist party found any kind of cooperation with the Social Democrats to be anathema. Yet the DNVP was perfectly positioned to take advantage of any discontent. It could claim governmental experience, both from the old empire and now from the Republic. It could portray itself as holding up old German virtues while promoting a paternalistic social policy in the model of Bismarck's. It is not a surprise that a radical right party advocating social policy came to power during the Great Depression. The shock is that it was the Nazi party, not the DNVP, that became the largest political party, and this peculiarity needs an explanation.

Luther now found it necessary to work with the SPD and use deficit spending to pull Germany out of the recession. For the first time, the constitutional budget mechanism functioned as intended. The system originated by Peter Reinhold and continued by Heinrich Köhler helped bring parties and interest groups together and restored prosperity to Germany. Budget-making would be done punctually and democratically from 1926 to 1928. Meanwhile, states and cities had found a way to make up for the loss of tax revenue by taking out enormous international loans. This alarmed Parker Gilbert, the American Agent General of Reparations under the Dawes Plan. His formal job

---

5. Charles Maier, *Recasting Bourgeois Europe: Stabilization in France, Germany, and Italy after World War I* (Princeton, 1975), p. 12.

6. Michael L. Hughes, *Paying for the German Inflation* (Chapel Hill, 1988), pp. 185-187.

was to watch over German finances, but few understood that his goodwill enabled Germany to build foreign confidence and attract loans. The alienation of Gilbert by the end of 1927 marked a fateful moment for the Republic. Germany could have averted many problems of the Depression, had Köhler made different choices in 1927.

Reinhold built his system on debt, but Germany could repay that debt if it created sufficient productivity growth. The debate over Weimar productivity has been a long and bitter one. Knut Borchardt charged that productivity was low and wages were excessive because of government intervention. Businesses were unable to make enough capital investments to increase productivity and economic growth. This made the Great Depression much worse in Germany. In Borchardt's view, Weimar was chronically ill, and political restraints made Keynesian-style stimulus impossible. Carl-Ludwig Holtfrerich analyzed his own set of economic data, using man-hour productivity numbers as opposed to Borchardt's weekly numbers, since the work week shrank in the Weimar era. Holtfrerich showed that productivity in the 1925-29 period rose 5.6% annually, a better number than the 1850-1913 average or that of the 1950s in the Federal Republic. Thus, wages matched the productivity gains. The collapse of the German Democratic Republic opened confidential legal records of businesses that are still closed in the West. Mark Spoerer's examination revealed that Weimar businesses were making far greater profits than they publicly reported. With these large profits, businesses should have had all the capital they needed to invest. Holtfrerich argued that as a percentage of the economy, investment in 1925, 1927, and 1928 matched the prewar average, while 1926 and 1929 were below the average.[7] It is true that productivity gains often take years to contribute to economic growth. It may be a sad irony that the productivity growth of the Weimar years may have only benefited the Nazi regime of the 1930s. It is going too far to say that "this revival provided Adolf Hitler with a splendid industrial machine and the money to finance massive rearmament."[8] The foreign credits were long since consumed by the time the Austrian corporal got his hands on power, but Weimar had built much of the modern plant that would produce tanks and planes.

The crisis of 1929-33 was entirely different and hardly related to the earlier crisis of 1912-24. This crisis was economic, beginning with the fall in farm prices and continuing with the Great Depression. This economic crisis became a political crisis when the DNVP, the main party of the farmers, failed

7. Knut Borchardt, *Perspectives on Modern German Economic History and Policy* (Cambridge, 1991), pp. 91, 144-157. Carl-Ludwig Holtfrerich, "Economic Policy Options and the End of the Weimar Republic," in Ian Kershaw, ed., *Weimar: Why Did Democracy Fail?* (New York, 1990), pp. 74-75. Mark Spoerer, *Von Scheingewinnen zum Rüstungsboom: Die Eigenkapitalrentabilität der deutschen Industrieaktiengesellschaften 1925-1941* (Stuttgart, 1996).

8. Chernow, pp. 250-251.

to win protectionist tariffs in 1927, and when the governments and major political parties of the 1929-33 period failed to take strong action against the Depression. The installation of the Hitler government, which promised and executed strong economic action, resolved the crisis. This second crisis marked a rebellion by those people who felt that the corporatist state had frozen them out of the system. Many who had regarded the political system with apathy and had not voted either in the old empire or the new Republic now trudged to the polls for the first time to vote against those they saw as exploiters. These people could include the elderly who had suffered in the Inflation and felt they had never received proper compensation. They could include women appalled at the smut and immorality coming out of Berlin. They could include farmers who blamed their declining incomes and bankruptcies on the failure of the government to support them. They could include young men and women who saw no prospect of employment. Whatever their grievance, these people turned from apathy to hostility against the entire political, economic, social, and cultural system, which they identified with the range of corporatist parties, from the Social Democrats to the Nationalists. Ultimately their preferred political party was the National Socialist.

This kind of backlash is hardly unique to Germany. The previous depression of the 1890s had seen the sudden rise and collapse of the Antisemite party in Germany. William Jennings Bryan organized a coalition of the dispossessed in the United States. In the 1930s, Scandinavia turned to a farmer/labor alliance that promoted a sweeping program of social and economic change. Germany had remarkably uninspired leadership. Brüning tried to revive the public-sphere style by preaching an elite esoteric brand of economics while cutting out some interest groups that opposed it. He held dangerously old-fashioned economic precepts and was determined to nationalize fiscal policy. By the late 1920s, several smaller states were choking on debt, and the Reich was trying to consolidate states further. Brüning coldly made the decision to cut transfers to the states further and was constantly pressing for a union of the Reich and Prussia, a move that would destroy federalism. Papen finally carried out that move by decree and within two years the states had lost all rights.

A close reading of the ever-shifting budget policy of the Hermann Müller and Brüning years reveals many missed opportunities. The argument that there were "no practical options" is specious. Müller received a budget plan that commanded a democratic majority, but he chose to resign instead. Wiser heads begged Brüning not to put a deflationary budget in by decree, but he persisted and then called for new elections without a second thought. He was not forced into his actions, nor is there much evidence that he was an evil genius ruining Germany deliberately in order to bring back the monarchy. On balance, Brüning comes across as a man of stubborn ideological beliefs, limited intelligence, and utter callousness.

After Brüning fell, Franz von Papen, a man of even less intelligence, had the sense to endorse several employment projects. The short-lived Kurt von

Schleicher regime was a last-ditch attempt to restore the societal corporatist state by bringing in labor unions as partners. Although the Nazis had campaigned as rebels against the corporatist system, they organized a form of state corporatism. The state was now the supreme power, and labor and business and agriculture were harnessed to its benefit. I end this book with the stabilization of the National Socialist regime and the easing of the Depression, but some have suggested that there was a third crisis that bloomed in the late 1930s as the fundamental contradictions of Nazi economic policy began to run up against one another and a stark choice between war and collapse became apparent.

The Weimar Republic continues to attract historians. It is fascinating not only as the prelude to the dreadful Nazi era, but as a time for experimentation in culture and society. There is a lingering sense of a new society being built and of a brief time when all things were possible. Its disastrous end makes the history of Weimar even more poignant. Alternative results have always been favorite toys in Weimar history. These are not exercises in nostalgia, for the same issues have come again. The end of the Cold War, the revolutions of 1989, and the subsequent collapse of the Soviet Union have again fostered a feeling that many more things are possible. Yet the same storm clouds are on the horizon as existed in the 1920s. Democratic mobilization and nationalist frustration have led to neo-fascist movements rising again, and the memory of the radical right's disastrous legacy seems to have faded. Scholars of the Weimar Republic can perhaps contribute something lest darkness falls again. Contrary to much recent historiography, I shall argue that Germany could have borrowed enough money to cushion the impact of the Depression and avert the catastrophe of Hitler.

# Chapter 1

# The Twelve-Year Crisis, 1912–1924

In the first years of the twentieth century, growing diplomatic isolation, budget problems, and consequent problems with the supply of money undermined the stability of the German government, society, and economy. The German nation ran large-scale budget deficits for the first time in its history and experienced a catastrophe: an uncontrollable inflation and a bankrupt government. This lesson would scar the German psyche. Some would say that the scars of the hyperinflation persist. The growing problems of the Wilhelmine empire culminated in a full-blown crisis beginning in 1912, when the Social Democratic Party (SPD) won the most seats in the Reichstag. This victory was largely due to resentment over regressive taxes voted to staunch the growing budget deficit. Germany did not resolve this crisis until 1924. The twelve-year crisis consisted of four factors: the international crisis that broke into the First World War, the monetary crisis that began when Germany legalized paper money, the fiscal crisis that became acute after 1900 when the budget could not keep pace with the needs of the nation, and a political crisis that began with the January 1912 elections. The main events of these twelve years including the war, the revolution, the reparations problem, and the Inflation were manifestations of these intertwined crises. Others have dealt with the international, political, and monetary crises. I will focus on the crisis of fiscal policy and its relationship to the other problems. This chapter will describe the twelve-year crisis. The next chapter will discuss the resolution of the crisis.

Germany had dominated the diplomatic scene in the 1870s and 1880s. Bismarck had woven complex alliances that began to unravel after Kaiser Wilhelm II asserted his power over foreign policy in 1890. By 1907, a series of blunders and miscalculations by the Kaiser and his advisers had placed Germany in a precarious situation. Its only firm ally was Austria-Hungary, while Russia and France were bound in a defensive alliance and both had signed treaties of friendship with England. Instead of trying to live with its neighbors peacefully, Germany seemed to become more erratic and threatening. Many military leaders felt that the only response to "encirclement" had to be war before the Russians recovered their strength from the Japanese War of 1904-5 and completed their railroad to the German border.[1]

Germany was also slipping into a monetary crisis. Modern monetary policy comprises two main aspects: interest rates and money supply. One can move interest rates up and down to control the price of money in the credit market. A high interest rate makes money expensive and discourages borrowing. A low interest rate provides easy credit and stimulates the economy. Money supply once depended on the supply of gold or other precious metal available for coinage. Paper money allowed a government to break those limits. A government "pumps money into the economy" by printing cash and then using it to buy government or private bonds. It takes money out of the economy when it sells those bonds and hoards the cash. Many European nations were slow to move to a paper money system after the French revolutionary government went overboard in printing and distributing the *assignats*, bonds that became paper money. The Reichsbank had issued notes since its creation in 1876, but generally these were of too high a denomination for general use. Barry Eichengreen suggests that the prewar monetary regime rested on two pillars: cooperation among the richest nations of the world and credibility. This credibility rested in turn on an elite form of politics that left industrial workers and antideflationary debtors with little or no influence. There had been moves in the 1890s to inflate the currency by basing the currency on both gold and silver (bimetallism) in Germany and the United States. The elite had defeated that suggestion, and gold discoveries in Alaska, South Africa, and Australia seemed to make it unnecessary. The defeat of bimetallism makes one question whether the East Elbian *Junkers*, long considered the backbone of Prussia and the empire, were still part of the elite, at least as agricultural leaders.[2]

The disruptions of the Russo-Japanese War and the Moroccan Crisis had affected the Germany money market as early as September 1905. The Russian ruble lost much of its value on the open market, and gold flowed out of the Reichsbank to Russia as the desperately high interest rates attracted investors. The Reichsbank raised its discount rate in response. As a precaution against a war draining its precious metal reserves, Germany decided in 1906 to print M200 million in 20M- and 50M-denominated notes to replace gold and silver coins. The Russians desperately needed foreign loans to cover their

---

1. Fritz Fischer, *War of Illusions: German Policies from 1911 to 1914* (New York, 1975), p. 173.

2. Barry Eichengreen, *Golden Fetters: The Gold Standard and the Great Depression, 1919-1939* (Oxford, 1992), pp. 10-30.

stupendous deficits and faced revolution at home. Germany delayed the Russian bond issue on the Berlin market, then forced it to compete with new Reich and Prussian loans. Russia was unable to raise enough money, investors only bought half of the German loan, and the Reichsbank's gold reserve still fell to its lowest level in twenty-five years. Had Germany been willing and able to support Russia in 1905-6, that nation might never have joined a Triple Entente. At least it would have created a reservoir of goodwill that both nations desperately needed between 1908 and 1914. The German government saw foreign bonds as a burden, not an opportunity.[3]

The growth of the American economy after 1896 and its insatiable need for gold tended to destabilize the system. Heavy American borrowing in the Panic of 1907 threatened to drain Great Britain's gold reserves. The Bank of England was forced to raise its discount rate to the highest level since 1873 and borrow gold from France. Germany's gold reserves again fell dangerously low, and the Reichsbank initiated a policy of building up its gold reserve. Some later interpreted this policy as a preparation for war, but one should consider these monetary problems. The hoarding of reserves took money out of the economy and threatened growth. From 1907 to 1910, the value of money in circulation fell approximately 4%. As of January 1, 1910, the Reich gave bank notes ranging in value from M20 to M1,000 the status of legal tender. A twenty-mark note still equaled the weekly wage for many, so most Germans conducted their business in coins. As Feldman points out, the government tried its best to encourage the use of paper money after 1908 because a metal-based currency would make it difficult for the government to fight a war if it broke out. It also favored noncash transactions. In November 1912, the Reichsbank imposed a premium for the export of gold, then issued more small notes, which now made up over 20% of all notes in circulation. The covering of the paper notes by gold, which had hovered around 50% for years, now slipped to 31%, the second-worst showing since 1876. The Reichsbank raised the discount rate to attract more gold. Thus the international crisis helped create a monetary crisis as the German people found themselves confronted increasingly with this suspicious currency.[4]

Fiscal policy, like monetary policy, can be the result of accident or design. A budget surplus means that the government has gathered more taxes than it has spent. When a government hoards surplus money or retires part of

---

3. Peter-Christian Witt, *Finanzpolitik des deutschen Reiches von 1903 bis 1913: Eine Studie zur Innenpolitik des wilhelminischen Deutschland* (Lübeck, 1970), pp. 145-151. Rudolf Kroboth, *Die Finanzpolitik des Deutschen Reiches während der Reichskanzlerschaft Bethmann-Hollwegs und die Geld- und Kapitalmarktverhältnisse (1909-1913/14)* (Frankfurt, 1986), p. 91.

4. Eichengreen, pp. 52-54. Witt, pp. 194, 327-329. Kroboth, pp. 61-71. Gerald D. Feldman, *The Great Disorder: Politics, Economics, and Society in the German Inflation, 1914-1924* (Oxford, 1993), pp. 26-30.

its debt, this has the same effect as reducing the money supply. One must cover a budget deficit by borrowing money from public or private sources or by borrowing from oneself, which amounts to printing money. Economists generally frown on the latter option, "floating debt." It is advisable to predict accurately the budget balance and plan ahead rather than catch up belatedly. Investors like to see a government with a plan, whatever the fiscal policy. Confident investors may extend more credit to a poor nation than uncertain investors will to a wealthy nation. Figure 1.1 shows the deepening crisis of confidence among investors. Bond prices move in the opposite direction of interest rates, so a fall in bond prices makes money more expensive and hampers economic growth. Falling bond prices make it harder for a government to sell its bonds because they indicate a fall in demand. From 1903 on, the German government faced a growing lack of investor confidence that made its interest rates higher than those of other wealthy nations and made it harder for the government to place bonds.

The German empire had difficulty from its beginning meeting expenses because its states raised and kept most revenue. Beyond a certain point the empire even had to surrender its own revenue to the states, chiefly customs duties and indirect consumption taxes. Only the states discussed progressive tax policies such as an income tax or inheritance tax. The Fiscal Year began on April 1, so that Fiscal Year (FY) 1889, for example, would run until March 31, 1890. Since that year the budget had been divided between an Ordinary Budget that taxes should cover and an Extraordinary Budget that loans would cover. The theory was that budget surpluses and deficits should mostly balance each other out, so that the national debt would grow very slowly, and short-term loans could cover the deficits until the next surplus. Because of accounting difficulties, the actual surplus or deficit would not be clear until some three or four years after the end of that particular fiscal year. Germany had legally limited its ability to fund deficits with printed money. Unlike other nations that could freely borrow in the short term to avoid cash shortfalls during the periods of the year when expenses exceeded tax revenues (especially the harvest season and the Christmas season), Germany was limited to M275 million in credit authority from the Reichsbank. Its other option was to sell short-term treasury bills, with or without interest rates, to private banks for cash. When firms began to balk at the growing amount of German debt, a decree of 1910 mandated that the insurance funds invest at least one-quarter of their assets in Reich and state bonds. A Prussian law of 1913 obliged savings banks to put 15% of their assets and 40% of their annual profits into public bonds.[5]

Germany's national debt rose from M2.3 billion to M4.2 billion during Bernhard von Bülow's term from 1900 to 1909. The portion of that debt not covered by treasury bonds or bills rose from close to zero to M713 million.

---

5. Witt, pp. 18-22, 39, 74, 321. Kroboth, pp. 51, 100-101.

**Figure 1.1**
**Measure of Confidence: German 3½% Bond Prices**

*Source*: Balderston, p. 188.

Germany's expanding domestic and imperial commitments, such as the Boxer Rebellion and the uprising in South-West Africa, began to strain the budget. Both the Reich and Prussian governments had difficulty floating their bonds on the German market to pay the costs. In FY04, the government repeatedly exceeded the legal limit of cash from the Reichsbank. Raising income was difficult. Chancellor Bernhard von Bülow had guided a tariff increase through the Reichstag in 1902, but many urban political representatives and export-oriented industrialists criticized it. Those forces were growing stronger. No one in the government seemed willing to unify tax policy, take income from the states, or impose a Reich income tax. The government in 1906 proposed a package of new consumption taxes and a Reich inheritance tax, but the Reichstag scaled back the consumption taxes. The debt crisis of 1905-6 and the Panic of 1907 made the situation even more dire. The German credit market was not strong enough to support the government's needs. Worse still, Germany in the late empire ran a persistent trade deficit equal to 3-4% of Net National Social Product despite tariff increases.[6]

    When the Reichstag rejected the FY07 budget for the Colonial Office, the Kaiser called new elections. The government whipped up patriotic fury

---

6. Witt, pp. 76-89, 119-126, 321, Table XV, 382-383.

against the Social Democratic and Catholic Center parties that had protested the brutality in South-West Africa, and the parties that generally favored the government scored gains. However, there was no more willingness to address the growing budget problems. The government overestimated income and "borrowed" money from the states to cover expenses. Only a strong economy and consequent growth in tax revenue prevented a catastrophe. By FY09 the Bülow government still faced a deficit of M500 million, more than 20% of the total budget, and a national debt of over four billion marks. A tax package featuring revenue enhancements in brandy, beer, tobacco, and inheritance duties, endured months of debate before a coalition of conservative, Catholic Center, and Polish parties in the Reichstag finally voted it down in June 1909. This triggered Bülow's resignation. Smaller taxes, a stronger-than-expected economy, and more loans covered the deficits. But the next three years showed that the fiscal problem had not yet become a full crisis. Despite continuing credit problems in FY10, the government increased the military, administrative, and social spending while running a small budget surplus. This encouraged the military to dream of vast expansion despite the opposition of the Treasury Department, which held new spending for FY11 to its lowest increase in the 1900-14 period.[7]

After the Reichstag shredded his tax package, Bülow wrote a prophetic parting shot: "The result may be regarded as the evil consequence of the Conservative attitude, which will then be seen as frivolous trifling with the interests of the Empire and the Fatherland. We shall meet again at Philippi."[8] For Bülow, the day of Philippi came on January 31, 1912, when general elections saw the Social Democrats sweep to victory. The demagogy of 1907 had increased the voter turnout and had paid off in the short term as new electors voted for the middle-class parties. But it was a Pyrrhic victory for the government. The Socialists' arguments for social justice and their attacks on Bülow's regressive tax package of 1909 swayed the lower-middle-class and working class voters who had turned out for the first time in 1907 to cast a patriotic ballot. The Social Democrats won most of the by-elections held after 1907. The Saxon and Baden elections of October 1909 saw the "black-blue" bloc of Conservatives and Catholics lose to the Socialists, progressives, and National Liberals (NLP). Calls rose up for a Reich-level parliamentary alliance. The NLP and the Progressive People's party saw an electoral disaster in the making and tried to limit the damage by calling for socialist participation in policy-making. The progressives went so far as to conclude a secret electoral pact with the SPD. The black-blue coalition suffered a crushing defeat in the

---

7. Ibid., pp. 192, Table XIII and Table XIV, 378-381. Politisches Archiv (PA), Auswärtiges Amt, Bonn, Wirtschaft Reparationen, Peace Treaty: Transferring Germany's Load, vol. 6, May 21, 1926. Kroboth, p. 83.

8. Bernhard von Bülow, *Memoirs* (Boston, 1931), vol. II, p. 585.

January 1912 elections. The German Conservatives lost about one-fourth of their seats, while the *Reichspartei* lost almost half of its mandates, although the combined conservative vote did not suffer much. The progressives increased their share of the vote but lost seats in the Reichstag. The Catholic Center held most of its mandates but suffered a fall in its popular vote. The SPD won 35% of the vote and replaced the Catholic Center as the largest party in the Reichstag.[9]

In most political systems, the government's defeat would have led to the resignation of the Chancellor and the formation of a new coalition. However, the peculiarities of the German political system meant there would be no immediate change. The government led now by Theobald von Bethmann Hollweg did not resign nor did it respond to the changes caused by the election. The government did not need to possess the confidence of the Reichstag, only that of the emperor. While the Reichstag had constitutionally guaranteed powers over the budget, it hesitated to use them, remembering the Prussian constitutional crisis of the 1860s, which Bismarck's aggressive foreign policy had broken. This ensured that the crisis would not end, but grind on. Figure 1.2 shows that the German bond market fell almost without interruption for the next eighteen months, accelerating the trend from 1903. The crisis would not end for another dozen years.

The budget debates reflected the change. The debate of 1911 had been a quiet one: the Reichstag had received the budget for FY11 on December 9, 1910, and had debated the general outline of the budget for five days. It reviewed the various departments and tax measures for the next three months. The final reading of the budget concluded on April 11 when the Reichstag approved it by voice vote. The exuberant Social Democrats now came into the Reichstag. Trouble began immediately over the election of a Reichstag President, the customary first item of business. The Catholic Center, Progressives, and National Liberals supported Peter Spahn from the right wing of the Catholic Center. The SPD nominated August Bebel, while the Conservatives backed Prince Heinrich Schoenaich-Carolath. Spahn was not able to secure a majority until the third ballot. Bebel picked up support on the third ballot from many National Liberals who then elected Philipp Scheidemann (SPD) as First Vice-President. This suited the Socialists because the rules stipulated that the President had to submit the credentials of the Reichstag to the Kaiser, an acknowledgment of the monarchy. Three days later, Spahn resigned under pressure. In the next round of balloting, 174 of the 374 ballots cast were blank as a Progressive was elected Reichstag President. The Kaiser refused to receive the officers unless Scheidemann attended. The Reichstag elected a Progressive as permanent President over Spahn, a National Liberal as First Vice-President

---

9. Witt, pp. 278, 345. Kroboth, p. 41. Fischer, p. 98.

**Figure 1.2**
**Measure of Confidence: German Monthly Bond Prices, 1909-1914**

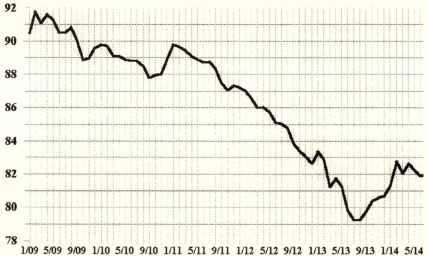

*Source:* Kroboth, p. 509.

over Scheidemann, and another Progressive as Second Vice-President over Scheidemann.[10]

The election result meant a stormier budget debate.  The first reading did not start until February 14.  The Reichstag Steering Committee refused to approve a Social Democrat as Budget Committee Chair.  Bethmann Hollweg had decided to bloat the budget with new army and navy bills.  He submitted the bills on April 15 in the middle of the budget's second reading.  Admiral Tirpitz believed that a naval bill would bring the old "cartel" of National Liberals, Conservatives, and Catholics together.  The debate was nearly as intense inside the government as in the Reichstag.  The Treasury Secretary drew up plans for a progressive inheritance tax, but the conservatives would not hear of it and forced his resignation.  The government proposed to break a recently enacted law dedicating budget surpluses to debt reduction by raiding the projected budget surplus for FY11.  Ernst Bassermann for the NLP and Mathias Erzberger for the Catholic Center introduced an amendment to the budget stating that the

---

10. *Verhandlungen des deutsches Reichstags (VdR). Stenographische Berichte*, vol. 262, pp. 3503-3723, vol. 266, pp. 6134-6268, vol. 283, pp. 3-14.  Beverly Heckart, *From Bassermann to Bebel: The Grand Bloc's Quest for Reform in the Kaiserreich, 1900-1914* (New Haven, 1974), pp. 199-205.

Chancellor propose a general wealth tax for Reichstag consideration within a year. The Reichstag also demanded hikes in the inheritance tax. The 1912 budget was not completed until May 22. The debate had weakened Bethmann Hollweg and thrown the Cabinet into turmoil.[11]

The 1912 budget debate revealed three distinct and conflicting alliances. One wished to centralize tax and budget authority and reduce the authority of the states. A second alliance of the propertied classes of the Center and the conservatives wished to preserve their assets, while a third alliance of the propertied and the socialists were willing to tax mobile capital. The struggle of these three groups would shape the 1913 debates. The government introduced the budget a week earlier than the previous year. The Bassermann/Erzberger amendment and Bethmann Hollweg's request for another boost in military spending after the Balkans War complicated the debate. The military bill would cost almost M1 billion for the first year and then about M200 million for maintenance each subsequent year. There was sharp disagreement on financing the first installment, and the government called a financial conference of the states. Saxony pressed for a loan to finance the military supplement, but Bethmann Hollweg shocked the conference by supporting a capital gains tax. The states of the Bundesrat agreed to forego M82 million of shared income annually to cover the maintenance costs and levy a one-time defense surcharge on capital and income. This would also have the virtue of satisfying the Bassermann-Erzberger Law. If it was not sufficient, the government could issue up to M600 million in Treasury transfers. Economist Heinrich Dietzel of the University of Bonn supported financing through credit alone since taxes would depress the economy and the military spending would not be a productive investment. The Reichstag was determined to cover spending with taxes, and that body's complicated alliances now went to work on the bill. The SPD pushed hard to make the German princes subject to taxation but failed. There was something in the final package for everyone: the centralizers won a direct Reich tax on capital gains, the left won the introduction of the principle of progressivity on the national scale, and the propertied avoided increased inheritance taxes. The 1913 budget was the first to use the view of Adolf Wagner, an economist at the University of Berlin and member of the Prussian parliament, that a budget should correct the maldistribution of the free market and achieve social justice. The budget proper was completed on April 28, but the debate over the military bill dragged to the end of June when the Chancellor gave final approval to the capital gains tax.[12]

---

11. Heckart, p. 206. Kroboth, pp. 121, 163. Witt, pp. 346-351. Fischer, pp. 136-137.

12. Kroboth, pp. 187, 210-227, 241, 270-274, 285. Fischer, pp. 185-189. John G. Williamson, *Karl Helfferich: Economist, Financier, Politician* (Princeton, 1971), p. 31.

The chronic German shortage of money had an adverse impact on the conduct of foreign policy. Germany could not compete with France or Britain in winning influence. The problems with the Russian credit in 1906, reminiscent of Bismarck's block on Russian credit in the late 1880s, harmed relations. In 1913, Germany had an opportunity to improve its standing in the Balkans by offering loans to Serbia and Greece but could not participate. Germany would have done better to put money into these projects instead of the enormous military supplement of FY13. Contracts tend to follow loans. Austria-Hungary alone absorbed one-quarter of Germany's European loans. Germany extended a loan to Bulgaria in July 1914. In Romania, ruled by a branch of the Hohenzollern family, the German position declined. German banks had held 64% of Romanian loans in 1895, but only 54% in 1915. Germany was unable to supply Greece with a loan of close to half a billion marks. Even in the Ottoman Empire, where German influence was growing, financial constraints forced German interests to take less of an oil and railroad concession than they might have gained. Wherever the Germans faltered, the French would be there with ready money to win influence. If for no other reason, this should have promoted a reform of German finances.[13]

Figures 1.1 and 1.2 show the slide into the twelve-year crisis. The year 1897 marked a peak in German bond prices, which fell during the Moroccan Crisis of 1905, the rejection of the Bülow tax package, and the elections of 1912. Could one argue that these were healthy developments? Rather than focusing on the conflict, one could see the engagement of the SPD as the end of its long estrangement. Reconciling this growing force could be productive, since the hostility of the Bismarck years and the neglect of the Wilhelmine years had not dimmed it. It was hardly the first time the Reichstag had rejected government initiatives. The difference was that instead of playing a negative role as it had in 1906 and 1909, the Reichstag was trying to wrest policy-making from the Cabinet's hands with determination not seen since the 1860s. That had led to a series of foreign wars. A generation of politicians had avoided challenging the government in such a direct manner. Germany could have resolved this crisis in a healthy manner by being more conciliatory in foreign policy. It could have saved its military money, corrected its fiscal policy, and liberalized its government to make the Cabinet responsible to the Reichstag. The slight uptick in bond prices from July 1913 to May 1914 seems to suggest that many investors believed the worst was behind. While some argue that the events of 1909-14 represented an evolution into a constitutional monarchy, others counter that Germany lurched into the First World War because of the domestic factors. G. Schmidt suggested that Germany was facing a state strike from above or a revolution from below. For many in Germany, the outbreak of war provided a welcome relief, but it would be going too far to

---

13. Fischer, pp. 292-307.

attribute the German declaration of war to these domestic tensions. There is no direct evidence and not much indirect evidence. Schmidt is surely correct that the Bismarckian empire had run its course and was on the verge of dramatic change.[14]

Little thought had been given to financing a war. The government expected that the 1914 war would be a repeat of 1866 or 1870: a quick victory and then an indemnity from the conquered foe. Popular myth said that the *Juliusturm* in Spandau held enough French gold from 1871 to pay for Germany's victory. No one knew what the war would cost. The *Juliusturm* gold covered only two days of fighting. The Reichstag unanimously passed a war credit of M5 billion with the full expectation of quick repayment. The Reichsbank's policies of hoarding gold and high discount rates proved prescient. The gold reserve, which had averaged M778 million in 1910, peaked at M1,370 million in July 1914. A run on the Reichsbank in the last week before the war persuaded the Reichstag to suspend gold convertibility. The mandates for insurance funds and savings banks to buy bonds also paid dividends even before the war as Prussia placed a loan of M600 million in February successfully. Patriotic fervor drew the investor into the bond market as nothing before the war. As the fighting continued, the expenditures grew steeper. M1 billion a month covered fighting in 1914, but the cost rose to M2 billion a month in 1915 and the first three-quarters of 1916. The government soaked up the tax revenue of the rickety fiscal system and then turned successfully to bond issues. While Adolf Wagner, "the Nestor of German financial science," called for new taxes and tax reform to cover the spending, Dietzel and new Treasury Secretary Karl Helfferich supported a credit policy. At the end of May 1916, M36 billion in bond issues had covered the war costs of M39.78 billion. Had the German army broken through at this time, the fiscal situation would have remained in balance and a moderate peace would have been possible though not likely. At the onset of war, the Reichstag had enabled the Bundesrat to pass emergency economic legislation on its own. It was inconceivable that the states would give up their monopoly on direct taxes. In 1914, the national revenue covered only 27% of expenditure. This fell to 7% in 1915 and 1916. France in the same years covered 40%, 19%, and 13% respectively from revenue. The British average over the war years was 28%.[15]

After the Battle of Verdun, victory was clearly far off, and Paul von Hindenburg became head of the Supreme Command. While Hindenburg may

---

14. Kroboth, pp. 308-317. Fischer, p. 199.

15. Fischer, p. 200. Kroboth, pp. 12, 52, 67, 106. Eichengreen, p. 70. Williamson, p. 31. Gerald D. Feldman, *Industry, Army, and Labor, 1914-1918* (Princeton, 1966), pp. 28, 63. Feldman, *Disorder*, pp. 30-40, gives a 1914 gold reserve figure of M 2.09 billion. Bruce Kent, *The Spoils of War: The Politics, Economics, and Diplomacy of Reparations, 1918-1932* (Oxford, 1989), pp. 26-49.

have been a hero to many, the investors of Germany were either unable or unwilling to throw good money after bad money in the German war effort. With great fanfare, the government lurched into the hugely inefficient Hindenburg Program. It aimed to double production of munitions and triple production of machine guns and artillery. All the pre-1916 trends accelerated: the government exempted more workers from military service, allowed the industries to have greater profits, and founded a new War Office, which stripped the Prussian War Ministry of its social and economic functions and subordinated the district commanders of Prussia to its wishes. From May 1916 to the end of the war, the regime spent another M120 billion. Bonds covered only M61 billion and revenue a mere M15 billion. The government slowly increased taxes starting in 1916 with increased consumption taxes and levied a turnover tax on each stage of production. The Reich covered the difference with printed money. The floating debt (that is, the portion borrowed from the government itself) from the Reichsbank rose to M48 billion. The growth of paper money had an especially negative effect because of its recent legalization. For most of the war, the government kept prices low by imposing piecemeal controls through the district military commanders of Prussia, first on food, then on a host of other items. Finally, it set up rent controls. The decline in quality and quantity of consumer items led to an increase in the savings rate, which provided a larger pool to buy German bonds. In the end it was not enough. The mark fell steeply in value in the currency markets. Its official exchange rate per U.S. dollar was M4.2 but the unofficial rate was M7 to a dollar by October 1918. In November 1918, the Kaiser fled Germany in the face of a revolution, and the war was over.[16]

The years before the war had shown a shift occurring in the old social, economic, and political alignments of Germany. Some analysts have followed the suggestion of Jürgen Habermas and focused on the evolution of the "public sphere" (*Öffentlichkeit*) existing between civil society and the state. In this school of thought, we may say that the Prussian monarchy and German empire had evolved in the nineteenth century to where the public sphere was publicly monitored but not publicly controlled. The war now began the next stage where the public sphere of social welfare state democracies became a field of competition among conflicting interests. This public sphere would now become an arena for settling conflicts with an unstable balance between the state and various interest groups. Politics, which had been a field mostly for conservative, liberal, or Catholic elites, was now going to change.[17]

---

16. Feldman, *Army*, pp. 149-152; *Disorder*, pp. 41, 57-59, 66, 83. Kent, pp. 49-60.

17. Jürgen Habermas, *The Structural Transformation of the Public Sphere: An Inquiry into a Category of Bourgeois Society*, reprint edition (Cambridge, Mass., 1989).

The war had joined strange bedfellows.    Yet an alliance between Wilhelm II and some Social Democrats was understandable.  The SPD wanted to see sweeping change in Russia.  Presumably the introduction of a parliamentary regime with free elections would lead to socialist gains in that industrializing nation as it had in most others.  The SPD also hoped that a demonstration of its loyalty might win major domestic concessions from the government.  It misjudged the Kaiser's government.  The government resisted a pledge on major political changes until the war turned sour and the revolution overthrew the Russian empire in 1917.  The regime also misjudged the SPD.  It believed that it could cow the party or buy it off with a few gifts.  It found that with each concession the SPD and the labor unions kept demanding more.    The government stalled, hoping that each offensive would be the last, but victory kept receding to the horizon.[18]

Labor won a major concession in 1916 with the creation of war boards, where the district military commanders would consult with labor leaders in settling disputes.  The unions saw this as the first step toward collective bargaining and formal recognition.  Not all of the district commanders accepted war boards, but it still had an impact.  The capstone to this process was the Auxiliary Service Bill passed in December 1916. During the passage of the bill, the SPD paid a cagey role, maneuvering to protect the rights of coalition, which amounted to de facto recognition of unions.  Rather than fight this provision, members of the Conservative party stayed home.  In many ways, the passage of this bill foreshadowed the history of the Weimar Republic.  There was a broad community of interest between industry and labor, mediated by the government.  Both sides had much to gain from this bill.  The industrialists would gain hefty profits, while the labor unions would regain many members lost up to this point in the war.  The Bill excluded the company-led "yellow unions" from the new workers' committees.  Even in the Krupp factories, a stronghold of yellow unions, the executives did not flex their muscles in the voting for committee representatives but left the yellow leaders to twist in the wind.  In October 1918, heavy industry agreed to collective bargaining.  The next month, industries cut support to the yellow unions.  The agreement between industrialist Hugo Stinnes and labor leader Carl Legien seemed to promise a new world.[19]

At times in the middle 1920s it appeared that industry and labor could rebuild this coalition.  One may draw a line from the Auxiliary Service Bill of 1916 to the Unemployment Insurance Bill of 1927, which  conservatives and socialists would support as well.  Yet the 1916 debate also foreshadowed some of the debates that would doom Weimar.  The two extremes in the Reichstag opposed the bill.  Here was the nucleus of anticorporatist rebellion, which would

---

18.  Fischer, pp. 524 and 540.

19.  Feldman, *Army*, pp. 87-92, 237-248, 323, 521-526.

become so important after 1928. The yellow unions would also wind up as supporters of the radical Nationalist Alfred Hugenberg against more moderate and cooperative forces that were willing to support the republic.[20]

The founders of the Weimar Republic had to pick up the pieces of a shattered fiscal policy. A budget is in surplus when all sources of income exceed expenses. Even loans taken before the end of the fiscal year may count as part of revenue. A classic budget deficit is one where some expenses need covering by loans. A deficit by itself does not lead to disaster as long as the debt is properly structured in a series of contractual loans that expire after a given period. What governments want to avoid is "floating debt," which is simply money printed to cover expenses. Germany paid for the last thirty months of World War I largely with printed money, and the floating debt's total of M48 billion was twenty-one times greater than 1914's entire tax revenue. The total debt (including bonds and structured loans) was a staggering M166 billion. Such numbers made the idea of a "fiscal policy" almost meaningless. Somebody had to pay this bill, and there were essentially four options. If the new government had tried to make the wealthy pay or repudiated the debt, it would require a sweeping expropriation. The wealthy also had ways to take their capital out of Germany. A second option would make the middle class pay through a process of inflation that would reduce the value of its fixed assets until the government could pay its debt at reduced cost. The third choice would burden the poor with crushingly regressive taxation, especially on consumer staples. This would be almost impossible in a democratic system. The fourth option was the old hope of making foreigners pay for the war. This would be difficult with military occupation looming, yet the Germans carried this out through inflation and repudiation of foreign debt. The inflation of the postwar period, while not a deliberate policy, was the inadvertent choice of most people who did not care for the other options. It would take a unique set of circumstances to unleash the hyperinflation of 1923. The socialists leading the revolutionary government turned to financial experts from the imperial period. The first Finance Minister of the Republic was Eugen Schiffer, who had served during the war in the Treasury Office. Schiffer's initial plan to the Council of People's Commissars seemed to follow Option 1: an 80% war-profits tax, a capital gains tax, and a higher income and inheritance tax. This plan angered the states and caused the rich to move their capital abroad. The government stopped well short of ordering expropriation. Perhaps if the revolution had continued and radicalized, the government would have ordered expropriation and diminished inflationary potential. Ironically, the desire of Friedrich Ebert,

---

20. Ibid., p. 237.

President of the new republic, to have a quick, stabilizing vote may have been a factor in the inflation.[21]

The chaos of the revolution of 1918 meant that the Scheidemann Cabinet did not take up the budget for Fiscal Year 1919 until March 11.  To keep the government legally funded, the Cabinet had to resort to four-month continuing resolutions, while it passed the rest of the budget department-by-department to the National Assembly.  The Assembly gave the Finance Ministry special spending powers to deal with the demobilization.  Although the piecemeal nature of the budget precluded any real fiscal management, the government began to wrestle with the taxes that would pay for the budget and reduce the debt.  Demobilization costs by January 1919 exceeded the entire Reich budget for 1913.  The baseline used was the last peacetime budget of 1913, but inflation had devalued money over six years.  The main sources of revenue would include a special war payment, a levy on capital, and the rayon tax.  The Ministry expected almost five times as much yield from taxes as before the war.  M2 billion would come from the turnover tax, which the Ministry would reform and expand to tax luxury goods at a 15% rate.[22]

Minister without Portfolio Erzberger challenged Schiffer, particularly over a new capital gains tax.  Although England had a 20% rate, Schiffer had proposed only a 10% rate for Germany.  Erzberger felt that this rate was too low and that it was unfair to tax the smallest capital-gains transactions.  The Cabinet backed Erzberger and inserted a "hardship clause."  As another way of balancing the budget, Erzberger suggested a unilateral revaluing of war loans from 5% to 4%.  As more of the piecemeal fiscal policy, the Cabinet allowed Schiffer to bring the tax proposals to the Committee of States and the National Assembly as soon as the Finance Ministry put them together.  In April, Bernhard Dernburg replaced Schiffer.  Dernburg gave the first comprehensive overview of Germany's postwar financial situation to the Cabinet on April 26.  He estimated the total war debt at a staggering M185 billion.  The impending loss of territories would cost the Reich M600 million of income.  Since the 1913 budget, revenue had grown M13.764 billion, but expenses had grown M18.029 billion.[23]

To plug the hole, the Reich took some M5.6 to 6 billion from the states and cities.  It also assumed control over some taxes from the states, and they found huge gaps opening in their budgets.  By September, the Assembly had passed many tax proposals but delayed others.  The Scheidemann Cabinet proposed another continuing resolution to last to the end of September.  The

---

21. Kent, p. 49. Feldman, *Disorder*, pp. 132-135. Hagen Schulze, ed., *Akten der Reichskanzlei. Das Kabinett Scheidemann* (Boppard, 1971), p. XXXI.

22. *Kabinett Scheidemann*, Doc. #9, p. 33. Feldman, *Disorder*, pp. 129-133.

23. *Kabinett Scheidemann*, Docs. #14a and #14b, pp. 48-59; #26, p. 112; #43, p. 175; #54b, pp. 229-231.

resolution only appropriated about M422 million, but it authorized the Finance Ministry to spend up to M6 billion on war-related and demobilization costs. The Assembly passed the resolution with hardly any debate because it was consumed with the burning problem of the peace treaty. The new Bauer Cabinet wrote the budget for the other half of the year and the Assembly passed it with little debate.[24]

Some socialists believed that only a command economy could solve the variety of problems. A "Dictatorial Committee" chaired by Economics Minister Rudolf Wissell called for a unified economic, financial, and social policy. The Wissell plan would nationalize key industries, use higher property taxes to create semi-public corporations, and give extra support to workers, especially those working in export industries. The non-Socialist parties opposed nationalization, and socialization ideas faded quite quickly. Wissell found himself isolated and resigned from the Cabinet in July 1919. Even without expropriation, Wissell had a point. The imperial government had mandated ownership of public bonds by insurance funds and by savings banks. It would not have been such a radical departure for the Weimar government to accelerate this trend. A Swedish law of 1903 forced private insurance companies to invest mostly in bonds and bills, while a 1924 banking law in that nation prevented banks from owning shares in joint-stock companies. In 1918, 44% of the assets of the Prussian savings banks had been in bonds, but by 1920, that figure would fall to 31%. The savings banks had showed their potential for being collection points of national capital, but that ended with the armistice. Had the government prevented the dumping of the securities or compelled the institutions to take more bonds, that could have served as a brake on inflation. Within a dozen years many private banks collapsed and the government had to nationalize them under different circumstances.[25]

Erzberger became Bauer's Finance Minister and generally opposed the more radical socialist plans. He had emerged in the years before the war as a leading financial expert of the Catholic Center and had pressed for a broader national tax structure, such as the general wealth tax he and Bassermann had proposed before the war. He wanted to put finances on a sound, tax-based footing and explained that the peace treaty and the Reich's financial duties had made a takeover of revenues necessary. This process had been advancing since

---

24. Ibid., Docs. #58, p. 256; #86, p. 378; #105, p. 436. Anton Golecki, ed., *Akten der Reichskanzlei. Das Kabinett Bauer* (Boppard, 1980), Docs. #60, p. 247; #62, p. 254.

25. Feldman, *Disorder*, pp. 145-155. Mats Larsson, "Overcoming Institutional Barriers: Financial Networks in Sweden, 1910-1990," in Youssef Cassis, Gerald D. Feldman, and Ulf Olsson, eds., *The Evolution of Financial Institutions in Twentieth-Century Europe* (Aldershot, UK, 1995), pp. 126-129. Paul Thomes, "German Savings Banks as Instruments of Regional Development up to the Second World War," in ibid., pp. 153-157.

the founding of the Reich.  In 1875, Reich tax revenue accounted for M240 million.  That rose to M822 million, or M15 per person by 1891, and then over M2 billion, or M32 per person by 1913.  Reich debt had escalated at a similar pace.  It was at M5.4 billion before the war added M151 billion.  Before the war, revenue had been split, with the Reich getting 41%, the states 22%, and the municipalities 36%.  Now the Reich would take 70%, the states 10%, and the cities 20%.  This represented a giant step toward fiscal union, but there was still a long way to go.  The debt situation, the growth of expenses, and the uncertainty of the economy would make revenue estimates extremely difficult.[26]

Shortly after sending this memo to the state and cities, Erzberger brought two major proposals to the Cabinet: an emergency progressive capital levy and an increase in the turnover tax from 5% to 6%.   Others feared that over time, property values would change so radically as to make the levy meaningless. Their fears were justified.  A year after the levy took effect, the government indexed it to inflation.  On the turnover tax, Erzberger tried to leave exports and certain items tax free, while raising the tax on luxury items.  The National Assembly passed both bills by the end of 1919.  The Emergency Capital Levy would take effect January 1, 1920, and the Turnover Tax changes would take effect April 1.[27]

State budgets remained a problem.  The Finance Minister laid out the essential problem: Reich spending would equal M17.5 billion with an allowance for the states and localities of M6.5 billion.  Erzberger expected the additional reparations bill to equal M2 billion a year.   The most optimistic revenue projections topped out at M8 billion.  His proposed levies would bring another M7 billion.  The only choice was to introduce an increased Reich income tax with a 30% capital gains tax tied to it.  Erzberger outlined a plan where the Reich would take exclusive control of the tariffs, consumption taxes, transportation taxes, and property taxes, while the states would keep exclusive control of production taxes and fees on land, building, and property.  The Reich and states would share the income tax, stamp tax, and turnover tax.  A Reich income tax made it necessary to create a unified tax administration.  Prussia supported Erzberger, but Bavaria deeply distrusted all of the proposals and pointed out that the Reich did not have the civil service to create a unified tax administration by Erzberger's target date of October 1.  Where would those officials come from?  Prussia agreed to support Erzberger's proposals as long as the Reich did not dismember the states or take autonomy from states and localities.  Against the votes of Bavaria, Baden, and Saxony, the Committee of States passed Erzberger's unification plan in August; the administrative changes came into effect in October.[28]

---

26. *Kabinett Bauer*, Doc. #17, pp. 71-78.

27. Ibid., Doc. #22, pp. 99-101.

28. Ibid., Docs. #24, pp. 105-116; #34, pp. 150-151.

The actual division of the income tax with the states took longer. The Cabinet accepted Erzberger's proposal. The income tax would be progressive with rates ranging from 10% to 60%. Those making less than 1,000 marks a year would be tax exempt. The Finance Minister had finally settled on a 10% capital gains tax, which would go the Reich alone. The Reichstag passed the State Tax Law in March 1920. By August, the Reich needed to fund M76 billion of debt. The main alternatives presented included a "premium loan," which would be free from the inheritance tax, or a forced loan, which would mandate that businesses and individuals prepay several years of taxes. The Reichsbank felt that a premium loan would not raise enough money considering the amount of capital fleeing Germany, but Erzberger warned that a forced loan would deprive businesses of needed capital. The Cabinet ultimately supported Erzberger and authorized a M5 billion eighty-year recallable loan at 2%. The Reichsbank opposed even this small loan and retorted that it would only raise M3.8 billion, of which half would be rolled-over war bonds; new capital would amount to less than M2 billion. Other small taxes would close the remaining gap. Because of the late 1919 budget measures, the Bauer Cabinet did not present the 1920 budget until March 12. At that point the Kapp Putsch broke out, and in the emergency the government had to resort to another continuing resolution to fund April through June of 1920. The caretaker Müller Cabinet passed a second temporary budget to cover July through September 1920.[29]

By the middle of 1920 things appeared to be settling down. Maier has written of a worldwide "Thermidor" as Germany, Italy, the United States, Britain, Spain, Austria, Hungary, and even the Soviet Union moved to the right in 1920-21. It had become clear that the Bolshevik Revolution was not the first wave of an inevitable revolutionary tide. Communist parties formed and dug in for the long haul. Industrialists and some older labor leaders again saw their interests converging. In March 1920 Germany received a ten-year credit from the Netherlands intended for purchase of food and raw materials. The collateral was steep: a 50% interest in the border coal mines. The New York market was buying and selling German bonds by the last half of 1919. Even the Kapp Putsch of March 1920 did not dent the German currency. In February 1920, a dollar had bought ninety-nine marks; by June it bought thirty-nine marks. An effective 90% devaluation was bad, but the trend was encouraging. Compromises with the army and industrial and financial interests along with heavy spending on demobilization had barely averted a civil war and full Allied occupation.[30]

---

29. Ibid., Docs. #49, pp. 197-198; #72, p. 287; #103-104, pp. 386-393; #186, p. 669. Martin Vogt, ed., *Akten der Reichskanzlei. Das Kabinett Müller I* (Boppard, 1971), Doc. #102, p. 258.

30. Maier, *Recasting*, p. 136. Feldman, *Disorder*, pp. 203-204, 216.

The turn to the right in the elections of June 1920 marked a key point in German history. The Weimar Coalition of Social Democrats, Catholics, and Democrats (DDP) lost its majority and never regained it. The first two years had seen a conflict between militant socialists and the nonsocialists. Future majority coalitions would feature conflicts either between socialists and the pro-business People's party (DVP) or between the business interests of the People's party and the Nationalist party (DNVP) against the social activists of the Catholic Center. Catholic Centrist Konstantin Fehrenbach became Chancellor with Joseph Wirth held over as Finance Minister from the Müller Cabinet. Wirth had enjoyed a meteoric rise. He had studied math and national economy, and by age thirty-four, he was a member of the Landtag of Baden. The next year he was a member of the Reichstag. After the war, he became Finance Minister of Baden and a member of the National Assembly.[31]

The Kapp Putsch, the caretaker Müller regime, and the election results had left fiscal policy in chaos. There was spending pressure to add more civil servants, and Ruhr businesses and unions were asking for a change in tax withholding. Wirth yielded on the last demand and allowed a reduction in the withholding rate for middle-class employees. Wirth confronted the Postal Minister, who had demanded sweeping raises for his workers and the rest of the civil service. Wirth threatened to resign unless he could cut the civil service budget. Fehrenbach persuaded Wirth to withdraw his resignation, and the Finance Minister began to build his institutional power. The Cabinet was about to take up the budget for Fiscal Year 1920 at last, and Wirth demanded guidelines, including the right to veto other ministries' budgets and a commitment to long-term reductions in the civil service. The railroad and postal service had to make sharp reductions in personnel and salary. He further demanded that all ministries register their compliance with these guidelines and that the government grant an official of the Finance Ministry special powers as commissar to check compliance. Wirth assured the Postal Minister that the commissar would not review the railroad or the postal service, since they were quasi-governmental bodies. While Erzberger had unified Reich finances under the Reich, Wirth had taken the next step and put all Reich finances under the umbrella of the Finance Ministry. The Ministry could now plan and execute a united fiscal policy.[32]

The Cabinet submitted the 1920 budget in September, five months after it should have become law. The draft balanced the ordinary spending at M29.8

---

31. Ingrid Schulze-Bidlingmeier, ed., *Akten der Reichskanzlei. Die Kabinette Wirth I/II* (Boppard, 1973), p. XXIII; Arnold Brecht, *The Political Education of Arnold Brecht: An Autobiography* (Princeton, 1970), p. 202.

32. Peter Wulf, ed., *Akten der Reichskanzlei. Das Kabinett Fehrenbach*, Docs. #50 (Boppard, 1972), p. 118; #71, pp. 186-187; #73, pp. 189-192; #85, pp. 222-229.

billion and would cover most of the extraordinary budget of M39.7 billion with new loans. Then the Allies raised their cost estimate of the army of occupation. Germany would need to borrow M67 billion for the extraordinary budget, the postal deficit, and the Reichsbahn. The Reichstag did not pass the 1920 budget until January 1921. Five days later, Wirth presented the draft of the 1921 budget to the Cabinet. The Fehrenbach government was getting a hold on fiscal policy. While taxes covered only 36.3% of the FY20's spending, they covered 44.5% of FY21. Nevertheless, the value of the floating debt had tripled to M272 billion. The yield from Erzberger's income tax and the special levy on capital was disappointing, largely because of tax evasion by the wealthy. The Reichstag passed the 1921 budget in July, only three months late. Budget-making was starting to return to normal.[33]

Germany had not been alone in putting off the financing of the war. Both Britain and France had borrowed heavily and faced the same options as Germany, but as victors they could burden the defeated. France had covered only 16.8% of expenses, while Britain had covered 28.5%. Britain owed the United States $4.7 billion, of which almost one-quarter would come due immediately. The French were in worse financial shape because they had refused to enact a meaningful income tax. There had been a general presumption that the losers would bear the costs, just as the French had suffered a 5-billion-franc indemnity in 1871. Article XIX of the Armistice provided for reparations and froze German gold and securities.[34]

On April 27, 1921, the Reparation Commission meeting in London finally announced that 132 billion Gold Marks (the 1913 value of the Mark) were outstanding in reparations. Germany would pay GM2 billion plus 26% of the value of its exports to the Allies each year to cover this. In the German FY1921, reparations accounted for almost one-third of all budget expenses. The German government was only collecting GM3 billion of revenue a year. The choices seemed stark: raise taxes to cover reparations and government expenses, cut spending to only the most vital necessities for the next forty years, or inflate the currency. Given the turmoil of the early years of the Republic, the first two options might well have led to the overthrow of the regime. It is understandable, if not excusable, that the government increasingly resorted to the third option. Analysts who are skeptical of German policy in this period note that Germany only had to pay amounts totaling GM50 billion, while the Allies put off the remaining GM82 billion for the future. Others have suggested that to

---

33. Ibid., Docs. #83, pp. 212-218; #108, pp. 274-276; #109, p. 277; #125, pp. 317-319; #151, p. 399; #156, p. 413. Feldman, *Disorder*, pp. 217, 347, 584. *Kabinette Wirth*, Doc. #44, p. 123.

34. France: 37.821 billion francs revenue, 224.862 billion francs expenditures 1914-1919; Britain: £2.733 billion revenues, £9.593 billion expenditures, Kent, pp. 26-49. Dan P. Silverman, *Reconstructing Europe after the Great War* (Cambridge, MA, 1982), p. 13.

fulfill the demands, Germany at this time would have needed a strong left-center coalition, import of foreign capital, high productivity, high taxes, fiscal discipline, and moderate inflation. The only other regime of fulfillment would have been a dictatorship that could compel payment.[35]

William McNeil has addressed Germany's ability to pay. He noted that French business interests rejected payment in kind with items such as coal. Sufficient global economic growth could have allowed Germany to pay reparations with ease. It also could have paid reparations, had it been willing to run a large trade surplus. Stephen Schuker suggests this would have been easy if Germany did not pay such high wages in the Weimar era, but he ignores the prewar trade deficit. Several economists have identified the relationship between budget surplus and a trade surplus. The trade surplus would have supplied Germany with the hard currency to pay the reparations. This situation would exist in 1924 and 1925. However, this degree of fiscal contraction led to high unemployment and threatened German political stability. Although the situation is not identical, economists have examined the transfer balance of France and Germany after 1871 and found similar results. France transferred roughly one-quarter of its Gross National Product to Germany over the course of thirty months. Half the money raised in bond issues came from outside France, but the French had to enforce a sharp reduction in consumption and investment spending. Within only six or seven years, the French had generated enough revenue to pay back the indemnity costs, while Germany, absorbing an amount equal to one-third of its Gross National Product, seemed to go on a consumption and investment binge and ran heavy trade deficits with France, Britain, and Belgium. Fritz Machlup compared the reparations problem to three other major transfers: British support for the enemies of Napoleon, the French indemnity of 1871, and American foreign assistance in the 1950s. Machlup found that German reparations payments as percentages of the economy or foreign trade volume were probably the least of the four transfer cases.[36]

Feldman stresses that political problems led to an acceleration of inflation precisely because the crisis seemed to have passed. Demand for

---

35. Kent, pp. 132-134. Stephen A. Schuker, *American "Reparations" to Germany, 1919-33: Implications for the Third-World Debt Crisis* (Princeton, 1988), pp. 14-19. Jon Jacobson, "The Reparations Settlement of 1924," in Gerald D. Feldman, Carl-Ludwig Holtfrerich, Gerhard A. Ritter, and Peter-Christian Witt, eds., *The Consequences of Inflation/Konsquenzen der Inflation* (Berlin, 1989), pp. 85-86.

36. Schuker, *"Reparations,"* p. 83. William C. McNeil, "Could Germany Pay? Another Look at the Reparations Problem of the 1920s," in Feldman et al., *Consequences of Inflation*, pp. 109-123. Michael Gavin, "Intertemporal Dimensions of International Economic Adjustment: Evidence from the Franco-Prussian War Indemnity," in John Komlos and Scott Eddie, eds., *Selected Cliometric Studies on German Economic History* (Stuttgart, 1997), pp. 34-45. Fritz Machlup, *International Payments, Debts, and Gold: Collected Essays* (New York, 1964), pp. 374-393.

clothes and food rose. During the Revolution, the government had issued a Demobilization Decree establishing unemployment relief. The Reich would pay half the cost, the states one-third, and the localities one-sixth. Labor Minister Heinrich Brauns promised a series of ordinances and noted that the Reichsrat was now working on a draft on comprehensive unemployment insurance. However, unemployment laws had set fixed payments, which the inflation had rendered worthless. The Bauer government had published decrees on work relief, but this proved to be more expensive than payments. It became easier to pay people than to maintain some variety of "workfare." There were also structural problems. John Kenneth Galbraith suggests that a root cause of twentieth-century inflation is the increased power of corporations and labor unions. The former have the power to set prices, while the latter force corporations to pass along some profit. Maier finds the keys to inflation in the organization of the workers and the failure to uproot the conservative elites.[37]

Many assign the main responsibility for the inflation to the leaders of the bureaucracy and particularly Reichsbank President Rudolf Havenstein. They believed that the reparations caused inflation. Stabilization would be impossible until a "final" reparations settlement. Havenstein claimed his hands were tied while the German money-printing presses ran continuously. He even mobilized the idle presses from the late Austro-Hungarian empire to keep cash flowing. When quantity theorists of money urged the Reichsbank to end the creation of new currency, Havenstein replied that the reparations were inflationary because they were exports that produced no balancing foreign exchange. To fight the returning surge of inflation, the Reichsbank needed to cut back on credit and hike the discount rate. Havenstein told the Reichsbank Curatorium in September 1920 that he could not raise the rate above 8-9%, which he said was the prevailing rate in the United States and United Kingdom. The sources of the time tell a different story. Usury laws limited American interest rates in most states to 6-8%, while the effective yield of British bonds was about 5% at this time. Economist Alfred Lansburgh criticized the Reichsbank for its low discount rate and its inability to market treasury bills. Only in June 1922, when Germany was on the precipice of disaster, was the discount rate raised to 6%. The bank should have raised the rate to double digits during the stabilization period to try to break the inflationary cycle and been prepared to raise it further in the later part of 1921 and 1922. This might have triggered a recession and caused incomes to fall. When the inflation accelerated, most real incomes fell anyway. The political instability of May 1921 caused by the London Ultimatum

37. Prussian State Archives (PrStA), Rep. 151, Abt. IA, #1074/6. *Kabinett Fehrenbach*, Doc. #80, pp. 204-207. Feldman, *Disorder*, pp. 232-235. John Kenneth Galbraith, *Money: Whence It Came, Where It Went*, revised edition (New York, 1995), pp. 275-276. Charles S. Maier, *In Search of Stability: Explorations in Historical Political Economy* (Cambridge, 1987), p. 202.

and a clash in Upper Silesia sparked the revival of "galloping" inflation. Fehrenbach resigned as Chancellor and Wirth took over that post as well. Between May and December 1921, the Mark lost another two-thirds of its value to stand at 192 to the dollar.[38]

The fiscal policy of the Wirth government was fundamentally sound. If one looks at the 1922 budget in Gold Marks, Wirth slashed spending from GM6.65 billion to GM3.95 billion and cut the deficit from GM3.68 billion to GM2.44 billion. However, the Wirth government also suffered a great loss in income, from GM2.98 billion to GM1.51 billion, from inflation and foreign-policy problems. After assuming the chancellorship, Wirth had to pay the demands of the London Ultimatum and try to reduce the debt. The Ultimatum poisoned Wirth's attempts to solve the financial crisis because the parties of the Reichstag were loath to approve tax increases that would go into the pockets of the Allies. As property values inflated, the yield on the property tax fell. By the end of July the Cabinet had agreed on a tax package, but it fell into a black hole as inflation rose and fiscal policy collapsed. The Cabinet did not send the bills to the Reichstag until October, and the Reichstag did not approve them until the end of March 1922. This was a fatal delay of eight months. As the deficit widened, Wirth had to propose another package raising fifteen taxes and featuring a forced loan, but the Reichstag did not approve this until July 1922. These taxes yielded very little revenue for 1922, and the rejection of a property tax angered the Allies.[39]

As the domestic economy crumbled, the Wirth government tried to stave off the Allied demands. The reparations payment of March 1922 drained the Reichsbank of most of its foreign exchange reserves and the Germans again pleaded poverty. Rescheduling followed rescheduling as the French began to discuss whether they should treat Germany as a financial colony. By the summer there was a growing fatalism that the government would not resolve the emergency and that the Allies would occupy the Ruhr valley. The assassination of Foreign Minister Walther Rathenau reduced international confidence in Germany even more. By the end of July, the mark was at one-tenth of its level of two summers before and less than 1% of its prewar value. The story of the collapse is well known: the mark continued to lose its value through the fall of 1922 and it became commonplace to use foreign currency in everyday transactions. The ministries fell to fighting with each other and with the

---

38. Feldman, *Disorder*, pp., 158, 256, 339-342, 386, 402-404, 451. *World Almanac and Book of Facts 1928* (New York, 1927), p. 862; Statistischen Reichsamt, *Finanzen und Steuern im In- und Ausland: Ein statistisches Handbuch* (Berlin, 1930), p. 743.

39. Williamson, p. 347. Fritz Blaich, *Der Schwarze Freitag: Inflation und Wirtschaftskrise* (Munich, 1985), Table 3, p. 164. *Kabinette Wirth*, Docs. #38, pp. 91-97; #40a-b, pp. 115-119; #58, pp. 155-157; #205, p. 565. Maier, *Recasting*, pp. 255-282.

Reichsbank. Politics became more extreme. Wirth resigned. It is impossible to guess how much German capital fled abroad during the crisis. Budget-making was truly a farce as the government put ten supplementary appropriations through the Reichstag in the 1922/23 fiscal year. The new Finance Minister, Andreas Hermes, asked for tax increases that again ran a seven-month gauntlet. Far, far too late, the Reichsbank raised the discount rate to 12% on January 8, 1923. By the end of the year, the rate would stand at 90%.[40]

Wilhelm Cuno had a solid financial background and became Chancellor in November 1922. He had been an official in the Treasury and the grain office during the war, then the leader of the Hamburg-America line. Cuno began with the confidence of the Reichstag stretching from the Social Democrats to the Nationalists. This last party had been formed out of the wartime wreckage of the Conservative, Free Conservative, and National Liberal parties. It was one of the most diverse parties in the Republic, as it included agrarian interests, industrialists, pan-Germans, racists, leaders of employees' organizations and other groups. The German National People's Party (DNVP) was especially attractive to civil servants. While the conservative parties of the empire had become exclusively East Elbian groups, the Nationalists had the opportunity to recast themselves as a mass movement. All that bound the party together was the memory of an unpopular empire. Most of the leaders of the party, such as Helfferich, Oskar Hergt, and Kuno von Westarp, had been officials in the government. They had lost their jobs with the Revolution, and though they hated the Republic, they desperately wanted to regain the levers of power. The Cuno Cabinet represented the first step in their journey back. They supported Cuno but did not enter the Cabinet. The Socialists had their chance in 1919-20, the center group had tried and failed in 1920-22, now the nationalists had their opportunity. There would be an immediate test.[41]

On January 11, 1923, the French and Belgians occupied the Ruhr. The Cuno government called for passive resistance and removed all restraints on spending. It would subsidize those workers who refused to labor for the occupiers. Numbers were calculated in millions, then billions, then trillions. It is ironic that this "cabinet of experts" turned out to be one of the most inept, and that Germany's economic collapse occurred under a man generally regarded as a successful business leader. The government refused to negotiate with the Allies while they occupied the Ruhr, and many believed (correctly) that Cuno

---

40. Feldman, *Disorder*, pp. 431, 450, 485, 640. Karl-Heinz Harbeck, ed., *Akten der Reichskanzlei. Das Kabinett Cuno* (Boppard, 1978), Docs. #68, pp. 229-230; #86, p. 284; #10, pp. 27-28; #55, p. 195. *Kabinette Wirth*, Doc. #369, p. 1038.

41. Feldman, *Disorder*, p. 490. Robert Grathwol, *Stresemann and the DNVP: Reconciliation or Revenge in German Foreign Policy, 1924-1928* (Lawrence, KS, 1980), p. 15. Otto Braun, *Von Weimar zu Hitler* (Hamburg, 1949), p. 32. Witt, p. 61, points out that of the forty-one districts won consistently by the Conservative or Reichspartei after 1890, all were east of the Elbe River. Maier, *Recasting*, pp. 354-355.

and his Foreign Secretary were heavily under Helfferich's influence. Cuno made few changes to Wirth's 1923 budget draft, but it was meaningless as inflation rendered the hard-won taxes of 1922 worthless. The Cuno Cabinet just watched the whirlwind. Not until July 25, 1923, was an action plan drafted, but it was reminiscent of Wirth's last tax package that had not come close to balancing the budget. Otherwise, all that the Cabinet could contemplate was another forced loan. Hermes believed that halting inflation was not possible, and his only suggestion was to raise the turnover tax each month. The Reichstag was now dutifully passing proposals almost as soon as it received them from the government. One law passed through the Tax Committee and the full Reichstag in less than forty-eight hours. In the emergency, all knew that this was no time for games.[42]

The end of the Cuno Cabinet came on August 12, not with a bang but with a whimper. Even without the inflation, investor confidence had plunged to a new low. The government floated a dollar-denominated loan, but investors purchased only one-quarter of the bond issue. The Cuno regime, which had billed itself as a government of economic experts, proved to be the most economically maladroit Cabinet in the history of the Weimar Republic, no mean achievement. The British rejected an attempt at arbitration by international lawyer John Foster Dulles. Finally, the Berlin printers went on strike rather than print more money. After nine months, the Cuno government resigned before a no-confidence vote would have brought it down. It was left to Gustav Stresemann to try to pick up the pieces.[43]

The early days of the Stresemann Cabinet were not much more steady than the final days of the Cuno Cabinet had been. Replacing Hermes at the Finance office was Marxist theorist Rudolf Hilferding. President Ebert chaired a chaotic meeting of the Cabinet Council that stretched into the early morning hours. Hilferding's best suggestion was another forced loan. In the next ten days, the Mark lost still more of its value as M256 trillion were added to the Reich's floating debt. At an August 30 Cabinet meeting, Stresemann and Agriculture Minister Hans Luther finally provided the leadership that Germany had been yearning for. Stresemann flatly ruled out any foreign assistance in the near future. While he believed that France wanted a solution to the Ruhr problem, Germany had to solve its own problems first. Luther, asserting himself over the flustered Hilferding, outlined the essential financial solution: the government must (1) reduce spending in the Ruhr, (2) strengthen the currency, and (3) introduce a new currency. With the emergence of Luther as

---

42. Feldman, *Disorder*, pp. 660, 700. Williamson, p. 373. *Kabinett Cuno*, Docs. #10, pp. 27-28; #224, pp. 662-666; #229, pp. 682-689; #235, pp. 702-706; #238, p. 713.

43. *Kabinett Cuno*, Doc. #128, p. 400; Feldman, *Disorder*, p. 654. Kent, p. 210.

a domestic manager to complement Stresemann's foreign-policy management, the end of the crisis was in sight at last. The inflation and uncontrolled budget deficits had been disastrous, but offered lessons to Germany. Though it was hard to tell among the ruins, the deficit spending had helped to stimulate economic growth.[44]

44. Karl Dietrich Erdmann and Martin Vogt, eds., *Akten der Reichskanzlei. Die Kabinette Stresemann I/II* (Boppard, 1978), Docs. #13, pp. 43-55; #33, pp. 155-168.

# Chapter 2

# The Soft Dictatorship and the Dawes Plan

Chastened by the hyperinflation, the government tried to avoid new deficits. By the end of 1923, the Weimar Republic seemed little different from the late empire. Both were "soft dictatorships." A constitution and an elected parliament were in place, but a few men held decision-making authority. President Ebert, Chancellors Stresemann and Wilhelm Marx, and Finance Minister Luther, not the Reichstag, held currency and tax power, The budget was written entirely by Luther and the Finance Ministry. If the former ministers of the Kaiser would return to their old offices, the cycle would be complete. The Nationalist party was poised to make an electoral breakthrough and might replace the Social Democrats as the single largest party in the Reichstag. But the Republic was more resilient than it appeared. The first steps to recovery were the end of passive resistance and the stabilization of the Mark. The Germans would finally get their monetary situation under control for the first time since 1909. They still had to stabilize the tax system, the international situation, and the political balance. By the end of 1924, they had succeeded in all these and brought the twelve-year crisis to its conclusion. The plan named after Charles Dawes provided for a bond issue, and international funds stabilized Germany. The bonds would symbolize the new hope of postwar reconstruction, cooperation, and reconciliation.

The soft dictatorship began with the passage of the Enabling Act of October 13, 1923. Nearly all sides had demanded dictatorial measures from the time that Stresemann had taken office in August. Stresemann put through eight emergency decrees under Article 48 of the Weimar Constitution from the end of September to the first part of October, but he craved even stronger authority. The Enabling Act allowed the Cabinet a free hand as long as it stayed intact. The Reich agreed to end passive resistance, but the next steps would be tricky.

The government bowed to business demands for an end to the eight-hour day, which cost them Hilferding's services in a cabinet reshuffle. To gain support from the SPD, Labor Minister Heinrich Brauns agreed to maintain the eight-hour day in principle but grant sweeping exemptions. The inflation had wiped out the union reserves, and the socialist leaders were concerned with the rising communist and fascist movements. Since the eight-hour day was legally in force only under demobilization decrees that expired in November 1923, there was very little given away. Brauns' program had other features as well: changes were made to the unemployment relief program to require contributions from employers and employees, a step toward the creation of unemployment insurance. Brauns also wanted to raise the rent tax level to bring it into accord with inflation and dedicate 15% of that tax to new housing construction. Replacing Hilferding at the Finance portfolio was Luther, who had emerged as *de facto* Finance Minister already. Luther had spent his career in the imperial civil service and had been mayor of Essen before joining the Cuno Cabinet as Agriculture Minister.[1]

Even as every group tried to blame someone else for the inflation, individuals have been quick to claim credit for the currency stabilization that began in the autumn of 1923. Arnold Brecht, then a ministerial director in the Prussian Interior Ministry, wrote in his memoirs that "I am one of the few members of the older generation who claims no credit for the currency stabilization."[2] It was Luther who took the initiative, worked out the details with other officials, and brought a plan to the Cabinet in September 1923. The government effectively raised taxes by valuing all payments on consumption taxes in gold marks. Luther fired 397,000 employees and cut the salaries of many others. The civil service released about one-third of the lower-scale workers and half of the contractual employees. The currency changeover occurred on November 15. By that time, the floating debt of the Reich had reached M191.6 quintillion, and the value of marks in circulation had reached nearly M400 quintillion. The Reichsbank ceased to discount Treasury Bills or to issue any more paper money. The value of the paper mark had reached a neat M4.2 trillion to the dollar so that the new Rentenmark was worth exactly one trillion old marks.[3]

---

1. *Kabinette Stresemann*, p. XXX; Docs. #97, pp. 416-431; #128, p. 543; #130, pp. 554-556. Feldman, *Disorder*, pp. 705, 745-6, 777, 800.

2. Brecht, p. 240.

3. For attempts to claim credit for Helfferich, see Williamson, pp. 383-393; for Hilferding, see William Smaldone, *Rudolf Hilferding: The Tragedy of a German Social Democrat* (DeKalb, IL, 1998), pp. 130-132; for Schacht, see Hjalmar Schacht, *Confessions of "the Old Wizard"* (Boston, 1956), pp. 164-172. Feldman, *Disorder*, pp. 753-760, 785-792. Edward N. Peterson, *Hjalmar Schacht: For and Against Hitler* (Boston, 1954), p. 54. *Kabinette Stresemann*, Doc. #186, p. 857.

The new currency brought a new figure into the government. Hjalmar Horace Greeley Schacht had been a director of the Nationalbank before the government named him Currency Commissioner on November 12. Schacht tried to emphasize the meaning of *Währung* not only as "currency" but also as "endurance" and "stability." If Germany stabilized its currency, general economic and political stability would not be far behind, no matter what the Allies decided. Havenstein had died three weeks earlier and President Ebert chose Schacht to head the Reichsbank because Schacht had been a charter member of the Democratic party. Karl Helfferich remained a fierce opponent of all Schacht's plans and was even more bitter after being denied the Reichsbank presidency.[4]

The Enabling Act expired when the Social Democrats left the Stresemann Cabinet in November 1923 and Stresemann resigned. Negotiations for a new government revolved around the role of the DNVP. Just five years after the revolution cast many of their leaders into political exile, the Nationalists seemed poised to resume their role as the party of government. As the Wilhelmine liberals had made their peace with the Weimar Republic in 1920, it seemed that the Wilhelmine conservatives were ready to do the same. But it became clear how much the DNVP had changed from the old conservative parties. It was a heterogeneous party including a leadership group of old imperial officials, a large agricultural faction, conservatives who had left the DVP when it became too moderate, mass organizations such as the German Employees' Union, and a significant racist faction. War and revolution had taken their toll on the self-confidence of the old imperial elite: the only things that held this amorphous group together were intense nationalism, a feeling of betrayal from the war, and the belief that the current government did not represent the true state of Germany. The Nationalists were largely responsible for the poisonous atmosphere that had led to the murders of Erzberger and Rathenau. Yet the aging leadership burned with a desire to return to the government and "put things right." At the end of November, the DNVP made concessions while negotiating with Catholic trade union leader Adam Stegerwald. It was willing to acknowledge the Weimar constitution as the basis of government, accept Stresemann as Foreign Minister and his policy of negotiating with the Allies, and would no longer call for the repudiation of the Treaty of Versailles. However, its demand for entrance into the government of Prussia ended negotiations.[5]

Wilhelm Marx, a leader of the Catholic Center, became Chancellor and retained Luther as Finance Minister. Brauns wanted to put through a new work-hours provision, and Luther had a new tax plan. Both insisted that only an

---

4. Schacht, p. 153. Peterson, p. 51.
5. *Kabinette Stresemann*, p. L. Günter Abramowski, *Akten der Reichskanzlei. Die Kabinette Marx I/II* (Boppard, 1973), pp. VII-VIII. Feldman, *Disorder*, p. 753.

Enabling Act would suffice.  Luther doubted that President Ebert would be willing to put through a massive tax program with Article 48, and others doubted that the Reichstag would pass another Enabling Act.  Marx decided that a vote on the enabling bill would serve as a vote of confidence in his government.  The Cabinet expected the SPD to vote down the second enabling bill and demand new elections.  The SPD said it might support the bill if there was Reichsrat oversight, but Brauns feared that this would allow particularist interests to decide the content of the decrees.  He proposed a compromise: the government would consult with a fifteen-man committee in the Reichsrat and the Reichstag before promulgating a decree.  On December 8, the Reichstag passed the Enabling Act with an expiration date of February 15.[6]

Since 1924, the conventional wisdom had agreed with Stresemann, Marx, and Luther that a soft dictatorship was necessary to achieve stabilization. Feldman suggests that the choice was a dictatorship or an enabling act.  He argues that some businessmen were taking a more radical line and had turned against the social compromises achieved during and after World War I.  Several men had approached the army commander about serving as emergency Chancellor.  The radical right toyed with the idea of restoring a House of Lords for all Germany, calling it a chamber of "productive estates."  But others have a point as well.  The expiration of the Demobilization Decree on work-hours would end the eight-hour day, and it should have been possible to forge a compromise not too different from Brauns' decree once the SPD climbed down from its high horse of rhetoric.  It is true that the Reichstag's delay in passing Wirth's tax package in 1921-22 had destroyed its effectiveness.  Since the Ruhr invasion, however, the Reichstag had been very quick to pass almost every piece of tax legislation the government had sent to it.  It passed all the main supplementary budgets of the Cuno Cabinet with little debate.  Although the Catholic Center and SPD rejected an increase in the turnover tax in June of 1923, they did support a package of tax increases to secure local budgets.  A six-part tax plan proposed on July 25, 1923, became law seventeen days later. It took just thirteen days from Cabinet meeting to printing of the law to raise railroad rates.  Only the Communists and a few individuals opposed these bills. The thorniest issue, as we shall see, was the revaluation portion of the Third Emergency Tax Decree, and the government was forced to compromise to such an extent that it is difficult to imagine that regular parliamentary procedure would have been worse.  The political leaders went back to the easy days of the empire and the heady days of demobilization much too quickly and set a precedent for the Nazi regime.  The choice was not soft dictatorship or hard dictatorship in 1923.  Hard dictatorship was not an option because of the occupation of the Ruhr.  It would have risked Allied occupation of the entire

---

6. *Kabinette Marx I/II*, pp. X-XII; Docs. #1-2, pp. 1-10; #4, p. 17; #7, pp. 35-37.  Feldman, *Disorder*, p. 802.

Reich. Though it was the more difficult path, the regime should have sought a democratic solution with the SPD, the DNVP, or both.[7]

Luther promulgated the First Emergency Tax Decree under Article 48. It required the advance payment of half of the installment of the Rhine-Ruhr Levy due in January and the portions of the turnover tax due in December and January. Both taxes were payable in Gold Marks. A Second Emergency Tax Decree immediately followed. It put all taxes on a gold basis, raised the turnover tax, and made prepayment assessments harder to evade.[8]

As 1923 ended, the German government was displaying new determination. No one was sure that the Rentenmark would succeed, the French still occupied the Ruhr, and immediate economic conditions were growing worse, not better. There were constant rumors of impending putsches or the appointment of a dictator. Support for the Weimar parties was ebbing while the Nazis and Communists grew stronger. In 1924 the twelve-year crisis came to its final chapter. Germany did not return to an authoritarian state in 1924, nor did it become a fascist or communist dictatorship. It renewed and fortified democracy. The Reichstag proved that it could act responsibly and pass controversial and necessary legislation. Within three years, the Nationalists had given up their monarchist dreams and grudgingly agreed to the new system. This remarkable turn of events came about with the passage of the Dawes Plan in 1924. The success of the parties in persuading the public to support the Plan, in contrast to the Treaty of Versailles, bolstered the moderate parties. By the end of 1924 they had stabilized the German economy and political scene, and the French were preparing to evacuate the Ruhr.

Luther knew that the first two Emergency Tax Decrees had not provided enough revenue. An unbalanced budget could threaten the new Rentenmark. Luther prepared a Third Decree, which would include a new form of rent tax, tax those corporations and entities that had profited from the inflation, and recast the financial arrangements among the Reich, states, and localities. The most controversial part concerned revaluation of public and private debts, insurance policies, and contracts. Luther had wanted no revaluation at all, which would leave everything at one-trillionth of its prewar worth. In the chaos of the last several years, original investors had sold many of their war bonds at a fraction of their value to speculators. Why should the government allow the same people who had helped to destroy the currency to reap profits on their bonds? However, the Catholic Church held many of these bonds and, through the Catholic Center party, exerted pressure for revaluation. The Supreme Court had said that there should be full restitution and the Justice

---

7. *Kabinett Cuno*, Docs. #98, pp. 309-312; #224, pp. 662-666; #238, pp. 712-714. Feldman, *Disorder*, pp. 736-742.

8. *Kabinette Marx I/II*, Docs. #10, p. 46; #20, pp. 100-101. Feldman, *Disorder*, p. 815.

Minister pushed energetically for higher revaluation. The other dispute was the use of the rent tax.[9]

Debate turned bitter.    Agriculture Minister Gerhard von Kanitz complained that agriculture could not bear the tax level, especially the one-time levy on undeveloped property.    Luther countered that he designed this tax to get revenue from inflated land values and hoped that rent tax revenue would allow the states to reduce the property tax.    Kanitz opposed revaluation because the inflation had wiped out farmers' extensive debts.    The Cabinet agreed that there should be some revaluation included in this decree.    The fifteen-man Reichstag Committee indicated its opposition.    The Social Democrats opposed any revaluation and the rent tax, while the Democrats asked for a 15% revaluation. The DNVP representatives stayed quiet at this meeting, but they seemed to agree with Kanitz that there should be no revaluation and joined the SPD in shattering a Committee agreement on revaluation.    The Cabinet contemplated asking for yet another Enabling Act but believed the Reichstag would not pass it.    New elections would not bring more cooperation, and Kanitz wondered if there were some way to postpone them.    Luther finally yielded on revaluation.    The Cabinet set a 15% revaluation rate and promulgated the decree just before the Enabling Act expired on February 15.    The revaluation conditions of the Third Decree were so onerous and restrictive that few expected to redeem any of the debt. The tax provisions included a rent tax allowing rents to rise from 40% of prewar value in April 1924 to 80% of value in December 1924; the rent tax would be 10% in April and 30% in December.    Luther saw the rent tax as an inflation-windfall tax that would be easy to collect and would yield much revenue. Eventually, Luther intended to have controlled rents exceed their prewar level.[10]

The Finance Ministry delayed the 1924 budget while it worked on the tax decrees and waited for the reparations experts to calculate occupation costs. Although it had imposed taxes through Article 48 and the Enabling Act, the Cabinet did not want to impose an entire budget using emergency powers. Budget Director Otto von Schlieben finally presented the tardy FY24 budget on March 14 while the Reichstag was still debating the decrees. This budget featured a large budget surplus to stabilize the new currency and placed sharp curbs on spending by the states and localities.    The Reichstag passed a continuing resolution on March 18 but had not considered the main bill when the government called elections.    Further continuing resolutions followed on June 12 and July 28.    The Reichstag did not pass the full 1924 budget until July 31, 1925.    To cover the budget until the tax decrees took effect, the German

---

9. *Kabinette Marx I/II*, Docs. #20, pp. 100-101; #30, pp. 127-129. Feldman, *Disorder*, pp. 816-818. Hughes, p. 34.

10. *Kabinette Marx I/II*, Docs. #67, pp. 258-259; #71, pp. 268-269; #90, pp. 322-324; #97, pp. 343-345; #103, pp. 360-361. Feldman, *Disorder*, pp. 816-818. Hughes, p. 46.

Golddiskontbank borrowed $25 million from Paul Warburg and the International Acceptance Bank.[11]

In November 1923 the Reparations Commission authorized a committee of experts "to consider the means of balancing the budget and the measures to be taken to stabilize the currency."[12] It chose Chicago banker Charles Dawes to head the committee. Dawes was a perfect choice. He was not in the government but had ties to the Republican party dating back to the 1896 campaign. He had served as the general purchasing agent of the American Expeditionary Force during the war and became the first director of the Bureau of the Budget under Harding. Britain and France understood that the U.S. government would support Dawes in all but name. Dawes decided that the priority was the stabilization of the German currency and placed the Reichsbank under international control. Germany could then raise its taxes to the Allies' level. He demanded that all German credit demands meet foreign approval to restrain the budget. This dovetailed neatly with Luther's priorities.[13]

Schacht worked hard to stabilize the Rentenmark, sabotage the French, and worsen relations between France and England. He secretly went to England and met with Montagu Norman, President of the Bank of England. Schacht persuaded Norman to guarantee a loan of GM500 million to the new Golddiskontbank, which would issue bank notes in inflation-resistant pounds sterling. Norman also agreed to refuse aid to France's separatist schemes for the Rhineland. Schacht's *fait accompli* infuriated members of the Dawes Commission. Dawes wrote of Schacht: "His pride is equaled only by his ability and his desire for domination. He frankly intimated that as long as he was President of the Reichsbank, he was the Reichsbank."[14] Schacht admired the committee for concentrating on economic rather than political matters. In his recollections, Schacht complained about having to sit on a "stool of repentance" surrounded by the Allies assembled at a semicircular table. Officials presented him with a questionnaire. "I do not know if that questionnaire was in any way comparable with the one we experienced after 1945, but . . . the number of questions cannot have been much smaller."[15] The committee quickly dispensed with the questionnaire. Germany had come before the conference as a defeated power but was now emerging as a partner, worthy of respect. There were still problems. When the committee was in Berlin, one expert told the Nationalist

11. *Kabinette Marx I/II*, Docs. #105. pp. 365-367; #111, pp. 380-381; #119, pp. 406-407; #123, pp. 410-411; #144, p. 463; #249, p. 874. Bundesarchiv Koblenz (BAK) R 43 I/877, pp. 39-66. Feldman, *Disorder*, pp. 831-832.

12. Charles G. Dawes, *A Journal of Reparations* (London, 1939), pp. VIII.

13. Ibid., p. 20. Stephen A. Schuker, *The End of French Predominance in Europe: The Financial Crisis of 1924 and the Adoption of the Dawes Plan* (Chapel Hill, NC, 1976), p. 172.

14. Dawes, p. 55.

15. Schacht, p. 192.

*Kreuzzeitung* that although he had not seen the poor neighborhood yet, he "had been completely astonished at the conspicuous luxury of certain circles, which aroused the suspicion in him that the German need had been greatly exaggerated."[16] The French wanted a reiteration of the Germans' war guilt, but the Americans refused.[17]

The committee released its report on April 9. The cover letter declared that the report had been written upon "the principles of justice, fairness and mutual respect," but warned that "the rejection of these proposals by the German government means the deliberate choice of a continuance of economic demoralization, eventually involving her people in hopeless misery."[18] The report adopted the standpoint of business, not politics. The German railroads would play a key role in the new reparations settlement. The experts valued them at GM26 billion. If GM11 billion in bonds were marketed with the railroads as collateral, the annual interest of 5% could be applied to reparations. Additionally, a joint-stock company would be created with the remaining GM15 billion. GM2 billion in preferred stock would be sold to the German public of which the German government would net one-quarter of the proceeds and the remaining three-quarters would pay reparations. The other GM13 billion would be offered as common stock. A board of fourteen German and four non-German directors would oversee the operations of the railroad. A non-German railroad commissioner would represent the interests of the bondholders. The only duty laid on the railroad would be to operate at a profit. The final contributions were to come from the interest on GM5 billion in bonds based on German industry, but not having any specific security. Any gap in payment should be closed with revenues from alcohol, tobacco, beer, sugar and customs duties. An agent for reparations payments would oversee the work of the commissioners for railroads, the Golddiskontbank, and controlled revenue, as well as the trustees for railroad and industrial bonds. If the experts' estimates proved correct, Germany would pay a billion gold marks the first year and increase its direct payments from the Reich's budget until the fifth year, when it would pay GM2.5 billion. In future years Germany would pay that same amount plus a supplement computed on the index of prosperity.[19]

The Dawes Plan provided more than a new payment schedule for reparations. An international loan to Germany would accompany the Plan. Germany would repay the loan of GM 800 million ($190 million) over twenty-five years. It would be sold in the form of bonds in markets across Western Europe and the United States. The bonds were to stabilize the new German currency and to forge links between the victors and vanquished of World

---

16. *Kreuzzeitung*, February 1, 1924.
17. Schuker, *Predominance*, p. 56.
18. Dawes, pp. 280-282.
19. Ibid., p. 303. Kent, pp. 252-253.

War I. While the reparation schedule had no fixed end date, most expected the arrangement to end when the last installment of the Dawes bonds was paid. This expectation would cap future reparations payments at about GM60 billion, a far cry from the GM132 billion of three years before. For international finance, the importance of the Dawes Plan was that it brought a mass of American investors into the foreign lending market for the first time, just as Barings' discount of French bills in 1819 brought in British investors, and the 1871 indemnity brought in French investors.[20]

The German government tried to ensure that the Dawes report would be as favorable as possible. Marx brought the Reichstag election date close to that of the French elections so that the expected gains for the German Nationalists would not help French Premier Raymond Poincaré hold on to power. Marx was willing to endure a long and bitter campaign in the hope that an upbeat report would give his coalition some badly needed credibility. The Nationalists condemned the new plan in their campaign. The *Kreuzzeitung* labeled the report as unacceptable and called for a system of guarantees, the withdrawal of the Allied troops from the occupied zones, the reassignment of war guilt, and a return to the business status quo in the Ruhr. Helfferich warned of a crushing economic load, the incapacitation of the economy through foreign control of vital sectors, and the continuing threat of occupation and sanctions. The government agreed to the report as the basis for further negotiations. The centrist party leaders promoted the plan as they stumped the country.[21] Marx opposed the takeover of the railroads, the introduction of the financial controls, and the sharp tax increases recommended by the Plan, but felt that "the United States has done the world a great service" and that the objections were not insurmountable. The Chancellor spoke optimistically of the future of German industry. Its productivity would enable the Reich to bear the heavy load, "But this will be impossible if business is destroyed again."[22]

The election result of May 4 was a disaster for the middle-of-the-road parties. The centrist parties (Catholic Center, People's party, Democratic party, and Bavarian People's party) comprising the government had held 189 seats in the 459-member Reichstag before the election and had drawn upon the support of 186 Social Democrats. These numbers would have been sufficient to pass the constitutional changes required in the Dawes Plan. Four years of unemployment, inflation, putsches, emergency decrees, and an increasingly uncertain international situation culminating in the invasion of the Ruhr pushed the German electorate toward the political extremes. The short Reichstag of

---

20. Charles P. Kindleberger, *Germany's Persistent Balance-of-Payments Disequilibrium Revisited* (Bloomington, IN, 1976), p. 29.

21. *Kabinette Marx I/II*, Docs. #124, pp. 411-412; #175, pp. 556-557. Grathwol, p. 24. *Kreuzzeitung*, April 18 and May 4, 1924.

22. *Kreuzzeitung*, April 20, 1924.

May-December 1924 would foreshadow the later problems of the Weimar Republic. Sixty-two Communists and thirty-two National Socialists were elected. The Social Democrats fell from 186 to an even 100, the Democrats lost eleven seats, the People's party lost twenty seats, and the Bavarian People's party lost five seats. The Nationalists were big winners as they gained two million votes and twenty-four seats above their 1920 totals.

The national results masked significant class and regional shifts. The DNVP had made a breakthrough in the western areas in 1920, but now began to shrink back to the East Elbian fastness of the old conservative parties, even as it consolidated its hold on that area. The urban middle class in handicrafts and commerce deserted the DNVP in droves. Many of these voters turned to the Nazis. The big gains for the DNVP came in East Prussia, Potsdam I, Frankfurt an der Oder, Pomerania, Breslau, Schleswig-Holstein, and Dresden. The DNVP was on the horns of a dilemma: it had won strong support among groups with very different interests. Its middle-class losses were more than balanced by gains among small investors and pensioners. A split in the DVP had enhanced the DNVP's urban vote. The liberal parties suffered losses in Bavaria and the East Elbian region and that made them eager to attract more agricultural support.[23]

The Nationalists demanded a role in the government, based on having the largest single bloc in the Reichstag if it included the ten representatives of the Landbund. The Nationalists overplayed their hand in the negotiations and confirmed the worst suspicions of their critics. There was also division within the party between the excitable chairman, Oskar Hergt, who seemed willing to enter the government, and the cool and inscrutable Count Kuno von Westarp, who many suspected of complicity in the Kapp Putsch of 1920 and saw as an implacable foe of the Republic. Hergt called for sweeping revisions in the Dawes Plan and pronounced the economic load unbearable. The DNVP wanted to enter the Cabinet not when it would have to take direct responsibility for stabilization, but rather when the hard work was complete. Hergt told Marx that the Nationalists would participate if the Prussian Cabinet would admit them, Stresemann were replaced as Foreign Minister, and a change in foreign policy were promised. Ebert had no choice and reappointed the old Marx Cabinet,

---

23. Thomas Childers, *The Nazi Voter: The Social Foundations of Fascism in Germany, 1919-1933* (Chapel Hill, NC, 1983), pp. 70-71, 85-87. Larry Eugene Jones, *German Liberalism and the Dissolution of the Weimar Party System 1918-1933* (Chapel Hill, 1988), pp. 215-216. Jones, "Democracy and Liberalism in the German Inflation: The Crisis of a Political Movement, 1918-24," in Feldman et al., *Die Erfahrung der Inflation/The Experience of Inflation* (Berlin, 1984), p. 40.

with the government parties now comprising 154 of the 472 Reichstag deputies and again dependent on Social Democratic votes.[24]

The rise of the radical right and left had blocked off almost a full quarter of the Reichstag from government support. The government claimed that the measures outlined in the Dawes Plan would require changes in the Constitution and thus a two-thirds majority. The Nationalists questioned this necessity. Article 48 decrees and enabling acts, the hallmarks of the soft dictatorship, were useless here. Robert Grathwol argues that Marx and Stresemann decided to press for this two-thirds majority for purely political reasons. On the domestic front, Marx wanted to force the Nationalists to take their share of the responsibility for this plan, so that they could not blame others for another "stab in the back," as they had after the ratification of the Treaty of Versailles. On the international front Schacht wanted to prove Germany's goodwill to the foreign community with an overwhelming, multipartisan vote of approval.[25]

The Cabinet would have to win over the Nationalists, or at least some Nationalists, to the Plan. Hergt seemed to be amenable if the government met certain conditions. Would the rest of the party follow its chairman? Marx and Stresemann needed to win some political guarantees from the Allies. They also had to convince the German electorate, which had registered its frustration in the May elections. The passage of the Dawes Plan by the Reichstag would be useless if voters repudiated the government in new elections and backed the National Socialists and the Communists. Marx would have to hope for a little luck in the coming months to quell three restless groups: the Allies, the Nationalists, and the electorate. The stakes were high: preventing another Allied ultimatum.

The Allies had postponed any negotiation over matters not resolved by the Dawes report until they had worked out a united front after French elections brought the left-of-center to power. The delay was fortunate because an issue appeared in Germany that would aid the government in dividing the Nationalists. The German farmers, many of whom supported the Nationalists, desperately needed credit. New techniques and machines would increase agricultural yields but were costly. Increased production would only add to the world surplus of some twelve million tons of grain and lead to a further fall in prices. Argentina, Canada, and even France were encroaching upon the German market. The

---

24. Grathwol, p. 13. Heinrich Köhler, *Lebenserinnerungen des Politikers und Staatsmannes, 1878-1949,* edited by Josef Becker (Stuttgart, 1964), p. 208. *Kabinette Marx I/II,* Docs. #199, p. 633; #206, pp. 659-661; #207, pp. 662-663; #212, pp. 671-673.

25. Grathwol, p. 41.

Nationalists drew much of their strength from the agricultural east, and if they did not satisfy their followers, they might lose to a more radical party.[26]

The government parties linked the agricultural crisis to the international business and political problems. Minister Kanitz detailed the government's recommendations. It urged passage of the Dawes Plan as a guarantee of quick credit and called for agricultural tariffs. When the voting on the Dawes Plan came down to the final, desperate days, the government could offer the Nationalists a powerful incentive for their votes: immediate consideration of the tariffs as soon as the Plan passed rather than a delay until after the election. The government sent its tariff proposal to the Reichsrat on July 3, but it was very careful because it knew that the SPD opposed these tariffs.[27]

The Allies and Germans met in London in August. The latest continuing resolution on the budget required passage by the end of July, but the DNVP demanded a debate on the subject of war guilt and asked the government not to sign an agreement unless it disowned the infamous Article 231 of the Treaty of Versailles. The French would only agree to evacuate the Dortmund zone when the Reichstag agreed to the Plan. The German delegation also won an assurance that the British forces would be withdrawn from the Köln zone quickly. The Allies would not allow the Germans to raise the war guilt issue, but even the most ardent Nationalists had to be impressed by the gains made by Germany at the London Conference. Marx had included a paragraph on war guilt in his concluding speech at the conference but decided to exclude it in his delivery, fearing it might upset the delicate agreements.[28]

The Germans were quietly ecstatic over their triumph at London. Marx and Stresemann appeared before the Reichstag Foreign Relations Committee. Hergt suggested that Germany could reach a better agreement and tried to discover what might happen if the Reichstag rejected the Plan. Marx left the matter slightly open, saying, "If the Plan is rejected and all possibilities are exhausted, then new negotiations might be opened." Stresemann warned that nothing good would come from a rejection. The President would call new Reichstag elections immediately. The government would not take any initiatives during the election period. "During this time the Finance Minister has to make sure that the lesser treaty remains in effect; during this time everything will be postponed: when the evacuation will occur, when freedom from payments will occur, and everything else."[29] Stresemann received a vote of confidence from

---

26. *Kreuzzeitung*, June 26 and June 28, 1924.

27. *Kabinette Marx I/II*, Docs. #228, p. 719; #235, p. 743; #243, p. 800; #262, Note #1, p. 915. *Kreuzzeitung*, June 28, 1924.

28. *Kabinette Marx I/II*, Docs. #259, p. 909; #262, p. 916. Schuker, *Predominance,* pp. 373-375. S. William Halperin, *Germany Tried Democracy: A Political History of the Reich from 1918 to 1933* (New York, 1946), p. 299. Grathwol, p. 46.

29. *Kreuzzeitung*, August 22, 1924.

his People's party, which had been willing to dump him as Foreign Minister the previous winter to win Nationalist support. It announced that its Reichstag delegation had accepted the agreements unanimously because it felt that the delicate economic and diplomatic situation made rejection impossible. Marx's presentation to the Reichstag was measured and sober: the London Conference was a success, but not a great success. His delegation had restored the idea of Germany as an equal negotiating partner with the Allies. He warned that rejection would worsen conditions in the occupied lands. "The rejection of the London Treaty would mean the destruction of all the hopes held by the German people and especially those of our brothers in the occupied territory." The premiers of both France and Belgium had promised to lift the Ruhr occupation by August 15, 1925, at the latest. What further guarantee could the Nationalists want? Most importantly perhaps, "the shift in American policy has brought it back into an active role in the European problem under the banner of the Dawes Plan."[30]

The fate of the Dawes Plan remained in doubt. The Nationalists might allow their members to vote independently, or they might absent their entire delegation and allow the Plan to pass without their approval. If the Nationalists voted the Plan down, perhaps the government would reverse its earlier position and claim that only a simple majority was necessary to pass the law. Only the Railroad Law absolutely needed a two-thirds' majority.[31] The Social Democrats were already talking of organizing a national referendum on the Plan if the Reichstag failed to adopt it. The dissolution of the Reichstag and new elections without the passage of the Plan might further aid the cause of extremism in Germany. The government had done everything in its power to promote the Plan and had the tools to achieve its passage. Only time would tell if the effort had been sufficient and the government had used the tools properly.

The Social Democrats had emerged as the strongest supporters of the Dawes Plan. They wanted to support the leftist governments in Britain and France, and they feared that prolonged Ruhr occupation and worsening economic conditions could hurt the trade unions further. They were concerned that a *Bürgerbloc* could impose worse conditions if the Reichstag rejected the Plan and inflation returned. Finally, they stressed national loyalty: the restoration of the occupied Ruhr, the reintegration of all German lands into a united trade zone, and a revision of the hated Versailles Treaty. The Plan would tax heavy industries at 20%, machine and electric industries at 17%, chemical industries at 8%, and textile industries at 7%.[32] The desire of the members of the Dawes Committee to raise German taxes to a level comparable to that of other European countries coincided with the desire of the SPD to shift

30. Ibid., August 23, 1924.
31. *Kabinette Marx I/II*, Doc. #277, p. 968.
32. *Vorwärts*, August 20, 1924.

the tax burden away from the lower classes. With American loans providing money needed for economic recovery, the Reich would no longer have to squeeze the capital out of the workers. The Social Democrats saw the acceptance of the Plan as the prelude to a new election, which would serve as a referendum on the Plan. The *Vorwärts* acted as if an election campaign had already begun with intense attacks on the Nationalists and the Communists. There was more than campaign rhetoric in these jabs. The SPD put pressure on the Nationalists to persuade them to accept the Plan. The Communists and the National Socialists would never vote for the changes, so everything depended on the DNVP. Hilferding emphasized that it was the Cuno government of 1923, considerably influenced by Helfferich, that had made the pledges embodied in the Plan that the Nationalists now opposed. "The opinion of the German Nationalists on the Dawes Plan is interesting, for the offers of the Cuno government would never have been made, if it had not secured the agreement of the German Nationalists for them. . . . At that time only we Social Democrats warned about the pledge of the Cuno government to turn over the railroads. . . . All other costs of the peace settlement would remain, so that the actual offer of the Cuno government would have added up to two and a half billion marks annually."[33] Hilferding concluded that the authorities would return the Reichsbahn after a period of thirty years. But who could guarantee that the French would ever return the Ruhr if the Reichstag did not endorse the Plan? Hilferding hammered away at Hergt. If the Nationalist leader would not support the Plan, he should propose an alternative. The socialists knew the weakness of the Nationalists, especially of Hergt. Having had a taste of influence in the Cuno government, the DNVP lusted to enter a new Cabinet.[34]

As the final vote approached, the prospects for passage of the entire Plan seemed dim. The Reichstag voted on the second reading of the Plan and passed all sections save that one dealing with the railroads. The government could muster only 248 votes in favor of the railroad law. It needed at least thirty more votes to gain the necessary two-thirds majority, but the rift in the DNVP was growing. There was particular conflict between urban and rural factions. Many Nationalist businessmen and political figures, especially from the Ruhr, tried to persuade party leaders to support the Plan. The list of those Nationalists who would vote for the Plan consists almost entirely of nonagrarian representatives. The Landbund allowed its members to vote their conscience. A few days before the final vote, the agricultural caucus of the DNVP's Reichstag delegation voted forty-two to three against the Plan. The catastrophic economic events of 1923-24 worried the urban Nationalists more than the agrarian interests, and the election of May 1924 had been an ill omen for the hopes of the former group. If Hergt and Westarp had not released the urban

---

33. Ibid., August 22, 1924.
34. Ibid., August 25 and 26, 1924.

and industrial representatives from party discipline, they might well have bolted the party and set up their own group or joined the People's party.[35]

The agrarian wing was clearly in charge of the DNVP. Both Hergt and Westarp opposed the Plan and voted against all readings of the railroad bill. The government saw that the key to success lay in persuading Hergt and Westarp to allow "free voting" by their delegation, rather than enforce party discipline. If the Nationalists could vote their "consciences," the nonagrarian representatives would be sufficient to give the government a two-thirds majority, pass the railroad bill and the entire Plan. This would avert the disaster of continuing stalemate, occupation of the Ruhr, and inflation. Most of the DNVP opposed the Plan for several reasons. There was continuing bitterness after the exclusion from the second Marx government. This gnawing resentment animated their opposition but was also their weak point, for Marx and Stresemann knew that the Nationalist leadership would do almost anything to get into the next government. Nationalist speeches focused on France's refusal to set a definite date for the evacuation of the Ruhr and the war-guilt issue. They hoped that since new discussions had altered parts of the Versailles Treaty, they could address the provisions that underpinned the Versailles punishments. If Germany could acquit itself on the war-guilt question, it could mitigate or even possibly eliminate the legal penalties prescribed as punishment for the guilt. Naturally, the Allies considered this matter to be closed and beyond the range of discussion. Stresemann and Marx had seen that this position was set in concrete for the moment and that attempting to change it was a waste of time. Nevertheless, the Nationalists tried to bring pressure to bear on the other parties. The tenth anniversary of the beginning of the war lay heavily over the debate. To appease the Nationalists, the People's party delegate Julius Curtius introduced an amendment for the mitigation of war guilt.[36] The Nationalist party office coolly replied that "The resolution of the DVP on the war-guilt question does not seem sufficient. The government would 'use every occasion to attempt to bring a correction on the war-guilt question.' But it must be demanded right now, at or before the acceptance of the London agreements, that the German recognition of war guilt will be revoked."[37]

There was also grumbling about the banking and financial provisions. Many felt that Schacht had displayed more loyalty in setting up the Golddiskontbank to his international banking friends than to his country. The agrarian interests suspected that these new arrangements would lead to higher interest rates and a systematic squeezing-out of farmers. One representative charged that Schacht "exceeded his authority to make an end to the inflation with the Rentenmark, but Schacht portrayed himself in the last campaign as the father of

---

35. *Kreuzzeitung*, August 28, 1924. Halperin, p. 200. Grathwol, p. 49.
36. *Kabinette Marx I/II*, Doc. #289, p. 1004.
37. *Kreuzzeitung*, August 27, 1924.

the Rentenmark.  He did not calculate enough agricultural credit."[38]  Schacht was cheating the farmers by charging an interest rate of 7%.  Nationalist delegate Paul Lejeune-Jung insisted that the load imposed by the experts was too great.  They expected German industry to bring in some five billion marks a year, "completely overlooking the fact that German industry suffers under a deadly capital shortage and a huge tax burden."[39]  The total load would amount to 40% of all German capital, according to his calculations.  The Plan would make German industry less competitive, and the lack of exports would reduce the amount of available foreign credit.  Hergt added: "Under some circumstances, the tax commission can even organize certain branches of taxes and direct German administration to execute them.  Will there be any German sovereignty left?  We are not an African tribe!  Even the loans carry no insurance."  If the loans did come through, they would only create "a false boom of proportionately short length.  The hangover would come right behind it."[40]

Some Nationalists contemplated a fantastic possibility.  In an article on the upcoming American presidential election and the Dawes Plan, the author speculated on the possibility of a victory by Progressive Senator Robert La Follette.  "The new third party of Senator La Follette has demanded the rejection of the Plan.  This is surprising since very few, except for the Jewish capitalists in America, have a pressing interest as to whether Germany accepts or rejects the Plan."[41]  The author attributed this interest to the strong support shown La Follette by the German-American community.  The article suggested that if La Follette won, the United States might demand renegotiation of the Versailles Treaty.  The author's knowledge of the workings of the American political system was questionable, but his implication was clear: if La Follette were elected with German-American backing, he would be obliged to change the terms of the treaties under which Germany had labored for the past five years.

In the end, the Nationalists did not take refuge in such fantasies.  The split within the DNVP and the government's concessions persuaded Hergt and Westarp to free their party members, and the final vote on the railroad law was 314 to 127 as a Nazi screamed "You band of traitors!  This is the darkest day in German history since November of 1918!"[42]  Forty-eight of the one hundred Nationalist deputies present had voted for the Plan.[43]

The major concession made by the government concerned the allocation of Cabinet seats in the next government.  The Reichstag passed a resolution that

---

38.  Speech by Dietrich, *Kreuzzeitung*, August 26, 1924.

39.  Ibid., August 27, 1924.

40.  Ibid.

41.  Ibid., August 29, 1924.

42.  Ibid., August 30, 1924.

43.  Maier, *Recasting*, p. 488.  Grathwol, p. 52.  *Kabinette Marx I/II*, Doc. #289, p. 1004.

after the next elections, the new government would allocate Cabinet positions based on the parties' proportions in the Reichstag. The government kept this promise and after the December 1924 election, five Nationalists entered the first cabinet of Luther after Marx proved unable to form a new government. There may have been agreements to seek higher agricultural tariffs, but after the passage of the Dawes Plan, the SPD moved to table the tariffs. The debate dragged on until there was no longer a quorum. The Reichstag adjourned and did not debate the tariffs again that year.[44] The SPD also opposed compensating the big industries of the Ruhr because they had profited from the inflation. The Allies evacuated the Ruhr within a year and withdrew from the Köln zone according to the Versailles schedule. The Reichstag passed a government-sponsored resolution that read in part: "The statement imposed upon us by overwhelming force in the treaty of Versailles, that Germany started the world war by her own act of aggression, is contrary to the facts of history. The government of the Reich states that it does not recognize this assertion."[45] However, Marx secretly sent a note to England and France explaining his reasons for supporting such a statement and insisting that he did not intend to forsake his legal obligations.

In retrospect, it seems that the Social Democrats' early and vocal support of the Dawes Plan went unrewarded. By supporting the Plan at the beginning, they sacrificed bargaining power that Hergt and the Nationalists used to their advantage. The passionate speeches and articles in *Vorwärts*, the huge demonstrations in Berlin, and all the exuberance were for naught as the "bourgeois bloc" closed in around the SPD. It would be almost four years until a Social Democratic government would take power. The socialist governments in Britain and France crumbled within a year despite the efforts of the SPD and the passage of the Dawes Plan. But it would be a grave mistake to characterize the adoption of the Plan as an empty victory for the Social Democrats. The Plan stabilized the economy of the Republic, and this diminished the wave of extremism of right and left spawned by the inflation. In the December 1924 elections, the Communists and National Socialists lost almost a million votes apiece. The Social Democrats' most important victory was in making the Reichstag governable again.

Maier identified the passage of the Dawes Plan as a key moment in Weimar history and the history of Europe between the wars. For him, it showed the triumph of corporatist and interest group forces. While the Right had to recognize trade unions, it shifted to the rationalization of factories and could try to exclude the socialists from political power. Maier also suggested that the limits to corporatism would depend on the availability of international capital. The inflation had brought big business and big labor together, but also

---

44. *Kabinette Marx I/II*, Doc. #288, p. 1002.
45. Halperin, p. 302.

spawned the Nazis and other parties as grass-roots rebels. Maier's analysis is quite good, but his conclusion only applied to the next year. As we shall see, the SPD was more effective as an opposition party than as a government party. Russell Leffingwell, an assistant to J. P. Morgan, identified the key problem in the entire Dawes arrangement that would haunt finance for the next seventy years: the Dawes loan was scheduled for a twenty-five-year period, but everyone expected the Dawes Plan to break down long before then.[46]

For the moment Leffingwell's gloom was ignored. The twelve-year crisis had ended: Germany had a new stable currency, Luther's tax decrees had given that currency solid fiscal backing, the French were pulling forces out of the Dortmund region, and would soon be evacuating other areas. The Plan would lead to a boom in exports because the Allies would no longer shun German goods out of lingering postwar bitterness.[47] This would be another boost for the economy. Most important, the old party of empire had been coaxed out of its cave to give a vote for the Republic. Parliamentary rule was now viable without decrees and enabling acts. The Republic could discard the soft dictatorship. The twelve-year crisis, which had begun with the rise of the Social Democrats, had now ended with the ascendancy of the Nationalists. The Reich seemed poised to resume the cautious balanced-budget policies of the Kaiserreich.

---

46. Maier, *Recasting*, pp. 580-592. Schuker, *Predominance*, p. 305.

47. Theodore Balderston, *The Origins and Course of the German Financial Crisis, November 1923 to May 1932* (Berlin, 1993), p. 97.

## Chapter 3

# Winter: The Luther/Schlieben Cabinet

The bonds mandated by the Dawes Plan were printed and sold to eager investors, primarily in the United States. The bonds found a protector when the American S. Parker Gilbert was named Agent General for Reparations. Gilbert's job was to ensure the maintenance of the payment schedule so that the bonds would return home on time and in order. The trauma of the inflation led the Reich to follow a very cautious spending policy and devise a tax system to provide enough revenue. For the moment, it would risk a surplus budget and possible recession. The lessons of deficit spending in the twelve-year crisis seemed to be entirely negative.

Hans Luther, the driving force on finance in 1924, prided himself on being a politician without a party. He had been born in Berlin, the son of a wood merchant, and joined the civil service at the communal level, first as a city councillor in Magdeburg, then as an executive secretary for the German and Prussian Congress of Cities, and finally as Mayor of Essen from 1918 to 1922.[1] He had played a dominant role in the stabilization of the Mark and the tax decrees that ended the fiscal and monetary crises. That had paved the way for the Dawes Plan, which ended the international and domestic crises. Luther had abolished the eight-hour-day law, slashed the civil service, and imposed a regressive rent tax. In the winter of 1924/25, Luther designed a tax-reduction program and replaced Marx as Chancellor. His Cabinet relied on officials who did not sit in the Reichstag. Otto von Schlieben received the finance portfolio because of his leadership of the budget office since 1920 and his membership in

---

1. Karl-Heinz Minuth, ed., *Akten der Reichskanzlei. Die Kabinette Luther I/II* (Boppard, 1977), pp. XIX-XXIV.

the DNVP. Although Luther did not retain the title of Finance Minister, Schlieben remained his subordinate. There would be no break with the policy laid down in 1923 until the beginning of 1926. The Luther/Schlieben era represents the formation of the corporatist model described by Charles Maier. Business tax reduction and tariff increases, especially on agricultural goods, marked the regime. Schlieben worked to protect the interests of large landowners by guiding tariffs through the Reichstag. The old alliance of rye and iron was returning. The revaluation settlement remained a contentious issue. As the year wore on, Schlieben suffered an increasing credibility problem because he had projected a large budget deficit and forced the states to accept a reduced share of revenue. It was clear by October that the budget was in surplus. The treaties of Locarno threatened to split the Nationalist party, which had to leave the Luther Cabinet to save its unity. By the end of 1925 Germany had slipped into a deep recession, and many wondered if another upheaval was imminent.

The Nationalists expected Cabinet positions since their votes had passed the Dawes Plan. Chancellor Marx launched an audacious scheme. He called for the expansion of the government to both the left and right by including the Social Democrats and the Nationalists in a *Volksgemeinschaft*. This would put into Cabinet form the coalition that had backed Cuno in 1922. The People's party had called for the inclusion of the DNVP. Marx doubted the DNVP's sincerity and suspected that it would sabotage the execution of the Plan and Stresemann's foreign policy. The SPD could be very difficult in full opposition to a government. Marx felt that the two would balance one another. If the Nationalists were to enter the Cabinet, they must pledge their support for the current line of foreign policy. Most of the Democrats opposed working with the DNVP and threatened to leave the government. They saw a new election as the only option. Westarp felt betrayed: in May and August the government had wooed the DNVP and considered a widening of the coalition to the right. Once the Reichstag adopted the Dawes Plan, Marx suddenly threw the SPD into the mix. Both Hergt and Westarp had said their delegation could vote for a positive endorsement of the Dawes Plan, if that is what it took to join. Agriculture Minister Kanitz echoed this: the government had morally bound itself to the Nationalists during the Dawes negotiations and Marx was indirectly bound as leader of that government. Stresemann believed that the negotiations with the Nationalists should continue because they were getting ready to abandon their radicalism. If a formal recognition of the Republic and the foreign policy of fulfillment split the DNVP, so much the better. Although the SPD newspaper *Vorwärts* had ruled out cooperating with the Nationalists, Marx felt all along that the SPD itself was more amenable. The People's party would not continue without the DNVP, and the Catholic Center would not continue without the DDP. The Democrats would not join a Cabinet without the Socialists. The process reached a stalemate by the end of October.   Ebert dissolved the Reichstag after only five months of life and called new elections.[2]

The 1924 budget was in limbo because only the Reichsrat had passed it.  Luther, the officials of the Finance Ministry, and the Cabinet had dictated that budget in violation of the Constitution.  Luther introduced the 1925 budget into the Reichsrat in November though Budget Director Schlieben complained that he had no solid estimates of revenues or spending.  He projected RM151 million more in revenue than in 1924, mostly from the impending sale of stock in the railroad.  The Reichsrat quickly adopted this budget.  Luther made some fiscal adjustments because his tax decrees had yielded more revenue than expected but had fallen heavily on German business.  The unresolved tariff issue complicated tax relief.  The Treaty of Versailles had forced Germany to extend the free trade provisions of August 1914 for five years after the ratification of the treaty.  That deadline was fast approaching, and the agricultural groups wanted the 1902 Bülow tariffs restored.  If the government enacted tax relief for industry, it might delay the restoration of agricultural tariffs until it judged the impact on revenue.   The Agriculture Ministry was alarmed at the just-concluded treaty with Spain, which it believed would lead to massive imports of French wine through Spanish reexport.  Kanitz tried unsuccessfully to get the Cabinet to reject the treaty and then to limit its term to just three months.  The Finance Minister prepared another Article 48 decree that would reduce the turnover tax, luxury tax, and prepayments for various businesses.  The only benefit for poorer Germans was that the decree raised the tax-free wage.  The government had again resorted to the ease of a decree rather than parliamentary negotiation.[3]

Maier suggests that the events of 1924 represent the formation of a corporatist model of government.  The inflation of the 1914-24 period and the revaluation brought big labor and big business (as debtors) together against the middle class (as creditors), and in most European countries the former emerged victorious in the revaluation issue.  This was a change from the bimetallism fights of the prewar years when the debtors' call for inflation went unheeded. The inflation and revaluation set a pattern for corporatist approaches to future issues.  The position of agriculture in this paradigm seems unclear.  Clearly most farmers had been big debtors and had clamored for credit and inflation back to the 1890s.  Kanitz had opposed high revaluation in the Third Emergency Tax Decree because this would hurt farmers.  To cement their place in the corporative system, the farmers needed either very high tariffs or very heavy

---

2. Grathwol, p. 31. *Kabinette Marx I/II*, Docs. #309, pp. 1074-1075; #311-312, pp. 1078-1080; #316-317, pp. 1088-1093; #319-320, pp. 1094-1096; #324, pp. 1102-1104.

3. *Kabinette Marx I/II*, Docs. #299, pp. 1031-1032; #315, pp. 1086-1088; #331, pp. 1116-1117; #344, pp. 1139-1142; #347, pp. 1150-1151; #349, pp. 1154-1159; #351, pp. 1163-1167.  Hans Mommsen, *The Rise and Fall of Weimar Democracy* (Chapel Hill, NC, 1996), p. 181.

subsidies until farm prices rose.  During the election campaign of autumn 1924, the DNVP called for 100% revaluation of debts in a bid to win more middle class support while ignoring its agricultural base on this issue.[4]

The elections of December 1924 did little to clarify the situation but did guarantee a more peaceful Reichstag as both Nazis and Communists lost seats. The Social Democrats regained their position as largest party in the Reichstag, but the Nationalists increased their vote total.  The other major middle-class parties (Democrats, Catholic Center, Bavarians, and People's party) also prospered.  The same conflicts continued.  The People's party withdrew from the government in Prussia until the Democrats and Catholic Center allowed the DNVP into the Prussian government.  Finally, the party leaders formed a Cabinet of personalities under Luther's leadership.  Kanitz remained Agriculture Minister.  Besides Schlieben, Nationalist newcomers to the Cabinet included Martin Schiele, a director of the *Landbund*, who became Interior Minister, and Albrecht Neuhaus, a former Prussian trade official who had resigned in 1920 rather than take a loyalty oath to the Weimar Constitution.[5]

Schlieben immediately introduced a transitional tax bill in anticipation of an overhaul of taxes and tariffs later in the year.  It would govern income and corporate taxes for 1924 and the prepayments for part of 1925 until the Reichstag passed new laws.  It replaced the progressive capital tax with a flat tax on capital and abolished the capital-gains tax.  It would also reduce the capital transfer tax, the land acquisition tax, and the stock exchange tax.  It would raise beer and tobacco taxes to compensate for the loss of revenue. Schlieben had been director of the budget office since 1920 but was inexperienced in devising taxes and estimating their yields.  He turned to the newly promoted State Secretary Johannes Popitz.  Popitz had begun his career in the Prussian administration, then had moved over to the Reich Finance Ministry after the Revolution.  At forty years of age, he was a rising star of the Weimar civil service.  Schlieben lacked personal ambition and was a safe pick for Luther, though he had threatened resignation and public embarrassment on a budget matter back in 1920, an unheard-of tactic in the imperial era.  Schlieben was not a gifted speaker and expected to have difficulty delivering the complex technical speeches that a Minister had to give.  He turned to Ministerial Director

---

4. Maier, *Recasting*, pp. 490, 591.  However, Maier, *In Search of Stability*, p. 203, and Balderston in his review of Feldman's *Great Disorder*, in *Central European History* 27 (1994), p. 216, say that the end of the inflation brought an end to the union-industry partnership.

5. *Kabinette Marx I/II*, Doc. #383, pp. 1259-1260.  *Kabinette Luther*, p. XXIV.  Maier, *Recasting*, pp. 485-486.  Jones, *German Liberalism*, p. 269.

Lutz Schwerin von Krosigk, also a member of the DNVP, and did not change his budget speech from Krosigk's draft.[6]

Luther's insistence on a balanced budget overrode complaints by some members of the government. Brauns pushed for raising the tax-free threshold, but Popitz warned that this would cost too much. The Bavarians objected to doubling the beer tax. Under the provisions of the Dawes Plan, if revenue from consumption taxes passed a certain level, Germany would pay a portion as reparation. Schlieben expected a budget deficit in 1926 and 1927 with almost RM200 million a year going to the Reparations Agent. He tied the final tax package to three other thorny issues: tariffs, revaluation, and the financial compromise with the states, which was up for renewal with the expiration of the Emergency Tax Decree. At the end of May, the Reichstag passed the Transitional Tax Bill by an overwhelming margin.[7]

The 1924 budget had collapsed into illegality and the 1925 budget was threatening to do the same. The Reichstag passed a bill continuing the previous spending to May 31 and later extended the deadline to the end of July. It also extended the financial compromise until June 30 and then to September 30. Reaching a compromise with the states was difficult. Prussia and Bavaria in particular wanted more revenue. Under the Luther/Schlieben proposal, the states would only get 75% of the yield from the income and corporate taxes. The Bavarian Prime Minister complained that without a larger yield, Bavaria would not have enough money for its social and cultural policies and would become a mere province. Luther and Schlieben insisted that the Reich was in "extraordinarily bad financial shape" despite the surplus budget in 1924. Schlieben told the Bavarian that it would be catastrophic if Germany ran a budget deficit because it would put the new currency into jeopardy (the Reichsmark had taken the temporary Rentenmark's place at the same value) and would anger foreign creditors.[8]

Schlieben was a fiscal conservative. He believed that a balanced budget was the only path to economic health, that a slight deficit was bad news, and that a large deficit would herald the return of inflation. By consistently underestimating tax revenues, Schlieben insured that a large deficit would be virtually impossible. The 1924 budget turned out to have a modest surplus, and the 1925 budget would have a surplus of almost RM900 million. Nevertheless, Karl Lothholz, Schlieben's successor at the budget office, suggested that it

6. *Kabinette Marx I/II*, Doc. #385, p. 1265. *Kabinette Luther*, Doc. #7, pp. 15-20. Hildmarie Dieckmann, *Johannes Popitz. Entwicklung und Wirksamkeit in der Zeit der Weimarer Republik* (Berlin-Dahlem, 1960), pp. 1-46. Lutz Graf Schwerin von Krosigk, *Staatsbankrott. Finanzpolitik des deutschen Reiches 1920-45* (Göttingen, 1974), pp. 25-31.

7. *Kabinette Luther*, p. XLVI; Doc. #22, pp. 55-56.

8. Ibid., Docs. #37, pp. 138-140; #42, p. 155; #89, p. 298; #124, pp. 437-439.

would be difficult to balance the FY26 budget because it would include reparations payments for the first time and might require new taxes. Lothholz ruled out loans or deficits for fear that they would undermine the currency, and inflation would return. By the summer of 1925 the Finance Ministry was still calculating a deficit for FY25 and preparing for sharp spending cuts in a later supplementary budget.[9]

The Reichstag dealt with the budget, the tax issue, the tariff issue, and the financial compromise in the summer of 1925. A separate tax on champagne was added to the wine tax. Schlieben felt the pressure from the states to yield on the financial compromise, but Luther strongly opposed any change from the 75/25 split on corporate and income tax. The Bavarian People's party (BVP) opposed the arrangement and forced the government to withdraw its beer-tax proposal. The government hoped that the Bavarians would agree to the revenue split if it asked for a lesser increase in the beer tax. The government won Bavarian support by guaranteeing a yield of RM1.5 billion a year from the turnover tax to the states. The states demanded more, and the Reich proposed a guarantee of RM2.1 billion from the turnover, corporate, and income taxes, almost one-third of the Reich's projected income. It scaled back the beer tax increase depending on the type of beer. The government agreed to dedicate one-third of the yield from the wine tax to subsidize the wine-growers. This fulfilled the pledge made during the Spanish treaty negotiations, Finally, to preclude any political mischief, the government parties agreed that if the Economics party and the Bavarian People's party voted for the beer-tax increase and the financial compromise, all the Bavarian representatives from the government parties would support it as well.[10]

These changes confounded Lothholz. The budget was four months overdue and the latest continuing resolution was due to expire on July 31, but Lothholz told the Cabinet that he had little idea of what income would be while the tariff, tax, and financial compromise issues remained unresolved. His sketch of the budget showed an income of RM6.73 billion and spending of RM7.5 billion. Mint income, the revaluation of public loans, and RM202 million of unspecified savings would cover most of this deficit, but Lothholz still estimated that he would need a RM202 million loan. As often happens, the Cabinet never got around to the spending cuts. Another continuing resolution extended the budget to October 31. The Catholic Center surprised the government by proposing a reduction of the turnover tax to 1% or exempting all necessities from it. Schlieben and Luther warned that this endangered the entire financial

9. Reports of the Agent General for Reparations in PA, Auswärtiges Amt, Aktennummer L 205, vol. 1, June 15, 1926. BAK R 43 I/877, pp. 39-54.

10. *Kabinette Luther*, Docs. #129, pp. 446-448; #132, pp. 450-452; #136, pp. 460-461.

compromise by jeopardizing the income guarantee to the states but finally agreed to reduce the turnover tax to 1%.[11]

The revaluation made the budget situation easier. The states and cities had taken advantage of the inflation to buy back many of their outstanding securities at low cost. The original creditors held only about one-quarter of the remaining debt. The Reich allowed these people to exchange their securities for new Reichsmark bonds valued at one-eighth of the original. Germany would not pay the other three-quarters until it finished paying reparations and then only at 15% value. The result was that Germany's annual domestic debt service was only RM500 million, one-sixth that of France, and one-twelfth that of Great Britain. After much wrangling, there were some adjustments made in private debt, but some circles were bitter that the DNVP had failed to deliver on its campaign promise of 100% revaluation. The agriculturalists were overjoyed. The inflation had reduced their prewar debt of M18 billion to RM3 billion.[12]

By the end of 1925, the government had set the principles of Weimar taxation. A glance at the main revenue sources from 1913 to 1925 reveals the clear impact of the Revolution and several periods of socialist government (see Table 3.1). First, the influence of the public sector had increased, as total tax revenue had more than doubled. Second, the central government in Berlin, rather than the states, controlled more tax revenue. The turnover tax and capital-transfer tax had grown the most. Next came the income/capital tax, then the new rent tax, and finally the real estate and inheritance tax. The only category showing a decrease was customs, suggesting the effect of the peace treaties and Germany's more liberal trade policy. If we divide the categories into "progressive" and "regressive" categories, we find that regressive taxation increased M3,167 million since 1913, while progressive taxation only grew M2,436 million. This can also explain some of the chronic economic problems of Weimar: consumers often did not have enough money to spend on goods. The positive effect of this regressive policy should have been the growth of an investor class able to buy German government bonds, but as we shall see this did not develop. This clearly shows the regressive impact of the Luther tax programs from 1923 to 1925. The government would introduce a more progressive policy in 1926.

The Dawes Plan had been a great success. The American portion of the GM 800 million Dawes Loan was oversubscribed tenfold even though

11. Ibid., Docs. #133, pp. 455-457; #139, pp. 466-468; #142, pp. 480-481; #146, p. 513.

12. Hughes, pp. 118, 184-185. Brecht, p. 277. Joseph Brandes, *Herbert Hoover and Economic Diplomacy: Department of Commerce Policy, 1921-28* (Pittsburgh, 1962), p. 190. Maier, *Recasting*, pp. 493-494. Friedrich-Wilhelm Henning, *Landwirtschaft und ländliche Gesellschaft in Deutschland, vol. 2 1750 bis 1986*, Second edition (Paderborn, 1988), pp. 204-205. Kent, p. 262, is mistaken when he sees 1925 as a triumph for particularism.

**Table 3.1**
**Tax Proportions in Budget Years 1913-1914 and 1925-1926 (in millions of Marks/Reichsmarks)**

|  | 1913-14 | | 1925-26 | |
|---|---|---|---|---|
| 1.Income and Capital Tax | 1,561.9 | 37.81% | 2,813.4 | 27.80% |
| 2.Real Estate/Inheritance Tax | 668.1 | 16.49% | 1,513.6 | 14.96% |
| 3.Rent Tax | -- | -- | 1,256.9 | 12.42% |
| 4.Turnover Tax and Capital-transfer Tax | 343.3 | 9.37% | 1,918.2 | 18.95% |
| 5.Transfer Tax | 45.4 | 1.12% | 384.1 | 3.80% |
| 6.Consumption and Expense Taxes | 775.4 | 19.14% | 1,161.1 | 15.92% |
| 7.Customs | 640.5 | 15.81% | 590.4 | 5.83% |
| 8.Miscellaneous | -- | -- | 32.6 | 0.32% |
| TOTAL | 4,651.4 | | 10,120.6 | |

*Source*: Dieckmann, p. 50.

investors had lost over a billion dollars on loans to Germany during the Inflation. Money began to flow despite the misgivings of J. P. Morgan and the Department of Commerce. Reich authorities saw a different danger as states and localities began to line up for loans. It was possible that Erzberger's work could be undone and the move toward Reich fiscal unity reversed if the states could compensate for their lost revenue by tapping the foreign loan market. In October 1924 Anhalt asked for a foreign loan of RM30 million to subsidize industry and housing, consolidate short-term debt, and balance its budget. Luther issued a decree under Article 48 giving the Finance Ministry and the Reichsrat veto power over foreign loans. The Cabinet approved the Ministry's proposal for an Advisory Board of experts to screen all applications for foreign loans. The Reich Finance and Economic Ministries, Reichsbank, and Prussian and Bavarian state banks all had representatives on this Board. It would set the interest rate and the amounts allowable under each loan. The United States had a large pool of investment capital waiting to be tapped. From April 1917 to July 1918, four Liberty Bond Acts had provided $10 billion of credit to the Allies, an amount roughly equal to the bonds sold by the Germans from 1914 to 1916. This brought many into foreign investing for the first time, and the experience only whetted their appetite for more investments.[13]

---

13. William C. McNeil, *American Money and the Weimar Republic: Economics and Politics on the Eve of the Great Depression* (New York, 1985), pp. 23, 59, 84. *Kabinette Marx I/II*, Docs. #347, p. 1151; #365, pp. 1206-1208; #381, p. 1253. Eckhard Wandel, *Die Bedeutung der Vereinigten Staaten von Amerika für das deutsche*

The selection of an Agent-General for Reparations proved to be difficult. Owen Young, a prominent member of the Dawes Committee, was an obvious choice, but he did not want to leave General Electric. James Logan from Dillon, Read openly campaigned for the job, but the British disliked him. Morgan asked Dwight Morrow to serve, but some were concerned that the Germans might object to someone so closely tied to Morgan. Coolidge also feared that a Morrow appointment might stir up German-American support for La Follette in the November elections, so he picked Seymour Parker Gilbert, Jr. Gilbert's mentors included Treasury Secretary Andrew Mellon, New York Federal Reserve Chairman Benjamin Strong, and Russell Leffingwell, the former treasury official now working for Morgan. Mellon had created the position of Undersecretary of the Treasury in 1921 for Gilbert, who was only twenty-nine.[14]

A speech by Frederick Kent, Vice President of Bankers' Trust, to the British Chamber of Commerce reflected the new optimism about Germany. Kent felt that Germany was in relatively good shape and pointed out that its per capita national debt was only $40 while the comparable French debt was $1,339. There was still too much "extravagant" spending on parks and swimming pools, and this was "a danger that should be corrected."[15] The Plan had worked well in the first year and transferred the necessary sums. The Dawes Plan led to the next step as Stresemann negotiated the Treaties of Locarno, which again renounced territories lost in the Versailles Treaty and agreed to arbitration with Poland and Czechoslovakia. When the Nationalists complained about the Treaty, the Foreign Minister won a further assurance that the Allies would evacuate the first zone of the Rhineland around Köln after ratification.[16]

The state governments, many containing Social Democrats, grew critical of Luther and Schlieben's budget policy as the surplus piled up. Schlieben had a credibility problem. He had pushed through the financial compromise with the states based on budget numbers that were nowhere near the mark. On October 2, 1925, Luther, Schlieben, and Schacht held a conference with the state prime ministers, finance ministers, and interior ministers. Schlieben informed the conference that there would be a surplus for FY25 but probably not a very large one, in contrast to liberal estimates of a RM1.2 billion surplus. Schlieben warned of the unpredictability of tax flows. Three tax laws operated in 1925: the Third Emergency Tax Decree, the transitional tax law, and the new tax laws of August. He was determined to resist loans and pay for

*Reparationsproblem 1924-1929* (Tübingen, 1971), p. 135.

14. Chernow, pp. 251-252. Schuker, *Predominance*, pp. 284-288. Kenneth Paul Jones, "Discord and Collaboration: Choosing an Agent-General for Reparations," *Diplomatic History* 1 (1977), pp. 118-139.

15. BAK R 43 I/275, p. 140-R.

16. *New York Times*, January 21, 1926, in PA Auswärtiges Amt, Büro des Staatssekretärs, Section C, vol. 11. Halperin, pp. 330-333.

all spending out of available income.  The Finance Minister criticized the cities sharply for unnecessary spending on new theaters, city halls, and stadiums, many of them financed by foreign loans.  The cities should use regular taxes if they really wanted these projects.  He also denied the hardship of the civil servants: "They know their income is higher than in the years before the war, in Prussia some 70% higher."[17]

Saxon Finance Minister Peter Reinhold sharply criticized Schlieben: "I believe we have the duty to state here . . . that we have taken out of the economy some three to four billion too much."  He felt that the faulty revenue estimates of Schlieben had driven the states to make faulty estimates of their own and that the heavy tax load on business had forced it to cut production and workers.  Reinhold went on: "I would use the reserves from last year to allow the economy to recover."  The government should have cut taxes when it confirmed that there was a budget surplus.  "I know that business bears a great measure of guilt because of its faulty investments, but none of us are free from blame."  The Saxon urged a cut of Reich personnel of up to 10%.  Tax simplification would help the economy.  Reinhold also supported Schacht in his call for tighter control of foreign loans.[18]

Schlieben replied that if he followed Reinhold's suggestion of using the surplus and a deficit resulted, then "a cry would go up in the press that I was a Finance Minister who could not count. . . . I fear that we have reckoned too highly."  He believed that income in 1926 would fall and thus make tax cuts impossible.  "It is self-evident in these uncertain times that we cannot calculate each pfennig and heller exactly.  It is only possible to say that the full yield will be so high: somewhat more here, somewhat less here.  We have in the budget a standing reserve of 100 million, so that we can always hope to have a surplus, as near as we can reckon."[19]

Germany fell into a recession in the autumn of 1925.  Unlike other events that reflected global economic problems, the German crisis of 1925-26 was confined to that country and thus traceable to specific policies and events. Schlieben's fiscal policy of building up huge surpluses, although a prime cause of the recession of 1925-26, was not the only one.  The tight monetary policy of Schacht also had a major role.  The Reichsbank's discount rate had hovered around 10% for the entire year and helped the commercial banks of Germany rebuild their cash reserves.  Since 1913, banks had lost 66% of their reserves and 70% of their stock capital.  Private capital was even more dear, with rates ranging between 12% and 14% during 1925.  Keynes attacked Schacht's monetary policy: How could Germany pay reparations when a tenth of its workforce was unemployed?  However, the price increases were running at an

---

17. *Kabinette Luther*, Doc. #169, pp. 607-626.
18. Ibid., pp. 627-641.
19. Ibid., pp. 651-653.

11% annual rate during the first six months of 1925, so Schacht's discount rate was probably either close to zero in real terms or even a little negative. Prices fell in the second half of 1925, and the overall increase for 1925 was 4%. Schacht also had to take account of the international interest rate structure established after the war: the United States generally had the lowest rates, then Britain, then Germany. To approach another country's level was to risk capital flight. In 1925, the American discount rate was 3½%, and the British rate was 5%. The effective floor for Germany therefore was around 6½%. As prices collapsed in the second half of 1925, Schacht should have taken swifter action, but generally his monetary policy was sound.[20]

Structural unemployment and the rationalization movement were other factors in the recession. The military provisions of the Treaty of Versailles created a small, poorly equipped army and threw many young men into the labor pool while not providing enough armament production to keep them working. Any economic slowdown meant that unemployment would skyrocket because there was rapid growth in the working-age population. From 1914 to 1927, the number of Germans aged 15 to 65 increased by 6.4 million. Another million joined this rank between 1927 and 1931. Rationalization meant that every sector of the German economy was trying to increase productivity while laying off employees. According to Brady, German heavy industry emerged from the war dangerously overexpanded. The collapse of the Stinnes industrial empire in 1925 set the stage for a complete reorganization of German industry. Brady examined each sector of the German economy to find out the extent of rationalization. Despite its great role in the economy, the coal industry scarcely reorganized itself at all. On the other hand, the chemical and potash industries presented the best examples of rationalization with their vertical and horizontal integration, the merger of firms into huge concerns, and the introduction of "scientific" American management techniques. I.G. Farben is the best-known chemical corporation that emerged out of this process. Rationalization also prevailed in the steel industry with the formation of the Vereinigte Stahlwerke. It controlled 40% of German raw-steel production while providing some 20% of Germany's total demand for coal.[21]

---

20.    Dieter Hertz-Eichenrode, *Wirtschaftskrise und Arbeitsbeschaffen: Konjunkturpolitik 1925/26 und die Grundlagen der Krisenpolitik Brünings* (Frankfurt, 1982), p. 14. McNeil, *American Money*, pp. 20-21, 115. *Kabinette Luther*, Doc. #244, pp. 946-973. *Neue Züricher*, February 5, 1926, in PA, Auswärtiges Amt, Büro des Staatsekratär, Sect. C, vol. 11. Fritz Blaich, *Die Wirtschaftskrise 1925/1926 und die Reichsregierung* (Kallmünz, 1977), pp. 72, 162. Lester V. Chandler, *Benjamin Strong, Central Banker* (Washington, DC, 1958), pp. 323-329.

21.    Blaich, *Wirtschaftskrise*, p. 15. Hertz-Eichenrode, p. 30. Werner Link suggests the Vereinigte Stahlwerke merger was only possible because of financing from American loans, "Der amerikanische Einfluss auf die Weimarer Republik in der Dawesplanphase," in Hans Mommsen, Dietmar Petzina, Bernd Weisbrod, and Dirk

The initial phase of rationalization in 1925 cost many workers their jobs and helped to trigger the recession. The increase in productivity eventually began to create enough jobs to bring the unemployed back. Brady, quoting Jürgen Kuczynski's productivity index, sees this figure rising from a base of 100 in 1924 to 116 in 1925, 125 in 1926, 133 in 1927, and 140 in 1928. The rationalization process played a key role in the societal corporatism of Weimar. Brady commented that the Social Democrats and Communists opposed capitalism, not rationalization. Both these parties had long called for greater centralized planning, and rationalization was a step along the road to centralization. Hilferding and others saw a highly centralized "organized capitalism" as a transitory stage to socialism. Brady also contended that rationalization usually resulted in wage increases. Maier, however, complains that rationalization increased productivity while reducing purchasing power. Gerhard Bry's figures seem to agree with Brady as wages rose 8% from 1913 levels to 1929 and 15% from 1925 levels. From 1925 to 1929 working hours per week also declined from 49.5 to 48.8. We shall revisit this productivity issue.[22]

The collapse of the Stinnes empire and concerns about future declines in corporate earnings undermined business and consumer confidence. The Consumer Price Index fell, bankruptcies increased rapidly and peaked in January 1926. The unemployment rate rocketed upwards. At first, the government was not alarmed by this, nor were international financiers. Schacht wrote to Shepard Morgan in Gilbert's office:

Last year there were only five thousand commercial failures in Germany. The normal number of commercial failures in Germany is nine thousand. A country that does not have a normal number of commercial failures is not in a healthy financial condition. It

Stegmann, eds., *Industrielles System und politische Entwicklung in der Weimarer Republik* (Düsseldorf, 1974), p. 495. Robert A. Brady, *The Rationalization Movement in German Industry* (New York, 1933), pp. XIX, 99, 249. George Hallgarten and Joachim Radkow, *Deutsche Industrie und Politik von Bismarck bis in die Gegenwart* (Frankfurt, 1974), pp. 184-185.

22. Heidrun Homburg, "From Unemployment Insurance to Compulsory Labor," in Richard Evans and Dick Geary, eds., *The German Unemployed: Experiences and Consequences of Mass Unemployment from the Weimar Republic to the Third Reich* (New York, 1987), p. 77. Brady, pp. 327-347. From 1925-29, productivity rose 25% in the coal mining industry, which makes one wonder how much effect rationalization had directly upon productivity, Werner Abelshauser, Anselm Faust, and Dietmar Petzina, eds., *Deutsche Sozialgeschichte* (Munich, 1985), p. 21. Smaldone, p. 117. Maier, *Recasting*, p. 544. Gerhard Bry, *Wages in Germany* (Ann Arbor, MI, 1960), pp. 17, 48.

is the business of the Reichsbank to shake the other four thousand bad apples out of the tree. A few months of real business recession and unemployment will be helpful.[23]

Both Schacht and Stresemann told Strong that they expected disorder because of a standard of living that was rising too fast and "too much extravagant food."[24]

In late October 1925 the Nationalists resigned from the government. They were reluctant to leave the Cabinet but unable to resist the outrage of the local DNVP chapters over the Locarno Treaties. This response surprised Luther because the ministers had participated in Cabinet discussions of the preliminaries of Locarno and had said they could persuade the Nationalists of the Treaties' benefits. When the Treaties were initialed, industrial leaders thought it better for the DNVP to split in half than to leave the government and open the way for socialist participation. Many members of the Nationalist Reichstag fraction did not think that withdrawal was the best answer. For a time the DNVP leaders considered suspending party discipline as they had for the crucial Dawes Plan votes. Westarp, who had replaced Hergt as DNVP Chairman, appeared to the Chancellor deeply shaken by his party's visceral reaction against Locarno. Westarp had assured Luther that the DNVP would not bring a motion of no-confidence or agitate for a dissolution. After Westarp left the DNVP in 1930 he revealed that he and a narrow majority of the fraction had wanted to stay in the Cabinet. Again, the DNVP's heterogeneous groups had affected policy. Schiele, the only minister who was also a DNVP Reichstag member, resigned with the greatest reluctance. Schlieben had worked under Luther as Budget Director and might have put personal relations above party loyalty. However, as Michael Stürmer points out in his analysis of the crisis, there were other factors contributed to the collapse of the coalition besides Locarno. Stresemann's Spanish trade treaty had upset agricultural interests vital to the DNVP's success and reopened the rift between the interests of the industrialists of the DVP and the landowners of the DNVP. In the end the ministers saw party discipline as more important and resigned. The DNVP voted as a bloc against Locarno and went into opposition. Almost immediately, however, it yearned to return to the government, provided certain conditions were met.[25]

For the second year in a row, there was a government crisis at

---

23. Stresemann and Schacht, quoted in Gerd Hardach, *Weltmarktorientierung und relative Stagnation: Währungspolitik in Deutschland 1924-31* (Berlin, 1976), p. 64.

24. Ibid., pp. 64-66. Balderston, *Financial Crisis*, p. 147. Blaich, pp. 21 and 72.

25. Halperin, p. 332. Jones, *German Liberalism*, p. 26, based on extensive documentation from the Historische Archiv der Gutehoffnungshütte in Oberhausen. Michael Stürmer, *Koalition und Opposition in der Weimarer Republik, 1924-28* (Düsseldorf, 1967), pp. 111-126. *Kabinette Luther*, pp. XXII-XXIV; Doc. #209, p. 807. Atilla Chanady, "The Disintegration of the German National People's Party 1924-1930," *Journal of Modern History* 39 (1967), p. 75.

Christmas. Democratic leader Erich Koch-Weser tried to form a Cabinet of the "Grand Coalition," but the SPD was profiting from its sojourn in opposition and declined to join. It might achieve its program (to restore the eight-hour day, increase unemployment benefits, delay rent increases, and use more of the rent tax for construction) more easily in opposition than in a coalition where the others would take it for granted. Luther returned to put together a new government. On social and economic policy, Luther tried to keep a balance by retaining Brauns, who was committed to expansion of social programs, with more business-oriented ministers such as Peter Reinhold of Saxony at Finance, and Julius Curtius, a Westphalian businessman from the People's party who became Economics Minister.[26]

Luther faced an impasse over the Interior Ministry. He intended to appoint Koch-Weser to the post, but ran into protest from the Bavarians, who objected to earlier antiparticularist statements by Koch-Weser. Luther and Koch-Weser had limited room to maneuver. Luther needed Democratic support and "could not do without Reinhold as Finance Minister."[27] The Democrats were not prepared for an election or another soft dictatorship. Koch went to the Democratic fraction and asked it to approve the Cabinet, with the Democratic mayor of Dresden, Wilhelm Külz, taking over the Interior Ministry. Koch argued that this was the only way. A return to the coalition of the Right would mean the end of Locarno. A Weimar Coalition (Catholic Center, SPD, and DDP) would push the DVP and DNVP together in opposition, and the SPD had thwarted the Grand Coalition by "refusing to take responsibility now."[28] Given his fondness for decrees, Luther might have tried to invoke Article 48 again. But there was no justification as there had been in 1923-24 for using Emergency Tax Decrees, and Luther would have alarmed many in Germany and abroad had he enacted an entire budget with Article 48. With the economy in a depression and getting worse, the Left would have made considerable gains had new President Paul von Hindenburg called a new election. Luther opted for the democratic approach: he would struggle with a minority coalition and rely on the two flank parties for majority support from issue to issue. Rumors were flying of another right-wing coup attempt, and the fear of a coup and/or dictatorship persuaded the republicans to bury their differences. As the vote of confidence approached, two options remained: the Luther government or new elections. The Catholic Center, Democrats, Bavarians, and People's party cast 160 votes in favor of the second Luther Cabinet, while 150 members, mostly

---

26. *Kabinette Luther*, p. LV; Docs. #246, pp. 985-987; #256, pp. 1009-1015. *Germania*, December 11, 1925. Stürmer, p. 145. Julius Curtius, *Sechs Jahre Minister der deutschen Republik* (Heidelberg, 1948), p. 61. Hertz-Eichenrode, p. 89.

27. BAK NL 12 (Koch-Weser), vol. 34, diary remarks of January 30, 1926.

28. BAK R 45 III, vol. 13, DDP Committee meeting of January 24, 1926, pp. 17-40.

Nazis, Nationalists, and Communists voted against, and 130 Social Democrats abstained. The government stood by the slimmest of margins.[29]

Maier's contention that the aftermath of the Dawes Plan saw the formation of a corporatist model of government has merit. The specter of revaluation hung over the Cabinet and there was acute embarrassment when the SPD introduced the identical language on revaluation that the Nationalists had proposed in 1924. The Nationalists' recruitment of Georg Best, a supporter of full revaluation, and their subsequent betrayal that led him to join the Nazi delegation work well as a case study of the Nationalists and the creditors. However, the industrialists and agricultural groups were far more important components of the Nationalist voting bloc. While they had broken their promise of full revaluation, the Nationalists had defended the agrarian interests effectively with their reintroduction of higher tariffs. But the corporatist equation did not preclude the SPD. Hilferding and other SPD leaders made a free choice not to participate in Koch-Weser's proposed Grand Coalition. As Maier points out, the SPD had considerable power from its position in Prussia and other states. Yet the corporatist control of revaluation was a Pyrrhic victory, as resentful creditors would eventually turn to the Nationalist Socialists who cast themselves as grassroots, anticorporatist rebels.[30]

The recession of 1925 forced a stark choice upon the German government. If it continued its orthodox fiscal policy, the recession could worsen into a depression and provoke a political crisis. The alternative was to try a reflationary policy of borrowing money to stimulate the economy. Could the government do this without reigniting inflation or had it drawn the wrong lessons from the early 1920s?

---

29. Historisches Stadtsarchiv (HSA), Köln, NL Wilhelm Marx, vol. 66, p. 39; Ernst Feder, *Heute sprach ich mit . . . Tagebücher eines Berliner Publizisten 1926-32* (Stuttgart, 1971), p. 30. Peter Haungs, *Reichspräsident und parlamentarische Kabinettsregierung: eine Studie zum Regierungssystem der Weimarer Republik in den Jahren 1924 bis 1929* (Köln, 1968), pp. 103-105. Richard Breitman, *German Socialism and Weimar Democracy* (Chapel Hill, NC, 1981), p. 139.

30. Maier, *Recasting*, pp. 491-515. Childers, pp. 165-166.

# Chapter 4

# Spring: Peter Reinhold as Finance Minister

In 1926 the Dawes bonds rested easily in the homes and safe-deposit boxes of their owners. There had been concern among investors in the fall of 1925 when the Nationalists left the coalition, but in the spring of 1926 the price of the bond rose again as demand exceeded available supply. Hans Luther had established a reputation for being a strong leader and having a taste for rule by decree. After the collapse of his center-right Cabinet, he made a sharp policy turn. Those who say that Marx and Luther assigned their highest economic priority to a balanced budget or that the SPD did not receive consideration in domestic policy are mistaken. First, the Weimar Constitution's budget provisions began to function democratically for the first time. The budgets had ranged from the tardiness of the Wirth years to the illegality of the 1924 and 1925 budgets. The Reichstag would pass the budget of 1926 in perfectly democratic fashion. It was the first budget to meet the constitutional deadline since 1911, before the twelve-year crisis. Second, as part of this resort to democracy, Luther had to reach out to the SPD and rely on its support to pass the budget. The SPD forced Luther to rediscover social policy. New programs relieved the recession by providing for emergency unemployment relief and new construction. Third, Luther and Reinhold moved away from the strict insistence on surplus budgets. Reinhold was willing to go "right to the brink of deficit," and many suspected that he went over that brink with a series of tax cuts that expanded upon the business tax cuts of the Luther/Schlieben Cabinet. Luther and Reinhold would work closely together until Reinhold became "like a younger son" to the Chancellor.[1]

---

1. Feder, p. 32.

The Reinhold policy was the most daring and experimental fiscal policy of Weimar and had consequences beyond Weimar's end.

German academic views on deficit spending predated even the empire. Eighty years of academic discussion now crystallized in the debate over the German budget of 1926. Peter Fritzsche has written that the history of the Weimar Republic is so compelling because of the sense that everything was possible. This is most true in economic policy. In the preface to his 1936 book *The General Theory of Employment, Interest, and Money*, John Maynard Keynes noted that classical economic theory was never as strong in Germany as in England. As far back as 1801, German writers such as Fichte challenged the fundamental assumptions of Adam Smith and the school of classical liberalism. Friedrich List asserted that the state's main goal was to maximize the well-being of its citizens. He added that the state could achieve this by intervening in the economy and providing generous credit. World War I shattered the old political and social certainties and caused a crisis in economic theory. The postwar world was split sharply between older Anglo-American economic theories and continental European economic theories. Some of this debate centered on the quantity theory of money. The Swedish economist Gustav Cassel believed that an increase in the money supply led to price increases and currency devaluation. Keynes and Irving Fisher agreed with him, but French economist Bertrand Nogaro dissented.[2]

Adolf Wagner had been a very influential economist in Germany before the war. British liberal ideas had originally influenced Wagner. By the 1870s he had joined the Zentralverein für Sozialreform and was the first important economist at the University of Berlin. He called himself a "state socialist" and claimed to hold a position between liberal and Marxist economics. Wagner demanded radical state intervention to prevent economic and social crises. His greatest influence came in trade policy, where he favored the agrarians' view because he believed that industrialism was a temporary phenomenon caused by rural overpopulation. Once emigration relieved the pressure, the traditional economy would reassert itself and need protection against Russian grain.[3]

Wagner had a longer-term influence that survived the war. Disciples of Wagner became prominent in the Prussian War Ministry with the outbreak of war. Before 1914, this "Nestor of finance" tended to favor those who supported a budget balanced by credit, rather than by taxes. Wagner and Adam Müller anticipated the ideas commonly attributed to Keynes. Keynes seems to have been generally unfamiliar with this school of thought. The hyperinflation

2. Peter Fritzsche, "Review Article: Did Weimar Fail?" *Journal of Modern History* 68, No. 3 (1996), p. 633. Avraham Barkai, *Nazi Economics: Ideology, Theory, and Policy* (New Haven, 1990), pp. 69-77. Silverman, *Reconstructing*, pp. 43-44.

3. Kenneth D. Barkin, *The Controversy over German Industrialization* (Chicago, 1970), pp. 139-144, 153, 178. Barkai, pp. 83-84.

had given credit creation a bad name, but Luther's new Finance Minister, Peter Reinhold, revived the policy. Reinhold had studied economics, especially American business-cycle theory.    He took a particular interest on the psychological impact of policy on the economic cycle.    Reinhold clearly followed the economic theories laid out by Wagner and Karl August Dietzel, who had removed the stigma from public credit in his 1859 book.[4]

Reinhold was the Finance Minister of Saxony and one of Schlieben's sharpest critics.  His father ran a publishing and paper-manufacturing concern, while his mother's family had connections to the Merck chemical interests. Reinhold held a doctorate in history.  Somehow, he avoided service in the war and built up his fortune in business.  Like so many Young Liberals of the prewar era, Reinhold split from Stresemann and the National Liberals and joined the Democratic party.  His mentor was Hermann Fischer, treasurer of the Democratic party and leader of the Hansa-Bund, who had led the Young Liberals before 1918.  Reinhold was the editor of the *Leipziger Tageblatt* before entering the Saxon government in 1924.[5]  He had first attracted Luther's attention in the fall of 1924 at a meeting of the state finance ministers to discuss the Dawes loan.  Many state ministers were dubious about the Reich's plans, but Reinhold worked on Luther's behalf at a reception, assuring them that as a former mayor, Luther would be sympathetic to the needs of the state and localities.  Reinhold concluded his apologia by telling the crowd that "the Finance Minister will be an old forty-eighter."[6]  Luther chuckled at the double meaning here: the first an assurance to liberals that Luther would follow in the traditions of the 1848 Frankfurt Parliament that had tried to unify Germany, the second a threat to invoke Article 48.  His quick-witted speaking ability and flexible mind appealed to Luther.  The Chancellor had asked Reinhold to serve as finance minister in January 1925, but Reinhold would not enter the Cabinet without his party's support.  Reinhold again attracted national attention with his stinging attacks on Schlieben at the conference of October 1925.  During the government crisis, Reinhold bid for the job by writing a front-page article for the *Berliner Tageblatt*.  He praised "the selfless sacrifice of Dr. Luther, who

---

4. Feldman, *Army*, p. 74.  Barkai, p. 104.  Blaich, *Wirtschaftskrise*, p. 107. Gisela Upmeier, "Schachts Kampf gegen die kommunalen Auslandsanleihen," in Karl-Heinrich Hansmeyer, ed., *Kommunale Finanzpolitik in der Weimarer Republik* (Stuttgart, 1973), p. 121.

5. *Deutsche Tageszeitung*, January 18, 1926, in BAK NL Luther, vol. 281. Bruce Frye, *Liberal Democrats in the Weimar Republic* (Carbondale, IL, 1985), p. 49. Hertz-Eichenrode, p. 91.  Dieckmann, p. 44.  See also Pünder's comments on Reinhold's campaign in BAK NL 57 (Stockhausen), vol. 24, January 2, 1926.  Kurt Sendner suggests that Defense Minister Otto Gessler brought Reinhold, his friend and fellow Democrat, into the Cabinet.  Blaich, *Wirtschaftskrise*, p. 106.  I have found no evidence that Reinhold and Gessler were particularly close.

6. Hans Luther, *Politiker ohne Partei* (Stuttgart, 1960), p. 305.

with his vision and energy . . . executed the correct tax and business measures that ensured the [stabilization] experiment's success." The main problems now were the absurd budget surpluses built up by Schlieben and the tight monetary policy of the Reichsbank. He proposed reversing both and concluded by saying that "a healthy economic policy can only be found on the foundations of a healthy fiscal policy."[7]

At thirty-eight, Reinhold was the youngest member of the Cabinet and was unknown to most political leaders and newspaper editors. The newspapers scrambled to review their information on the young Saxon. The *Berliner Tageblatt* called him "a man who combines ideas with unwavering energy and successful parliamentary talent" and noted that he had balanced the last Saxon budget.[8] The *Berliner Volkszeitung* praised his care for the entire working class and his creation of jobs and bread for the jobless. To help small and medium businesses Reinhold had set up the Saxon Landespfandbriefanstalt, a reservoir for private capital to attract credits for private business. He also founded the Sächsischen Werken, a state-owned company to use Saxon brown coal for light and power. It was now producing power at the cheapest rate in all Europe and exporting electricity.[9]   On the other hand, the newspaper of the large landholders, the *Deutsche Tageszeitung,* said: "During his term Dr. Reinhold was exposed to the sharpest, most legitimate criticism because of his compulsive attempts at socialization with absurd wastes of money, which not only failed to produce a single practical success but also imposed unbearable agricultural taxes. One can easily see which areas Herr Reinhold will tax."[10]

Luther did not change his policies immediately. He still hoped to straddle all the parties and interest groups, opposing the Nationalists on foreign policy while keeping to their line on domestic policy. However, the new Luther Cabinet could not maintain this balance because of the challenges of unemployment and a housing shortage.   Both would require considerable spending by the government.   A new fiscal policy was the answer to both challenges.   A large tax cut for business would pull Germany out of its self-induced depression.   Vastly expanded state spending, supplemented by Reich grants and paid for indirectly by American loans, would repair the infrastructure and provide for public housing.   A new fiscal policy, radical at the time but quite familiar to us now, would result in massive public debt and trade deficits.

The first challenge was the recession, which had deepened into a depression. By January 1926, 23% of union workers were unemployed. Even

---

7. *Berliner Tageblatt*, January 1, 1926, in BAK NL Luther, vol. 280.

8. *Berliner Tageblatt*, January 5, 1926, in Bundesarchiv Potsdam (BAP) R 8034 II/968.

9. *Berliner Volkszeitung*, January 8, 1926, in ibid.

10. *Deutsche Tageszeitung*, January 18, 1926, in BAK NL Luther, vol. 281.

during the good times certain areas and cities had problems of structural employment. In the big cities, Mannheim had the highest level of structural unemployment, while Stuttgart had the lowest. For regions, the Rhenish Palatinate had 5.5% structural unemployment, while Württemberg had 1.8%. The recession/depression of 1925 particularly affected the mining, heavy industry, manufacturing, and trade and transport sectors. Calls came from everywhere for job creation, from Köln to Bavaria to Königsberg.[11] An increase in unemployment-support pay became inevitable.[12]

The shortage of living space posed a second challenge. Private capital had played the biggest role in construction before the war, and government efforts varied widely from state to state. The diversion of labor and material to the war effort had brought construction to a standstill. The prevalence of rent control in the large cities and the domination of renters in city politics hindered a postwar revival. In 1922 the Reichstag had passed a formal national rent control law covering pre-1918 units. The government had estimated a shortage of 1.5 million homes in 1920. The housing law of June 1921 provided loans and grants and covered them with a rent tax on pre-1918 housing. The tax proceeds would be split on a four-to-one basis between the Reich and the states. The inflation cheated the hopes of Brauns and other supporters of public housing. Public authorities built or reconstructed about 250,000 units in 1920-21, but the tax money was worthless after that. The hyperinflation of 1923 wiped out the credit societies. Only the government could assist major construction. The Third Emergency Tax Decree of 1924 imposed a rent tax of 30% as part of the budget stabilization process, but almost none of these funds were dedicated to housing. Moreover, landlords paying this tax could raise their rents to 80% of prewar value. The Luther government of 1925 did not deal

---

11. Karl Heinrich Pohl, *Weimars Wirtschaft und die Aussenpolitik der Republik 1924-1926* (Düsseldorf, 1979), pp. 154-156. Blaich, *Wirtschaftskrise*, p. 15. Hertz-Eichenrode, pp. 21-24. BAK R 43 I/2030, pp. 148, 202-204, 242, 300, and 362. *Kabinette Luther*, Docs. # 222, pp. 851-855, and #236, pp. 910-915. For a detailed description and statistical charts of the unemployment problem during the recession of 1925/26, see C. Edmund Clingan, "Breaking the Balance: The Debate over Emergency Unemployment Aid in Weimar Germany, 1925-6," *Journal of Contemporary History* 29 (1994), pp. 371-384.

12. Under the 1924 unemployment law, only those who had contributed at least thirteen weeks of state health insurance were eligible for benefits. This excluded both the long-term unemployed who had exhausted their support and lower-middle-class white collar and self-employed workers, who did not make the health insurance contributions. The maximum period was twenty-six weeks with an extension to thirty-nine weeks possible, Richard J. Evans, Introduction, in Evans and Geary, p. 4; as a result of these restrictions, the percentage of unemployed ineligible for benefits would vary from 8% to 23% depending on the business cycle, Merith Niehuss, "From Welfare Provision to Social Insurance," in ibid, pp. 63-76.

with the problem because it feared that large amounts of spending could trigger another round of inflation. Before the war some 57% of the funds spent on construction had come from banks as mortgages, 17% from taxes, and the remaining 26% came from the capital of landlords. After the war public financing jumped to 58%, with organized capital covering only 30%, and the landlords' capital funding 12%. By 1925 housing was in crisis, and both official and anecdotal accounts told a horrifying story.[13]

The government linked the housing and unemployment problems. Brauns presented a program for underemployment. If a worker was unemployed three days out of six at a firm, he would receive an extra day's pay of unemployment support; if four or more days were lost, then he would get two days of support. This support would kick in only after eight days of underemployment and would not last for more than six weeks. The Labor Ministry calculated the cost of this at RM13.5 million per month. The Cabinet resolved to hold the line on unemployment support against the expensive motions of the Communists and Social Democrats. Originally, this program would only apply to firms with more than twenty workers, but the Reichstag Social Policy Committee forced the level down to ten. On February 16 the committee also raised some support levels for unemployment. A construction plan took shape as Reichstag pressure built. Brauns planned for RM1.5 billion of credit to go to mortgages. The Labor Minister called for building at least 150,000 new four-room apartments in 1926. Reinhold wanted to use only 15-20% of the rent tax for construction and avoid foreign loans. Luther tried to get more information on the availability of skilled workers and materials. The Economics Ministry opposed a housing and job-creation program, and the Cabinet was deadlocked until the Reichstag intervened.[14]

Although the Reichsrat had already approved Schlieben's budget draft, Reinhold and the Cabinet decided to submit an entirely new 1926 budget for Reichstag consideration because of the economic downturn. He dropped the

---

13. Dorothea Berger-Thimme, *Wohnungsfrage und Sozialstaat. Untersuchungen zu den Anfängen staatlicher Wohnungspolitik in Deutschland* (Frankfurt, 1976), pp. 31, 177, 220, 243. Silverman, "A Pledge Unredeemed: The Housing Crisis in Weimar Germany," *Central European History* 3 (1970), p. 121. *Kabinette Wirth*, Doc. #148, Note #1, p. 412. *Kabinett Fehrenbach*, Doc. #135, pp. 347-349. Hertz-Eichenrode, pp. 137-138. Feldman, *Great Disorder*, pp. 816-818. From 1925-29, 40% of house construction was aided in some way by the state, Abelshauser, Faust, and Petzina, p. 184. For a detailed account of the Reich's 1926 construction program, see Clingan, "More Construction, More Crisis: The Housing Problem of Weimar Germany," *Journal of Urban History* 26 (2000), pp. 630-644.

14. *Kabinette Luther*, Docs. #278, pp. 1079-1080; #279, p. 1082; #287, pp. 1113-1115; #289, pp. 1116-1120; #293, pp. 1130-1131. BAK R 43 I/1409, pp. 131-138R, 259; R 43 I/2345, pp. 201-202, 215-225; BAK NL Gessler, vol. 51, February 1, 1926.

conservative Schlieben policy of surplus budgets and used some of the previous years' surpluses in the new budget.  If necessary, the budget would run a deficit.  Beyond that, the Cabinet held three conflicting points of view.  Luther, Reinhold, and Economics Minister Curtius all supported tax cuts for business, Labor Minister Brauns supported new spending programs, and Stresemann did not care either way as long as there was a budget deficit.  The budget surpluses had led Parker Gilbert to think that perhaps the Dawes Plan had undervalued Germany's ability to pay reparations.  The main features of the Cabinet proposal were tax cuts for business.  The Cabinet also asked the Reichstag to raise the quarterly allowance of cash from the Reichsbank.  The bank allowed the government an allowance of RM100 million for cash to pay immediate bills, but the government had to repay the balance within three months.  Luther and Reinhold asked for and received an additional RM300 million of cash reserves in order to give the government more flexibility.[15]

Reinhold brought this proposal to a skeptical Reichstag and showed his oratorical skill by mixing analytical insight with humor.  Referring to a recent article by Keynes, "A Finance Minister's Paradise," he suggested that the current financial situation resembled the entrance to hell, not paradise.  He brought the house to its feet as he concluded:

I am not the minister of fortune but the minister of need. . . .  For our generation, only redoubled frugality and strengthened work will ease our burden. . . .  The road that lies before us will be narrow and laborious for all, with milestones of sacrifice and privation. But we must travel along it and bear our fate together.  At the end stands the goal that I believe all of us will find: a new height with the old freedom of the German nation.[16]

He told the Reichstag that loans would need to cover the tax cuts and asked for RM370 million in loan authority.  It was always difficult to estimate spending, and governments did not always use all of their loan authority.  I will argue later that the "Reinhold Loan" of 1927 did not cover this original budget but rather the supplementary budget that the Reichstag passed at the end of the year.

The next six weeks of debate saw Luther and his Cabinet gradually give way on social spending, especially on housing and unemployment.  Oskar Hergt said that the DNVP would continue to oppose Stresemann's foreign policy and would not support the new budget.  The Social Democrats and Catholic Center members were more supportive, but demanded more social spending.  Reinhold

---

15.  *VdR*, vol. 406, *Drucksache #1731*.  *Kabinette Luther I/II*, Docs. #281, pp. 1085-1086; #286, pp. 1103-1112; #292, Note #14, p. 1128.  S. Parker Gilbert, *Report of the Agent General for Reparations*, November 30, 1925.  For a blow-by-blow account of the passage of the 1926 budget from Cabinet proposal to final Reichstag approval, see Clingan, "The Budget Debate of 1926: A Case Study in Weimar Democracy," *European History Quarterly*, 30 (2000), pp. 33-48.

16.  *VdR, Stenographische Berichte*, vol. 388, p. 5411.

had originally earmarked only RM40 million for general unemployment relief and RM60 million in job creation. The Reichstag slowly worked its will. On February 20, it raised the rates of unemployment support. The Center and Bavarians won abolition of the wine tax and a delay in the scheduled increase of the beer tax. To pay for this, the Reichstag scaled back the Cabinet's proposed reduction in the turnover tax, a tax on each stage of production, from 0.6% to 0.75%. The Reich and the states would dedicate 15-20% of their shares of the rent tax to housing, and the Reich made a short-term RM200 million construction loan to the states. Finally, the SPD supported the budget on the conditions that the government delay a scheduled increase in controlled rents and extend the term of unemployment support from twenty-six to thirty-nine weeks. In the final votes the Nationalist motion to cut the rent tax was rejected 98 to 251, with the Economics party and the *völkisch* groups supporting it. The Communist motion to abolish the turnover tax was rejected 33 to 140 with the Nationalists and Social Democrats abstaining. On March 27 the Reichstag accepted the 1926 budget on a voice vote, and Reichstag President Paul Löbe announced with delight that for the first time since 1911 the Reichstag had passed the budget before the April 1 deadline. The party leaders, beginning with Hermann Müller of the SPD, went over to the ministers' bench to congratulate Reinhold on a job well done.[17]

It is worth speculating about what result would have occurred had there been no stimulus package in 1926. Would the German economy have recovered on its own? Would lower interest rates have ended the recession? We must consider that the German economy was in a recession in 1925-26 and slipped into an economic downturn that would become the Great Depression in 1928-29. The growth of 1926 and 1927 was the exception, not the rule. It is entirely likely that Germany in the late 1920s could have remained in the economic doldrums with too little economic growth to employ an expanding labor force. This was the economic history of Britain through much of the interwar period. Critics later attributed the German recovery to the English coal strike and the subsequent labor difficulties, but this seems overstated. The German recovery took place over many sectors. Others might say that Germany should have saved the budget surplus of 1924 and 1925 for the Great Depression, when it desperately needed money. This ignores the fact that slow growth or contraction in 1926 and 1927 probably would have consumed the surplus anyway because of lower tax revenues and greater spending needs. Had Luther and Reinhold not taken swift action, the jump in unemployment would have led to a deflationary spiral and the loss of foreign confidence. Monetary policy would have been unable to break the spiral, as demonstrated in 1930-31. The Depression simply would have been more drawn out. It is impossible to guess the political impact

---

17. Ibid., vol. 389, pp. 6799-6857. Curtius, p. 34. *Berliner Tageblatt*, March 28, 1926.

of a longer Depression. Would it have simply moved up the timetable for the Nazi seizure of power? Would the Communists have been in a stronger position? Could the Social Democrats have forged a Scandinavian-style farm-labor alliance? If Hitler came to power anyway, could the government have financed Hitler's economy without the examples of Weimar's deficit financing? All these are unknowable.

The passage of the budget marked a turning point in the government of Germany. Unlike the previous Luther Cabinet, the new coalition had appealed to the Social Democrats and made considerable concessions to the SPD to gain passage. The *Berliner Tageblatt* noted that the Chancellor had returned to power with the idea that he would work with shifting majorities, presumably working with the Nationalists on domestic policy and the Socialists on foreign policy. On the budget, however, Luther had sided with the SPD to gain a majority, leaving the DNVP to abstain sullenly. Within four months of the rancorous fight over Locarno, a broad coalition had come together. It was no accident that it was the calmest budget debate since the Social Democrats became the single largest party in the Reichstag in 1912, an event that led to the sharp right-left conflict inherited by Weimar. Theodore Balderston suggests that the competing demands of Reichstag parties swamped Reinhold's coherent program, but the budget of 1926 still had the outline that Reinhold had proposed seven weeks before. The speed of the budget's passage was even more remarkable, given the complexity of Reinhold's program and the recession/depression of the winter of 1925-26. The change in the Reichsbank law allowed the government to draw upon RM400 million in reserves. After fifteen years of bitter conflict and legislative deadlock, the German people, as represented in interest groups and Reichstag parties, were becoming reconciled to a social republic. The idea of a *volksgemeinschaft* stretching from the Nationalists to the Socialists, as broached by Wilhelm Marx in late 1924, seemed closer than ever to reality.[18]

The debate of 1925 over the financial compromise had ended in a victory for the Reich over the states, cementing the principles laid down by Erzberger. States were perpetually short of funds, especially after the compromise of 1925. Reinhold had brought to Berlin the state mentality of borrowing money to balance the budget. The coalition that had appeared during the debate over the 1926 budget asserted itself during the late spring and summer on the Reich, state, and local levels. The pattern of a broad agreement on deficit spending to fund social programs and job creation was repeated in areas as different as Centrist Catholic Köln, Conservative Catholic Bavaria, and

---

18. *Berliner Tageblatt*, March 26, 1926. Balderston, *Financial Crisis*, p. 224. Mildred B. Northrup, *Control Policies of the Reichsbank, 1924-1933* (New York: Columbia University Press, 1938), p. 28. *VdR*, vol. 409, Drucksache #2370. BAK R 43 I/635, pp. 33-38.

Socialist Protestant Prussia. The loans to fund these programs came largely from the United States. Government stimulation of the economy began to improve the economy, but a desire grew to accelerate growth. Job creation became the leading priority, eclipsing even the idea of fiscal responsibility that had dominated thinking since the inflation of 1923. The Cabinet forced the miserly Advisory Board on Foreign Credits to consider job creation during its deliberations.

In the spring of 1926 the stream of foreign loans became a flood. The Board approved only 65% of proposed city loans in part or in whole by the end of 1925; in the first four months of 1926 this rate fell to 53%. This drove the towns into the domestic market and they soaked up whatever domestic capital was available. The cities did not mind high interest rates because the inflation had wiped out their debts. They now had a clean slate. The Reichstag had provided an incentive for capital-hungry businesses and governments to go abroad for loans by relieving the loans from tax burdens. If corporations would refrain from seeking loans on the Berlin market, the government would give them significant tax exemptions. Entities seeking loans abroad would gain approval from the Advisory Board and then receive the tax exemption from the Reichsrat and the Reichstag Budget Committee. The hope of the government was that this would loosen the domestic market so that the Reich and states could offer their own loans domestically and thus avoid any conflict with the Dawes Plan authorities. While Gilbert did not have veto power over foreign loans, he would not approve any attempt by the Reich to float another long-term loan abroad because it would conflict with the Dawes bonds he was sworn to protect.[19]

Monetary policy also eased at last. Schacht had urged private bankers to rebuild their inflation-ravaged reserves by holding interest rates high. The central committee of Reichsbank directors and leading private bankers called for a change in policy in January 1926. They deemed that the situation had changed in the previous month: more foreign currency was coming in, money circulation was stronger, and thus there was more chance for long-term credit. It lowered the discount rate from 9% to 8% and eased credit. Imports had fallen by one-third since October 1925 as the recession took hold. The currency was clearly in no danger. In March it lowered the discount rate to 7½%. The Reichsbank was a follower, not a leader, in monetary policy. It had only cut the discount rate by 1½% while the daily money rate fell 3.6% from December 1925 to April 1926. On June 6 the Reichsbank reduced the discount rate to 6½%.

---

19. James, *Slump*, pp. 46-52. Michael L. Hughes, "Equity and Good Faith: Inflation, Revaluation, and the Distribution of Wealth and Power in the Weimar Republic," (Ph.D. diss., University of California, Berkeley, 1981), p. 264. McNeil, p. 138. BAK R 2/2008, March 16, 1927.

Despite the reduction of rates, the money market was no more liquid than in the early spring.[20]

Mayor Konrad Adenauer of Köln was very successful in obtaining foreign loans. He had gotten a short-term loan in the winter of 1924-25, when credit was especially scarce, because of personal connections. In late 1925, Köln concluded an agreement with the underwriters Blair and Company and the Chase National Bank to lend the city $10 million (RM42 million) at 6½%, repayable over twenty-five years. The loan's main intents were expansion of the electrical and gas works and construction of a suburban rail network. By the end of 1927 Adenauer had run up RM222 million of debt (a nation-leading 316 Marks per capita). Köln's long-term debt was RM115 million, of which RM35 million was foreign debt. The city's total income in 1926 was only RM81.4 million. Adenauer's city was in the shakiest financial position. Berlin had a total debt of RM569 million, but this only amounted to RM141 per capita, and its long-term debt was RM333 million with RM243 million from foreign sources. Berlin's annual income was RM400 million. Köln's debt per capita far outstripped that of other large Prussian cities. Of the five Prussian cities with over a million residents Frankfurt trailed Köln with RM237, then came Berlin, Breslau at RM136, and Essen at RM54. If one removes any controls for size to find small cities with big loans, only Mainz rivaled Köln as the leading debtor. (See Table 4.1.) Adenauer plowed the money borrowed from domestic sources (and therefore not answerable to the Advisory Board) into such popular projects as park expansion and construction of stadiums, housing, canals, and roads. These labor-intensive projects contributed enormously to Adenauer's popularity and nearly propelled him to the Chancellorship in 1926. Other mayors such as Gustav Böss in Berlin and Ludwig Landmann in Frankfurt, presiding over leftist coalitions as Adenauer did, followed his lead. Reinhold's debt was nothing compared to this. Eventually Köln was unable to pay off its debts when the economic downturn of the late 1920s reduced public income. Despite this, Adenauer's popularity remained unscathed and he went on to greater things.[21]

Heavy borrowing was not the policy of left-of-center coalitions alone. The conservative regime in Bavaria became notorious for its reckless fiscal ways. William McNeil has told this story incisively, but some portions are worth closer examination. In the summer of 1925, Bavaria contracted with the New York firms of Harris, Forbes, and Company and the Equitable Trust Company for a $25 million loan at 6%, repayable over twenty-five years. The Advisory Board approved only $15 million on these terms. According to the proposal, RM36 million would go for hydroelectric programs, RM10 million for

---

20.   McNeil, pp. 21, 122.    BAK R 43 I/641, pp. 4-12.    Blaich, *Wirtschaftskrise*, p. 168. James, *Slump*, p. 37. Hardach, pp. 68-69.

21.   McNeil, pp. 8, 70, 245-248. BAK R 2/2006, June 12, 1926.

**Table 4.1**
**Per Capita Urban Indebtedness as of November 1, 1927 (populations of 80,000 or more)**

| Prussia (including occupied lands): | | Bavaria: | |
|---|---|---|---|
| Köln | 316.33 | Augsburg | 161.74 |
| Mainz | 311.87 | Munich | 116.27 |
| Frankfurt | 237.10 | Saxony: | |
| Bonn | 219.48 | Dresden | 183.04 |
| Darmstadt | 218.11 | Leipzig | 86.43 |
| Offenbach | 208.66 | Chemnitz | 84.50 |
| Altona | 202.31 | Baden: | |
| Barmen | 187.31 | Mannheim | 270.20 |
| Duisburg | 171.20 | Karlsruhe | 242.63 |
| Elberfeld | 148.86 | Württemberg: | |
| Düsseldorf | 145.45 | Stuttgart | 131.27 |
| Aachen | 141.49 | | |
| Berlin | 141.47 | | |
| Breslau | 136.18 | | |
| Magdeburg | 130.44 | | |
| Kassel | 118.28 | | |
| Halle | 116.59 | | |
| Königsberg | 108.04 | | |
| Bochum | 102.60 | | |
| Kiel | 98.11 | | |
| Stettin | 89.97 | | |
| Hannover | 66.86 | | |
| Gelsenkirchen | 58.18 | | |
| Essen | 53.92 | | |

*Source*: BAK R 2/20151a.

the Rhine-Main-Danube Canal, and another RM10 million for state-owned businesses such as salt plants, iron works, and basalt quarries. As McNeil points out, Bavaria's real need was to cover RM23 million in short-term debt. The Bavarians returned in July 1926 for their second slice, the $10 million deleted by the Advisory Board. The state asked for a nineteen-year loan at 6.5%. The ostensible spending goals were eight water and electrical projects, but the money actually paid off old debts. One Reichsbank director felt that the effective yield was a bit high, but he would not block the loan. The Board warned that while it recognized that there had been insufficient domestic capital in 1925, Bavaria should look to German capital in the future. The Bavarians followed this advice and took a $10 million short-term loan from the Dresdner Bank in December 1926.[22]

Given the history of German budgets up to this point, one may wonder why the American investment houses were so bullish on Germany. A speech given by H. M. Addinsell of Harris, Forbes to the Philadelphia Bond Club in May 1926 is revealing. Addinsell assured his audience that Germany now had the "most stable currency in Europe" and had the will to pay reparations, that its industry was in excellent operating condition, that it had balanced the budget and had its best harvest since the war, and that its energy production was now three times the 1913 level. He brushed off the recession: "the inevitable readjustment which was foreseen by economists has taken place and the curve of German trade and industry is now turning upwards." American investors had a unique opportunity because this strong economy was suffering a capital shortage. Investors could gain high returns with very little risk. "Most of the [German bonds] are better than most of our domestic issues--the public utility bonds, for example, have much larger factors of safety in physical property, earnings, etc.--and when the public becomes reassured as to the moral and political risk, the proposition of 50% more income than is obtainable from comparable home investments will attract more and more investors." Finally, Addinsell addressed what he called the "moral risk":

As an ex-member of the American Expeditionary Force, I was certainly "from Missouri" when I first went to Germany in 1924. I have become convinced . . . that fundamentally it is a good moral risk. I think that our prewar conception of the German people (leaving out the *Junkers*) as a reliable, industrious, and enterprising people, is and was the true one. . . .   The military ministry that led them into the disastrous war is discredited and discarded. After all, the war has been over seven years and the passions and prejudices engendered by the conflict are dying out.[23]

Both public and private corporations attracted American money. One public corporation was the Rhine-Main-Danube Corporation, which floated $6 million in bonds through Lee, Higginson and the J. Henry Schroeder Banking Corporation. This project would dig a 375-mile canal linking Aschaffenburg on the Main to Passau on the Danube with up to thirty-three high-energy dams. Bavaria and the Reich government were the main backers of this company. An example of a private issue was a $25 million bond issue handled by Schroder and Dillon, Read for the Rheinelbe Union, a consortium of large iron, steel, and coal producers in the Ruhr. These bonds converted short-term debt into long-term debt and increased working capital.[24]

---

22. BAK R 2/2022, pp. 205-218, Advisory Board meeting of July 14, 1926. McNeil, pp. 251-253.

23. PrStA, Rep. 151, Abt. IA, #2595, vol. 2.

24. BAK R 43 I/655, pp. 185-187.

There was a vocal minority opposed to European loans in general and German loans in particular. Grosvener Jones, the Chief of the U.S. Department of Commerce's Finance and Investment Division, and its commercial attaché in Berlin, Charles Herring, both saw long-term loans to German industry as dangerous. Herring condemned the Germans for "their beggar psychology, the natural tendency of the race for self-pity, the national desire to get something somehow without a too scrupulous regard to ways and means of obtaining or repaying it . . . to beg, borrow, or steal something from Uncle Sam, the rich man of the neighborhood."[25] By the end of 1925, the State Department was quietly circulating these negative evaluations to bankers, but they had no impact.

In the middle of the recovery, Hans Luther was suddenly forced out as Chancellor. The immediate cause was a fight over the display of the imperial flag, but it was an odd issue for an astute politician such as Luther to stumble over. There has long been speculation about what (if anything) was the real reason for Luther's fall. Perhaps Luther himself was weary of all the political wrangling that the democracy required now that decrees were no longer necessary. After another failed attempt to build a Grand Coalition under Adenauer, Stresemann urged Marx to become Chancellor again. Marx was reluctant but the Foreign Minister held out support of the People's party for the eventual inclusion of the Social Democrats. Hindenburg also wrote to Marx urging him to take the job. On May 16, Marx went to visit the President to ask for more time. It was an awkward moment for both men since it was their first meeting since the election in which Hindenburg had edged Marx to win the presidency. Hindenburg tried to ease the tension by saying, "Who would have thought we would be negotiating together?"[26] On May 20 the Reichstag approved what Hermann Müller called "the Luther Cabinet without Luther."[27] Marx left his portfolios as Justice Minister and Minister for Occupied Regions vacant for the moment in hope that the Social Democrats would join in a Grand Coalition and take these slots. Stresemann had shrewdly urged Marx to become Chancellor, knowing that Marx's loose management style differed markedly from Luther's. Stresemann had complained privately that Luther had always remained a mayor: he had taken leadership on the tax issue away from the Finance Ministry and had given foreign-policy declarations instead of the Foreign Minister. Marx believed in simply letting the ministers make their own policies with only the loosest form of coordination.[28]

---

25. Brandes, pp. 184-185.

26. HSA, Köln, NL Marx, vol. 70, p. 5.

27. *Berliner Tageblatt*, May 20, 1926.

28. Hugo Stehkämpfer, *Nachlässe Wilhelm Marx* (Köln: Neubner, 1968), p. 420. Rudolf Morsey, ed., *Die Protokolle der Reichstagsfraktion und des Fraktionsvorstandes der deutschen Zentrumspartei 1926-33* (Mainz, 1969), Document # 44, p. 41. Ulrich von Hehl, *Wilhelm Marx 1883-1946. Eine politische Biographie* (Bonn, 1987), pp. 378-383. BAK R 45 III/20, meeting of DDP Board of Directors, May 20, 1926.

Peter Reinhold gained sole control over financial policy with the resignation of Chancellor Luther.  As part of his plan to reduce bureaucracy, he forced out the meddlesome State Secretary David Fischer.  Reinhold was determined to continue with his program.  The government's new trade and tax policies were beginning to take effect.  Reinhold's analysis was that the economy suffered from a shortage of capital and that the government's job was to pump capital in, as it had with tax cuts, loans to the railroads, export credits to the Soviet Union, and the house-building plan.  Reinhold admitted that creating capital was a difficult task.  If the government had raised taxes, this would only have worsened the economy and led to a "vicious circle."  The government would have to borrow money to fund the deficit, as he had told the Reichstag in February.  He hoped that market conditions and interest rates would support this loan.  Reinhold reminded his critics that, in contrast to Schlieben, his estimates on income and spending had been accurate so far.[29]

Reinhold was less confident privately.  He had presented a memo to his colleagues in May on the finances.  The minister was alarmed at the increasing demands for spending that had mushroomed in the last several weeks.  The final budget deal had increased unemployment spending by RM200 million.  The Reichstag Committee on Social Policy wanted to add another RM40 million.  There were demands from Reichstag committees and subcommittees for more support for the occupied regions, wounded veterans, and retired persons.  Reinhold decried the view of the Reichstag that there was plenty of money around.  He would probably need some RM400 million in loans at the end of the year, but if spending escalated, the deficit would be unavoidable and unmanageable.  As the Finance Ministry began to draft the budget for FY27, Reinhold urged the utmost fiscal restraint.   He stressed that reparations payments would require additional funds while the surplus from the 1924 and 1925 budgets used in 1926 would be unavailable.  He asked his divisions to write the budget in the same spirit of austerity used in the winter of 1923-24.[30]

By the late spring of 1926 the German economy was responding to the relaxation of the fiscal and monetary policy by the Luther government, but the recovery was sluggish.  Unemployment had peaked in February at a little over two million.  It fell to 1.7 million in May.  By June 1926 there were still 1.75 million persons out of work.  This figure towered above the mere 673,000 recorded as unemployed just the previous November.  Other economic indicators reflected this.  Bankruptcies had peaked in February but had fallen 50% by June.  Temporary receiverships had peaked in January but were down two-thirds

PA, Auswärtiges Amt, Stresemann Papers, vol. 37, Aktennummer 7326, May 14, 1926.

    29.  *Berliner Tageblatt*, July 18, 1926.

    30.  Günter Abramowski, ed., *Akten der Reichskanzlei. Die Kabinette Marx III/IV* (Boppard, 1987), Doc. #7, pp. 13-16.   BAK R 43 I/877, pp. 290-296. Hertz-Eichenrode, p. 111.

in June. During the summer both figures would decline by another 50%. The stock market index rose rapidly from 103.8 in May to 145.1 in September. By every measure, the economic downturn had ended during the spring of 1926, when the government reversed its economic policies, but the German economy was still mired.[31]

Labor Minister Brauns was another beneficiary of Luther's departure. As unemployment remained high in the summer of 1926, calls grew for more government involvement. Brauns, who had been so isolated in the discussions of 1925, now moved to center stage with his schemes for putting the jobless to work. In June, Brauns outlined a new comprehensive plan on job creation. The Labor Ministry foresaw extra employment by the railroad and post office by means of special loans, new projects on canal and street construction, cultivation of wasteland, and construction of agricultural settlements and urban housing. Financing would be difficult, but loans could cover part of the plan, especially the Transport Ministry's canals. Finally, Brauns proposed that the Cabinet create a new Ministerial Commission under the chairmanship of the Labor Ministry. The unemployed had already made many gains in 1926: higher benefits, money for part-time unemployment, an extension to thirty-nine weeks and, as of May 1, fifty-two weeks in special cases.[32] Unemployment remained high in certain areas where many had already exhausted their benefits.[33] In July, representatives from the Labor, Finance, Economics, Transport, Post, and Agriculture Ministries agreed to create more emergency work, especially in

---

31. Salomon Flink, *The German Reichsbank and Economic Germany* (New York: Harper and Brothers, 1930), p. 173. Blaich, *Wirtschaftskrise*, p. 21. Heinz Habedank, *Die Reichsbank in der Weimarer Republik* (East Berlin: Akademie-Verlag, 1981), p. 15.

32. Hertz-Eichenrode, p. 152. *Kabinette Luther*, Doc. #355, pp. 1336-1337. *VdR, Stenographische Berichte*, vol. 289, pp. 7262, 7633-7659. *Kabinette Marx III/IV*, Docs. #30, p. 70; #40, pp. 94-95. BAK R 43 I/1412, pp. 102-107; R 43 I/1413, pp. 182-R, 277-282.

33. Districts where average length of unemployment had exceeded twenty-six weeks by September 1926:

| City | Average weeks | City | Average weeks | City | Average weeks |
|---|---|---|---|---|---|
| Berlin | 73 | Heidelberg | 34 | Erfurt | 30 |
| Köln | 73 | Hanau | 33 | Kaiserslautern | 29 |
| Hamburg | 53 | Stuttgart | 33 | Speyer | 29 |
| Frankfurt | 51 | Offenbach | 33 | Worms | 29 |
| Breslau | 47 | Wiesbaden | 31 | Leipzig | 28 |
| Munich | 43 | Höchst am Main | 31 | Hannover | 28 |
| Darmstadt | 41 | Mainz | 31 | Mannheim | 28 |

Source: BAP R 401/529, p. 41.

housing. The states would match these funds. There would be a special fund for agricultural housing. The government would lend money to the railroads to build roadbeds and bridges, expand depots, and improve vehicle yards. Funding for a canal program would go into a supplementary budget measure. The government should appropriate RM160 million in immediate supplementary spending on emergency work, railroads, and agricultural settlements. The post office would take an RM80 million loan independently to employ more people. It also endorsed Brauns' Ministerial Commission proposal.[34]

The Ministerial Commission first met on July 13. Finance Ministry Director Lutz Schwerin von Krosigk calculated that the ministries had allocated at least RM1.37 billion to job creation. Krosigk doubted that foreign loans could finance much of this, but Commission Chairman Oskar Weigert insisted that funding must be found somewhere and was supported by Hans Schäffer of the Economics Ministry. Another Ministry Director from the Finance Ministry, Alexander von Brandt, said that the Advisory Board on Foreign Credits had insisted that all loans should go to productive purposes. Brandt feared that states and cities would now use the cover of job creation as a way to fund any number of projects and urged fiscal responsibility on the Commission. Weigert neatly turned the tables on Brandt by noting that the views of the Commission and the Advisory Board on what were "productive" loans might vary, and he resolved to talk to the Board. At the next Advisory Board session, Wolfgang Reichardt of the Economics Ministry suggested that the Board did not have to change its guidelines but that from now on a representative of the Labor Ministry would be present to give his views on how a given loan might affect job creation. The Reich Economics Council also formed a committee to fight unemployment and proposed a RM50 million program of road construction and a ten-year canal-building plan that would cost RM825 million.[35]

The first seven months of 1926 had seen a marked shift in fiscal policy. The Reinhold tax cuts and social spending increases gave the economy a considerable lift. State and local authorities also provided stimuli. Attempts to make the *de facto* Grand Coalition into a real one proved fruitless. The SPD did not want to be part of a government for another winter. It calculated that two and a half million would be jobless then, with up to 20% enrolled in the government's new job-creation program.[36] The government clearly allowed the socialists direct economic and social influence. The SPD chose to stay out of the government in this period. Marx noted that the Cabinet seemed stable even without a Grand Coalition. His one worry was over the People's party, which

---

34. BAK R 43 I/1414, pp. 28-38. *Kabinette Marx III/IV*, Doc. #53, pp. 120-121. Hertz-Eichenrode, p. 169.

35. BAK R 43 I/2031, pp. 242-245R.    BAK R 2/2022, pp. 205-218. Upmeier in Hansmeyer, p. 162. BAP R 401/657, p. 54.

36. *Kabinette Marx III/IV*, Doc. #64, pp. 144-145. BAK NL Pünder, vol. 27, pp. 84-89.

had made the opening to the Nationalists in December 1924 to force Marx out and might do so again.[37]  Even with Luther's departure, the coalition in favor of massive deficit-spending projects had gained strength during the late spring and early summer of 1926.  Luther's ouster enabled Brauns to put larger spending schemes into motion.  Reinhold could not hold the line on spending. States and cities, no matter their political composition, repeated the pattern of deficit spending and generous social programs.  Marx was correct about both the stability of the Cabinet and the DVP's opening to the DNVP, but the fall and winter of 1926-27 would prove remarkable as the already broad coalition would grow again to encompass for a time industrial interests and the Nationalists themselves.  The Reich had averted a political crisis and the revival of extremism in 1926 by using a countercyclical policy with an explicit and precise plan to use credit to fight the recession.  Germany in the winter of 1925-26 provided a preview of the Great Depression to come.  Reinhold provided a preview of what would come to be known as "Keynesian economics" by cutting taxes and raising spending to pull the Reich out of its economic rut. Unfortunately, when the real Depression came, Germany did not embrace this solution immediately.

---

37. Pohl, p. 240. *Kabinette Marx III/IV*, Doc. #64, pp. 144-145.

# Chapter 5

# The High Summer of the Weimar Republic

The Dawes bonds were more popular than ever. Foreign investors clamored for them after the Reichstag accepted Reinhold's budget plan. From January to May 1926, the price of the bonds rose by 35%. The national government absorbed the lessons of the 1926 budget and was eager to take another step. It could use controlled deficit spending to put more people to work and to enhance its position in Europe. In a continent desperate for reconstruction capital, Germany seemed to have a goose with golden eggs. In the fall of 1926 the Weimar Republic came closest to dispelling the clouds that had cloaked it since its inception. The Luther/Reinhold budget had brought the economy out of recession, put 250,000 more Germans to work, strengthened the German Mark, and enhanced the government's ability to deal with foreign and domestic problems. The Republic functioned normally, and disparate groups responded in the autumn months. German industry seemed more inclined to accept the Weimar parties, including the Social Democrats. The Nationalists yearned to return to the government and were willing to soften some of their positions. The Germans and French discussed a deal to exchange cash for early French withdrawal from the occupied regions. The debate over fiscal policy continued as the government brought a huge supplementary budget to the Reichstag. Finally, the issue of unemployment relief brought three strange bedfellows together as the Communists, Socialists, and Nationalists united to vote for higher payments. Political stability was a delicate compromise among business, agriculture and labor. This compromise in turn relied on economic prosperity and a continuing flow of loans from abroad. In 1926 the Republic tried to cash this prosperity in nationalist coin by using its economic clout to regain territories lost in the war. Had the Republic succeeded in establishing its nationalist credentials and assuaging those insulted by Versailles, the early 1930s might have gone in a very different direction. By the end of 1926 the German goose was showing signs of fatigue and Marx's centrist coalition had fallen.

The flow of international capital after 1924 had made the Finance Ministry more important than ever. Reinhold entered the charmed circle of international finance and diplomacy previously reserved for Stresemann, Schacht, and Luther. Stresemann and Reinhold made the first official moves toward a revision of the Dawes Plan. They were concerned about both the load of RM2.5 billion a year slated to begin in 1928-29 and the Plan's lack of an official end date.[1] Reinhold decided that an approach to Gilbert should start on the issue of "small-improvement notes." The financial crisis in France had become dramatically worse, and J. P. Morgan's extensive French loans were in jeopardy. The German railroad could sell these notes ostensibly to make repairs and improvements. Marketing these short-term notes would pump a quick RM55 million into France because it took about half of the sale proceeds under the reparation agreements. Stresemann did not want money going to France without any concessions and opposed the plan in its original form, but dropped his opposition to the "small-improvement notes" when an intriguing possibility arose during the negotiations. Ferdinand Eberstedt, the European representative of Dillon, Read, told Stresemann in July that a general French-German understanding was possible. Although revision of the Dawes Plan was not feasible, Eberstedt suggested that Dillon, Read could market some $1 billion worth of railroad bonds to give the French a massive infusion of capital. If France could get this, the French Premier "would not have the slightest interest in continuing the occupation."[2] This would be the essence of the deal: German consent to market the railroad bonds in exchange for French withdrawal. Eberstedt was extremely confident because he had just marketed bonds for large German businesses. Although Gilbert's support was not necessary, it was important that he not oppose the plan. Public attacks would scare off the investors in New York whom Eberstedt saw as the prime targets for the bond issue. This tantalizing prospect would haunt the Atlantic community throughout the fall of 1926.[3]

Rumors of a deal began to filter out in August. The Whaley Eaton letter of August 31 predicted that RM2 billion of the railroad bonds would be marketed to finance an American, English, and French stability plan. Strong denounced the plan and warned the French to make sure that Dillon, Read could

---

1. There seems to have been an unofficial understanding that the Dawes Plan would end in 1950, when the last payment of the 1924 loan was due. *Akten zur deutschen auswärtigen Politik (ADAP)*, Series B: 1925-33, vol. I, 2 (Göttingen, 1966), Doc. #193, pp. 454-457, November 12, 1926.

2. Gustav Stresemann, *Vermächtnis* (Berlin, 1932), vol. II, p. 451.

3. *ADAP*, Series B, vol. I, 1, Docs.# 244, pp. 579-580; #255, pp. 603-604. *Kabinette Marx III/IV*, Docs. #35, pp. 83-85; #37, pp. 88-90; #69, pp. 168-170; #75, pp. 181-188. Hallgarten and Radkow, p. 186. Wandel, p. 51.

carry it out before they deserted Morgan.  To some, it seemed that German economic diplomacy was now working to reverse the result of the war with moves to buy back Eupen and Malmédy from economically-troubled Belgium, to subsidize Poland for alterations in the Danzig corridor and France for the Saarland.  The Poles were particularly alarmed.  The Polish Mark had collapsed in an inflation similar to the German experience and had been replaced by the new zloty.  The Poles had asked Dillon, Read for a stabilization loan in the summer of 1925, but the underwriter had refused.  The Poles blamed the failure on the Germans as the zloty began to slide in value.  The Germans linked any trade agreement with Poland to better treatment of Germans in Silesia, but the Poles suspected, with some justification, that the Germans wanted Poland's finances to deteriorate until it made territorial and trade concessions.  Back in January Schacht had harangued an American expert on the Polish economy at the Berlin railroad station to turn him against a stabilization loan.[4]

The German Ambassador to Washington, Ago von Maltzan, was concerned that there was a false impression of Germany's ability to pay reparations.  Stories appeared describing the Berlin stock market boom.  The generally smooth course of payments under the Dawes Plan had also encouraged this impression.  The *Saturday Evening Post* portrayed Germany in rosy terms. It looked at the spending on public works such as the new stadium in Frankfurt and the Danube reservoir and declared German industry to be larger than in 1913 and found that this prosperity came mostly from foreign loans.  This made it more difficult for Stresemann to plead poverty.   Stresemann privately complained: "Just because the state of Prussia spends 14 million Marks on the building of the Berlin Opera House, the world assumes that we are overflowing with money.  No victorious state has done anything like this."[5]  Maltzan wrote of Germany's poverty compared to the United States.  Germany had a per capita income of $200, while the U.S. figure was $650.  Americans drove 16 million automobiles while Germans only had 175,000.[6]

Germany was not a poor country.  Measuring national wealth was not a science undertaking in the 1920s, although everyone agreed that the United States was the leading economic power with about $321 billion in national wealth.  If one accepts Maltzan's proportions and other estimates, Germany's national wealth would be about $60 billion (RM252 billion).  France was also

4. Wandel, pp. 49-63.  Neal Pease, *Poland, the United States, and the Stabilization of Europe, 1919-1933* (Oxford, 1986), pp. 36-63.  Whaley Eaton Letter, August 31, 1926, PA, Auswärtiges Amt, Wirtschaft Reparationen, Aktennummer L253, Peace Treaty: Germany's Financial and Economic Position, vol. 5.

5. Stresemann letter to Karl Jarres, August 23, 1926, PA, Auswärtiges Amt, Wirtschaft Reparationen, Aktennummer L253, Peace Treaty: Germany's Financial and Economic Position, vol. 5.

6. *Saturday Evening Post*, September 4, 1926.  Wirtschaft Reparation 6, U.S. Economic Relations with Germany, October 23, 1926.  Krosigk, p. 48.

at about $60 billion, and Great Britain claimed $80 billion. A recent estimate of 1925 GDP agrees: British GDP was about 30% of the American level, France at 23%, and Germany at 20.4%   From 1925 to 1929, American loans to Germany exceeded repayment by $842.5 million. Due to the stabilization, the recession, and the thaw in international relations, Germany's trade balance ran a surplus of RM965 million from November 1925 to August 1926. The budget surpluses of 1924 and 1925 and the turn to deficit spending of 1926 had enabled the Germans to monetize a considerable amount of this trade surplus, and they had a unique opportunity now to use this spare cash as a diplomatic tool.[7]

In September Stresemann had sought his colleagues' opinion on marketing RM1.25 billion in railroad bonds to buy back the Saarland and Eupen-Malmédy and gain early evacuation from the Rhineland. French Foreign Minister Aristide Briand visited Berlin on September 11 to prepare for the meeting in Geneva, where he wanted to discuss all matters of concern to the two countries, including the occupation of the Rhineland, revision of the Dawes Plan, and most especially the Saarland. Briand's aide gave a more detailed description: Briand wanted to discuss the evacuation of the second and third zones of the Rhineland and the Saar but feared upsetting French public opinion. In Briand's view the Rhineland had to remain under some loose French control, but the troops could be withdrawn. After the opening session of the League of Nations, Briand and Stresemann left Geneva and drove to the French border. Guards held curious journalists at the frontier, but word leaked out that the foreign ministers had stopped at Thoiry, a small French village just across the border.  Briand and Stresemann began by discussing the major problems outstanding between France and Germany: the Saar, the Rhineland, Eupen-Malmédy, and relations with the Soviet Union. Stresemann mentioned the possibilities of revising the Dawes Plan and the opposition within the Cabinet to marketing the railroad bonds.  Briand repeated his earlier desire for a full settlement of problems and maintained that he had the full support of the Foreign Affairs Committee of the Chamber of Deputies for his position. Stresemann was willing to stabilize the franc but did not want to stabilize his old antagonist Poincaré.  Briand agreed but believed that the new government could not survive very long.  At the first meeting Stresemann and Briand agreed on further discussions and to send French technical experts to Berlin at the beginning of October.[8]

---

7. *World Almanac 1928*, pp. 295-296.  Cleona Lewis, *America's Stake in International Investment* (Washington, DC, 1938), p. 393. Balderston, *Financial Crisis*, p. 137.  Angus Maddison, *Monitoring the World Economy, 1820-1992* (Paris: Organization for Economic Cooperation and Development, 1995), pp. 148-150.

8. *ADAP*, Series B, vol. I, 2, Docs. #82, pp. 179-81, note #1, September 11, 1926; #88, pp. 188-191, September 17, 1926.  Werner Link, *Die amerikanische Stabilisierungspolitik in Deutschland* (Düsseldorf, 1970), p. 401.

The foreign ministers then considered specific goals. Briand suggested that the French could evacuate the Saar and the entire Rhineland. Stresemann mentioned his problems with the Economics Ministry in the Cabinet and the Nationalists in the Reichstag. Even two more years of occupation would be intolerable. Stresemann insisted that evacuation must be immediate as Briand nodded supportively. Briand turned to the financial need of France: could Stresemann get the money to France quickly? The German foresaw the marketing of RM1.5 billion of 7% bonds as the maximum feasible sale. France would get 52% or RM780 million (9 billion francs) under the provisions of the reparations agreements. In addition, Germany would pay a flat fee of RM300 million to recover the Saar mines, and presumably a plebiscite deciding control of the Saar would follow quickly if France did not simply return the area. Thus France would have an infusion of one billion Marks (about 12 billion francs) to stabilize the currency. France could withdraw six thousand troops immediately, but complete and immediate evacuation of the Rhineland would be difficult because there was no housing in France for them. Stresemann boasted that his foreign policy had the backing of three-quarters of the German people. Belgium would receive RM120 million as its share plus a RM120 million loan for the return of Eupen-Malmédy.[9]

Stresemann transmitted news of the conversations at Thoiry to Berlin. He had not discussed revision of the Dawes Plan but had also avoided any discussion of a final settlement in the east. He had insisted that France withdraw its last soldier by the middle of 1927, and Briand had apparently agreed. Chancery State Secretary Hermann Pünder felt that the financial burden would be bearable, with a 50-to-75-million-Mark payment each year on top of the lump sum needed for the Saar. Pünder also believed in Briand's authority to negotiate: Poincaré had not phoned Briand once in Geneva. Marx found this news too good to be true and mentioned that Stresemann had just told him that Briand and Poincaré did talk at least once by phone while Briand was at Thoiry. Pünder said that Stresemann was considering the doubts of Curtius and Reinhold on the question of transfers and suggested that the Finance Minister could exercise a veto over the plan if he found it too exorbitant. Reinhold himself was visiting Paris as part of his summer vacation and talking with Poincaré. The German Embassy in Paris was none too pleased about the minister conducting personal diplomacy, but the Foreign Ministry saw an opportunity to probe Poincaré's feelings privately.[10]

---

9. *ADAP*, Series B, vol. I, 2, Doc. #94, pp. 202-210. For the British reaction, see the memos in *Documents on British Foreign Policy (DBFP)* 1919-1939, Series IA, vol. 2 (London, 1968), pp. 403-411.

10. *ADAP*, Series B, vol. I, 2, Doc. #95, pp. 210-236. PA, Auswärtiges Amt, Büro des Staatssekretärs, Section Fab (Thoiry), vol. 2, pp. 14-15, 145-149.

Despite the initial euphoria, serious flaws emerged in the Thoiry Plan. A German Foreign Ministry representative met with the American Embassy Councillor DeWitt Clinton Poole. Poole would not give a definite opinion until he knew the precise facts but remembered that Gilbert had generally opposed early mobilization of the railroad bonds. This was vital because the Thoiry Plan would fail without American cooperation. The French Cabinet continued to support negotiations, although the conservative Louis Marin stated ominously that Thoiry depended on the settlement of certain unspecified questions. France had no plan ready to market the bonds. Montagu Norman took a very negative position. The thorny problem of the settlement of the French war debt to the United States also loomed larger. The American government wanted ratification of the Mellon-Bérenger Treaty, but there was strong opposition in the Chamber of Deputies. Schacht dismissed Thoiry as "a romantic episode." French military leaders opposed early evacuation of the Rhineland. The Belgian Queen Elizabeth was a Wittelsbach who generally stood against any scheme hatched by the republic that had displaced her family.[11]

Stresemann nevertheless urged swift negotiations, and the Cabinet set up a special Thoiry Committee. On September 28 the Foreign Ministry State Secretary, Carl von Schubert, met with Lord D'Abernon, the British Ambassador, to give him the details of Thoiry. D'Abernon thought that the price of the Saar might be a bit high, but Schubert thought it a fair price considering that France might give up the plebiscite. Norman maintained that all the financiers of London and New York stood behind him, but financier Carl Melchior made inquiries and found three willing to carry the bond issue. James Logan of Dillon, Read offered to underwrite the loan, although the Mellon-Bérenger problem made American approval unlikely.[12]

The American position remained crucial. President Coolidge said at a press conference that the Thoiry matter was not fit for the government's intervention. American capital would have to decide whether to become involved. This implied that the government might not make the bond issue dependent upon the ratification of Mellon-Bérenger. Assistant Secretary of State for Western European Affairs William Castle delivered a different message. The

---

11. *ADAP*, Series B, vol. I, 2, Docs. #97, pp. 234-236; #98, pp. 236-238; #103, pp. 242-245; #106, pp. 251-253. Wandel, pp. 70-71. *DBFP*, p. 430. Schacht quoted in an October 7 memo from Lord D'Abernon to the British Foreign Office, *DBFP* 1919-39, Series IA, vol. 2, p. 424. Rudolf Breitscheid also informed Stresemann of Schacht's opposition, PA, Auswärtiges Amt, Stresemann Papers, vol. 43, October 7, 1926.

12. *ADAP*, Series B, vol. I, 2, Docs. #105, pp. 247-253; #114, pp. 265-267; #117, pp. 275-279; #120, pp. 283-284. The Thoiry plan would have sold $320 million worth of bonds in New York, larger than any similar loan to date, New York *Herald Tribune*, September 26, 1926, from PA, Auswärtiges Amt, Wirtschaft Reparationen 14 (Commercializing Reparations Notes), vol. 3. Kent, p. 270.

government greeted the reconciliation of France and Germany with "relief and the greatest satisfaction" but insisted that ratification must come first. Foreign Ministry aide Karl Ritter went to New York to scout out opinion and found a mixed situation. The general American impression of German finances was very positive because of the budget surpluses of 1924 and 1925 and the agreement on the small-improvement notes. However, investor opinion was very cautious about France and saw ratification of Mellon-Bérenger as a necessity.[13]

Gilbert was noncommittal. He expressed strong reservations and doubted that France would evacuate the Rhineland early, but he did not campaign against it as Norman was doing. It has been suggested that Gilbert, with his close ties to the Morgan bank that had sunk so much capital into France, was willing to turn a blind eye to protect Morgan's money. Gilbert had attacked the 1925 American ban on further loans to France. However, it is just as important to see that Gilbert still held a noninterventionist view: if the signatories of Versailles and the Dawes Plan wanted this, they should have it. He was relieved that the Germans had not used the railroad bonds to reopen the reparations question. Privately, Gilbert was confident that the market would not accept the bond issue before France ratified its debt treaty with the United States and stabilized the franc. He visited Schubert and suggested that all France had to do was ratify the treaty and get a regular loan from the United States. He called the partial mobilization "not impossible" but would go no farther. France forced the pace by applying to the American Department of State for permission to market the bonds. This required a multilateral application from the other Allies. England refused, while Italy had no instructions and declined to join the French. Schubert was astonished that the French had acted so rashly since British Foreign Secretary Austen Chamberlain opposed special treatment for France. Chamberlain was under pressure from certain Conservatives who believed that the continental powers were ganging up against British industry.[14]

By mid-October the Thoiry Plan was fading. At the second meeting of the Thoiry Committee, Curtius asked if Germany could still buy the Saar mines if the rest faltered. Schacht complained that Dillon, Read could not lead a consortium on such a large issue; the loan needed Morgan's prestige. Briand remained optimistic even as everyone else was losing faith. Ratification of the French-U.S. debt treaty seemed necessary, and suddenly opinion in Paris began calling for additional German concessions in the East. Talks went around in a

---

13.    PA, Auswärtiges Amt, Büro Reichsminister, Section 27 (USA), Aktennummer 3087, vol. 6, p. 9. *ADAP*, Series B, vol. I, 2, Docs. #129-130, pp. 300-303.

14.    *ADAP*, Series B, vol. I, 2, Docs. #112, pp. 263-265; #131, p. 303; #135-#137, pp. 310-317; #139-141, pp. 320-325. Harold James, *The Reichsbank and Public Finance in Germany 1924-1933* (Frankfurt, 1985), p. 51. Gilbert's telegram of September 24 to Strong and Mellon quoted in Wandel, p. 68. Link, 402.

circle until by December the French denied that they had ever explicitly mentioned evacuation of the Rhineland.[15]

The fate of Germany and of interwar Europe turned on the aftermath of the Thoiry meeting. Had the Thoiry Plan been successful, it would have given the Weimar Republic a considerable boost in prestige. It would have lessened the stain of the Treaty of Versailles and strengthened the tradition of liberal nationalism. The public would see the tangible benefits of Stresemann's policy of fulfillment instead of the concessions. The parties comprising the coalition of the middle would have derived some benefit from this, and participation in the government might have become a political asset rather than a liability. Reduction of the national injury of 1919 would have undercut fascism in Germany. Instead, the failure of Thoiry left a sour taste in everyone's mouth as they turned back to the issues of domestic politics and especially the question of coalition building. Thoiry was the climax of the policy of 1925-26 where Germany used its fiscal strength to humble other currencies such as the franc and the zloty and to press foreign governments for concessions in other areas. The American loans had created this strength. As Gilbert became aware of this, he was increasingly concerned with the proliferation of loans.

The new budget politics promised breakthroughs on domestic affairs as well. The Reinhold policy appealed to both business and labor with its tax cuts, job creation programs, and extended unemployment benefits. As long as both groups believed that the economy was expanding, they could put aside their differences and work together. Even as Stresemann and Briand negotiated over the future of Europe, Reinhold and Paul Silverberg held out a new and bright future for Germany.

On September 3, 1926, the RdI (National Federation of German Industry) began its annual convention in Dresden. It had been a key force for moderation after 1923. It worked for the passage of the Dawes Plan and tried to keep the Nationalists in the government after the signing of Locarno. RdI President Carl Duisberg welcomed the delegates and guests. He set the tone for the convention by lamenting the adversarial relations between employers and workers and urged conciliation. Curtius greeted the convention in the name of the government. He wanted all classes to work together and pool their energies to promote the German economy. Ludwig Kastl, Executive Director of the Federation, continued this theme by reminding listeners of the active role of the RdI in the passage of the Dawes Plan.

Reinhold delivered the keynote speech. A Cabinet meeting in Berlin had delayed him. He caught the train to Dresden and rushed to the hall, having had

15. *ADAP*, Series B, vol. I, 2, Docs. #144, pp. 331-334; #156, pp. 363-365; #160, pp. 375-377; #221, pp. 513-514.

no time to prepare a formal speech.[16]   He began by recounting the situation when he took office: overtaxation, an iron industry suffering from French dumping of cheap steel, the coal industry in trouble.  He had thought it absurd that well-run industries had been forced to pay high taxes to subsidize inefficient ones.  He had sought a correct basis for fiscal policy because "it seemed wrong to me that we of the present have had to carry the entire load and that we had the right to ask later generations to bear this burden."[17] He discussed the tough negotiations to win approval of the tax package in the spring and then reminded the audience of the important reduction of the bureaucracy.  Cheers rose as he revealed the approval of the reduction in Finance Ministry personnel and the "small-improvement notes" agreement with Gilbert.   Reinhold renewed the German government's pledge of full loyalty to the provisions of the Dawes Plan but insisted that it must acknowledge Germany's economic needs.

The attention of the giant assembly grew as Reinhold concluded:

I am characterized by the entire public as an optimist.  If being an optimist means that I judge Germany's present and future position to be rosy, then I am certainly not an optimist.  I see endless difficulties and a very hard path.  If being an optimist means that I consider the position of the Reich's finances as favorable, then I must reject this energetically.  I will be happy if I succeed in avoiding a deficit.  There can be no speech on the favorable position of the Reich's finances.  But if being an optimist means believing in the future, then I declare enthusiastically that I am an optimist.  I believe in Germany and I believe in Germany's future.  I believe in the nation, at whose forefront stands the leader [Hindenburg] before whose exemplary loyalty to the people and the fatherland we all bow down in reverence.  We will take our Reich to a better future and must travel the difficult path in work that will lead to freedom.  I know that the way is difficult but we must travel it, whatever our political beliefs, united as one because my firm conviction holds that at the end of this road stands the goal for which we all strive: the reconstruction of our nation, the old German greatness, and the new German freedom.[18]

A roar of approval rose from the assembly.  Reinhold sat down, but the stormy applause would not cease.  Finally, the Finance Minister had to return to the lectern to acknowledge the crowd.  Duisberg gave Reinhold a special word of thanks that only brought the crowd to its feet again.  People were still talking about the speech the next day when they gathered to hear the main speech of RdI director Paul Silverberg.

The Reinhold speech whetted the delegates' appetite for the main address.  Unlike Reinhold, Silverberg was not a stirring speaker.  He read from his text in a monotone, yet when he was done, there was strong applause.  Silverberg's subject concerned the relationship of the working class to industry,

16.  Curtius, p. 40.

17.  *Berliner Tageblatt*, September 4, 1926.

18.  *Kabinette Marx III/IV*, Doc. #76, note #2, p. 189.

a subject touched upon the night before by Kastl and Curtius.  He denounced maneuvers of parties done for purely political reasons and praised Reinhold and his program.  Finally, he urged industrialists to cooperate with labor leaders and mentioned the former labor leader Carl Legien and Friedrich Ebert as exemplars of responsible socialism.  Industry could not rule against the working class nor could it rule without the working class.  Industry and labor would have to work together.  The applause for Silverberg at the end of his speech showed that this view had strong support in the RdI.[19]

Silverberg was known as a progressive industrialist, a member of the People's party with some ties to the Catholic Center party.  He had welcomed unions back in 1917 and  believed that, except for a few weeks before and after the November Revolution of 1918, the German General League of Unions (ADGB) and SPD had always been reasonable.  Others at the convention disputed Silverberg.  A Nationalist Reichstag deputy, Wilhelm Jakob Reichert, rose to argue that cooperation with the Left was no guarantee of material prosperity.  "The leftist governments of Prussia and Saxony have created no El Dorado."[20]  He extended his attack to parliamentary government as a whole.  Silverberg replied that attitudes such as Reichert's drove most workers to vote against the DNVP.  Die-hard opposition to the entire system was irresponsible because business enterprises had to deal with the Reichstag.  In this exchange Silverberg seemed to get the better of Reichert.[21]

Reinhold and Silverberg followed up their speeches over the next month.  At the Congress of Salaried Employees, the Finance Minister insisted that "capital and labor belong together."  Reinhold revealed that he would be pushing for further tax reductions for the next fiscal year and liberal trade treaties to reduce tariffs.  The government would find more administrative savings and reduce property taxes.  Silverberg gave a second speech on October 1 to the Congress of the Union on the Protection of Communal Business Interests in the Rhineland and Westphalia (the Langnamverein) in Düsseldorf.  Silverberg wanted business and labor to reach agreement on all important questions.  Duisberg, Carl Friedrich von Siemens, and Hans von Raumer supported Silverberg and all represented export-oriented industries, reflecting the old split.  Fritz Thyssen strongly opposed Silverberg.  Paul Reusch, Executive Director of the Langnamverein and a leading Ruhr industrialist, held a curious position in the middle.  It seems clear from the archival record that Reusch disagreed with Silverberg and worked with Reichert to organize opposition in the Langnamverein.  But he publicly stated in Düsseldorf that he agreed with Silverberg's main point of not working without or against the working class.  His only

---

19. *Berliner Tageblatt*, September 4, 1926.

20. Ibid.

21. Feldman, *Army*, p. 382; David Abraham, *The Collapse of the Weimar Republic*, Second Edition (New York: Holmes and Meier, 1986), p. 128

disagreement, he said, was that Silverberg referred specifically to the SPD, which Reusch felt was not the only party of the "workers of hand and head." Silverberg then stood up and said that he and Reusch agreed. There was no consensus as to who got the upper hand at Düsseldorf: the liberal *Berliner Tageblatt* said Silverberg received more applause while the conservative *Kölner Zeitung* reported that Silverberg received scanty applause while Reusch and Thyssen received the main cheers.[22]

Liberals saw the Silverberg speech as a turning point in the history of the young republic. Big business was finally accepting ideas that had been floating around since the time of Wirth and Rathenau. The editor of the *Berliner Tageblatt* issued a hearty welcome to the industrialists supporting the Republic. The paper of the Catholic Center, *Germania*, was more skeptical. If the RdI was serious, then it should cut off all funding to the "fatherland associations." Catholic labor union leader Adam Stegerwald remembered that the young Kaiser Wilhelm II had said something similar back in 1890. Hugenberg's *Lokal-Anzeiger* sneered at the "utopia in Dresden" while expressing its "astonishment and full surprise." At the DNVP Congress in Köln the industrial committee, led by Hugenberg, predictably condemned Silverberg. The trade unions welcomed the speech but doubted that Silverberg had anything resembling unanimous support. The *Vorwärts* rejected Silverberg's plea for an end to class warfare, but some socialists welcomed the speech.[23]

The role of the Silverberg speech in the history of Weimar has been much disputed as part of the larger debate over the role of big business in the Republic and in the rise of the Nazis. Over the last twenty-five years it has become fashionable to say that the Silverberg speech was meaningless, that it was a speech given by one industrialist with no backing, and that the speech made a big splash in the liberal newspapers but nothing emerged from it. Bernd Weisbrod suggested that the RdI itself was not that important because the more conservative heavy industrialists had enough influence to keep the federation paralyzed while they pursued their own agenda in the Langnamverein. Accordingly, Weisbrod looked more at the Langnamverein speech and saw Thyssen's scathing attack on Silverberg as symbolic of the feelings inside the Langnamverein. Weisbrod insists that nothing came of the Silverberg speech and that Duisberg eventually had to pull back as well. He cites the Labor Ministry's continued resistance to the return of the eight-hour day as proof that conservative corporate interests still ran the Weimar Republic. In a similar vein

---

22. Dick Geary, "Employers, Workers, and the Collapse of the Weimar Republic," in Kershaw, p. 96. Abraham, pp. 62, 130. Feldman, "The Social and Economic Policies of German Big Business 1918-1929," *American Historical Review* 75 (1969), p. 53. *Berliner Tageblatt*, October 1 and 2, 1926.

23. *Berliner Tageblatt*, September 5, 7, and 8, 1926. *Kölnische Zeitung*, September 8, 1926, Archiv für Christliche Demokratie, Konrad-Adenauer-Stiftung, Sankt Augustin, NL Stegerwald, Karton 003. *Kreuzzeitung*, September 6 and 9, 1926.

Dirk Stegmann emphasized the attacks on Silverberg by the socialist trade unions, the right wing, and the conservative *Landbund*. Some anti-Semites attacked Silverberg's religious heritage. The executive board of the RdI was unable to unite on an endorsement of the speech, which showed that Silverberg did not speak for all. Harold James discounts Silverberg as a human weather vane, shifting according to the prevailing wind. The wind of 1926 may have favored cooperation and moderation, but an extremist gust would turn everything around.[24]

Some, including Christian Lammers of I. G. Farben and the Catholic Center and Deutsche Bank chairman Werner Kehl, believed that the Silverberg's real intention was to strengthen the wing of the Nationalists that favored a return to government. This is the crucial area in which we find the impact of the Silverberg speech. It is easy enough to take the speech at face value, prove that the era of peace and light in labor-management relations did not begin, and therefore say that the speech had no effect. It is easy enough to take the eight-hour day as a litmus test and claim that each refusal of the eight-hour day was proof of a government of reaction. The purpose of this study is to take a close look at the actual events and to examine the entire period. When we look at the internal struggles of the DNVP that had flared up since it left the government over Locarno, and when we place the Silverberg speech into the context of the previous day's speech by Reinhold and the Finance Minister's policies, we begin to see a picture emerging of government systematically responding to the needs of interest groups and of a policy of inclusion and reconciliation for the vast majority of the German population. Business had good reason to cheer Reinhold: since he had become Finance Minister German stocks had risen 61%. Some specific stocks had even more spectacular results between January 2 and November 2 of 1926: I. G. Farben had risen 215%, Rheinstahl 291%, Siemens 224%, and the Deutsche Bank 79%. Historians cannot restrict social policy to the status of the eight-hour day and ignore the mass construction of low-income housing and job-relief programs and a general improvement of infrastructure taking place in 1926. The working families living at the time would not have done so. Weisbrod is wrong: something did come of the Silverberg speech. It was a step along the path traveled by the DNVP from 1924 to 1927 that ended with the Nationalists abandoning some of their most treasured beliefs in return for entrance into the government. It also had an impact on the evolution of social policy. The Reich Economics Council began to come around to the idea of unemployment insurance. One member concluded

---

24. Bernd Weisbrod, "Economic Power and Political Stability Reconsidered: Heavy Industry in Weimar Germany," *Social History* (May 1979), pp. 242-258. Dirk Stegmann, "Die Silverberg-Kontroverse 1926: Unternehmerpolitik zwischen Reform und Restauration," in Hans-Ulrich Wehler, ed., *Sozialgeschichte Heute* (Göttingen, 1974), pp. 594-610. Although Silverberg's heritage was Jewish, he had been baptized a Protestant. James, *Slump*, p. 167.

that based on Silverberg's speech, unemployment insurance was a bitter necessity.[25]

One should also not ignore the impact of the speeches on international opinion, especially the opinion of the international bankers who provided the money to keep the economy afloat. The *New York Times* ran a four-part series in September praising Germany's recovery and government and proclaiming it "the soundest country on the continent." Reinhold had told American newsmen that he expected no budget deficit and this too made Germany an attractive investment. In an article on the RdI meeting, the *New York Times* called Reinhold "the Jupiter among the several oratorical stars." The October issue of *Foreign Affairs* also featured articles by Henry Robinson and John Foster Dulles that were generally favorable to the present course of foreign loans. Dulles served as counsel to the underwriting firm Harris, Forbes, which had just completed a contract with the State of Prussia to offer a huge loan and was hardly a disinterested party.[26]

Not everyone in the audience at Dresden cheered Reinhold's speech. As he listened, the customary scowl on Heinrich Brüning's face deepened. Brüning had long harbored doubts about Reinhold's fiscal policy. He believed that Reinhold intended the tax cuts mostly for the large capitalists rather than the ordinary people and that Reinhold's policy of "pushing the budget to the brink of deficit" was unsound and could lead to inflation. One should try to put a humanitarian face on Brüning's view. He was the main sponsor of the "lex Brüning" that freed the poorest Germans from the income tax in 1925 and feared that Reinhold's budget deficits might lead to the repeal of the law. Brüning found a willing coconspirator in Popitz. Reinhold's vigorous leadership had taken away much of Popitz's authority. Popitz doubted Reinhold's budget management and use of credits. The prosperity credited to Reinhold was but a mirage caused by the English coal miners' strike. When the State Finance Ministers met in Berlin, Brüning and Popitz approached Heinrich Köhler, the Finance Minister of Baden, who they believed was a more pliable man. Popitz told Köhler that the ministry must be taken from the Democrats to avoid more

---

25. Stegmann, pp. 604-605. Balderston, *Financial Crisis*, 207. Speech of Heckert (KPD), *VdR, Stenographische Berichte*, vol. 391, p. 7911. BAP R 401/528, pp. 351-353.

26. Lincoln Eyres, *New York Times*, September 9, 1926, PA, Auswärtiges Amt, Wirtschaft Reparationen, Peace Treaty: Germany's Financial and Economic Position, Aktennummer L253, Volume 5. Washington *Evening Star*, August 14, 1926, New York *Times*, September 4, 1926, Letter from Dieckhoff of Washington Embassy to the Foreign Office, September 18, 1926, PA, Auswärtiges Amt, Wirtschaft Reparationen, America's Position and Critique of Dawes Plan, Aktennummer L201, vol. 7.

"Reinhold waste." Brüning said that he would back Köhler for the post when the next Cabinet reshuffle took place.[27]

Upon returning from the Dresden meeting, Brüning wrote a lengthy letter to Marx attacking Reinhold's speech and suggesting that Reinhold had assailed the fiscal policy of 1923-24 when Marx had been Chancellor. Brüning said that he was not criticizing the Finance Minister but attempting to convey the real state of finances in 1924 and 1925. Brüning felt that it was imperative for the government to maintain a reserve fund. This reserve would pay off the Dawes Plan and provide socially necessary spending, such as paying off the liquid creditors of the Reich, rebuilding the social-insurance system, repairing damage in the Ruhr, improving the pay of civil servants, and resettling the east. Brüning supported Popitz's view of the economic improvement as solely due to the coal strike. Reinhold's latest move on the small-improvement notes made loans for Fiscal Year 1926 inevitable. Brüning concluded by stating that a continuation of this policy would only reduce the future freedom of the government and urged Marx to uphold the Catholic Center's position as the party of continuity in foreign policy and responsibility in fiscal policy. Pünder wrote to Reinhold and reiterated the strong support of the Chancellor for "most of your program and aims" but expressed concern about the Dresden speech. Marx was unhappy about criticism of the emergency tax decrees of 1923-24 because the Democrats had supported them at the time. Reinhold replied that his position had been misinterpreted and that he did support those measures. Stabilization had been necessary. He pledged his support for a balanced budget. Pünder then replied to Brüning that he must have misunderstood the Finance Minister, who had intended no criticism of the previous Marx government.[28]

Since it had bolted the Luther Cabinet over Locarno, the DNVP's political fortunes had fallen. It had been shut out of the budget negotiations in March. The DNVP wanted to govern but was more politically isolated than ever. The Dresden Congress of the RdI showed that even industry was deserting it. The party had suffered a string of electoral defeats, including the loss of the government in Mecklenburg-Schwerin, a Nationalist stronghold, and a bad defeat in Saxony. (See Table 5.1.) Larry Jones points to the Saxon results in particular as a harbinger of the DNVP's loss of votes to revaluation parties in 1928.[29] Even the 1926 referendum on the princes' property had been a defeat

---

27. Köhler, p. 189. Dieckmann, p. 62. Köhler had previously spoken of his distrust for the DDP to Ernst Feder in Feder, p. 61.

28. *Kabinette Marx III/IV*, Docs. #76, pp. 189-196; #77, pp. 196-198. BAK R 431/2359.

29. *Berliner Morgenpost*, September 10, 1926, in BAP R 8034 II/9014. Larry Eugene Jones, "Inflation, Revaluation, and the Crisis of Middle-Class Parties: A Study in the Dissolution of the German Party System, 1923-28," *Central European History* 12 (1979), p. 166.

**Table 5.1**
**State Election Results from Mecklenburg-Schwerin and Saxony**

| | | | Mecklenburg-Schwerin | | |
|---|---|---|---|---|---|
| | February 17, 1924 | | December 7, 1924 (Reichstag) | June 6, 1926 | |
| Party | (%) | Seats | (%) | (%) | Seats |
| SPD | 22.8 | 15 | 34.2 | 39.9 | 20 |
| DNVP | 28.9 | 12 | 26.6 | 22.6 | 12 |
| Völkisch | 19.3 | 13 | 11.9 | 9.4 | 5 |
| DVP | 7.3 | 5 | 10.6 | 8.4 | 4 |
| KPD | 13.6 | 9 | 6.0 | 6.6 | 3 |
| DDP | 3.6 | 2 | 5.9 | 3.0 | 2 |
| NSDAP | -- | 0 | -- | 1.7 | 0 |
| Others | 1.5 | 1 | 4.8 | 8.4 | 4 |

| | | | Saxony | | |
|---|---|---|---|---|---|
| | November 5, 1922 | | December 7, 1924 (Reichstag) | October 31, 1926 | |
| Party | (%) | Seats | (%) | (%) | Seats |
| SPD | 41.8 | 40 | 35.2 | 32.1 | 31 |
| DNVP | 19.0 | 19 | 20.5 | 14.5 | 14 |
| DVP | 18.7 | 19 | 15.4 | 12.4 | 12 |
| KPD | 10.5 | 10 | 11.1 | 14.5 | 14 |
| DDP | 8.4 | 8 | 7.2 | 4.7 | 5 |
| NSDAP | -- | 0 | 2.6 | 1.6 | 2 |
| Center | 0.9 | 0 | 1.0 | 1.0 | 0 |
| Others | 0.2 | 0 | 7.2 | 18.5 | 18 |

*Sources*: Jürgen Falter, Thomas Lindberger, and Siegfried Schumann, eds., *Wahlen und Abstimmungen in der Weimarer Republik, Materialien und Wahlverhalten 1919-1933* (Munich, 1986), pp. 97-99. Reichstag results obtained from percentages for District 35 (Mecklenburg) and Districts 28 (Dresden-Bautzen), 29 (Leipzig), and 30 (Chemnitz-Zwickau). *Deutsche Reichsanzeiger*, December 22, 1924.

of a kind. That was a radical Socialist and Communist proposition that would have confiscated nearly all property held by the former princes in Germany. The Nationalists strongly opposed this and urged people to defeat the measure simply by staying home. Under the rules of the Weimar Constitution half of all registered voters had to vote affirmatively in order for the measure to pass. Although the measure did not gain 50%, it did exceed the percentages received by the Social Democrats and Communists in the 1924 elections. Thirteen electoral districts gave the proposition at least 40%. In Westarp's home district of Potsdam II, 49% voted yes. The Marx government had been embarrassed when Catholic Center strongholds such as South Westphalia and East Düsseldorf gave strong votes for the measure.[30] (See Table 5.2.)

The position of agriculture had steadily deteriorated, despite the debt reduction of the inflation and the Luther/Schlieben tariffs. In a September 1926 speech to the Pan-German League, Landrat von Hertzberg noted that total indebtedness had grown by RM600 million in just the first six months of 1926. There was a total agricultural debt of RM3.7 billion, not including another billion in foreign debt. The DNVP's standing also fell. Agricultural interests had not received the hoped-for improvements in the aftermath of the Dawes Plan, and the Land Leagues began to break with the position of the DNVP. The Brandenburg *Landbund*, for example, chided the DNVP for reacting too strongly against the Locarno Treaties. Some Leagues even said that the DNVP should have supported the expropriation of the princes' lands.[31]

The Nationalist Party Congress gathered on September 9, just five days after the Silverberg speech. In preparing for the congress, Westarp had suggested that he wanted to work with the other middle-class parties but blasted the Catholic Center for its "leftist policies." In June the Nationalists had voted for a miners' insurance and pension bill that would require a contribution of ten to thirty million Marks a year from mine owners. This vote had infuriated Thyssen and Reusch, who withheld part of the industrialists' contribution to the DNVP. The DNVP had tried to forge some additional links with the People's party and especially with the right wing led by Ernst Scholz. The Nationalist and People's parties had made an alliance in the State Council, the upper house of the Prussian Parliament. Now the two parties attempted to create an alliance in the Prussian House of Representatives against the dominant Weimar Coalition. Karl Jarres of the People's party and Wilhelm von Gayl of the Nationalists attempted to work out an agreement during the fall, much to Stresemann's displeasure. They hoped that a solid rightist bloc might unseat the Otto Braun government, which did not control an absolute majority of the House and had to rely on the tolerance of the People's party or covert support from the Communists.[32]

The 1926 Nationalist Congress put a special emphasis on labor, with the Reichstag deputy Wilhelm Koch (Düsseldorf) calling for better economic and social policy and especially for improvements in housing and agricultural settlements. Koch had led the National Association of German State Workers

---

30. *Kreuzzeitung*, June 21, 1926. Stresemann noted an immediate softening of the DNVP's position by late July, PA, Auswärtiges Amt, Stresemann Papers, vol. 95 (DVP), undated.

31. BA Potsdam R 8048/147, p. 89. Chanady, p. 76.

32. *Kreuzzeitung*, September 8, 1926. William L. Patch, *Christian Trade Unions in the Weimar Republic* (New Haven, 1985), p. 110. Stresemann, *Vermächtnis*, vol. II, pp. 412-419. Eric Dave Kohler, "Otto Braun" (Ph.D. Dissertation, Stanford University, 1971), p. 257.

**Table 5.2**

**1924 SPD/KPD Vote and Affirmative on Princes' Referendum as
Percentage of Registered Voters**

| District | December 1924 SPD/KPD % | June 1926 Yes % | +/- |
|---|---|---|---|
| 1.East Prussia | 22.22 | 20.28 | -1.94 |
| 2.Berlin | 39.49 | 63.56 | 24.07 |
| 3.Potsdam II | 32.20 | 49.14 | 16.94 |
| 4.Potsdam I | 32.50 | 47.76 | 15.26 |
| 5.Frankfurt/Oder | 24.36 | 26.78 | 2.42 |
| 6.Pomerania | 24.17 | 23.58 | -0.59 |
| 7.Breslau | 28.14 | 32.05 | 3.91 |
| 8.Liegnitz | 28.87 | 34.24 | 5.37 |
| 9.Oppeln | 12.91 | 24.40 | 11.49 |
| 10.Magdeburg | 37.36 | 42.59 | 5.23 |
| 11.Merseburg | 33.52 | 39.40 | 5.88 |
| 12.Thuringia | 32.64 | 40.86 | 8.22 |
| 13.Schleswig-Holstein | 28.26 | 35.03 | 6.77 |
| 14.Weser-Ems | 22.50 | 28.02 | 5.52 |
| 15.East Hannover | 25.10 | 27.58 | 2.48 |
| 16.South Hannover/Brunswick | 32.96 | 37.93 | 4.97 |
| 17.Westphalia-North | 22.64 | 33.04 | 10.40 |
| 18.Westphalia-South | 28.84 | 44.36 | 15.52 |
| 19.Hesse-Nassau | 27.70 | 40.17 | 12.47 |
| 20.Köln-Aachen | 16.09 | 34.16 | 18.07 |
| 21.Koblenz-Trier | 10.88 | 17.81 | 6.93 |
| 22.Düsseldorf-East | 26.16 | 41.84 | 15.68 |
| 23.Düsseldorf-West | 19.01 | 33.69 | 14.68 |
| 24.Upper Bavaria-Swabia | 17.98 | 20.68 | 2.70 |
| 25.Lower Bavaria | 12.28 | 12.54 | 0.26 |
| 26.Franconia | 24.06 | 26.69 | 2.63 |
| 27.Palatinate | 22.62 | 27.97 | 5.35 |
| 28.Dresden-Bautzen | 34.24 | 44.56 | 10.32 |
| 29.Leipzig | 39.97 | 51.90 | 11.93 |
| 30.Chemnitz-Zwickau | 37.36 | 45.43 | 8.07 |
| 31.Württemberg | 20.36 | 34.04 | 13.68 |
| 32.Baden | 17.78 | 36.64 | 18.86 |
| 33.Hessen-Darmstadt | 29.44 | 40.01 | 10.57 |
| 34.Hamburg | 34.35 | 52.53 | 18.18 |
| 35.Mecklenburg | 33.87 | 34.47 | 0.60 |
| TOTAL | 26.70 | 36.39 | 9.69 |

and Employees, was active in the German railroad union before the war, and was a senior Christian National union leader.    The Working Committee of German Nationalist Industrialists urged the government to control spending but insisted that social policy and unemployment were the biggest problems. Representative Bernhard Leopold said that the government's job-creation plan was a good idea but did not go far enough.    Ernst Oberfohren repeated that Reinhold's policies merely followed Schlieben's tax reduction and insisted that the Nationalist ideas had a positive influence on the tax package.    Finally, he mourned the heavy burden of the income tax on the middle classes, implying that a tax cut might be in order.    Suddenly, the Nationalists who had opposed the Reinhold program were echoing the Finance Minister.[33]

Westarp's speech tried to steer a middle ground between the new conservative social policy advocated by Koch and Walther Lambach, the DNVP's liaison to the Nationalist "yellow" trade unions and Reichstag whip, and the old reactionary policy.    Westarp continued to reject Locarno and received especially loud applause when he asserted that monarchist sentiment had not waned in Germany.    He insisted that a party in opposition had the duty to shape the government, not reject everything out of hand.    He reiterated the party's "recognition of the Republic," the lukewarm endorsement of the Weimar constitution given by the DNVP in 1925.    Nationalist participation in the government would depend on the position of the Catholic Center.    If that party would give its support to a responsible Cabinet of the center-right, the Nationalists could return to the government.[34]

In contrast to states such as Bavaria and cities such as Köln, Prussia had refrained from requesting foreign loans.    The state had not taken a foreign loan in over a hundred years and this habit persisted.    As the Reich first cut back on its sharing of taxes with the states and then pushed for more social spending, the Prussian government dedicated more funds to social spending.    In the summer of 1926 Prussian Prime Minister Otto Braun had tried to cover the growing deficit by raising taxes, but the Communist, Nationalist, and People's party representatives had blocked that.    When the government forced the Advisory Board on Foreign Credits to consider job creation, Braun saw a chance to gain a large foreign loan.[35]

The Advisory Board had debated in March 1926 a proposed Prussian loan from Harris, Forbes of New York, which would spend $20 million on electrical improvements, deepened ports, expanded mining, and eastern settlement.    The Prussian representatives argued that the domestic bond market was too weak to sustain such a loan.    Rudolf Karlowa, the liaison to Gilbert,

---

33.    *Kreuzzeitung*, September 9, 1926.

34.    *Kreuzzeitung*, September 10, 1926.

35.    *Frankfurter Zeitung*, September 13, 1926, in BAP R 8034 II/4601. McNeil, pp. 50-52.

worried about the reaction in Washington. Many Americans doubted that the loans to Germany were going to productive purposes. The Board decided to check with Gilbert and reduced the loan to $15 million. These problems convinced Braun to take his loan to the domestic market instead. In February, Prussia had issued three-year notes at 6.5% for RM30 million. In April an identical note issue took place. An extra RM140 million for unemployment relief and RM17 million for the police opened a new deficit and Prussian Finance Minister Hermann Höpker-Aschoff negotiated a new American loan.[36]

In September 1926 the Advisory Board met to consider Prussia's new request, based on the changed guidelines taking account of job creation. Prussia would raise any money cut by the Board on the domestic market. Braun had proved that the Board could not control Prussian state loans. Prussia, unlike other states, pressured its cities to keep their requests for foreign loans to a minimum, so that while over half of the German population lived in Prussia, Prussian municipal borrowing accounted for less than a third of the total of foreign loans going to cities. On a per capita basis, the indebtedness of Prussian cities was still below the German average. The Board felt helpless and approved the full $20 million loan. It would have a twenty-five-year term at 6.5%. About RM59 million would go to special electrical projects. Another RM23 million would go to expand harbors. The Board conceded that these projects would be important for creating jobs but did mention the Prussians' ability to go to the domestic market and felt that it was important that this loan not go onto the Berlin bourse where it might put pressure on interest rates.[37] (See Table 5.3.)

The German War Payments Commission described the Prussian loan to Gilbert. This was the first Gilbert had heard about any proposed loan, and he immediately made inquiries on Wall Street about it. Although he did not see the prospectus being prepared by Harris, Forbes, what Gilbert learned was thoroughly alarming. He had previously advised Höpker-Aschoff that under Article 248 of the Treaty of Versailles all loan repayments must take a secondary position to the payment of reparations. This ordering of priorities hindered loans because investors feared that in a financial crunch the limited funds would have to go to reparations and the loan would go into default. To speed German stabilization in 1924 and ease the acceptance of the Dawes bonds, the negotiators had agreed to give repayment of that loan priority over payment of reparations. Harris, Forbes now said that there were no legal limits on

---

36. BAK R 2/2126, pp. 386-394. Link, p. 394. *Berliner Tageblatt*, May 22 and June 26, 1926.

37. BAK R 2/2091, September 4 and September 24, 1926. McNeil, p. 120. Per capita urban indebtedness by state, December 31, 1926 (in RM): Baden 183, Hesse 140, Württemberg 122, Saxony 111, Bavaria 98, Oldenburg 98, Prussia 81, Thuringia 72, Mecklenburg-Schwerin 61, Brunswick 59, Anhalt 48. *Frankfurter Zeitung*, January 27, 1927, in BAP R 8034 II/1982, vol. 9.

**Table 5.3**
**The Structure of Prussian Debt, 1926**

| Description | Due | Amount (RM) |
| --- | --- | --- |
| Domestic Loans | | |
| 5% Fertilizer Loan of 1923 | 1928 | 16,294,950 |
| 5% Roggenwert-Loan of 1923 | 1928 | 3,936,457 |
| 6½% Treasury Notes of 1926 | March 1, 1929 | 30,000,000 |
| 6½% Treasury Notes of 1926 | October 1, 1930 | 30,000,000 |
| 6½% Treasury Notes of 1926 | October 1, 1930 | 40,000,000 |
| One to three-month treasury transfers | | 122,710,500 |
| **Foreign Loans** | | |
| 6½% Loan of 1926 | September 15, 1951 | 84,000,000 |
| GRAND TOTAL | | 326,941,907 |

Source: *Frankfurter Zeitung*, September 13, 1926, in BAP R 8034 II/4601.

Prussia's ability to raise foreign currency, which was untrue, and implied that the Prussian loan would be on a par with the Dawes loan and thus have precedence over reparations. Gilbert wrote to Reinhold asking him to correct Höpker-Aschoff and the New York bankers on this loan.[38]

The only response made was on a related issue, a $15 million loan to Berlin for elevated and underground rail systems. In a letter to the Prussian Interior Ministry the Finance Ministry informed it that the authority had been trimmed to $12 million, but also expressed concern about the "security" as explained in the proposal. The Finance Ministry did not respond directly to Gilbert until November 27. It had sent copies of Gilbert's letter to all the states but maintained that Gilbert and the Reparation Commission were wrong in their interpretation of priorities in Article 248. The American renewed his objection and reminded the Ministry of the legal opinion of Sir William Leese, the counsel to the Dawes Plan negotiators, on this matter.[39]

It was clear to the bankers and the Prussians that they needed heavy legal artillery to refute Leese's argument and dissuade Gilbert from his opposition. In New York, Harris, Forbes contacted its general counsel Sullivan and Cromwell and asked for a different opinion that would support the firm and Prussia. John Foster Dulles, a member of the negotiating team at Paris, prominent in Republican Party circles, and the managing partner at Sullivan and Cromwell, wrote the brief refuting Leese and released it on January 10, 1927.

---

38. BAK R 2/2513, September 20, 1926.
39. BAK R 2/2002, pp. 8-11. R 2/3211, pp. 173-178.

Dulles charged that Leese and Gilbert had made an overly broad interpretation of Annex 6, Section VII, of the Dawes agreement, which called for "control of foreign exchange." Dulles complained that the Dawes Plan had not been written in solid legal language. It had been written "colloquially" and contained any number of gray areas. In the French translation of the Plan the word "control" did not even appear. Gilbert's other objection, based on Article 248, was also groundless. Dulles implied that the Agent General's argument was contradictory, founded on a broad interpretation of Annex 6, Section VII, and a strict interpretation of Article 248. If Gilbert won on his strict interpretation of Article 248, all government activities would become subject to commission approval since all revenue and payment could be "prioritized." Dulles referred to specific Paris sessions to prove that the Allies had no intention of such control, and thus Gilbert's interpretation violated the original intent at Versailles. Finally, even if this were true at the time, the Treaty implied relaxation of the terms after May 1921.[40]

Dulles concluded that the Transfer Committee and Reparations Commission were placing "a construction not warranted by either French or English texts and which has consistently been repudiated by word and act during the past seven years."[41] The Dulles brief led Gilbert to back off temporarily, although he did not admit error. The Prussian and German governments had won this round, but it had been at a cost. Much of Gilbert's good will had disappeared during this debate. Throughout 1927 Gilbert would have one fight after another with the German government until Gilbert reminded the Germans of his power by trying to block the Prussian loan of 1927 and issuing a memo highly critical of German fiscal policy. These actions, combined with other events, destroyed the ability of the Germans to gain further long-term loans from the United States and began the slide of the Weimar Republic into the abyss.

The Reichstag had been in recess while the government put the job-creation programs into effect and the Thoiry negotiations had inspired and then dashed hopes for an early withdrawal of the Allied forces. The political landscape had changed with the referendum on the settlement with the princes, the Reinhold and Silverberg speeches to the RdI, and the Nationalist party congress. The major issues, however, remained the same: unemployment relief and social spending. The Labor Ministry had sent a memorandum in October to the various state agencies informing them that long-term unemployment would probably last well into the fall and urging them to enact emergency make-work projects. The government promised that it would aid associations of localities for this purpose.[42] The Chancery also circulated a memo detailing requests for

---

40. Ronald W. Pruessen, *John Foster Dulles: The Road to Power* (New York, 1982), pp. 70-73. BAK R 2/3211, pp. 186-205.

41. BAK R 2/3211, p. 200.

42. BAK R 43 I/2032, pp. 96-99.

a second supplementary budget.[43]  The Reichstag had provided RM400 million of loan authority for the 1925 and 1926 budgets combined.  Now the government requested another RM540 million of authority, including the temporary loan for housing that the Reichstag had enacted in March.  In essence, this meant that the estimated deficit of the 1926 budget had reached RM940 million, which seemed staggering to some.  Credits from the Reichsbank and Reichspost, surpluses from previous years, and some one-time savings could cover most of it, but part would remain uncovered.  On the spending side the most pressing item was funding the RM200 million needed for housing.  Small revenue increases and windfalls in revenue unanticipated in the March budget would cover the ordinary budget of RM229 million.  In the ordinary budget, RM60 million in continuing spending would go to labor mediation and unemployment relief.  RM42 million in one-time spending would go to the Interior Ministry for its projects.  Credits would cover 70% of the total budget.[44] (See Table 5.4.)

Economics Minister Curtius expressed concern over the size of the loan that might be necessary if revenue did not increase to meet the uncovered spending in the extraordinary budget.  Pünder also feared "a collision with the money market."[45]  To allay Curtius' fears, Finance Ministry Counselor Othmar Fessler reported that the uncovered deficit would be RM400 million, which could be balanced by a RM250 million cut in industrial subsidies and RM150 million from the working out of revaluation.  If the uncovered deficit rose higher, the Finance Minister had the power to cut back on the purchase of foreign exchange up to an additional RM500 million.  Fessler noted that "an almost limitless requisition of reserves would be justified" to ensure that reparations creditors did not notice the difficulties with the Reich finances.[46]

Reinhold presented the supplementary budget to the Reichstag on November 9.  The ordinary budget contained funding for worthy programs such as flood relief, aid to the Rhineland wine-growers and the Saarland, and an additional RM60 million for jobless relief on top of the RM200 million of the first budget.  The Finance Minister discussed his dilemma in finding money to cover the new spending.  He did not want to increase the same taxes he had cut in the regular budget.  By a budget gimmick the "small-improvement notes" treaty with Gilbert would add a little revenue in the short term.  The budget cut RM80 million from the bureaucracy.  Tariffs and several other taxes had yielded more revenue than anticipated.  Reinhold then lauded the job-creation program.  The Reich could not allow millions of workers to sit around without work or worth.  The RM200 million in temporary credits would build 40,000 dwellings

43.  The Reichstag had passed a first supplementary budget of negligible spending in July.

44.  BAK R 43 I/877, pp. 342-343.

45.  *Kabinette Marx III/IV*, Doc. #92, note #7, p. 259.

46.  Ibid. and R 43 I/877, pp. 351-352.

**Table 5.4**
**Breakdown of 1926 Supplementary Budget--Draft of October 19**

| | |
|---|---:|
| Ordinary Budget | |
|   Spending | |
|     Continuing | 105,388,418 |
|     One-Time | 123,159,900 |
|    Total | 228,548,318 |
|   Income | 228,548,318 |
| Extraordinary Budget | |
|   Spending | |
|     Labor Ministry | |
|       Housing and Settlements | 215,000,000 |
|       Labor Arbitration/Unemployment Relief | 130,000,000 |
|     Loan to Reichsbahn | 100,000,000 |
|     Transportation Ministry | 38,241,000 |
|     Debt Repayment | 12,348,000 |
|     Financial Administration | 41,955,470 |
|    Total Spending | 537,544,470 |
|   Income | |
|     Credit under Housing Law of March 26, 1926 | 200,000,000 |
|     Additional Loan Authority | 337,544,470 |
|    Total Income | 537,544,470 |
| | |
| TOTAL BUDGET | 766,092,788 |

This breakdown does not include approximately RM96 million in reparations payments and RM117 million in domestic war payments, which were covered by their own income.

*Source*: BAK R 43 I/1415, pp. 282-286. *Kabinette Marx III/IV*, Doc. #92, note #3, pp. 257-259.

while employing 120,000 of the 150,000 construction workers registered as unemployed. This in turn would save the Reich some RM84 million in unemployment-relief payments. The Reich would invest in railroads, the post office, and rural housing. The government's program had already yielded results. In February a total of 4.39 million persons had been receiving aid of some kind. As of October 15, this was down to 2.7 million. Reinhold admitted that the additional loan authority could lead to economic danger if governments used loans for unproductive purposes. He asked for an amendment to the Reichsbank law to increase the ability of the government to borrow from the bank and admitted that the government would eventually have to market a loan. "As you see from this presentation, we have maintained the full tax cut without turning other tax screws and this will be the case in the future. We will push very hard to the brink of deficit but will maintain an absolutely secure financial situation."[47]

What did this whirl of numbers mean? The government's estimate of revenue could not be more accurate than Schlieben's had been the year before. What had changed was the Cabinet had confidence in its ability to spend and to fund that spending. Without this confidence, the Reich would never have dared to propose a supplementary budget of one-tenth the size of the regular budget. It was pleased with the success of the main budget and wanted to drive down unemployment and stimulate the economy. Fessler and the Finance Ministry had opened the vistas of unlimited resources for the Reich to draw upon to keep the picture of orderly finances and the flow of foreign loans. The budget was not simply a mechanism for accounting revenue and spending. It was an exercise in public relations. If the Germans predicted that enough revenue would come in to meet their spending, it would come in. The spending in turn would keep enough Germans at work and happy to ensure political stability. To critics, this sounded like a shady game at a carnival. They called for a realistic approach and austerity. Should investors have taken alarm had they known the precise state of German finance in November 1926, when the supplementary budget appeared? Gilbert's chief concern was that the repayment of loans (labeled "B" on Table 5.5) exceed the proceeds for loans (labeled "A") for any given year. Table 5.5 shows the final reckoning of the budget, including all supplementary budgets. Despite Reinhold's tax cuts, revenues increased almost 5% in FY26. This alone was enough to cover the increased social spending for the fiscal year. The new loan would increase debt service. This impressed both investors and Gilbert. While the surplus at the end of the year was not what it had been a year before, Reinhold had succeeded in cutting taxes and raising social spending. Germany only needed about one-third of the requested credit authority. The precise fiscal balance of Germany at the end of 1926 is difficult to gauge and became the object of later attempts to fix the numbers. Balderston, modifying Gilbert's figures, found that Germany ran a budget deficit in both 1925 and 1926, a fact confirmed by no German source. Balderston's budget and debt numbers suggest that Germany should have been suffering a 1930-style cash shortage plugged only by the Reinhold loan of 1927.[48] But no one in the government felt such a shortage, and the desperation of 1929, 1930, and 1931 was absent. The recession and the surplus trade balance of the winter of 1925-26 would seem to confirm all reports at the time of a large budget surplus. The

---

47. *VdR*, *Stenographische Berichte*, vol. 391, pp. 7971-7977.

48. Balderston, *Financial Crisis*, pp. 226-228, has an extensive chart with the fiscal balance. I have tried to replicate his results following his footnotes, but the FY25 revenue comes up at least RM150 million short, while the expenditures exceed the Gilbert numbers consistently without any explanation. Footnote #4, p. 228, says "There is an unexplained difference of RM 242 million in respect of the 1926/27 deficit between the figures here and the Agent-General's."

**Table 5.5**
**Gilbert's Budget Statements, 1924-1927 (billions of RM)**

|  |  | 1924-25 | 1925-26 | 1926-27 |
|---|---|---|---|---|
| **Revenues** | | | | |
| Tax Revenues | | 7.3220 | 6.8560 | 7.175 |
| Administrative Revenues | | 0.4350 | 0.4780 | 0.515 |
| Surplus Brought Over | | | 0.6720 | 0.782 |
| Proceeds of Loans | A | 0.3553 | | 0.329 |
| **TOTAL** | | **8.1123** | **8.0060** | **8.801** |
| **Expenditures** | | | | |
| Payments to States/Communes | | 2.7704 | 2.5956 | 2.626 |
| General Administrative | | 1.5210 | 1.8840 | 2.156 |
| Social Spending | | 0.2590 | 0.5070 | 0.811 |
| Internal War Charges | | 2.1080 | 1.5130 | 1.496 |
| Execution of Dawes Plan | | | 0.2913 | 0.550 |
| Capital Investments & Grants | | 0.1116 | 0.3910 | 0.483 |
| Reduction of Debt | B | 0.4500 | 0.2620 | 0.421 |
| **TOTAL** | | **7.2200** | **7.4439** | **8.543** |
| Balance | | 0.8923 | 0.5621 | 0.258 |

*Source*: Schuker, *Reparations*, p. 26.

preliminary estimates of credit authority turned out to be exaggerations because of the increase in tax revenue fostered by Reinhold's stimulus program. By official figures, the tax revenue excluding customs and consumption taxes fell only 1.25% between FY25 and FY26 while total revenue rose 10-14%, depending on whose figures you follow.[49]

The government had devoted much of the supplementary budget to jobless relief but was under heavy pressure to add more. Thanks to the stimulation of the economy, joblessness had fallen below the 10% level, but long-term unemployment and underemployment remained serious problems. Külz had decided that the "normal" level of unemployment was one million by adding 700,000 who would have served in the army to the prewar norm of 300,000. The DNVP's shift to support more unemployment relief and insurance in the fall of 1926 was a strong indicator of that party's growing moderation. With its old base of industry and agriculture turning cooler, the DNVP sought to expand its base into the urban labor force. Unemployment had fallen from 1.75 million in July to 1.5 million by September, but deep pockets of distress such as Berlin and Düsseldorf remained. Brauns continued to feel the pressure

---

49. Hertz-Eichenrode, p. 112. Balderston, *Financial Crisis*, pp. 226, 268. Gilbert has 10%. *Verhandlungen deutsches Reichrats*, 1928, Drucksache #79, says 12.1%. Balderston, p. 226, has 13.6%.

of the SPD for more action. His Labor Ministry urged localities to pursue job-creation measures. The Reich would offer aid to associations of localities for distribution to those out of work who had exhausted their support. Under no circumstances would this aid surpass the previous relief payments.[50]

The Cabinet discussed revisions in the unemployment-relief law in October. It increased the payroll tax on business and created an "emergency stock" of unemployment insurance sufficient to cover 400,000 unemployed for up to three months. While Brauns had to compromise in the Cabinet with more conservative interests, the Social Democrats in the Reichstag introduced steeper benefit increases. Curtius was particularly concerned about a new measure called the "emergency work-time" bill, which he saw as a backdoor attempt to reassert the eight-hour day. This bill would mandate payment of overtime wages for all workers who toiled more than forty-eight hours (six eight-hour days) in a week. The Catholic Center, Democrats, and Bavarians all wanted more than the Cabinet was prepared to give.[51]

The Nationalists presented the Cabinet with its greatest headache. Wilhelm Koch told the Reichstag's Social Policy Committee that the DNVP would not be exceeded by any other party in the area of care for the jobless. The Nationalist representatives tended to abstain on the more radical measures. While this killed one Communist proposal to raise the support level by 50%, it passed another that added fourteen- and fifteen-year-olds to the lists of eligible workers. The SPD's 30% raise would mean that some unemployed would receive support close to their old wages while some would get more. The government might claim that this killed incentive, but to the SPD it would be worthwhile if it averted the illness, murder, and suicide associated with poverty. The Nationalist Georg Schulz also scoffed at the government for treating unemployment as an acute illness instead of a chronic one. He drew unaccustomed cheers from the left as he announced that the DNVP would vote against the government's plan. Brauns stressed to the Reichstag how much the government had compromised, but his bill was doomed.[52]

The Reichstag voted on amendments on November 8. When the 30% raise came up, the SPD demanded a roll-call vote. Reichstag President Löbe announced the results: 205 in favor of the amendment, 141 opposed, eight abstentions. Chaos swept the chamber: the Nationalists had voted for the amendment! Shaken, Brauns rose to announce that the government probably could not survive the execution of this motion as the Communists yelled for the

50. *New York Times*, October 2, 1926, PA, Auswärtiges Amt Wirtschaft 6, U.S. Economic Relations with Germany. BAK R 43 I/2032, pp. 71-72R, September 22, 1926, and pp. 96-103, October 5, 1926. PrStA Rep. 151, IC, 11901, vol. 1. Stürmer, p. 163.

51. BAK R 43 I/1415, pp. 232-233, October 5, 1926. *Kabinette Marx III/IV*, Docs. #87, Note #5, p. 243; #93, pp. 260-262; #97, pp. 269-270; #100, pp. 276-277.

52. *VdR, Stenographische Berichte*, vol. 391, pp. 7887-7906.

Cabinet's resignation.   Westarp then spoke in an attempt to explain the Nationalists' change.  The SPD had not expected the amendment to pass and certainly had no idea how to pay for it.  Its representative on the Social Policy Committee had asked the DNVP to end its obstruction and now it had complied. Since the government parties were moving closer to the SPD anyway, why not give the Socialists' program a chance to work?  When the eligibility question rose again, the DNVP would support the Communists and Nazis.  There should not have been such shock.  The Executive Committee of the *Reichslandbund*, the agricultural ally of the DNVP, had urged more social policy to broaden the base of working-class support.[53]

Matters grew worse as the floor leader of the Catholic Center, Theodor von Guérard, rose:

Guérard: The acceptance of the Müller motion has changed everything.  The government wishes to pull the legislation.

(Left: Hear! Hear! Shady business!)

Guérard: I move to pull this item from the agenda.

(Communists: Racketeering!)

Rädel (KPD): I believe that I speak in the name of all of the unemployed when I say that they are sick of this political comedy.

(Roll call occurs.)

Löbe: The vote is 140 Yes, 140 No, and 52 abstentions.

(Many shouts and confusion.)

Löbe: The motion fails.

(Left: Bravo!)

Leicht (Bavarian People's): I move to transfer this matter back to the Committee.

(Roll call occurs.)

Löbe: The vote is 149 No, 138 Yes, and 28 abstentions.[54]

As the Reichstag accepted the other articles, the representatives from the government parties left the chamber as the Communists taunted them.   A Catholic Center deputy suggested the absence of a quorum and then walked out. The Reichstag in the Weimar era had often seen the Left or the Right walk out, but seldom had the two groups faced each other across rows of empty seats in the middle.  By seventeen votes the extremes failed to achieve a quorum, and Löbe had no choice but to set an agenda for a new "legislative day" to start in eight minutes without unemployment on the agenda.[55]

The ministers decided to put the government's motion into effect as an ordinance with the approval of the pertinent Reichsrat committee.[56]  However, the government's problems had only begun.  Quite separately from unemploy-

---

53.  Patch, p. 112.

54.  *VdR, Stenographische Berichte*, vol. 391, pp. 7953-7954.

55.  Ibid., pp. 7954-7955.

56.  *Kabinette Marx III/IV*, Document #109, pp. 304-305.

ment relief, the Social Policy Committee was considering the long-delayed unemployment-insurance bill.    Following Westarp's lead, the Nationalists supported every generous Communist, Socialist, or Nazi motion, leaving the government in the minority.    The tactics were particularly obvious at one meeting of the Committee.   A Nationalist deputy, described by the *Vorwärts* as "a constant enemy of the workers," made no vote on a Socialist-Communist motion until Lambach shouted from the audience, "The Count has ordered it!" The representative then voted with the SPD and KPD (Communist Party of Germany).[57]   The Catholic Center and Democratic parties were deserting the government on aspects of the supplementary budget.   The Reichstag added RM117 million, including the subsidies for general and long-term unemployment, and accepted the budget by voice vote on December 17.[58]

Germany in 1926 had seen classes coming together.   The working classes had long taken a moderate view, although the SPD often resorted to biting rhetoric.    Industrialists, led by Silverberg, reverted to a position of paternalism and supported social programs.   As Stegerwald had noted, there was nothing new here: this approach dated back at least to the time of Bismarck.   It was unusual to see the *Landbund* backing social policy.   The change in class relations was reflected in the change in party relations.   The Nationalists in particular moderated their view on spending, unemployment relief, and foreign policy.   The key to the construction of this political community was spending: increased spending for housing and rural settlements, job creation, and public works.   The growth in spending was in turn made possible by two developments: a new attitude by the Finance Ministry toward fiscal policy as it pushed for deficit spending, and the *laissez-faire* attitude of Parker Gilbert, protector of the Dawes bonds, who had stood aside as billions of Marks in foreign loans flooded into Germany and financed any number of projects.   Many Germans, with the important exception of Reinhold, did not recognize how vital Gilbert's goodwill was.   Reinhold had pushed for the "small-improvement notes" to please Gilbert.    The Prussian loan of 1926 marked a turning point.    When Höpker-Aschoff and Dulles ran roughshod over Gilbert, they created a powerful enemy who would increasingly attack Weimar's fiscal policy and eventually bring an end to the "golden age" of the Republic.   While the government had been unable to press its fiscal advantage in foreign policy, it still held to the lesson that deficit spending, managed properly, could enhance the budget and produce revenues to balance the deficits in part.

---

57. *Vorwärts*, November 11, 1926.
58. *VdR, Stenographische Berichte*, vol. 391, pp. 8549-8551 and 8614-8651.

# Chapter 6

# Autumn: The Köhler and Hilferding Years

The end of the 1920s saw confidence in the Dawes bonds ebb. The government's policies were more careless, and the bonds lost their protector when the Young Plan eliminated Parker Gilbert's job. Investors pulled out their bonds and began to sell them. The clash over unemployment payments at the end of 1926 made a change in government almost inevitable. A minority coalition of the middle was no longer tenable. The Chancellor turned first to the Social Democrats, but that party did not want to enter another coalition as junior member and chose instead to make an issue of the illegal rearmament of the Reichswehr. This forced the Cabinet into the arms of the Nationalists. After long negotiations the Catholic Center went into a coalition with the DNVP, but the Democrats declined this alliance and with them left Peter Reinhold. A new Finance Minister Heinrich Köhler alienated Gilbert almost immediately. Even as the Germans estranged the most important player in the new system of fiscal policy, their attempt to cover the deficit with an internal bond issue failed. The system cracked after Köhler insisted on an unreasonable raise for the civil servants. Many in Germany refused to accept the lessons of 1926 and clung to the orthodox fiscal policies of balanced budgets. Spending seemed to spiral out of control in 1927 and 1928. When another economic downturn began in 1929, the government passed an unrealistic budget and then seemed surprised when it had to enact stopgap borrowing measures. Then it fatally tried to turn back to the old orthodoxy. Rather than achieve a balanced budget, this policy put Germany on a treadmill of higher deficits and ever more budget cuts. Rudolf Hilferding, who returned to the Finance Ministry after the SPD's victory in the May 1928 elections, and Popitz found themselves increasingly trapped by fiscal measures until they resigned at the end of 1929.

Even as the government tottered, Reinhold had decided that something had to be done about excessive spending by the Reich, states, and localities. The Reichstag had ignored his pleas to restrain spending on the supplementary budget. Schacht had complained since October that the influx of foreign money was destroying the ability of the Reichsbank to control credit and the money supply. In his November report on the course of reparations payments, Gilbert criticized the use of foreign loans for "unproductive" goals such as unemployment relief. Two options were possible: reducing the Reichsbank discount rate to discourage foreign investment or suspending the tax breaks given to foreigners who purchased German bonds on the New York market. The corrective mechanism of allowing the mark to sink in value was not an available option. Ultimately, the government used both measures. Foreign-loan problems multiplied daily. Gilbert was complaining about the Prussian loan. The Reichsbank Directorate sent a letter to Reinhold formally requesting restrictions on the tax breaks. It was alarmed at the growing indebtedness to foreigners. Conditions had changed since the establishment of the tax breaks in 1925. Then, the domestic credit market had lain in ruins and long-term loans seemed impossible. Now, the directors believed, some long-term loans on the Berlin market might be possible.[1]

On December 4 the Finance Ministry suspended the tax breaks. Reinhold also made efforts to limit spending by trying to reduce the appropriation for settlements in the east and by fighting a Catholic Center motion to provide Christmas bonuses for civil servants and wounded veterans.[2] Having sponsored a huge tax cut in the spring and stood by while the Labor Ministry put programs for job creation and housing in place, Reinhold finally was taking action against new spending. The suspension of the tax breaks might end foreign borrowing, but it also ran the risk of driving government and industry into a domestic credit market that was too weak to handle the load. Clearly this was the time to build a debt structure for the Reich domestically with a proper mixture of short-term and long-term debt. One cannot build such a structure overnight. The Reich needed to market a quantity of short-term bills and prove its ability to redeem them before it could expect investors to buy long-term bonds. Instead, the government held to the old pattern of selling short-term debt to institutions and only selling bonds to the public. The failure to build a debt structure was critical in the fall of the Republic.

After the suspension of tax breaks and the reduction of the Reichsbank discount rate from 6% to 5% on January 11, 1927, Reinhold believed that the time was right for the government to issue bonds to finance the deficit. Since

---

1. McNeil, pp. 137-140. January 10, 1927 description of Gilbert's report with comments by Hugo Ferdinand Simon, *ADAP*, Series B: 1925-33, vol. IV, Doc. #18, pp. 34-40. BAK R 2/2002, pp. 8-11. BAK R 2/2007, November 23, 1926.
    2. *Kabinette Marx III/IV*, Docs. #141, pp. 414-420; #152, pp. 440-445.

his first speech to the Reichstag as Finance Minister, Reinhold had maintained that loans should cover the extraordinary budget. After the Reichstag passed the supplementary budget, it was clear that there would be a budget deficit. Also, the course of government negotiations suggested that the Democrats would probably not be in the next Cabinet, so Reinhold had to act quickly if he wanted to put the finishing touches on his program. If Reinhold placed the loan successfully, it would open new horizons of financing spending for Germany. It would have used fiscal tools to affect the business cycle and improve the economy. If the bond issue failed, however, Germany would be facing a fiscal problem with vast deficits that would require massive tax increases, deep spending cuts, or a new international arrangement similar to the Dawes loan of 1924-25.

The Cabinet discussed the proposed loan on January 27. This meeting was of questionable legality since the Reichstag had expressed no confidence in this government in December, but a later protest from the Budget Committee was brushed aside.[3] Reinhold wanted to raise RM200 million from public and semi-public institutions such as the post office and railroads and RM300 million in a bond issue. He expected that the bonds would bear a 5% interest rate while being issued at 92% of par value. The bonds would appear in a range of denominations to appeal to both large and small investors. Reinhold wanted to get the bonds out while the discount rate was very low and before many governments and businesses tried to borrow money on the Berlin market. The Cabinet unanimously agreed that Reinhold should conclude negotiations for the loan.[4]

The bond issue was Reinhold's last action as Finance Minister. During the debate over the supplementary budget, the SPD raised the issue of secret military training and brought down the government. The Nationalists were feeling more pressure than ever from their agricultural supporters to rejoin the government. In 1926 some 27,000 hectares of land had gone into bankruptcy. Of these, 63% were estates of greater than 200 hectares, which formed the backbone of DNVP support, mostly in East Prussia, Pomerania, Brandenburg, and Silesia. Sellers only realized 75% of the prewar value on these estates. The Brandenburg *Landbund* had called for reentry into the government. Negotiations lasted for more than a month. The Catholic Center would only form a coalition with the Nationalists if they agreed to obey the Weimar constitution, follow the foreign policy of fulfillment including the Dawes Plan, Locarno, and Thoiry, and commit to a generous social policy. The Nationalists would have to pledge "unconditional protection" to the republican colors and

---

3. After 1928, the Reichstag prohibited a caretaker government from raising loans.

4. *Kabinette Marx III/IV*, Doc. #174, pp. 508-512. Hertz-Eichenrode, p. 112. Reichsrat 1928, Drucksache #105.

oppose any associations trying to undo the Republic. On social policy they had to endorse an expansion of labor law, especially labor protection for mine workers against employers. The DNVP would have to back work-time laws and support ratification of the Washington Treaty mandating the eight-hour day when other Western European nations ratified that treaty. Until ratification occurred, the Nationalists would have to vote overtime pay for workers who exceeded that time. The DNVP would have to promote a concerted effort against joblessness and finally lend its full support for the enactment of a long-delayed unemployment-insurance act. Alfred Hugenberg tried to block Nationalist participation in the Cabinet, but found scant support.[5]

The Democrats declined to join this coalition for fear that the Catholics and Nationalists would push through laws on religious instruction and higher tariffs. All eyes turned to the Democratic members of the Cabinet. Reinhold said that he would remain as Finance Minister only if Hindenburg, Stresemann, and Marx urged him to stay for reasons of foreign policy. He would serve as an expert minister with no ties to the DDP fraction. Marx felt this was unwarranted, although he personally laid "great value" on Reinhold staying on, the Chancellor suspected that the Nationalists and People's party members did not want him to remain.[6] Reinhold chose to leave and never held government office again.

Wilhelm Marx sent a telegram to Karlsruhe asking Heinrich Köhler, who had become Prime Minister of Baden in November, to come to Berlin as Reich Finance Minister. Köhler had been born in Karlsruhe and risen in both political and civil-service circles. Since 1913 he had been a member of the Baden Landtag. His specialty had been customs and tax service, and during the war he had been a financial administrator in occupied Belgium. In 1920 he had succeeded Wirth as Finance Minister of Baden.[7] Köhler arrived as a man with a mission: to undo Reinhold's mistakes. Reinhold's fiscal policy "was wholly in the hands of big business and the great banks without a care for the interests of the poor."[8] He had joined the Marx Cabinet on the condition that the "big-business policy" of Reinhold would end, and that he would not enforce DNVP demands conflicting with his "republican and democratic sense." He was willing to support the DNVP farm policy because this would strengthen the Weimar state and better the lot of the poor. The Reich and the states would have to sort out their financial relations (again), and finally he demanded substantial raises

---

5.  Hertz-Eichenrode, p. 188. Ross McKibbon, "The Myth of the Unemployed: Who Did Vote for Hitler?" *The Australian Journal of Politics and History* 15, no. 2 (1969), pp. 31-32. Chanady, p. 76. *Kabinette Marx III/IV*, Doc. #177, pp. 515-523. Stürmer, p. 188. Grathwol, p. 193.

6.  BAK NL 5 (Pünder), vol. 33, p. 61. *Kabinette Marx III/IV*, p. XLVIII and Doc. #177, pp. 515-523. Von Hehl, p. 400. Haungs, p. 130.

7.  BAK R 43 I/1307, p. 275. *Kreuzzeitung*, January 29, 1927.

8.  Köhler, p. 189.

for the long-suffering civil servants.  He knew that this would not meet with Gilbert's approval, but he had nothing but contempt for the American: "Before the gate, nay, inside the German house itself, sat the overlord of our war-enemies, the American Parker Gilbert, to keep alert that nothing might happen to disturb the Dawes payments.  It was clear to me that the most painful [cuts] to the budget and absolute adherence to the reparations payments must be my first duty."[9]  Köhler saw himself as surrounded by enemies.  He accused Reinhold, Stresemann, Briand, Austen Chamberlain, and Gilbert of membership in a Masonic conspiracy against him.  "I had learned that [Gilbert] had meddled in an unforgivable way in government-building to place his [lodge] brother Reinhold in the new Cabinet."[10]  He described the Democrats as "representatives of Jews and industrial capitalists."  "At my entrance into national politics they were very irritated that their representative Reinhold had just lost his influential position as Finance Minister, although he declared himself willing to join the DNVP Cabinet as Finance Minister, and . . . Gilbert had the tastelessness to undertake steps to try to keep Reinhold in his post."[11]

Brauns' goals for the Labor Ministry were little changed from the previous Cabinet: job creation, rural settlements, an unemployment-insurance law, a labor-protection act, regulations on working hours, and housing construction.  Köhler gave priority to a civil-service raise.  He also wished to reduce the sugar tax to take a regressive tax from the backs of the poor.  During Reichstag debate, Westarp claimed that the new government represented the fulfillment of the goals laid out at the DNVP congress in September.  He pledged Nationalist defense of the Republic's land, constitution, flag, and colors as the Left laughed.  Finally, he made a strong endorsement of Marx's economic and social policy.  The Communists immediately forced the Nationalists to prove their loyalty by demanding withdrawal from the League of Nations.  Reversing two years of official opposition, every Nationalist voted to uphold Germany's membership.  The government received the confidence of the Reichstag by a vote of 236 to 174 with eighteen abstentions.  The only member to break party ranks was Joseph Wirth.  Although the Nationalists had accepted the manifesto he had drafted, Wirth could not bear to give his vote to the "black-blue bloc."[12]

Köhler presented the 1927 budget on February 16 and delivered a stern message.  He warned that the Reichstag must tightly guard spending because the government had used part of the 1926 reserves to cover the supplementary budget.  Germany would have to pay more in reparations than the year before.

---

9.  Ibid., p. 192.

10.  Ibid., p. 242.

11.  Ibid., p. 215.

12.  BAK R 43 I/1498, pp. 163-169.  *VdR, Stenographische Berichte*, vol. 393, pp. 8789-8825, 8890-8893.

Köhler admitted a false appearance of balance in the budget.  The government had hoped that unemployment insurance would be in place by April 1 and had not included unemployment relief in the budget.  RM200 million would cover that expense.  The Cabinet would also bring proposals increasing payments to civil servants, wounded veterans, and small pensioners later in the year.  Köhler urged tax simplification and consideration of a reduction in the sugar tax.  As with the 1926 budget, loans would cover the extraordinary budget, which would again contain job-creation measures in the Labor and Transportation Ministries, agricultural settlements, and additional payments to widows, orphans, and invalids.  The Left jeered when Köhler announced that the military budget would grow.[13]

Although it was only a small part of the speech, Köhler caused the greatest stir outside Germany by suggesting that a time would come soon when Germany could not pay reparations and would need to revise the current agreements.  He also referred to the insecurity from an unknown end date for the Dawes Plan.  The Chancellor had to face countless sharp questions from the foreign press, which demanded to know whether Köhler's speech marked a change in the government's position.  One American writer asked specifically if this speech meant that Germany would move for a revision in the Plan.  American reaction to Köhler's speech was very negative.  The *New York Times* saw this as a challenge to the Dawes Plan.  Senator William Borah, Chairman of the Foreign Relations Committee, asserted that Köhler was trying to have an impact on the Senate's debate on a bill to release German assets seized during the war.[14]

Köhler attempted to quell the growing firestorm by giving a "clarifying" interview.  The Finance Minister claimed that he had never intended to deny Germany's responsibility under the Dawes Plan.  For a man who had once been Press Secretary in Baden's Interior Ministry, he had a distressing habit of putting his foot in his mouth.  Criticism of the Germans continued to grow in the American press.  Maltzan warned that there was uneasiness over the size of the military budget and tried to show that, as a percentage of budget outlays, the Germans spent far less than Britain or France.  Shortly after Köhler's budget speech and the "clarifying" interview, the New York *Herald Tribune* ran a six-part series by John Elliot, the newspaper's Berlin correspondent, who described a prosperous country that had fully recovered from the ravages of inflation and depression.  Growing beer and tobacco consumption showed that luxury goods were again widespread.  Stocks had been soaring, with the *Frankfurter Zeitung*'s stock index growing 136% from January 1925 to January 1927.  British Foreign

13. *VdR, Stenographische Berichte*, vol. 393, pp. 9005-9033. Köhler, p. 231. Dieckmann, p. 69.

14. BAK NL 57 (Stockhausen), vol. 38, February 17, 1927. American reaction described in BAK R 43 I/275, p. 256, February 19, 1927.

Secretary Chamberlain also took exception to Köhler's "veiled threat" against the Dawes Plan and felt that this would make evacuation of the Rhineland more difficult.[15]

With Reinhold gone and the new Finance Minister suspect in the eyes of many abroad, Schacht reassumed the leading role in German foreign economic policy and domestic monetary policy. In March he gave the first report to the Cabinet on currency and finance since December 1925. He spoke of the precipitous decline in German interest rates since the last report and estimated that some RM1.7 billion of foreign investment had come into the Reich in 1926. Schacht warned that two recent developments could endanger the current liquidity: frantic speculation in the Berlin bourse and an overabundance of short-term funds held by private banks. Both dangers fed upon each other, as investors used short-term money to buy stocks on margin. Any sudden reversal or panic could lead to a financial catastrophe. Schacht then lectured the Cabinet on fiscal policy, an area outside his jurisdiction. He complained that the Reich should be more careful in its spending, and in particular criticized the projects on unemployment insurance, housing, settlements in the East, transportation improvements, and unemployment relief. Had the ministers been more careful, the bond issue would have been unnecessary. Since the Reichsbank had lowered its discount rate to 5%, the money market had tightened up, and already the Prussian State Bank had raised its rate. Schacht criticized the Reinhold loan indirectly while saying that he did not believe it proper to criticize a public measure. He claimed that he had no idea that this loan had been under consideration because he had been on vacation. The long-term market was still far too weak to support such a large loan. Popitz was attending the meeting in Köhler's absence. He resented Schacht's intrusion into the preserve of the Ministry and rebuffed Schacht. The bond issue had been necessary to cover spending through April 1, Popitz explained. Schacht interrupted to maintain that the Reichsbank could have covered the funds, and Popitz shot back, "Not all 500 million!" Schacht concluded by urging the Cabinet to consider strict regulations for the Bourse to bring the money market back into order and foil speculation.[16]

Schacht's critique was largely correct: the bond issue was failing. Demand for the bonds by the brokerage houses had been moderate in the first days of the issue, and within a week over 80% had been sold in small chunks. By mid-February the bond issue was oversubscribed, with official bodies,

---

15. Maltzan's comment of February 21 and New York *Herald Tribune*, February 21-26, 1927, in PA, Auswärtiges Amt, Wirtschafts Reparationen, Aktennummer L253 (Peace Treaty: Germany's Financial and Economic Position), vol. 6. Büro Staatssekratär, Section C, vol. 12, p. 133. *DBFP 1919-1939*, D, vol. 3, Doc. 143, pp. 212-213, April 11, 1927. Stresemann, *Vermächtnis*, vol. III, p. 137.

16. *Kabinette Marx III/IV*, Doc. #195, pp. 577-610. Upmeier in Hansmeyer, p. 163.

insurance companies, and savings banks taking the bulk. The real trouble began when these institutions and other brokers tried to market the bonds to the public. They immediately fell from 92% to 89% after their official offering date of April 5. There were several essential problems. The first was that the interest rate was too low. The effective yield for the Reich bond in April was 5.79% compared to 7.26% for various public loans and a mortgage rate of 8.61%. Reinhold had erred in setting a 5% interest rate, though it followed the Reichsbank's new discount rate and the monthly rates for money on the open market. Table 6.1 shows that eight other loans similar to the Reich loan were placed on the Berlin market in February 1927 and all of them bore a rate of at least 6%. Reinhold himself later admitted that he set the rate too low but also blamed an excessive capital gains tax for discouraging investment. Reinhold also made a serious mistake on the term of the bonds. In his report of June 1927, Parker Gilbert made a penetrating analysis of the bond issue and its failure. The long-term market had little excess capital available, and after the bond issue it had even less capital to foster long-term development. Gilbert agreed with Schacht about the excess of short-term capital. This misalignment of funds had been evident in January, and Reinhold should have placed his loan in treasury bills, repayable in a matter of months. Reinhold's bond issue had made the situation much worse because it had soaked up long-term capital while the Reich and the brokers deposited their cash proceeds in banks, which could use the money for speculation and short-term investment. However, it is probably going too far to maintain that this loan harmed the private sector by diverting capital from it. If this had been the case, there should have been a general increase in German and global bond yields. The opposite occurred: bond prices rose in the first quarter of 1927, and no weakness appeared until the fourth quarter of the year.[17] (See Figure 6.1.)

Rather than cut its losses and admit its error, the government inaugurated a secret policy of subsidizing the price by repurchasing the bonds at a higher price. In August, the Finance Ministry admitted defeat and raised the rate on the bonds to 6%. For want of a single percentage point, enormous damage had been done to the government's financial prestige. Gilbert was later

---

17. *Berliner Tageblatt*, February 8, 15, and 16, 1927; *Germania*, February 12, 1927. Dieckmann, p. 67. PrStA Hauptabteilung I, Rep. 77, Titel 733, vol. 5, p. 107. BAK R 45 III/6, pp. 172-199. Parker Gilbert, Report of the Agent General for Reparations, June 10, 1927, PA, Auswärtiges Amt, Wirtschafts Reparationen, Section 14 (Transfers), Aktennummer L205, Reports of the Reparations Agent, vol. 3. As Undersecretary of the Treasury, Gilbert's specialty had been converting debt. Krosigk, p. 35. Feldman, "Industrialists, Bankers, and the Problem of Unemployment in the Weimar Republic," *Central European History*, 25 (1992), no.1, p. 79. Balderston, *Financial Crisis*, pp. 206-210.

**Table 6.1**

**Comparable Loans Also Listed on the Berlin Market in February 1927**

| Loan | Amount (in millions) | Rate | % of Par | Time |
|------|------|------|------|------|
| German Reich | 500.0 | 5% | 92.00% | 1935-59 |
| Bavaria | 75.0 | 6% | 97.75% | to 1953 |
| Deutsche Sparkasse und Giroverband | 10.6 | 6% | 98.00% | 1932-61 |
| Emschergenossenschaft | 5.0 | 6% | 97.00% | 1932-53 |
| Kelberg | 1.5 | 6% | 95.75% | to 1932 |
| Pforsheim | 6.0 | 6% | 96.75% | 1932-56 |
| Gewerbe Brockdorf Nietleben bei Halle | 5.0 | 6% | 95.00% | 1932-57 |
| Gorkauer Societätsbrauerei | 1.0 | 7% | 95.00% | Not listed |
| Sächischer Gusstahl Döhlen | 4.0 | 6% | 94.00% | Not listed |

*Source*: *Berliner Tageblatt*, March 10, 1927.

told that such an extraordinary step had been taken only twice before: in Germany before the Revolution and in Guatemala.[18]

Tables 6.2 and 6.3 indicate two different ways of viewing the FY27 budget: the first was the official accounting by the German government, the second the budget summary of Parker Gilbert. While the numbers and categories differ, they show a considerable increase in spending from FY26. Most of this came in two categories: RM250 million more in Dawes Plan payments and RM350 million in additional transfers to the states. Gilbert was particularly annoyed at the state transfers. The bare record makes it appear that Reinhold's proposal represented a budget freeze from FY26. However, a few notes of caution are in order. The transfer to the states had not yet been determined because it depended on tax revenue. Reinhold had also removed much of the cost of unemployment relief on the assumption that an insurance program would begin in 1927. He was correct, but there were additional costs that he did not include. Unemployment insurance also accounts for part of the steep fall in the Labor Ministry's budget and Gilbert's category of "social spending," as the Ministry took it (temporarily) "off budget." Reinhold defended himself by saying that he had inserted money for relief. The budget negotiators in 1927 did manipulate the numbers. They closed the budget gap by gimmickry: raising tax estimates by RM270 million and drawing upon RM190

---

18. McNeil, pp. 145-146, says the government spent RM70 million supporting the bond issue. PA, Auswärtiges Amt, Aktennummer K516 Finanzwesen 2: Loans and Bonds, vol. 3, September 3, 1927. *Verhandlungen deutsches Reichsrats* 1928. Drucksache #105, September 10, 1928.

**Figure 6.1**
**Measure of Confidence: German 8% Mortgage Bond Prices**

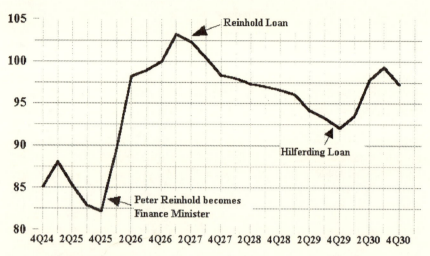

Source: Balderston, p. 206.

million from a special working capital fund. The Reichstag passed this budget on March 26. The precise budget situation did not seem dire to anyone. The RM900 million of credit authority granted during Reinhold's term had been covered partly by the bond issue, while the rest was not needed because tax revenues exceeded expectations. Gilbert's barometer of health, debt repayment exceeding new debts, continued to show positive signs.[19]

By May 1927 the coalition had solidified, and the Nationalists were ready to fulfill their promise to uphold the Republic and support progressive legislation. The new Marx Cabinet was already a political success. The economic scene was more troubling. Köhler had proved to be much less adroit than Reinhold, and Gilbert remained suspicious. Schacht had warned of real dangers, and the Reichsbank President took drastic action to achieve his desired remedies. This action led to the crash of the Berlin stock market and the loss of confidence in Schacht by many inside Germany. But his reputation abroad remained sterling and he played a key role in the bankers' summit of July that would help usher in the Great Depression. On the political side, the Nationalists supported construction and labor legislation, including the unemployment-insurance law. They even voted to renew the Law for the Protection of the Republic, which Wirth had aimed at them in 1922. The issue of more

19. *Kabinette Marx III/IV*, Doc. #210, pp. 656-658. BAK R 45 III/6, pp. 172-199. *Vorwärts*, March 25, 1927; BAK R 43 I/878, pp. 55-68.

**Table 6.2**
**The 1927 Budget (millions of RM)**

| Category | FY26 Spending | Reinhold 1927 Proposal | Final FY27 Spending | Change from 1926 |
|---|---|---|---|---|
| **ORDINARY BUDGET:** | | | | |
| **Continuing spending:** | | | | |
| President | 0.587 | 0.622 | 0.671 | 0.084 |
| Reichstag | 7.132 | 6.712 | 7.765 | 0.633 |
| Ministries, Chancery, and Chancellor | 0.685 | 2.697 | 2.623 | 1.938 |
| Foreign Office | 60.858 | 59.332 | 68.954 | 8.096 |
| Interior Ministry | 22.772 | 23.322 | 25.328 | 2.556 |
| Ministry for Occupied Regions | 5.715 | 8.379 | 7.977 | 2.262 |
| Economics Ministry | 9.083 | 11.572 | 11.186 | 2.103 |
| Reich Economics Council | 0.716 | 0.671 | 0.723 | 0.007 |
| Labor Ministry | 706.212 | 369.452 | 359.311 | -346.901 |
| Defense Ministry | 536.837 | 572.28 | 583.596 | 46.759 |
| Justice Ministry | 10.162 | 10.965 | 11.891 | 1.729 |
| Agriculture Ministry | 9.539 | 7.373 | 9.794 | 0.255 |
| Transport Ministry | 104.475 | 101.578 | 105.837 | 1.362 |
| Retirement Pensions | 1,456.949 | 1,465.823 | 1,630.963 | 174.014 |
| Auditing Office | 2.137 | 2.266 | 2.848 | 0.711 |
| Debt Service | 340.373 | 493.095 | 491.064 | 150.691 |
| Finance Ministry | 419.385 | 436.308 | 471.617 | 52.232 |
| Financial Administration (including transfers to states, war pensions, and miscellaneous) | 3,805.745 | 3,949.152 | 4,586.645 | 780.900 |
| Post Ministry | 0.038 | 0.038 | 0.041 | 0.003 |
| Sub-Total | 7,499.40 | 7,521.637 | 8,378.834 | 879.434 |

**Table 6.2 continued**

**One-time Spending:**

| | | | | |
|---|---|---|---|---|
| Reichstag | 0.468 | 0 | 0.428 | -0.040 |
| Ministries, Chancery, and Chancellor | 0 | 0 | 0.075 | 0.075 |
| Foreign Office | 4.668 | 0 | 2.294 | -2.374 |
| Interior Ministry | 63.478 | 0 | 78.761 | 15.283 |
| Ministry for Occupied Regions | 18.511 | 0 | 41.347 | 22.836 |
| Economics Ministry | 10.063 | 0 | 8.163 | -1.900 |
| Labor Ministry | 29.609 | 204.248 | 284.818 | 255.209 |
| Defense Ministry | 80.537 | 73.757 | 61.975 | -18.562 |
| Justice Ministry | 0.374 | 0 | 0.184 | -0.190 |
| Agriculture Ministry | 113.278 | 0 | 14.296 | -98.982 |
| Transport Ministry | 56.889 | 65.982 | 69.833 | 12.944 |
| Retirement Pensions | 5.316 | 0 | 1.403 | -3.913 |
| Debt Service | 13.394 | 0 | 36.062 | 22.668 |
| Finance Ministry | 19.705 | 0 | 41.806 | 22.101 |
| Financial Administration (including transfers to states, war pensions, and miscellaneous) | 438.317 | 469.384 | 479.338 | 41.021 |
| Sub-Total: | 854.607 | 813.371 | 1,120.783 | 266.176 |

**EXTRAORDINARY BUDGET:**

| | | | | |
|---|---|---|---|---|
| Interior Ministry | 0.036 | 0 | 0 | -0.036 |
| Economics Ministry | 0.003 | 0 | 0 | -0.003 |
| Labor Ministry | 179.769 | 195.000 | 232.204 | 52.435 |
| Defense Ministry | 29.174 | 61.750 | 60.419 | 31.245 |
| Transport Ministry | 66.376 | 118.000 | 76.194 | 9.818 |
| Debt Service | 10.353 | 0 | 11.561 | 1.208 |
| Finance Ministry | 2.118 | 0 | 2.500 | 0.382 |
| Financial Administration (including transfers to states, war pensions, and miscellaneous) | 593.447 | 622.460 | 368.651 | -224.796 |
| Sub-Total | 881.276 | 997.210 | 751.529 | -129.747 |
| GRAND TOTAL | 9,235.283 | 9,332.218 | 10,251.146 | 1,015.863 |

Sources: *Verhandlungen deutsches Reichrats* 1928. Drucksache #79. *Berliner Tageblatt*, January 7, 1927.

**Table 6.3**

**Gilbert's Budget Statements (billions of RM)**

|  | 1926-27 | 1927-28 | Difference |
|---|---|---|---|
| **Revenues** | | | |
| Tax Revenues | 7.175 | 8.490 | 1.315 |
| Administrative Revenues | 0.515 | 0.471 | -0.044 |
| Surplus Brought Over | 0.782 | 0.259 | -0.523 |
| Proceeds of Loans        A | 0.329 | 0.123 | -0.206 |
| Transfers from Special Working Fund | | 0.190 | 0.190 |
| Industrial Charge | | | 0.000 |
| **GRAND TOTAL** | **8.801** | **9.533** | **0.732** |
| | | | |
| **Expenditures** | | | |
| Payments to States/Communes | 2.626 | 3.016 | 0.390 |
| General Administrative | 2.156 | 2.296 | 0.140 |
| Social Spending | 0.811 | 0.766 | -0.045 |
| Internal War Charges | 1.496 | 1.560 | 0.064 |
| Execution of Dawes Plan | 0.550 | 0.899 | 0.349 |
| Capital investments & Grants | 0.483 | 0.267 | -0.216 |
| Reduction of Debt        B | 0.421 | 0.512 | 0.091 |
| **GRAND TOTAL** | **8.543** | **9.316** | **0.773** |
| Balance | 0.258 | 0.217 | -0.041 |

*Source*: Schuker, *Reparations*, p. 26.

agricultural tariffs, however, proved to be a very thorny one for the fourth Marx Cabinet.

Despite the economic difficulties and the problems of the government in balancing the budget, the Berlin Bourse was enjoying great success. Fueled by the low interest rates of the Reichsbank, the unattractiveness of the bond market since the internal loan of the Reich, and its own growth, the Bourse began a dizzying rise. At the beginning of 1927 the *Berliner Tageblatt*'s stock index had measured 143.3. By February it stood at 163.0, about a 14% increase. The market stalled as investors tried to sort out the real strength of the Reich's bond issue. By the end of March, stock prices in the electricity, banking, textile, fertilizer, and cement sectors had all exceeded their 1913 levels (see Table 6.4). In April, with the release of the bonds to the general investor, the speculative frenzy took over. The index rose from 154.9 on March 18 to

**Table 6.4**
**Stocks by Sector, 1927**

|                | Jan. 6 | Feb. 4 | Mar. 4 | Apr. 29 | May 13 |
|----------------|--------|--------|--------|---------|--------|
| Automobiles    | 117.0  | 126.0  | 124.1  | 141.2   | 126.0  |
| Banking        | 193.3  | 225.0  | 208.2  | 195.9   | 176.4  |
| Brewing        | 216.6  | 259.2  | 256.1  | 289.4   | 258.4  |
| Chemicals      | 154.3  | 159.6  | 150.7  | 156.9   | 138.2  |
| Coal           | 189.2  | 249.2  | 231.1  | 227.7   | 195.7  |
| Construction   | 136.1  | 158.7  | 154.4  | 187.1   | 161.8  |
| Electricity/Gas| 141.7  | 163.5  | 163.3  | 177.7   | 150.1  |
| Iron           | 129.5  | 153.6  | 139.9  | 154.1   | 127.4  |
| Machines       | 117.0  | 136.3  | 128.1  | 140.1   | 116.2  |
| Metals         | 124.9  | 139.5  | 135.9  | 146.7   | 125.1  |
| Paper          | 165.4  | 189.6  | 182.5  | 199.3   | 176.7  |
| Railroads      | 103.5  | 113.5  | 108.1  | 106.6   | 92.9   |
| Shipping       | 147.5  | 163.7  | 154.5  | 167.9   | 141.5  |
| Sugar          | 120.7  | 141.0  | 135.5  | 138.3   | 125.4  |
| Textiles       | 140.9  | 181.8  | 175.9  | 215.1   | 183.5  |

*Source*: *Berliner Tageblatt*, February 14, March 21, May 30, 1927.

a high of 177.3 on April 29. Construction and textile stocks led the way, while banking stocks lagged. At the beginning of May the market became a little soft from profit-taking but remained high at 175.4.[20]

Schacht became increasingly alarmed as the stock market rose higher and higher. The Cabinet had no intention of tightening fiscal policy. The new spending and budget gimmicks of the 1927 budget offered no debt relief. On May 5, Schacht met with the Cabinet to discuss the recent trends in the stock market since the suspension of tax breaks for foreign loans, the internal national bond issue, and the reduction of the discount rate. At the end of 1926 the currency position of the Reichsbank had been good, with some RM3 billion held in reserve. Since then RM700 million had fled Germany. A continuing hemorrhage would shake foreign confidence in the currency and could lead to devaluation. The greedy borrowing of the states had strained the internal money market. Schacht urged the government to draft a bill to reduce stock speculation.[21]

The Cabinet greeted Schacht's tirade tepidly. It promised nothing to the Reichsbank President but asked him to confer with Gilbert. Schacht was not satisfied and took unilateral action. He demanded that the private banks reduce

---

20. *Berliner Tageblatt*, February 14, March 21, April 5, May 16, 1927.
21. *Kabinette Marx III/IV*, Doc. #226, pp. 709-712.

their funding of stock-market investments or face a cutoff in federal funds. On May 12 the banks announced that they would cut their stock-market credit by 25%. Schacht justified his action to Montagu Norman by stating, "I totally lost control of the market, as our portfolio went down to almost nothing."[22] Schacht's action was catastrophic for the stock market. It had been in a slight downturn since the beginning of May, when the speculative cycle had eased. There was a sudden and dramatic selloff. The stocks that had prospered most during the boom felt the bust most acutely (see Table 6.5). The directors of the exchange board panicked, closed part of the exchange, and suspended trading in the worst-hit issues. This had never happened before in the history of the Berlin Bourse. The directors had rejected a full shutdown, although brokers traded little as they stood around on the exchange floor discussing the situation. Members of the Cabinet endorsed Schacht's action. Curtius said later: "Essentially, I agreed with the Reichsbank President as he tried to end this wave [of stock speculation]. I remain undecided whether he chose the proper method."[23] The move frightened foreign investors, and German reserves lost another RM110 million.[24]

The private banks were angry at Schacht's tightening of credit. They sent out a public communiqué that Schacht had acted for no reason and had caused a great disturbance. Schacht claimed that the banks themselves had caused the damage by announcing the credit tightening publicly instead of working with the Reichsbank. The next session of the exchange was quieter, but the banks insisted that they were not harming the economy. Some suggested that this rash act might have destroyed Schacht's influence. Foreign reaction varied. The *Wall Street Journal* called the crash a "tragic adventure" and described Schacht as "the pitiless dictator." The *New York Times* saw the crash as causing a "temporary strain" but expected it "to bring about beneficial readjustment in the long run." The *Financial Times* suggested that the crash showed the impossibility of executing of the Dawes Plan. The *Financial News* of London, which had always been suspicious of the Germans in general and Schacht in particular, saw this as a ploy to increase the pressure for a revision of the Dawes Plan and urged the Reichsbank to use interest-rate increases instead of credit restrictions to regulate capital flow. It summed up recent nervousness in the global marketplace: "With the recent Japanese crises, it indicates that the world is far from having settled down from its postwar

---

22. Quoted in Hardach, p. 77.
23. Quoted in McNeil, pp. 150-151.
24. Johannes Houwink ten Cate, "Hjalmar Schacht als Reparationspolitiker 1926-1930," *Vierteljahrschrift für Sozial- und Wirtschaftsgeschichte* 74, no. 2, p. 196. Hardach, p. 79. *Berliner Tageblatt* and *Kreuzzeitung*, May 13, 1927. Link, p. 407.

**Table 6.5**
**Banking and Industrial Stocks Worst Hit by the Crash of May 1927**

|  | May 7 | May 12 | May 13 |
|---|---|---|---|
| Allgemeine Elektrische Gesellschaft | 214.75 | 197.00 | 173.00 |
| Berliner Handels-Gesellschaft | 282.25 | 263.50 | 245.00 |
| Commerz Bank | 213.50 | 199.50 | 182.00 |
| Darmstädter Bank | 280.00 | 257.50 | 231.00 |
| Deutsche Bank | 190.00 | 177.25 | 170.00 |
| Disconto-Gesellschaft | 184.50 | 173.50 | 163.50 |
| Dresdner Bank | 199.37 | 184.37 | 170.00 |
| Farbenindustrie | 339.00 | 314.00 | 290.25 |
| Gelsenkirchen Bergwerks | 186.75 | 181.12 | 166.75 |
| Hamburg-Amerika | 153.50 | 144.50 | 131.12 |
| Harpener | 254.50 | 228.75 | 200.25 |
| Norddeutsche Lloyd | 158.00 | 146.25 | 141.00 |
| Reichsbank | 175.75 | 170.25 | 165.50 |
| Vereinigte Glanzstoffe | 705.00 | 643.00 | 517.00 |
| Vereinigte Stahlwerke | 157.75 | 150.50 | 145.00 |

Source: *Financial News*, May 14, 1927, PA, Auswärtiges Amt, Sonderreferat Wirtschaft, Section Finanzwesen 24 (Börsewesen).

financial difficulties."[25]  On June 10, the Reichsbank raised its discount rate to 6%.  The *Herald Tribune* saw this as another game to avoid the Dawes payments.  In later months the market continued to drift lower, with the index reaching 133 by November, a 25% drop from its peak.[26]

The market had stabilized when Gilbert issued his June report on the state of the German budget, economy, and reparations payments.  It was deeply critical of the entire budget process.  The Reparations Agent had never been happy with the extraordinary budget.  He now attacked Germany's abuse of this gimmick.  He made a long analysis of the Reich loan of February 1927 and its failure.  By June the government had already slapped restrictions on the resale of the bond until August 15, but despite this attempt to slow transactions, the bond had fallen to well below 90% of par.  The only praiseworthy developments were the increases in the German savings rate and money in circulation.

---

25.  *Berliner Tageblatt*, May 13 and 14, 1927.  Hjalmar Schacht, *My First Seventy-Six Years* (London: Wingate, 1955), p. 230. *Wall Street Journal*, May 14, *New York Times*, May 15, *Financial Times*, May 16, and *Financial News*, May 16 and 17, 1927, from PA, Auswärtiges Amt, Sonderreferat Wirtschaft, Section Finanzwesen 24 (Börsewesen).

26. New York *Herald Tribune*, June 15, 1927, PA, Auswärtiges Amt, Büro Staatssekretär, Section C, vol. 12, pp. 231-232. Hardach, p. 79.

Some in the Cabinet believed that the attacks of Gilbert and Schacht were no coincidence. Stresemann suspected that Gilbert's criticisms of the budget were identical to the ones that Schacht had been making for the past two years. Köhler insisted that Schacht's reforms were impossible. He was angry at the increase in interest rates. Schacht had promised the three ministers that he would not raise the rates, had read Gilbert's report, and immediately had raised the rates, making the rescue of the bond issue impossible. Stresemann demanded privately that the Cabinet exclude Schacht from its meetings. He had vented his fury by scratching Roman numerals into papers. The ministers were even angrier when they learned that Schacht had left the meeting to go to a dinner party, loudly proclaimed that Köhler was incompetent, and urged the return of Hans Luther to the Finance Ministry. Pünder had to chuckle at this suggestion, for Köhler and several others had lobbied for Luther to take Schacht's job. Schacht had then given a comic account of the day's meeting, saying that the ministers resembled a group of "drenched poodles." The Reichsbank President had seen reports in left-wing newspapers that he would retire in 1928 because of intestinal illness, and refuted these rumors.[27]

It was clear to all observers that the attempt to reduce the influx of foreign capital by suspending the tax breaks on foreign loans and reducing the Reichsbank discount rate had not worked. The failure of the bond issue had proved that government and business could not turn to the domestic market for investment capital and funds to cover the budget deficit. On June 4 the Finance Ministry lifted the suspension and again provided for tax breaks if businesses took loans abroad. The loans had to be for "productive" purposes and the Advisory Board for Foreign Credits, the Reichsrat, and the Tax Committee of the Reichstag would have to approve them. The Advisory Board modified its previous stance and now declared construction to be nonproductive. The Directors of the Reichsbank urged Marx to reduce demand for foreign loans. They warned that the currency was in danger. The reserves had risen by RM900 million in 1924, RM250 million in 1925, and RM600 million in 1926 but had fallen by a billion Marks in just the first six months of 1927. They blamed this trend on the increase in foreign loans combined with a stagnation in exports. An acid test appeared immediately. Berlin was trying to gain a RM4 million loan for street expansion and the construction of a streetcar system. This would run for a thirty-year term at 6% face value. The Reichsbank was dead set against it. Its representative on the Advisory Board pointed out that since 1925 the city of Berlin had doubled its budget while France and other

---

27. Parker Gilbert, Report of the Agent General for Reparations, June 10, 1927, in PA, Auswärtiges Amt, Wirtschafts Reparationen, Section 2A: Germany: Question of German Credit, supplement to vol. 3. *Kabinette Marx III/IV*, Docs. #254, pp.805-806; #257, pp. 810-823. Upmeier in Hansmayer, p. 164. Köhler, p. 243. Schacht, *Seventy-Six Years*, p. 231. Stresemann, *Vermächtnis*, vol. III, p. 257.

countries were scaling back spending to the prewar level. He was overruled by the other members of the Board, which did trim the loan.[28] Despite all the warnings and Schacht's unhappiness, business would resume as usual.

While trust in Schacht had collapsed in Germany, the Reichsbank President remained highly respected abroad. On July 6, 1927, Schacht, Strong, Norman, and Charles Rist, the Deputy Governor of the Bank of France, held a secret bankers' summit at the Long Island mansion of Ogden Mills, the Undersecretary of the U.S. Treasury. They discussed six items: (1) the financial position of Paris *vis-à-vis* New York and London, (2) the extraordinarily great movement of gold among these markets, (3) technical procedures between the Treasury Department and the Federal Reserve in buying gold, (4) gold shipments to New York, (5) the possibility that the gold standard could be responsible for the problems in capital flow, and (6) coordination of interest rates. There were two essential problems. The first was France. Just a year before, France had been the financial basket case of Western Europe and the franc had been in free fall. The pathetic state of the currency had driven the French to consider abandoning the Treaty of Versailles for a quick infusion of German cash at Thoiry. During the winter of 1926-27, Poincaré had stabilized the franc at four cents by adopting Strong's terms for the Bank of France and rationalizing the tax structure. In eighteen months Poincaré reduced the national debt by two-thirds. Suddenly, the Bank of France contained too many reserve funds. It had bought £100 million sterling during the stabilization period. Norman, disliking the French and knowing that the French recognized this dislike, was deathly afraid that the bank might suddenly convert this currency into gold and put great pressure on the pound. In May the French had begun this conversion into gold, triggering the conference. The second concern was over international interest rates, especially the German rate. The failure of the German bond issue and Schacht's increase of the discount rate were ominous signs. The British rates remained high, perhaps artificially high, to protect their currency. Schacht might have to raise his rate to 7% or 8% to protect his reserves. The alternative was a devaluation of the mark, which could set off another inflationary cycle and therefore was not considered.[29] Strong saw only one possibility: "I personally believe that unless we can reduce our market rates, bank rates in Europe must advance beyond their present level. It would

---

28. McNeil, p. 161. *Kabinette Marx III/IV*, Doc. #260, pp. 818-825. BAK R 2/2101, pp. 35-45R and R 2/2026, Advisory Board sessions of June 28 and June 29, 1927.

29. Chandler, *Benjamin Strong*, pp. 371-375. Henry Clay, *Lord Norman* (New York, 1957), p. 227. Martin Wolfe, *The French Franc between the Wars, 1919-1939* (New York, 1951), p. 61. Andrew Boyle, *Montagu Norman* (London, 1967), pp. 198, 226-227. McNeil, p. 163.

be their way of protecting the gold reserves."[30]    High interest rates in Europe would stunt economic development and could bring on another recession.

Strong moved quickly to take command of both situations. He brought the French into line by threatening to flood the gold market with American reserves, which would lower the value of the French gold. Instead of draining British gold reserves, the Federal Reserve would offer the French the same price for their pounds sterling as the Bank of England had given them. The Federal Reserve would also lower its own discount rate to 3.5% to discourage foreign investment in the United States and encourage American investment abroad. He hoped that capital would stay put in Britain and Germany, and those countries would not have to raise their interest rates to stimulate foreign investment. A rise in American prices would also help the international trade balance, and the Federal Reserve system purchased $340 million in securities to put more cash into circulation. It seemed that the decision had been an easy one and that the international financial situation in the wake of the crash of the Berlin Exchange was still sound. In retrospect this easy decision was disastrous. In the two years following the agreement to lower interest rates, borrowing and speculation ran rampant on Wall Street. Instead of encouraging American investment in German bonds, the change encouraged a wave of borrowing. Underwriters had led unwary investors step by step from Liberty Bonds to German municipal and industrial bonds and now plunged them into the high-risk world of the stock market. Easy money and minuscule margins for downpayment brought speculators by the thousands. When the Federal Reserve tried to follow the same path as the Reichsbank by raising interest rates and mandating an increased margin, the same result occurred as in Berlin on May 13. This time it occurred in the world financial center of New York rather than the lesser center of Berlin, and the fall prefaced the collapse of the entire global financial system.[31]

While Schacht and the others sowed the seeds of economic chaos in New York, the government was passing a great deal of productive legislation. It was again using spending policy to carry out social improvements and boost its popularity. The Labor Ministry unveiled its latest construction program to coordinate RM2.5 billion in public and private funds to build about 250,000 apartments in 1927.[32] In the summer of 1927, the unemployment-insurance bill finally became law. When the Nationalists wrecked the government's unemployment-relief and insurance programs in November 1926, they effectively committed themselves to supporting a generous program. To gain entrance into the new Cabinet they had also pledged their full cooperation. The

---

30. Quoted in Hardach, p. 82.

31. Chandler, pp. 376-377. Clay, p. 236. Link, p. 411. Wandel, p. 106. Boyle, p. 231. Galbraith, p. 177. Charles P. Kindleberger, *Manias, Panics, and Crashes: A History of Financial Crises*, revised edition (New York, 1989), pp. 79-80.

32. BAK R 43 I/2346, pp. 479-485, June 27, 1927, outlined the proposed financing for construction.

spring had been very productive for labor legislation. In 1926 the DVP had stalled a bill on overtime pay mandating that employers pay their workers time-and-a-quarter for all work over forty-eight hours a week. In April 1927, the Reichstag passed the bill 195 to 184 though many members of the DVP "took sick" and industrialists objected strenuously. A general labor-protection act had passed the Reichstag in June, and a special law protecting miners seemed assured of passage. The proposals of the Socialist trade unions in particular led to remarkable cooperation between the SPD and a government featuring the DNVP. Brauns' unemployment-insurance bill was very simple. There would be three stages of relief for the unemployed. The first would be insurance, funded by employer and employee payments fixed at 1.5% of the worker's wage. There would ten wage-classes adjusting the insurance payment to the worker's salary of the previous three months. When insurance ran out, the worker could apply for "crisis support." The states would pay 20% and the nation would pay 80% of the contributions to this fund. If the unfortunate person still could not find a position, he could apply for locally funded welfare. There was also a provision for underemployment insurance, taken partly from the temporary program of the winter of 1925-26. The SPD could only complain that the government was trying to make social policy without the Social Democrats. Walter Lambach crowed that the DNVP's social policy had proven so good that even the Communists could not complain much. On July 7, 1927, the law on labor mediation and unemployment insurance passed 355 to 47. Only the Communists and right-wing Nationalists did not support it. It was a landmark of the time, but Erich Eyck later noted that only the insurance and "crisis-support" funds could only support a maximum of 1.1 million at a time when 1.3 million were out of work.[33]

Perhaps the most remarkable development of the fourth Marx Cabinet was the renewal of the Law to Protect the Republic. The Reichstag had enacted this law in the searing days following the murder of Rathenau. It mandated sanctions against organizations, especially right-wing organizations, which opposed the Republic. The DNVP had correctly seen this as a measure aimed at it and had protested vociferously, especially against Section 23, which forbade the return of former Kaiser Wilhelm II to German soil. Many in the SPD

---

33. Stürmer, pp. 210-211. See also Patch, pp. 116-117 and John A. Leopold, *Alfred Hugenberg. The Radical Nationalist Campaign against the Weimar Republic* (New Haven: Yale University Press, 1977), p. 40, for the views of the Catholic Center and Nationalists, respectively. Leopold cites Thyssen, Emil Kirdorf, and Vögler as being especially opposed. von Hehl, p. 389. Maier, *Recasting*, p. 512. Heidrun Homburg, "From Unemployment Insurance to Compulsory Labor," in Evans and Geary, p. 77. Blaich, *Schwarze Freitag*, p. 64. VDR, *Stenographische Berichte*, vol. 393, pp. 11234-11333, 11366-11368; vol. 413, *Drucksache #2885*. Erich Eyck, *A History of the Weimar Republic* (Cambridge, MA, 1962-1963), vol. 2, p. 135. James, *Slump*, p. 53, says the bill only covered 800,000 persons.

feared that the DNVP-influenced Cabinet would fail to renew the law when it expired in July 1927, so Prussia attached the law to the Reichsrat's version of the Reich penal bill. Marx proposed a compromise: the Law should be extended for two years without any amendments. The DNVP could tell its supporters that it expected the law to expire then and would not bother with Section 23. Hergt, now Justice Minister, doubted that this would fool the DNVP or its voters. The DNVP finally agreed to extend the law. To Hergt's distress, the government motion did not specifically mention a review of Section 23, which the leftist press dubbed the "Lex Westarp." On the final vote, thirty-six Nationalists were absent. Among the notable switchers from 1922 were Hergt, Westarp, Schiele, Reichert, and Oberfohren. Only the Nazis, Hannoverians, and Communists voted no. Westarp tried to make the best of it by saying "no one among us is so silly as to regard the immediate restoration of the monarchy as a task for the present."[34] President Hindenburg was reluctant to sign the bill but relented after Marx threatened to resign.[35]

The Cabinet had more difficulty with the tariff issue. The centrist government of 1926 had amended the strict tariff law of 1925 by including some lower rates in amendments to a trade treaty with Sweden. The *Landbund* saw itself in a position of strength with Schiele back in the Cabinet as Agriculture Minister. In a lengthy letter to Marx, it demanded an increase in the tariffs of potatoes, grain, and sugar and gradual elimination of tariff-free status for frozen meat imports. It also wanted protection in treaties with France, Czechoslovakia, Spain, Canada, and especially Poland. Beyond that, the *Landbund* wanted credits for local improvements and relief from debt. These demands sabotaged the negotiations with Canada. Agricultural interests also raised the import tariff on French grain while accepting a quota of French wine imports. However, the People's party, especially Curtius and Stresemann, worried that higher agricultural tariffs would hurt German industry. The RdI supported the reduction of 559 tariff rates.[36]

The tariff law of 1925 and the provisions of 1926 were due to expire in July of 1927. Those laws had set tariffs at RM30 per ton of rye and oats, RM35 per ton of wheat, and RM22 per ton of corn. Schiele wanted additional rises in the basic tariffs for wheat, bacon, sugar, and potatoes. The Cabinet agreed to raise the tariffs for sugar and potatoes but the Reichsrat rejected this. Westarp warned the Catholic Center that the coalition would collapse if it

---

34. Quoted in Chanady, p. 80.

35. *Kabinette Marx III/IV*, Docs. #213, p. 665; #220, Note 6, p. 679; #227, pp. 712-714; #230, #232, and #233, pp. 730-743. *Vorwärts*, May 18 and 19, 1927. Josef Becker, "Josef Wirth und die Krise des Zentrum während des IV. Kabinette Marx, Darstellung und Dokumente," *Zeitschrift für die Geschichte des Oberrheins* 109 (1961), p. 380.

36. *Kabinette Marx III/IV*, Docs. #15, pp. 32-33; #193, Note #9, pp. 572-573; #199, pp. 620-621; #213, pp. 663-666; #264, p. 833.

opposed the Cabinet's resolutions. The final tariffs raised duties to RM50 a ton on oats, rye, and corn and extended them until 1930.[37]

The agricultural lobby was still not satisfied. As prices, especially meat prices, continued to fall in the summer and fall of 1927, the number of bankrupt farms increased, and the *Landbund* asked for credits and debt relief for them. Schiele complained in January 1928 that agriculture was at the very end of its strength with a total debt of RM7 billion. It was losing an additional RM1-1.25 billion a year. It needed a foreign loan, but the problems with Gilbert made this impossible. Popitz did not give him much hope: the best Schiele would get was a temporary credit, but only if the prospect of a foreign loan existed. The government declined to put it into the 1928 budget. Landowners were furious that they had not received more. They launched a tax boycott in the spring of 1928 that was most widespread in Schleswig-Holstein.[38]

In a speech to Catholic Center party members at Essen on October 30, Chancellor Marx recounted the accomplishments of his government. The party that had opposed the Republic (the DNVP) now stood by the Weimar Constitution.[39] But outside forces, particularly the combination of Schacht and Gilbert, began to fragment the alliance. Köhler compounded his blundering on the budget with a bloated raise for the civil servants. Prussia asked for another foreign loan and enraged Gilbert. The Reparations Agent issued a stinging memorandum on October 20 and jarred American investor confidence. All the efforts of the underwriters could not restore it. The crash of the Berlin bourse and the decline of German bond values in New York revealed the stark condition of the German economy. Despite a German charm offensive, the system had cracked.

Heinrich Köhler was determined to help the civil servants of the Reich from the day he took office. In the days before World War I, their pay had been low, but they enjoyed considerable prestige and job security. The events of 1923 vitiated job security, but there were more civil servants in 1925 than there had been in 1907. The inflation and revaluation had narrowed the gap between salaried employees and industrial workers. The sudden change in the fortunes of the bureaucracy was felt in the universities, where many students had enrolled to gain the credentials needed to join the civil service. The evaporation of these guaranteed lifetime jobs left many would-be professionals floundering. In the budget debate of 1927, Köhler had been confident that the money would be found to fund a supplementary budget that would feature a raise for the civil servants. Most expected that the government would ask for raises averaging 10% to 15%. At a speech before a meeting of the Reich and state civil servants

---

37. Ibid., Doc. #268, Note #5, p. 842. James, *Slump*, p. 265.

38. *Kabinette Marx III/IV*, Doc. #400, pp. 1257-1258. James, *Slump*, pp. 255-259.

39. BAK NL Pünder, vol. 95, pp. 189-191.

in Magdeburg, Köhler apparently got carried away with himself before his old comrades and pledged the government's support for a program that would raise the average salary by 25%. This appalled many. Koch-Weser did not see how the Democratic party, which had many civil servants as members, could possibly fight such a popular bill. Their officials' union had merged with the Catholic Center's union in October 1926. The People's party and Nationalists also expressed doubt over the amount of the raise. The Social Democrats had decided at their Kiel party Congress in May to woo white collar workers and civil servants and supported the bill.[40]

The Prussian civil servants would gain the same percentage raise as the Reich civil servants, which meant that as much as the bill bloated the Reich budget, it would bloat the Prussian budget.[41] Köhler was confident that he would need no new taxes to pay for the raise. The income received so far in the year had exceeded the estimates in almost every category. Although Gilbert had not objected earlier to a proposed 10% raise, he now warned that this larger raise would cost over a billion Marks a year and endanger German credit. These lavish increases angered Stegerwald because there was nothing similar for his unions. He wanted to see a system of untenured temporary employees supplant the old-fashioned civil service. Increasingly, the position and rhetoric of the Christian trade unions came to resemble those of the socialists in their demands for huge wage increases. Brüning, the general manager of the Catholic unions, also complained because of his fear of an unbalanced budget and his union connection. Köhler charged that Stegerwald had a lifelong dream of merging the Catholic and Socialist trade unions and saw the issue as a means to that end. The rifts in the Catholic Center almost sank the measure. The parliament defeated an amendment of Hermann Müller that would have linked civil service wages to workers' wages. The vote was 189 to 200 with seventeen abstentions. Thirteen Catholic Centrists broke ranks and voted for the amendment and ten members from the Bavarian People's party abstained, but eighteen negative votes from the Democrats doomed it. The Reichstag approved

---

40. James, *Slump*, p. 41. L. E. Jones, *German Liberalism*, p. 251; Maier, *Recasting*, p. 513. Konrad H. Jarausch, "The Crisis of German Professionals, 1918-33," *Journal of Contemporary History*, 20 (1985), p. 384. Hermann Fischer, "Die Finanzen des Reiches," *Zehn Jahre deutsche Republik*, ed. Anton Erkelenz (Berlin, 1928), p. 440. A. Barteld, "Die deutsche Beamtenbewegung," ibid., p. 349. BAK R 43 I/1424, pp. 110-112. Patch, p. 119.

41. In a joint Cabinet session of the Reich and Prussia, the following increases were agreed to on September 10: Groups thirteen and fourteen would receive RM1,500; group eleven would receive an 18.3% raise; group ten 22.9%; group nine 20.5%; group eight 24.1%; group seven 17.4%; group six 21.3% to 21.8%; group five 15%; groups three and four 10.2%, group two 17.8%, and group one 17.7%. Note that in the German system the higher the number, the lower the rank and the pay. BAK R 43 I/1424, pp. 159-164R.

the raise 333 to 53, but there were sixteen abstentions, including Brüning, Ersing, and Stegerwald.    Prussian Premier Braun worried about the budget impact, but because of the overwhelming vote, the Reichsrat had no right to overrule the Reichstag.[42]

The civil-service raise had numerous ill effects.  Gilbert estimated a direct impact on the Reich's budget of RM325 million additional annual spending, including RM155 million in salaries and RM170 million in pensions. But when he added the parallel increase in the states, localities, railroads, and postal service, he estimated additional spending of between RM1.2 billion to 1.5 billion.  Table 6.6 takes the most conservative estimate of the impact of the raise and ends before the reductions in salaries and personnel of the Brüning years. One may presume that the states and communes would not have needed all the money transferred by the Reich were it not for the raises.  A saving of up to RM200 million would change the amounts needed to cover loans and reduce the debt.  The key number is the surplus generated for FY29, when everything fell apart.  The civil-service raise was the first great crack in the German fiscal system.  The loss of Gilbert's support marked the second great crack because it brought an end to the steady flow of American long-term loans.

Though Gilbert's patience had worn thin by September of 1927, the Prussian government pushed ahead with another foreign loan.  Höpker-Aschoff told Köhler he could not delay a loan.  The Prussian Landtag had passed measures appropriating RM80 million more for construction and RM100 million in productive unemployment-relief, and the uncovered debt of the state had grown dangerously large.  Prussia would not consider an internal loan because of the weakness of the domestic market since the Reinhold loan.  Harris, Forbes would again lead the consortium in New York.  Prussia had contracted for a $30 million loan to run for twenty-five years at a 6% face value.  The loan would cover agricultural demands and harbor expansion, so its productivity "cannot be doubted."[43]

The conflicts among the desires of Prussia and the Reparations Agent and the needs of the German economy led to an open fight on the Advisory Board.  The representative of the Reichsbank did not believe that foreign loans benefited the German economy and that loans to localities were especially suspect.  This was the same line that Schacht had been peddling for a year and a half, but now he was stepping up his attack. He would seek a tightening of the

---

42.  BAK NL 5 (Pünder), vol. 95, pp. 195-200.  Wandel, p. 168, from the official *Wirtschaft und Statistik*, quotes a RM380 million deficit for FY27.  Balderston, *Financial Crisis*, p. 226, says the deficit was RM457 million.  Krosigk, p. 38.  Braun, p. 232.  Patch, pp. 119-124.  James, *Slump*, p. 168.  Köhler, pp. 257-259.  Haungs, p. 55.  Von Hehl, pp. 425-426.  *VdR, Stenographische Berichte*, vol. 394, pp. 12116-12125.

43.  BAK  R 2/2009, October 3, 1927.  R 2/2091, September 17, 1927, described the Prussian requests.

Table 6.6

**Direct Impact of Civil-Service Raises on Reich Budget (billions of RM)**

| Gilbert's Budget Statements--Actual | | | | **Adjusted by Gilbert's estimates for raises in BAK R 43 I/276, p. 30.** | | |
|---|---|---|---|---|---|---|
| | 1927-28 | 1928-29 | 1929-30 | 1927-28 | 1928-29 | 1929-30 |
| **Revenues** | | | | | | |
| Tax Revenues | 8.490 | 9.025 | 9.096 | 8.490 | 9.025 | 9.096 |
| Administrative Revenues | 0.471 | 0.626 | 0.815 | 0.471 | 0.626 | 0.815 |
| Surplus Brought Over | 0.259 | 0.217 | -0.704 | 0.259 | **0.298** | **-0.449** |
| Proceeds of Loans   A | 0.123 | 0.101 | 1.192 | 0.123 | 0.101 | 1.192 |
| Transfers from Special Working Fund | 0.190 | 0.062 | | 0.190 | 0.062 | |
| Industrial Charge | | | 0.150 | | | 0.150 |
| **GRAND TOTAL** | 9.533 | 10.031 | 10.549 | 9.533 | 10.112 | 10.804 |
| **Expenditures** | | | | | | |
| Payments to States/ Communes | 3.016 | 3.413 | 3.299 | 3.016 | 3.413 | 3.299 |
| General Administrative | 2.296 | 2.401 | 2.399 | 2.296 | 2.401 | 2.399 |
| Social Spending | 0.766 | 1.101 | 1.345 | 0.766 | 1.101 | 1.345 |
| Internal War Charges | 1.560 | 1.915 | 1.752 | 1.560 | 1.915 | 1.752 |
| **Restriction of Civil-service Raises to 10%** | | | | **-.081** | **-.325** | **-.325** |
| Execution of Dawes Plan | 0.899 | 1.220 | 0.665 | 0.899 | 1.220 | 0.665 |
| Execution of Young Plan | | | 0.410 | | | 0.410 |
| Capital Investments and Grants | 0.267 | 0.334 | 0.305 | 0.267 | 0.334 | 0.305 |
| Reduction of Debt    B | 0.512 | 0.502 | 0.673 | 0.512 | 0.502 | 0.673 |
| **GRAND TOTAL** | 9.316 | 10.886 | 10.848 | **9.235** | **10.561** | **10.523** |
| Balance | .217 | -.855 | -.299 | **.298** | **-.449** | **.281** |

*Source*: Schuker, *Reparations*, p. 26.

Advisory Board's guidelines. Furthermore, he would oppose all loans to public corporations.  Krosigk worried that the Prussians and Harris, Forbes were making the same claims for security that so upset Gilbert the year before.[44]

---

44.  BAK R 2/2091, September 20, 1927.

The Board approved the Prussian loan, but Köhler warned Pünder of the change in Reichsbank opinion.   Embassy Councillor Alfred Vallette recounted the attacks by the press in London on loans to Germany.  This came at a time when long-term foreign loans had strengthened.  The rise in the discount rate had restored incentive for foreign investors.  From January to April 1927 German public and private concerns had offered only RM140 million in long-term credits.  From June to August this had shot up to RM650 million, including RM400 million from the United States alone.  Foreign loans for 1927 were now only RM270 million behind the pace of 1926.  The new Prussian proposal set off a firestorm.  Gilbert was incensed.  Since January, when he had protested the 1926 Prussian loan and Dulles had countered him, he had seen Köhler condemn the Dawes Plan and the government ignore his warning against excessive raises for the civil servants.  It was futile to appeal the decision of the Board.  The Germans knew how strongly he felt about the priorities of payments and had gone ahead anyway.  The Reparations Agent turned to Washington to ban the marketing of the Prussian loan in the United States.  He repeated the complaints of the year before and added a new reason: the firm opposition of the Reichsbank to this loan.  Dulles, again acting as general counsel for Harris, Forbes, sought to obtain a personal opinion from Assistant Secretary of State Castle.[45]

The crisis over the Prussian loan led Schacht to issue an ultimatum and withdraw his representative from the Advisory Board.  Schacht told the leaders of the German Congress of Cities that he wanted foreign loans brought under control.  He did not care about unemployment or if the jobless rioted and spilled blood.   Both Gilbert and the British officials noted that the Reichsbank President's mood swings were becoming more violent and feared that Schacht was scheming to undermine the entire reparations agreement.  Schacht's moves made reconsideration of the guidelines and organization of the Board inevitable.  Schacht was angry that the Cabinet had not yet answered his letter demanding a reduction in public debt and a reform in administration.  Pünder suggested expanding the Advisory Board to include a representative from the business community or another high official.  Curtius condemned Schacht for raising the discount rate to 7%.  The Economics Minister would not stand for any veto by the Reichsbank.  Höpker-Aschoff noted that it was not the State Department that stood against the loan, but Schacht and Gilbert because they thought it in conflict with Article 248 of the Treaty of Versailles.  Prussia had already cut the amount for the loan from RM200 million to RM120 million on Schacht's recommendation.  What would it take to satisfy him?  Prussia welcomed sharper guidelines against borrowing by localities.  The Braun government had long tried to police

---

45. BAK R 2/2091, September 21, 1927. *Kabinette Marx III/IV*, Doc. #301, pp. 929-930. *ADAP*, Series B: 1925-33, vol. VI, Docs. #224, pp. 488-490; #235, pp. 509-511.

the loans by the communes in its area, but other states had not been as diligent. Prussia's debt was smaller and better structured than that of Bavaria (see Table 6.7). Curtius noted that Article 248 obliged neither the Reichsbank nor the government to block a loan in conflict with the treaty guidelines. Marx sharply rebuked Schacht. Schacht assured the Chancellor that there were no more disputes, but he felt bound by a promise he had made to American bankers in 1925 to maintain austerity on the Advisory Board.[46]

Prussia received loan approval in October as it found a way of harmonizing the language of Versailles and the Dawes Plan. The press expected another billion Marks of Prussian communal loans, but Schacht was determined to prevent that. The Cabinet wrote new guidelines for the Advisory Board that were more amenable to Schacht's way of thinking and removed the representative of the Labor Ministry. It would make a concerted effort to deny short-term loans to localities and local associations. From October 1927 to May 1928 the Advisory Board blocked all new foreign loans for states and localities.[47]

Gilbert now took his campaign to a new level. He drafted a lengthy memorandum reiterating his previous objections to German fiscal policy and sent it to the leading officials of the government. Word would undoubtedly leak out and make it more difficult for the Germans to raise funds abroad. Gilbert enclosed copies of his 1926 letters on the security of the Prussian loan of that year and a March 1927 letter opposing the budget plan to increase transfers of income to the states. Gilbert said his purpose was to call "attention to the dangers involved in the present economic situation, in the hope that by doing so fully and frankly at this time I may render some service to the German government and to the German economy as well as to the international situation generally."[48] The Reparations Agent stressed gradual improvements in the standard of living and gradual wage increases. Germany needed to repair its capital reserves by providing incentives for savings and by maintaining a well-ordered public finance. Although Gilbert admitted that an economic crisis had not yet occurred, he urged the government to clean up its act, especially on the civil-service raise. The American traced the beginning of the problem to the passage of the supplementary budget for 1926, which had added nearly a billion Marks to the budget, for a total of RM8.534 billion. The draft budget for 1927 contained RM8.525 billion, almost equal to all expenditures for 1926. The negotiations had added another RM600 million. The budget debate and the new unemployment-payments law mandated further assumptions of spending by the

---

46. Upmeier in Hansmeyer, p. 165. McNeil, pp. 173-174. See especially Gilbert's letter of September 8, 1927, to Strong, cited in James, *Slump*, p. 61, and Wandel, p. 106. *Kabinette Marx III/IV*, Docs. #310, pp. 955-960; #312-313, pp. 961-982.

47. *Kabinette Marx III/IV*, p. LXXXI. *Berliner Morgenpost*, October 11, 1927, in BAP R 8034 II/4601. BAK R 43 I/656, pp. 318, 324-328.

48. BAK R 43 I/276, p. 23.

**Table 6.7**
**The Structure of Prussian and Bavarian Debt, 1927**

## PRUSSIAN LOANS

| Description | Due | Amount (RM) |
|---|---|---|
| **Domestic Loans** | | |
| 5% Fertilizer Loan of 1923 | 1928 | 16,294,950 |
| 5% Roggenwert-Loan of 1923 | 1928 | 3,936,457 |
| 6½% Treasury Notes of 1926 | March 1, 1929 | 30,000,000 |
| 6½% Treasury Notes of 1926 | October 1, 1930 | 30,000,000 |
| 6½% Treasury Notes of 1926 | October 1, 1930 | 40,000,000 |
| One-to-three-month treasury transfers | | 70,000,000 |
| **Foreign Loans** | | |
| 6½% Loan of 1926 | September 15, 1951 | 84,000,000 |
| GRAND TOTAL | | 274,231,407 |

## BAVARIAN LOANS

| Description | Due | Amount (RM) |
|---|---|---|
| **Domestic Loans** | | |
| 6% Loan of 1927 | 1953 | 63,000,000 |
| 7% Treasury Notes | | 50,000,000 |
| **Foreign Loans** | | |
| 6½% Loan of 1925 | 1945 | 63,000,000 |
| 6½% Loan of 1926 | 1945 | 42,000,000 |
| 6½% Loan of 1927 | | 63,000,000 |
| 5% Treasury Notes of May 1927 | June 1928 | 84,000,000 |
| | | 365,000,000 |

*Source*: *Berliner Lokal-Anzeiger*, September 21, 1927, in BAP R 8034 II/4601.

Note: Prussia owed RM129 million and Bavaria RM15 million to public creditors (Reich and states), *Finanzen und Steuern*, p. 296.

national government and gave more tax revenue to the states. Finally, the Finance Minister's proposal for the civil servants would cost the Reich RM155 million in salaries and RM170 million in pensions, but this increase would filter down to the states, communes, postal service, and railroads, and add another RM1.2 billion to 1.5 billion annually. The Agent General was mortified to hear discussions of yet other expenditures contemplated by the government. A plan to compensate German citizens for property confiscated abroad would cost up to a billion Marks. A proposed school law would probably add considerable expense, especially for the states and localities. The Reich had set a bad example for these other governments, which had gorged themselves on foreign credits since 1925. He welcomed the decision to revise the guidelines for the Advisory Board. In conclusion, Gilbert praised the energy and industry of the

German people, which had accomplished many positive goals since the passage of the Dawes Plan. All might be for naught if public spending were not checked.[49]

Köhler attempted to dismiss the memo as a repetition of Gilbert's June report. Furthermore, he urged that the Cabinet keep the memo secret since "Gilbert wanted it that way." Brauns and Stresemann wanted at least partial publication of the memo, and Curtius suggested the preparation of a "counter-memo" to refute Gilbert. Gilbert read Köhler's assertion in the newspapers and replied that the German government could do as it pleased and urged publication to avoid confusion in the newspapers.[50] Köhler's credibility had been completely destroyed. His name had become synonymous with incompetence, and the reparations expert in the Foreign Ministry called him "that old muddle-headed fool."[51] Köhler responded on October 26 by reassuring the Budget Committee that he would not require new taxes to pay for the civil-service raise. If the economy remained healthy, the Reich would gain RM300 million above the estimated revenue. The Reich would save RM95 million in unemployment relief alone since the jobless rate was falling. In total, there would be RM500 million more available for spending; the Reich could pay for the civil-service raise easily. He did concede that Fiscal Year 1928 would be difficult to manage with at least RM500 million more needed, mostly for reparations.[52]

As the German government debated its response to Gilbert's memo, Wall Street recoiled from its impact (see Figure 6.2). Prices of German bonds fell. The brokerage houses that still held a large volume of German bonds began a campaign to counteract Gilbert's negative assessment of the German situation. British Ambassador Robert Lindsay said that "every bank in the eastern United States seems to have indulged in German loans."[53] Leading the charge was Harris, Forbes. Its October 25 daily letter to salesmen emphasized the bonds for the German Central Bank of Agriculture: "We all know how important it is that Germany be made self-supporting so far as possible from the standpoint of foodstuffs. . . . Never mind that many of your customers already have their quota of foreign bonds. The country is full of people to whom we have not yet sold any foreign bonds and it is our job to find them."[54] The next

---

49. BAK R 43 I/276, pp. 21-44.

50. BAK R 43 I/1424, p. 322. McNeil, p. 183, charges that Köhler's assertion of Gilbert's desire for secrecy was a "total fabrication."

51. McNeil, p. 185, recounts a number of scathing comments by prominent personalities against Köhler.

52. BAK NL Pünder, vol. 95, pp. 195-200.

53. Lindsay to Chamberlain, *DBFP*, 1919-39, Series IA, vol. 4, Doc. #24, pp. 57-59.

54. Harris, Forbes, "Daily Letter to Salesmen," October 25, 1927, from PA, Auswärtiges Amt, Wirtschaft Reparationen, Aktennummer L199, Priority Questions, vol. 1.

**Figure 6.2**
**Measure of Confidence: German and American Bond Prices on the U.S. Market**

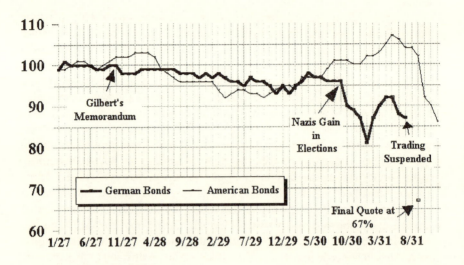

*Source* : Balderston, p. 210.

daily letter continued this theme. The discussion of the priority question was "mainly academic," and Harris, Forbes predicted that it would fade away within thirty days. If clients expressed doubt about the German economy, salesmen should point to a recent *Wall Street Journal* article on the robust state of Germany. On October 27 the firm added a new article from the *New York Times* to its argument. The *Times* had reported that the American share in German loans had fallen from 75% to 53.6%. It saw this as reflecting a growing wariness in the United States toward the Germans. Harris, Forbes emphasized the positive: the English share had grown from 8% to 17% and the Dutch share from 12% to 20.4%. These countries were "closer to the German situation" and had poured much money into Germany recently, accounting for the decline of the U.S. share.[55] Harris, Forbes kept issuing daily letters to its salesmen with titles such as "German fundamental conditions improve," emphasizing Köhler's revised revenue estimates. As the aftershock of Gilbert's memo roiled the market, the letters took on a harder edge. On November 9 the letter informed the salesmen that German municipal indebtedness was no more than one-fifth of the prewar total. It reported the comments of a high official at Harris, Forbes: "The great big job that we have on our hands at the present time is to sell these bonds and there is no use in trying to hide the fact. Now

---

55. Harris, Forbes, "Daily Letter to Salesmen," October 26 and 27, 1927, ibid.

we cannot sell these bonds if we quit on them. Fundamentally, the situation has not changed at all, and the market situation is the result of a lot of newspaper comment."[56]

The *Economist* noted "signs of private extravagance and of maladministration of public finance" during the last twelve months.[57] Walter Bell of Harris, Forbes and Robert Hayward of Dillon Read both gave statements reiterating full confidence in the Germans. The brokers played up Senator Carter Glass' attack on the State Department. Glass, the ranking Democrat on the Banking Committee, said that the department had no right to restrict commerce by approving or disapproving loans. The trustees of the large brokerages feared a torrent of lawsuits from angry investors if prices plunged. The Guaranty Trust Company also sent out a special letter of assurance, as did J. Henry Schroeder and Company, a longtime ally of the German government. One unidentified New York trust company did send out a letter urging its clients to dump all their German securities, but generally the brokers lined up to defend the bonds. This gave truth to the old maxim that a banker who gives out a small loan acquires a debtor while he who gives out a large loan acquires a partner. By the end of November the prices for German bonds had stabilized at a level of about two to eight points below their October prices. The brokers had prevented a crash, but there was little prospect that the market would accept any more long-term issues in significant volume. While Germany placed more debt on foreign markets in 1928 than it had in 1927, it was mostly short-term. Most of the German bonds sold in the first three months of 1928 were from public utilities. After June of 1928, French short-term money replaced American long-term bonds as the most popular form of credit.[58]

The Germans finally sent their response on November 6. It was generally conciliatory. The government would delay a compensation bill at least a year, it would fully fund any school law, and it promised sharper control over state and local loans and administrative simplification. It insisted that the loans had gone for productive purposes. It would pare down the extraordinary budget and finally settle the financial compromise with the states when there was a "normal" year to act as benchmark. Wall Street was not impressed, and the French suspected German duplicity. The Germans received secret information suggesting that the British government did not agree with Gilbert and felt that

---

56. Harris, Forbes, "Daily Letter to Salesmen," letter of November 9, ibid. These letters were apparently given to Karl Ritter of the Foreign Office by Franklin Stallforth, the European representative of Harris, Forbes.

57. The *Economist*, November 19, 1927, ibid.

58. Press statements from Bell and Hayward; Glass quoted in the *Literary Digest*, November 5, 1927, p. 13; *New York Journal of Commerce*, November 16 and December 8, 1927, all in ibid. Also see Sonderreferat Wirtschaft, Finanzwesen 2: Loans and Bonds, vol. 3, Note of November 2. Balderston, *Financial Crisis*, pp. 205-213. McNeil, p. 198. James, *Reichsbank*, p. 105.

his memo had been counterproductive. Strong also felt the Reparations Agent had gone a bit too far. He argued that Gilbert must preserve the market for "sound and reasonable" German loans, and urged cooperation in devising "reasonable and proper measures to protect our investors."[59]

The system responsible for Germany's prosperity was collapsing. The underwriters, long the best friends of the German government, recognized that something had changed. Dr. Bernhard Endrucks, the representative of J. Henry Schroeder and Company, wrote that the firm had used its "full strength" to enhance the world position of the German economy. It had tried to increase exports while decreasing imports to gain a favorable trade balance and prevent capital from flowing out. It had tried to protect German credit. Now Germany was facing difficulties, the balance of both trade and payment was unfavorable, and a turnaround seemed impossible.[60]

Although officially optimistic and defiant, Köhler privately was very pessimistic. He conceded that Gilbert had been correct. In January 1928, Köhler brought a RM500 million supplementary budget (to the FY27 budget) before the Reichstag. Most of this went to pay for the civil-service raises. RM190 million from operating funds and the RM400 million Reichsbank allowance would cover it. The Finance Ministry did cut the extraordinary part of the 1928 budget, as promised in the "countermemo" of November. By the time the Reichstag began to debate the FY28 budget, Köhler was looking at an uncovered debt of about a billion Marks (see Table 6.8). The situation was not as bad as it appeared at first light. The Reich never needed half of the credit authority requested by Reinhold, so the true level of the uncovered credit was only RM386 million. It could remain uncovered until 1929. Köhler wanted a special committee for budget reductions, but the Interior, Labor, Transport, and Agriculture Ministries fought this idea tooth and nail. This forced Köhler to make small reductions in the 1927 Supplementary Budget still before the Reichstag. Köhler's concern over the debt situation could not have been that deep since he increased aid to agriculture and some pensions in the new budget. Although its coalition collapsed over the defeat of the school bill in February 1928, the Marx government still made sure the budget was finished punctually. The opposition SPD had no interest in blocking this budget. The government issued about RM100 million in 7% Treasury transfers and medium-term notes to cover the new budget and previous allowances. When Brüning helped put Köhler in the Finance Ministry, he thought there would be a cautious and solid fiscal policy. The 1928 budget would have been difficult to balance simply

59. HSA Köln, NL Marx, vol. 72, p. 74, October 25, 1927. *ADAP*, Series B: 1925-33, vol. VII, Docs. #63, pp. 148-150; #78, pp. 180-181; #82, Note #3, p. 188. Link, p. 417.

60. PA, Auswärtiges Amt, Aktennummer K516 Finanzwesen 2: Loans and Bonds, vol. 3, November 15, 1927.

**Table 6.8**
**The Structure of Reich Debt, December 31, 1927**

| Credits Authorized | | Covering | |
|---|---|---|---|
| Treasury Transfer of 1923 "K" | 554,054 | Treasury Transfers of 1923 | 10,981,577 |
| Treasury Transfer of 1923, due 9/2/35 (Gold Loan) | 17,702,626 | Rentenbank | 344,295,541 |
| 6% Treasury Transfer of 1923 | 1,190,209 | 1927 "Reinhold Loan" | 452,500,000 |
| Rentenbank Loan | 763,403,428 | Miscellaneous | 3,444 |
| FY25 Laws of 3/27/25 and 1/30/26 | 62,369,301 | | |
| Construction Law of 3/26/26 | 200,000,000 | | |
| FY26 Budget Law of 3/31/26 | 293,824,650 | | |
| Supplementary FY25 Budget Law of 5/22/26 | 37,630,699 | | |
| Second Supplementary FY26 Budget Law of 1/18/27 | 345,964,470 | | |
| Total | 1,722,639,437 | | 807,780,562 |
| Uncovered | 914,858,875 | Need to cover | 75,069,755 |

*Sources*: *Verhandlungen deutsches Reichsrat* 1927, Drucksache #39. Reichsrat 1928, Drucksache #105. PrStA Hauptabteilung I, Rep. 90, Abt. E III, 1, #2, vol. 5.

because the Dawes Plan demanded higher payments, but Köhler's excessive civil-service raises threw it deeply out of balance. Many budget problems of the next three years would come from trying to swallow the FY28 deficit. Another problem was that the amount of debt repayment stopped growing. While the Germans could argue that they were taking less in loans (Gilbert's "A") as well, debt repayment is always an excellent way to build investor confidence. Köhler should have added another RM110 million to debt reduction, simply to reassure investors after the shaky Reinhold loan. With a lower raise and a higher debt repayment, Germany would have returned to a surplus budget in 1929 and entered the Depression with more investor confidence.  It also would have averted the immediate cause of the confrontation with Schacht that triggered the Christmas crisis of 1929.[61]

It is important to review the economic and financial situation before the elections that ushered in a new government.  For the next four years, government leaders would complain that they were forced to take drastic actions because of the actions of their predecessors, notably Reinhold and Köhler. Analysts have charged that the excesses of the mid-1920s made the Depression much worse for Germany.

There are several ways of looking at the budget and debt in 1928. Table 6.8 shows the government's own figures.  At first glance, the amount of uncovered debt seems quite large.  One must bear in mind that there was a two-year grace period for covering debt because revenues credited to the fiscal year would continue to trickle in.  What seemed to be debts of RM940 million from the Reinhold era turned out to be RM411 million fifteen months later.  The grace period also meant that the government only had to cover credits through FY25 as of March 31, 1928.  That amount was only RM75 million, which Köhler covered with Treasury transfers and medium-term Treasury notes.  We must use the same qualifiers when examining the total Reich debt.  The official total was RM7.66 billion (about 9% of Net National Product), but more than RM5 billion of that was debt from before the stabilization revalued at 15% and subject to so many conditions that it was never repaid. (See Table 6.9.) Germany's debt service was far less than that of either Great Britain or France. Balderston maintains that the Reich ran a deficit every year, but he arrives at those numbers by excluding the proceeds of the Dawes Loan of 1924 and the subsequent use of the funds over the next several years.  His omission of this from the annual cash figure along with credits from the Reichsbank creates a misleading impression.

Comparing budget estimates also raises the problem of whether to include state, local, and public institutional spending.  Raymond Cohn compared budgets used by Harold James (who says that the Reich/social insurance fund deficit for FY27 was RM160 million, and for FY28 RM387 million), Richard Overy (who finds the Reich FY28 deficit at RM2,063 million), and Walther Hoffmann (who used different calculations to find a total government deficit of RM1,440 million in 1927 and RM771 million in 1928).  These wildly varying figures, to which we may add Gilbert's report of a FY28 deficit of RM859 million and FY29 deficit of RM298 million, depend on whether one uses Reich figures alone or additional public budgets.  Balderston's "consolidated fiscal balance" shows a RM2.39 billion and RM2.2 billion deficit for FY28 and

61. *Kabinette Marx III/IV*, Docs. #330, pp. 1031-1034; #418, pp. 1304-1306; #422, p. 1313; #426, pp. 1321-1333. Dieckmann, p. 69. Reichsrat 1930, *Drucksache* #24.  Blaich, *Schwarze Freitag*, p. 92.

**Table 6.9**

**The Development of Total Reich Debt, 1927-1929 (in Reichsmarks)**

|  | 1927 | 3/31/29 | 12/31/29 |
|---|---|---|---|
| Prestabilization Debt | 5,247,834,500 | 5,086,146,225 | 4,936,900,000 |
| Treasury Transfer of 1923 "K" | 587,950 | 501,400 | 400,000 |
| Treasury Transfer of 1923, due 9/2/35 (Gold Loan) | 18,785,644 | 18,341,787 | 18,300,000 |
| 6% Treasury Transfer of 1923, due 12/1/32 | 1,263,024 | 1,252,629 | 1,252,629 |
| Rentenbank Loan | 810,107,205 | 655,605,128 | 550,600,000 |
| Debt at the Reichsbank | 208,408,000 | 190,340,000 | 190,340,000 |
| Dawes Loan | 903,539,546 | 877,136,192 | 826,700,000 |
| 5% "Reinhold Loan" of 1927 | 470,000,000 | 500,000,000 | 500,000,000 |
| 7% Treasury Transfer of 1928 |  | 23,130,000 | 23,130,000 |
| 7% Debt-Notes 1929-32 Law of 3/31/28 |  | 79,600,000 | 79,600,000 |
| 2/8/29 Treasury Transfers for Romania |  | 45,000,000 | 30,000,000 |
| 7¼% Credit Line of Dillon Read |  |  | 210,000,000 |
| War Damage Liquidation Certificates |  |  | 957,600,000 |
| 7% "Hilferding Loan" of 1929 |  |  | 183,000,000 |
| 7% Treasury Transfers of 1929 |  |  | 132,200,000 |
| Nondiscountable Treasury Certificates |  | 200,000,000 | 952,600,000 |
| Bills Discountable at Reichsbank |  | 383,000,000 | 375,000,000 |
| Special Loans |  | 135,000,000 | 117,100,000 |
| TOTAL | 7,660,525,869 | 8,195,053,361 | 10,084,722,629 |
| Real Debt | 2,412,691,369 | 3,108,907,136 | 5,147,822,629 |
| Publicly Held Debt | 1,373,539,546 | 1,377,136,192 | 1,509,700,000 |
| Short- and Medium-Term Debt | 229,044,618 | 1,076,165,816 | 2,129,922,629 |

*Sources*: *Verhandlungen deutsches Reichsrat* 1930. Drucksache #24. *Finanzen und Steuern*, p. 294. S. Parker Gilbert, Report of the Agent General for Reparations, May 17, 1930 (London, 1930).

FY29 respectively. His comparable Reich figures are RM1.38 billion and RM827 million. What are we to make of all this? We can see the general direction of the budget, but the degree of the deficit is quite different. I have decided to focus on the Reich budget, and its related social insurance budgets to a lesser degree. First of all, these budgets are more precise. More research is needed to see if the actual budgets of the states and localities match the consolidated reports of the Statistical Office. The second reason is that during the Depression the Reich's budget policy had a powerful impact on the policies of the states. Reich budgets increasingly overshadowed the states with the end of the period of easy foreign credit. Cohn introduced the new wrinkle of the "high employment budget" to put all of the contrasting budget numbers into context. This economic theory calculates the surplus or deficit that would have occurred with the existing tax rates and government spending if employment was at its maximum. Cohn takes the 1937 German Net National Product (NNP) as a baseline for maximum employment and finds that even with this, the FY28 budget ran a deficit between 0.3% and 2.4% of the economic baseline. This is roughly equivalent to the deficits of the United States during the late 1970s. What is startling is that Cohn suggests that an increasingly restrictive fiscal policy began in 1929. This shows that the fiscal policy of 1926-27 had not inflicted lasting damage at all. The real problems would begin with the excessive civil-service raises of 1928 and then the start of the Depression in 1929.[62]

But could the earlier fiscal policy have caused or contributed to the German Depression? For Balderston, the credit squeeze of 1927-28 was the real beginning of the Depression in Germany. The further decline of fixed investment and the stock market drove economic decline. Harold James notes five basic weaknesses in the Weimar economy: (1) an over-organized industrial sector that tended to cut production first instead of prices, (2) the continued *Junker* domination of agriculture, leading to protective tariffs, (3) a rigid wage structure due to labor unions, (4) employer complaints about taxes, and (5) the ongoing drain of reparations. James makes clear that many of these problems were not unique to Germany. Unlike Britain and France, however, Germany had escaped from its heavy burden of debt. In 1931, only 2.9% of the German budget was dedicated to debt service, a significant increase over 1925, but paltry compared to Great Britain, which devoted 28% of its budget to debt service. If one counted reparations as a German form of "debt service," even a full Dawes payment of RM2.5 billion only amounted to 10% of the total German federal, state, and local budget. On the other hand, German taxes took 26% of

62. Brecht, p. 277. Brandes, p. 190. Mommsen, *Rise and Fall*, p. 185. Balderston, *Financial Crisis*, pp. 226-234, 268. Raymond L. Cohn, "Fiscal Policy in Germany during the Great Depression," in Komlos and Eddie, eds., pp. 274-281.

the national income compared to 22% in Britain, 18% in France, and 11% in the United States.[63]

Over the last twenty years, critics have claimed that excessive taxes and spending by the Weimar governments and excessive workers' wages damaged the economy. They have cited two areas: capital shortages and productivity. Businesses complained about taxes: Duisberg pointed out in 1927 that 309 of the 850 companies listed on the Berlin Bourse paid no dividend and that the average dividend yield had fallen from 10% in 1913 to 6.75%. However, company profits had grown enormously during the war. The companies studied by Gerald Feldman reported a 34% growth in earnings from 1913 to 1918 and a lesser growth in dividends. Most modern companies prefer to keep their dividend yields low so that they may reinvest profits in the company. We should also note that 1927 yields would be peculiarly low because of the doubling of stock prices since 1925. The stock price rises and attracts investors. Microsoft, for example, has never offered dividend payments. The natural place to assess the supply of capital and demand for capital is interest rates. We have already noted that German rates were higher than those in the United States or Britain. Fixed currency rates also excluded that form of adjustment. Balderston argued that the tight monetary policy and high interest rates of the Reichsbank and the weakness in the internal market were due to the inflation. Interest rates had to be kept high to keep capital from flowing out, and credit had been "annihilated" during the inflation, especially by the liquidation of state debt. The only occasions when Germany's discount rate approached world levels were January to June of 1927 and January of 1929, and both times the Reichsbank's reserves suffered.[64] The balance of payments abroad was also generally in deficit causing a further outflow of capital. One could consider higher interest rates an additional "debt service" from the war. Whichever set of economic numbers one takes, government revenues as a percentage of the economy clearly fell from 1926 to 1929. Firms seemed to get all of the capital they wanted. If there was a capital squeeze, it was a *chronic* squeeze dating back before the war. There was pressure on the German bond market in the years before 1914 and Germany did not have enough public or private capital to effect an economic foreign policy. Interest rate premiums were greater than Britain's but not as high as Poland's, and the German private and public sectors had reached an

---

63. Balderston, *Financial Crisis*, pp. 156, 217. James, *Slump*, pp. 17-21, 48. Tax figures from PA, Auswärtiges Amt, Wirtschaft Reparationen: America's Position and Critique of Dawes Plan, vol. 9, April 16, 1927.

64. *New York Times*, Sept. 7, 1927 from PA, Auswärtiges Amt, Wirtschafts Reparationen, Section 2A: Germany: Consideration of German Credit, vol. 2. Feldman, *Army*, p. 469. Balderston, "The Origins of Economic Instability in Germany 1924-1930: Market Forces versus Economic Policy," *Vierteljahrschrift für Sozial- und Wirtschafts-geschichte*, 69. Band, Heft 4 (1982), p. 493.

accommodation in the years before 1930. The reasons for the collapse are to be found in specific events of 1930 and 1931.

Did the increase of public and private sector wages hurt productivity? Knut Borchardt charged that wages exceeded productivity in the Weimar years. This cut profit margins, discouraged investment, and made German export goods too expensive for the world market.[65] This thesis led to a cottage industry comparing different measures of wages and productivity. We may start with some basics. The percentage of men and women in the active labor force (employed and unemployed) grew.[66] However, the work week decreased from 49.8 hours in 1924 to 48.8 hours in 1929. Therefore, the overall productivity of the population may have grown with regular employment replacing army drudgery, but the productivity of the *workforce* fell. Due to the monetary upheaval of the twelve-year crisis, many Germans who had been living off financial assets had to get jobs. James notes that in 1927 hourly wages increased 9%, while productivity grew 5%; in 1928, the comparable figures were 12% and 4.8%. Carl-Ludwig Holtfrerich, the most persistent critic of the Borchardt thesis, argues that productivity looks better when measured on a man-hour basis. This shows a 5.6% annual increase from 1925-29, superior to the 1.8% annual increase of 1850-1913 or the 4.7% annual growth of the Federal Republic in the 1950s. Balderston splits the difference: productivity exceeded wages in 1925-26, but was exceeded in 1927-28. It all depended on the sector. He found no detectable decline in competitiveness until 1930. Clearly we are not arguing over huge differences. James suggested there was a catchup process: from 1880-1913, German wages constantly lagged behind productivity gains, especially right before the war. Balderston noted that wages rose faster from 1924 to 1929 (60%) than in the entire post-depression period from 1893 to 1913 (55%). On the other hand, Mark Spoerer has found legal records suggesting that corporate profits were larger than reported.[67]

The beginning of the Depression did not hit Germany any worse than the rest of the world. The postwar financial system with its gold standard and fixed exchange rates encouraged the misappropriation of global capital and was too rigid to accept gradual changes. The fall in the price of farm goods harmed a still-significant sector of the world economy that employed 30.5% of the

65. Knut Borchardt, *Perspectives on Modern German Economic History and Policy* (New York, 1991), pp. 144-177.

66. Labor force participation grew from 90.5% of the age cohort in 1925 to 93.1% in 1933, according to Detlev Peukert, "The Lost Generation," in Richard Bessel and E. J. Feuchtwanger, eds., *Social Change and Political Development in the Weimar Republic* (London, 1981), p. 174. Balderston, *Financial Crisis,* p. 11, using different numbers, says participation increased only from 1925 to 1930, then fell.

67. Bry, p. 48. Holtfrerich, p. 83, and James, p. 38, in Kershaw. Balderston, *Financial Crisis,* pp. 58-59, 81; "Economic Instability," p. 501. James, *Slump,* pp. 194-197. Spoerer, pp. 109-111.

German workforce and accounted for 16% of the NNP. Growing trade protection dampened commerce and all economic activity. There was a recession at the end of 1927 in Australia and the Dutch East Indies. Germany and Brazil declined in the last part of 1928, and Argentina, Canada, and Poland all succumbed in the first half of 1929. Canada, Australia, Argentina, and Brazil responded by suspending the gold standard, but Germany did not. The German Depression was not the result of excessive spending, taxes, debt, or wages.[68]

The trend to the left of the previous four years was confirmed in the national elections of May 1928. The November 1927 state elections in Braunschweig had seen a stunning breakthrough for the SPD. In 1924, it had received 36% of the vote in the Reichstag elections and 38% in that state's elections. The princes' referendum had received only a 38% affirmative vote, perhaps due to a lingering loyalty to the Welf family. Now the SPD won 48% of the vote. Joining the government had not helped the Nationalists. As Chanady found, the "transition from convenient opposition to responsible government brought to the surface latent structural and ideological cleavages which . . . became a potent cause of disintegration."[69] Throughout 1927 there were constant rumors of an imminent split. The *Breslauer Zeitung* reported that the Pan-German League had opposed joining the government and that twelve DNVP Reichstag members were about to leave the party. The *Kölner Zeitung* reported that the monarchists would set up their own party because of the DNVP's disloyalty.[70]

Germany's agricultural calamity deepened. The agricultural interest payments as a percentage of sales had grown from 5.6% in 1925-26 to 8.3% in 1927-28. The Thuringian *Landbund* broke with the DNVP and established a party that would win 2% of the nationwide vote in 1928. The Mecklenburg *Landbund* also felt it needed to take strong action. The SPD's support in Mecklenburg-Schwerin grew from 23% in 1924 to 40% in 1926 and 41% in May 1927 while in Mecklenburg-Strelitz it grew from 23% in 1923 to 34% in July 1927. The *Landbund* demanded that its candidates should head the DNVP list, that those candidates would be free to ignore the Nationalist party line, and that a *Landbund* leader be added to the local DNVP directorate. When

---

68. James, *Slump*, p. 246. Eichengreen, pp. 222-241, draws from Hoffmann's work which finds a 1.6% growth rate for all 1928 and 4.2% shrinkage in 1929. Compare this to Maddison, p. 180, who states a 2.3% and 1.2% growth for each respective year. Thus Maddison pushes the start of the downturn back by six to nine months. Looking at the tax revenues, it seems clear that Germany was in a recession by April of 1929 that probably began at the end of 1928, so I lean to Hoffmann and Eichengreen here.

69. Chanady, p. 65.

70. *Vossische Zeitung*, November 11, 1927; *Breslauer Zeitung*, February 15, 1927; and *Kölner Zeitung*, March 2, 1927, in BAP R 8034 II/9014.

negotiations broke down, the Mecklenburg *Landbund* ran its own list of candidates and won 6% of the local vote. Three weeks before the election, Westarp addressed a half-empty sports arena in Berlin.[71]

The Social Democrats and Communists gained seats, while the Nationalists lost almost one-third of their support. In a Reichstag of 491 members, the SPD held 153 seats, the Democrats 25, and the Catholic Center 62, a total that left the Weimar Coalition just six seats shy of a majority. The SPD's gains were distributed nationwide, with only South Hannover/Braunschweig and Mecklenburg showing stunning gains for it. The growth of the SPD in Mecklenburg showed that the party's new policy of giving free legal aid and technical advice to farmers was bearing fruit. Although it had targeted urban workers in the elections, the tiny Nazi party did better in the farming regions because of the anger that the DNVP had not done enough on tariffs.[72]

However, both the DDP and Center had grown further apart from the SPD than in the heady days of 1919, and the fear of a Communist revolution had also faded. The Center held the fewest number of seats it would have between 1871 and 1933. In retrospect, perhaps the Socialists should have tried a minority government as Otto Braun did in Prussia, but that probably would not have dissuaded the Catholic Center from making trouble or demanding the Prussian Premiership. There were also health concerns over Braun since his wife had suffered a stroke in 1927 and he had collapsed at his desk. The Center pulled Heinrich Brauns out of the government against his will after his eight years of service as Labor Minister and allowed Guérard from the Catholic Right to serve as Transportation Minister and observer in the Cabinet. Marx had fallen ill in the spring of 1928 and stepped down as party Chair. Monseigneur Ludwig Kaas of the right wing defeated Stegerwald for the party chairmanship.[73]

The elections devastated the Nationalists. Not only had they lost a third of their vote, but the decline was huge in some areas. They lost badly in the three Saxon districts, especially to the revaluation parties, and suffered heavy losses in Schleswig-Holstein, East Hannover, and Mecklenburg. Since 1920 the Nationalists had lost strength in Saxony, Württemberg, Hesse-Darmstadt, and Thuringia, while gaining strength in Potsdam II and Pomerania. After its

---

71. James, *Slump*, p. 267. *Deutsche Tageszeitung*, March 26, 1928, *Mecklenburg Nachrichte*, April 13, 1928, *Der Abend*, April 12, 1928, in BA Potsdam R 8034 II/9014. Jürgen Falter, Thomas Lindberger, and Siegfried Schumann, eds., *Wahlen und Abstimmungen in der Weimarer Republik, Materialen und Wahlverhalten 1919-1933* (Munich, 1986), pp. 97-99. BA Potsdam R 8034 II/5119, p. 66.

72. Wolfgang Michalka and Gottfried Niedhart, eds., *Deutsche Geschichte 1918-1933* (Frankfurt, 1992), p. 277. James, *Slump*, p. 260. Mommsen, *Rise and Fall*, p. 319.

73. Becker, p. 422. Breitman, p. 141. E. D. Kohler, p. 314. Mommsen, *Rise and Fall*, p. 249.

postwar breakthrough, the DNVP was shrinking back to its roots as an East Elbian party. Westarp's policy of cooperation became the focal point of criticism. Hugenberg complained to the Count that he could no longer distinguish the DNVP from the DDP. Heinrich Class said the present DNVP seemed willing to support Wilhelm Marx for President and Adenauer for Chancellor. The *Jungdeutschen* paper was one of the first to call for Westarp's ouster. It wanted to see a younger leader. Westarp was reelected fraction leader in July with Oberfohren and Hans Lindeiner-Wildau as deputies, the same team that had supported the entry into government and the exclusion of the Kaiser. But trouble was brewing at the local level. Hugenberg decided to challenge Westarp for chairmanship of the party, and local DNVP chapters in fifteen of the thirty-five districts supported him. Even at the end of August, it was felt that Westarp had the upper hand as a Hugenberg-inspired attempt to expel Walther Lambach from the party failed. Lambach had offended the Hugenberg wing by commenting on the decline of monarchism as shown in the referendum of 1926 and called for a new popular conservatism that could appeal to German youth. The local association of Westarp's home district did expel Lambach. At the party congress of October 1928, Westarp declined to run again as chairman. Even without opposition, Hugenberg only won the chairmanship by a bare majority. Hugenberg now returned to the total opposition of the early 1920s. Cheering Hugenberg on was a group of heavy industrialists centered in the Ruhr who had opposed Silverberg's call for moderation in 1926, opposed the overtime pay rule backed by Westarp, and locked out workers in 1928. This group was determined to wreck the corporatist order and pursue a policy of social confrontation, not cooperation. Josef Becker has seen this as a key moment. The fourth Marx Cabinet had broached the question whether the DNVP could become a conservative state party. The election of Hugenberg provided a negative answer.[74]

The Social Democrats had not run on a platform of massive spending increases since the government had enacted most of their desired items. Their initiatives were limited to extending the term of unemployment insurance or crisis support. The new Müller government did not enact even these mild measures. Rudolf Hilferding, who had gained a reputation as a lightweight in 1923, returned to the Finance Ministry. This dismayed several socialists. Otto Braun privately called him a "Slovenian racketeer." Carl von Ossietzky called him "a man without a shadow," typical of the burned-out conservatism of an older generation of socialists.[75] Hilferding blocked any attempt to raise crisis

---

74. BA Potsdam R 8048/396, pp. 1-7; R 8048/151, p. 2. *Jungdeutschen*, May 30, 1928, in ibid., R 8034 II/9014, vol. 6; *Frankfurter Zeitung*, July 3, 1928, *Berliner Tageblatt*, July 11, 1928, *Germania*, August 30, 1928 in *Ibid.*, vol. 7. Leopold, pp. 46-52. Mommsen, *Rise and Fall*, pp. 256-257. James, *Slump*, p. 173. Becker, p. 361.
    75. Quotes from Smaldone, p. 148.

relief because the budget had too much spending. In contrast to the previous years, the socialist government proposed no massive supplementary budget for 1928.[76]

The 1929 budget had problems from its inception. The income from tariffs and consumption taxes had fallen throughout 1928, and Hilferding projected a deficit of RM683 million because of RM416 million additional spending and RM268 million less in income. He also saw a RM80 million deficit in the Extraordinary Budget. Hilferding was determined that there would be no deficit. An uncovered deficit would endanger the flow of foreign loans and the payment of reparations at a time when negotiations to revise the Dawes Plan were pending. The fall in tax revenue, Schacht's report in November 1928 of a fall in prices, and a doubling of people on relief should have sent alarm through the government, but there was not a murmur about stimulus. Agricultural problems and a tight monetary policy were choking the economy. Schacht had held the discount rate at 7% since October 1927 and his vaults now held the highest amount of gold and foreign currency since the stabilization. He regarded this as necessary to cover the foreign indebtedness, but neither he nor Hilferding appreciated that this was RM2.7 billion not being used productively. Hilferding's 1929 budget was very modest. Although he foresaw no uncovered spending, the debts from the previous extraordinary budgets were RM1,886 million, and the government had only converted RM908 million into covering loans (see Table 6.10). It only had to convert RM140 million immediately by law, and there was some breathing space: the credit line at the Reichsbank was RM210 million below its limit. The real problem would come in 1930, which would need to cover FY27. That would add up to RM300 million in credit need.[77]

Hilferding's bigger problem was covering the ballooning FY28 deficit, caused largely by the excessive civil-service raises. He proposed several tax hikes, including an increase in the beer tax, to close a projected gap of RM739 million. The spending budget had now gone over RM10 billion, with RM2.5 billion dedicated to reparations. He did not ask for an increase in the loan authority for foreign policy reasons. When other ministers challenged this, the Finance Minister sniffed that the Cabinet had agreed to a balanced budget two months earlier and it was too late to change things. Issuing bonds out of the insurance fund or cutting RM100 million in transfers to states and localities would be an alternative to raising taxes, especially the beer tax so odious to the Bavarians. The Cabinet brushed these suggestions aside and endorsed all of the

---

76. Martin Vogt, ed., *Akten der Reichskanzlei: Das Kabinett Muller II* (Boppard, 1970), p. XLVIII; Doc. #17, pp. 66-68.

77. *Kabinett Müller II*, Docs. #57, pp. 194-199; #59, pp. 203-212. In August 1928, 654,539 were registered as receiving relief, by November it was up to 1,131,574, and would be 1,832,552 by December. PrStA Hauptabteilung I Rep. 90, Abt. EIII, 1, #2, vol. 5.

**Table 6.10**
**The Structure of Reich Debt, March 31, 1929**

| Credits Authorized | | Covering | |
|---|---|---|---|
| Treasury Transfer of 1923 "K" | 472,494 | Treasury Transfers of 1923 | 10,981,577 |
| Treasury Transfer of 1923, due 9/2/35 | 17,284,358 | Rentenbank | 344,295,541 |
| 6% Treasury Transfer of 1923 | 1,180,423 | 1927 "Reinhold Loan" | 452,500,000 |
| Rentenbank Loan | 617,808,605 | Miscellaneous | 3,453 |
| FY25 and FY26 Allowances | 411,300,154 | Treasury Transfers of 1928 | 100,485,248 |
| Fiscal Year 1927 | 298,329,696 | | |
| Fiscal Year 1928 | 539,709,250 | | |
| Total | 1,886,084,980 | | 908,265,819 |
| Uncovered | 977,819,161 | Need to cover | 139,780,215 |

*Sources: Verhandlungen deutsches Reichsrat* 1930. Drucksache #24.

tax increases, even when Post Minister Georg Schätzel told it that the beer-tax increase was unacceptable to the BVP.[78]

The Bavarians pulled out of the coalition. The Center suspended its participation and demanded three Cabinet posts. The budget was in limbo. The People's party stayed in the Cabinet but opposed the new taxes; it renewed its old demand for inclusion in the Prussian Cabinet. For two months, the stalemate persisted as the jockeying over positions in the Reich and Prussia continued. With the budget tied up, the Cabinet revived the old practice of a continuing budget for three months. This was a very bad sign. A Cabinet reshuffle ended the freeze, but the budget came under withering criticism from Brüning, who preferred cuts in the Foreign Office and the Defense Ministry to raising any taxes. Hilferding grew angry as the Reichstag chopped his budget to pieces. Instead of the real taxes proposed by the Finance Minister, the Reichstag simply raised the estimated yields. He would not agree with Stresemann's suggestion to use the Reichstag numbers as the basis of negotiation. Müller backed his fellow Socialist. Complicating matters was the government's reluctance to fund the first installment of a pocket-battleship.[79]

---

78. *Kabinett Müller II*, Docs. #102, p. 359; #106, pp. 365-369.
79. Ibid., Docs. #142, p. 463; #159, Note #2, p. 507; #165, pp. 524-530.

The budget worsened along with the government's relationship with Schacht. During the winter of 1928-29 the Reichsbank cut the discount rate to 6½% but was alarmed as gold began to flow out of the country. As the economy turned down, the tax yields missed their targets, and the government borrowed more from private concerns. The Golddiskontbank took out a $30 million rediscount credit with Dillon Read and had the right to extend it to $50 million (RM220 million) until July 1930. The Reich had sold RM400 million and Prussia RM125 million of Treasury bills to a bank consortium. The flow of gold became worse after February 1929 when the Bank of England raised its benchmark rate to 5½%. Short-term American interest rates were around 4½%, while long-term rates were at 3½%. There was again an insufficient spread among the New York, London, and Berlin markets. The economy had fallen into recession by April 1929, yet Schacht said Germany was in a technical bankruptcy that only a tighter monetary policy could solve and raised the discount rate to 7½%.[80]

With Schacht insisting on tight money and Hilferding and Popitz insisting on tight fiscal policy, Germany encountered a growing cash crisis. Balderston points out that a cash crisis was something alien to Britain and France with their well-structured debt systems. Gilbert had been amazed at Germany's trouble with short-term Treasury bills. Rather than an increased loan-authority from the Reichsbank, Hilferding took a short-term loan of RM180 million from a banking consortium. Popitz had to present a lengthy list of stopgap measures, based on different assumptions of what would finally emerge from the Reichstag. Even with all of this, he warned that RM200 million remained uncovered in the fourth quarter of 1929. The government estimated a FY30 gap of RM423 million. Popitz tried to urge passage of the beer-tax increase and a 20% surcharge. One must remember that Germany had faced this before. The government had gotten around a cash shortage in May and June 1926 by amending the Reichsbank Law to raise the credit limit from RM100 million to RM400 million.[81]

Local finances were also worsening. Hesse was reporting difficulties in early 1928. Köhler granted Hesse a short-term loan of RM1.5 million, which it was supposed to repay in four months. Instead of repayment, the Reich transferred another RM1.5 million in July and an equal sum in September. There was little debate when Hilferding brought these before the Cabinet. Hesse's debt soon approached RM25 million. By the end of 1928, Mecklenburg-Schwerin reported its second straight large deficit and expected the FY29 deficit to be higher still because of a fall in tax revenues. Suggestions

80. Ibid., Docs. #123, pp. 418-421; #182, pp. 585-586. Eichengreen, pp. 214-220. James, *Slump*, p. 57.

81. Balderston, *Financial Crisis*, p. 275. *Kabinett Müller II*, Doc. #187, pp. 601-606. Hertz-Eichenrode, pp. 110-111.

ranged from the Reich taking over the administration of the states' justice systems to a full merger with Prussia.[82]

Hilferding resorted to another domestic bond issue in 1929 after contracting for several private short-term loans. The revenue situation was worsening rapidly. In May, he had sketched a plan to offer a RM500 million loan at 7%. He believed that this rate would compare favorably to other international loans and would appeal to foreign creditors. It would also support the deflationary policy of the Reichsbank. Given Schacht's monetary policy and a discount rate of 7½%, however, his rating of the bond was already too low. Curtius warned that dumping this much paper on a weak market would depress prices. Stresemann did not want the Reich to issue these bonds until after the latest round of reparations' negotiations. Popitz, looking at the cash balance, pleaded that a loan was the only possible solution, supplemented by loans from the railroads, the post office, and Prussia. The representatives in the Reichstag had refused to act responsibly. The bond issue was a catastrophe and raised only RM187 million. The government withdrew most of the bonds.[83] The government had supported the Reinhold bond prices in 1927, but the 1929 loan failed so miserably that such support was impossible. The Reich would not try another long-term issue during the Weimar period.

The greatest pressure on the budget came from unemployment insurance. The 1927 law had never anticipated so many unemployed. It had assumed that the Reich would enact a job-creation program as it had under Reinhold and Brauns to keep people off the jobless rolls, but Hilferding had doubted the efficacy of that program and resisted large-scale proposals. The government patched the hole in the insurance fund with a series of loans, but "reform" soon became the word of the day, meaning an increase in the premium paid by employers and employees or cuts in benefits. The framers of the law had also made an error in creating a pay-as-you-go system, which could not support itself in a time of high unemployment. They should have provided safeguards since the recession of 1925-26 was still fresh in their minds, but they likely assumed that a crisis would be short-lived because the government would fight it as vigorously as the Luther/Reinhold government had. By January 1929 there were 1.9 million Germans on unemployment insurance and another 138,000 on crisis relief. In March, the government had lent the unemployment insurance fund (Reichsanstalt) RM288 million to cover its losses. The growth of unemployment worsened the budget crisis. At the end of June 1929, the government extended another RM370 million credit but stated that would be the final support. The Cabinet established an experts' committee to create a

---

82. *Kabinette Marx III/IV*, Doc. #453, pp. 1388-1389. *Kabinett Müller II*, Docs. #9, p. 27; #75, pp. 260-263.

83. *Kabinett Müller II*, p. LVII, and Doc.#193, pp. 628-631. James, *Reichsbank*, p. 105.

program that would take the heat off the political parties, especially the SPD, which opposed benefit cuts, and the DVP, which opposed tax hikes.[84]

By August, the unemployment issue had deeply divided the Cabinet. Popitz warned that unemployment would be up to 2.5 million by the winter. Labor Minister Rudolf Wissell was willing only to cut benefits for the highest wage classes and wanted to raise the premiums on workers and employers by 0.75%. He was convinced that 1930 would bring relief as a fall in birth rates would be reflected in the labor force. The experts called for raising the premium by 0.5% and cutting benefits more deeply. Economics Ministry State Secretary Ernst Trendelenburg opposed any raise in the premiums. Popitz warned that other deficits were looming: RM50 million in military pensions, RM20 million in crisis relief for those who had exhausted their unemployment benefits, and RM34 million in invalid insurance. The Cabinet generally supported Wissell's draft and refused attempts to limit the increase or the term of the premium increase. Wissell had wanted to make unemployment insurance a part of the ordinary budget, but Popitz refused to include a RM100 million loan in his draft budget for FY30. In October Wissell asked for RM234 million in the general budget. Stresemann suggested that the Cabinet link the payments to other issues to resolve them more easily. The Germans had won a modification in the Dawes Plan, which was named after American Owen Young. The Young Plan would cut more than one-quarter of the annual payments the Dawes Plan had demanded over the next five years. The immediate savings in the Young Plan could subsidize the insurance fund, and then the government could raise other taxes to support the budget. This would save everyone's face. By September, some members of the DVP were hinting that they would support a smaller raise in the premium. The Cabinet now looked at a broader financial program with a short-term program to plug the immediate leaks.[85]

Hilferding and Popitz opposed using the Young Plan savings for unemployment because there were other needs. The Supplementary Budget for FY29 merely covered the deficits. There was already a RM130-150 million shortfall in income for FY29 on top of the deficit. The government needed yet more money for occupation costs, the Belgian Mark treaty, and the gaps in the pension fund. Hilferding and Popitz wanted to use the Young Plan's savings of RM704 million in FY30 to fund an extremely ambitious five-year financial plan. It would cut the sugar tax in half, reduce the income tax rates while exempting entirely those making under RM1,800 a year, and aid businesses by reducing their taxes. This program would have been a very good start to fighting the economic downturn, but Popitz and Hilferding were determined to keep the

---

84. James, *Slump*, p. 54. *Kabinett Müller II*, Docs. #196, p. 640; #213, p. 694.

85. *Kabinett Müller II*, Docs. #262, pp. 848-853; #274, pp. 881-888; #277, p. 894; #280, pp. 899-900; #298, pp. 955-957. Kent, p. 302.

revenue neutral. This meant raising other taxes, and the Finance Ministry took square aim at the beer tax and the states' share of revenue. That made it quite unlikely to pass the Reichsrat, and the Bavarians would never support it. The Finance Ministry missed a golden opportunity to reform and structure German debt. By the end of 1929, German domestic debt was RM3.3 billion. RM953 million were treasury transfers without any interest rate, RM683 million were the long-term bonds of 1927 and 1929, and RM236 million were held in interest-bearing treasury transfers. It had drawn on credit authority from the Reichsbank. The remainders were mostly war payments without a specific due date. The Reich had still not sold any bills or notes to the public. The German government also owed a billion Marks in foreign debt, mostly from the Dawes loan. Despite the obvious growth in short and medium debt between March and December 1929, the economy was shrinking more rapidly. This is a classic case of unplanned, piecemeal deficit spending, which is very inefficient at stimulating the economy. The government needed to get ahead of the cycle fast with a big tax cut or a large-scale employment program.[86]

Had Hilferding made up the revenue shortfall of RM400 million by selling short- and medium-term debt instruments at reasonable interest rates to the public, the program would have sailed through the parliament. Germany would not have averted the Depression, but the economy would have received a stimulus, and the later budget crises would not have been so severe. This program also had no bearing on the immediate problem with unemployment insurance. Indirectly, it could have served as an incentive to the DVP to back the higher premium increases, but there were enough interests alienated by the tax proposals that they could bury the entire program and the government.[87]

This is precisely what occurred. The Cabinet again postponed the unemployment issue. The Cabinet declined to add RM25 million for job creation in the supplementary budget for FY29. In the late fall of 1929, the Cabinet found itself beset by the next round of negotiations to fine-tune the Young Plan. Stresemann died on October 3, and Curtius succeeded him. The government had not resolved the unemployment issue, the supplementary budget, or the financial program, and the 1930 budget draft was running late. Tempers grew short and work overwhelmed the financial part of the civil service. Hilferding had not been up to the task in 1923, but now was showing skill and patience. His colleagues marveled at the change, but suspected that the Finance Minister had drifted far from socialist ideals. His opposition to Wissell and insistence on sound finance led many to wonder if he had become the puppet of Johannes Popitz. Hilferding had never promoted something like the Financial Program before and yet here he was pushing aid to business. The greatest strain was on Schacht. In the growing crisis, he expected the

---

86. Statistischen Reichsamt, *Finanzen und Steuern*, p. 294.
87. *Kabinett Müller II*, Doc. #305, pp. 968-978.

government to turn to him as the savior.  In his own eyes, he had saved the currency in 1923 and caused the Berlin bourse to crash.  He did not understand that the latter event had caused the government to regard him as dangerously erratic.  Foreign adulation constantly boosted his ego.  He now publicly demanded that the government make deep budget cuts.  If necessary, all transfers to the states should cease.  To Hilferding, this talk was madness.  The Reich had a cash deficit of RM1.5 billion.  (This was a drop in the bucket compared with Britain's short-term debt of RM16 billion equivalent, but Britain had structured its short-term debt, and Germany had not.)  Hilferding told Schacht that he could not get rid of the mistakes of 1925-26 in a year.  The Finance Minister claimed that loans had never properly covered the job-creation program, although we have seen coverage for all FY26 spending.  Most of the current budget went to civil servants or to relief spending.  Cuts in either would lead to a political firestorm.  Schacht piously retorted that politics was the business of the Cabinet; he only took responsibility for the Reichsbank and as a negotiator for reparations.  He then made the direct threat: without spending cuts, the Reichsbank would cut off its credit.  Hilferding begged Schacht to be neutral on a new foreign loan, but the Reichsbank President would not cooperate.  The government got over the immediate crisis by having the Reichstag authorize RM465 million in credits.  Where the credit would come from was unclear.[88]

By December, Müller and Hilferding wanted an immediate program raising the unemployment premium and the tobacco tax as well as a long-term tax-cut package.  The Reich had to make RM1,700 million in cash payments and had only RM1,370 million to cover them.  It expected to extend RM150 million in credits to the unemployment fund to cover the first three months of 1930. Schacht demanded that the government pay RM500 million into the sinking fund before he would support any loans.  Schacht's point was not absurd, but it was ill-timed.  More payments into the sinking fund would make more credit available to the German government.  We have seen that Germany paid very little in debt service compared to other nations.  Devoting another 5% of the budget to debt service was not unreasonable.  A prudent policy might have included tax cuts, the sinking fund payment, and financing with a well-structured program of foreign and domestic short-, medium-, and long-term debt.  It is always better to plan ahead and have the initiative than to be catching up perpetually.  Schacht would relent, then harden again.  The parties of the Reichstag were little better.  When Brüning, Curt Hoff of the People's party, Johann Leicht of the Bavarians, and Reinhold of the Democrats all pledged to support the immediate program, Rudolf Breitscheid suddenly objected on the

---

88. *Kabinett Müller II*, Docs. #309, pp. 988-990; #323, p. 1050; #367, pp. 1210-1215; #371, p. 1233. James, *Slump*, p. 59. The authorization vote was 239 to 138; PrStA Hauptabteilung I Rep 90 Abt EIII, 1, #2, vol. 5.

SPD's behalf. The Cabinet and the party leaders were now regularly meeting late into the night. Hindenburg talked to Schacht, but the Reichsbank leader would not back down. The confrontation became ugly on December 16, when Schacht claimed that he alone represented a constituency of forty million people. The government should have listened to him over the past five years. Interior Minister Carl Severing angrily said that Schacht was demanding the impossible. After Schacht left the room, Chancellor Müller suggested another possibility. Dillon, Read had offered a short-term loan of $125 million (RM525 million), but with an effective yield of 7½%. Schacht and Gilbert had blocked it in October. Schacht was obviously against it, but perhaps they could win Gilbert's support.[89]

Considering Gilbert's view on loans, this was remarkably naïve. Hilferding and Müller met with Gilbert on December 18, but found that the American agreed with Schacht on many points. As Müller outlined his desperation, Gilbert replied that things did not seem so tragic nor did he believe the government to be in danger. Young Plan savings would cover the 1928 and 1929 deficits. Germany was discussing a RM500 million loan with the Swedish "match king" Ivar Kreuger. The proposed tobacco tax would raise another RM220 million, which could be put into the sinking fund for FY30. Schacht wanted RM280 million in cuts or taxes. The government wanted instead to gain a bridge credit from Dillon, Read. Why go abroad? A cash deficit of RM300 million was not that great. The domestic market could cover that. Once again, the Reparations Agent tried to nudge the Cabinet toward selling short-term debt. After the Reichstag adopted the immediate program and settled the unemployment insurance fund, the government should ask the Reichsbank to organize a domestic syndicate to take over the cash deficit. "A government is never weaker than when it must beg for foreign credits and is never stronger than when it refuses foreign credits offered on unfavorable terms."[90] If the Cabinet resorted to domestic financing, Dillon, Read might come back with a better offer. Finally, the government should pledge controls on the spending side by naming a nonpolitical official to police spending. Ambassador to Washington Friedrich von Prittwitz relayed word from Clarence Dillon: his firm would not extend any loan before July 1930 without support from the Reichsbank. Worse still, the French government warned that this could damage the reparations negotiations. Schacht was obviously pulling out all the stops to sabotage foreign loans, and the Cabinet was both furious and helpless. On December 19, the Cabinet surrendered to Schacht. It would cut the transfers to the states and augment the sinking fund in the FY30 budget. The Reichsbank would organize a small German bank consortium to assume the cash debt. Most expected that

---

89. *Kabinett Müller II*, Docs. #374, pp. 1238-1244; #378, p. 1249; #380, pp. 1254-1255; #387, pp. 1266-1267; #390, pp. 1272-1277. James, *Slump*, p. 57.

90. *Kabinett Müller II*, Doc. #391, p. 1279.

this would get the government through at least the first half of the next year. The Reichstag passed the provisions on December 22. These events badly damaged the credibility of Hilferding and Popitz. The People's party was now prepared to vote for a motion of no-confidence in Hilferding and its ministers told Müller that unless Hilferding resigned, they would quit and try to bring down the government.[91]

To sum up, there were any number of good suggestions to fight the deepening depression and the accompanying financial crisis in 1929. The government should have increased the FY30 sinking fund payment without quarreling with Schacht. It should have pushed through the tax cut as proposed by Hilferding, Popitz, and the DVP, but without any balancing income. The revenue shortfall from these measures should have been covered, as Gilbert suggested, by sales of short-term bills to the public and to private consortia. Finally, the government could have covered the insurance fund as needed by raising the premium or extending more credits. These were not insoluble questions, nor do they require some wisdom gleaned years after the fact. All these suggestions were made by prominent men in powerful positions. All it required was the flexible and creative thinking shown by the Cabinet just three years before. The Grand Coalition would have held together for up to another year.

By the longest night of the year in 1929, Stresemann was dead, Hilferding and Popitz were gone, and Schacht would soon be gone. Of all bond issues on the Berlin market, 55% were below parity for the first time since September 1926. Fiscal policy and coalition building had again gone hand in hand, but not in the positive sense of 1926. Now the collective nervous breakdown of the Müller Cabinet had swallowed up fiscal policy and the entire political system.

---

91. Ibid., Docs. #391-392, pp. 1277-1289; #395, pp. 1292-1294; #398, p. 1297. Kent, p. 320.

# Chapter 7

# Infinite Illusions: Fiscal Policy under Brüning

In 1930 panic-stricken investors unloaded their Dawes bonds after the Nazi party made big gains in elections. The prices sank ever lower. Even after the markets suspended trading, one might sell a Dawes bond to a speculator at a fraction of its face value. Without their protector Parker Gilbert, the bonds were left to the vagaries of a bear market. The Germans and their government had learned enough lessons from the fiscal regimes and economic conditions since 1912. The example of 1926 was still fresh in memory: the government had announced in advance that it was borrowing money to fight the recession with tax cuts. When it settled the accounts, it needed less than half of the credit authorized because economic recovery had boosted tax revenue. From 1930 to 1932, the government of Heinrich Brüning ignored these lessons. It insisted on balancing the budget and reducing debt by raising taxes and cutting spending. Not only did this policy hurt millions of people and drive them to the political extremes, it worsened the budget and created a permanent sense of crisis. Table 7.1 summarizes the fiscal crises of the Depression and compares the possible solutions with the actual resolutions. At the end Brüning had to use credit in the worst possible way: to cover the deficits of 1930 and 1931 retroactively. Had Brüning simply planned for this credit at the outset, Weimar democracy could have been saved.

The civil-service raise of 1927 had many baneful effects. Besides the sharp memo of Parker Gilbert and the deleterious impact on the Reich and state budgets, it led to the election of Heinrich Brüning as Catholic Center Reichstag leader. When Stegerwald condemned Köhler's proposal, he alienated a large segment of the party's leadership. Stegerwald had been the favorite to succeed Marx as party chair, but the civil-service faction blocked his appointment, and the party chose the conservative prelate Ludwig Kaas. Stegerwald took Marx's other post as Reichstag floor leader as a consolation prize. He resigned as

**Table 7.1**
**Fiscal Problems During the German Depression, 1929-1932**

| Time | Nature of Problem | Possible Solutions | Actual Resolutions |
|---|---|---|---|
| February-April 1929 | FY29 budget: RM683 million deficit projected initially, grows to RM739 million | Tax increases; spending cuts; long-term loan; sell short-term debt to public or private concerns; increase Reichsbank credit limit | Beer-tax hike; continuing resolution Apr-June 1929; long-term bond issue; debt sold to private concerns; raise tax revenue estimates |
| December 1929 | Depression worsening; Hilferding/Popitz tax cut proposal | Finance tax cuts with credit; balance reduction in sugar, income, and business taxes with hikes in consumption taxes | No major tax cut enacted; resignation of Hilferding and Popitz |
| December 1929 | Cash shortage of RM330 million from revenue shortfall in regular and unemployment-insurance budgets | Insurance premium hikes; tax increases; spending cuts; foreign loan from Dillon, Read; sell short-term debt to public or private concerns | Reichsbank-organized bank consortium to extend loan; cut in transfers to the states |
| March-July 1930 | FY30 budget; initial projection of RM657 million deficit | Tax increases; premium increases; spending cuts; limit subsidy to unemployment insurance; forced loan; cuts in civil-service salaries; long-term loan; sell short-term debt to public or private concerns; increase Reichsbank credit limit. Hansa-Bund: massive tax cut, spending cut, and job-creation program. | Decree of July 26, 1930: Tax and premium increases, especially poll tax, income tax, and tobacco tax; cuts in unemployment support; spending cuts; cuts in civil-service salaries; establishment of Öffa, which provides RM50 million for job creation |
| September 1930-March 1931 | FY31 budget; initial projection of RM900 million deficit | Tax increases; premium increases; spending cuts; limit subsidy to unemployment insurance; cuts in civil-service salaries; sell short-term debt to public or private concerns; foreign (France or U.S.) short-term credit; use another RM205 million in Reichsbank/railroad/post credit authority | Premium increase; tax surcharge; cut in salaries; budget cuts; cut in transfers to states; $125 million Lee, Higginson loan; RM125 million in treasury bills renewed |

| May-June 1931 | Shortfall in FY31 revenue projected at RM782 million | Tax increases; premium increases; spending cuts; cuts in civil-service salaries; sell short-term debt to public or private concerns; foreign (France or BIS) short-term credit | Decree of June 5, 1931: Budget cuts; tax hikes; salary cuts; RM100 million for job creation; call for treaty revision; RM250 million in Treasury bills renewed |
|---|---|---|---|
| May-September 1931 | Bank crisis from withdrawal of funds | French 10-year $500 million credit; short-term $100 million BIS credit; raise interest rates; law against capital withdrawal | $100 million short-term credit from BIS; takeover of Danat and Deutsche Banks; sharp hike in interest rates; law against capital withdrawal; temporary market shutdown |
| September-October 1931 | Help for unemployed in winter 1931/32; unemployment-fund deficit of RM146 million; English devaluation | Budget cuts; relief for states and cities; reduce pensions; rent tax cut; interest rate cut; cuts in civil-service salaries; extend FY31 to July 1, 1932; build suburban settlements; foreign and/or domestic credits | Decree of October 6, 1931: Budget cuts, especially term of unemployment relief; relief for states and cities; reduce pensions; rent tax cut; interest rate cut; cuts in civil-service salaries; extend FY31 to July 1, 1932; build suburban settlements |
| November-December 1931 | Gap of RM600 million in FY31 budget | Tax increases; cuts in civil-service salaries; budget cuts; foreign and/or domestic credits | Decree of December 14, 1931: cuts in civil-service salaries; budget cuts; massive hike in turnover tax |
| March-May 1932 | Cash crisis | Foreign and/or domestic credits; Wagemann RM3 billion job-creation plan; "WTB Plan" of RM2 billion for job creation | RM1.3 billion in treasury-transfers authorized to cover FY30 and FY31 deficits; RM135 million job-creation plan |
| June 1932 | FY32 budget; total deficit estimated at RM1.62 billion | Tax hikes; budget cuts; premium increases; foreign/domestic credits | Salt tax; massive cuts in unemployment aid; premium increase |
| July 1932 | Cash gap of RM125 million | Tax hikes; budget cuts; credits | Bank consortium extended credit |

leader of the Catholic unions but only served as floor leader for a few months before leaving to become Müller's Transport Minister. To take his place, the Center's Reichstag deputies chose Brüning. This seemed logical: Brüning had been Stegerwald's assistant first in the Prussian Welfare Ministry, then in the unions. Brüning had emerged after 1924 as the party's budget expert. He had studied philosophy and history at the University of Strassburg, where Prussian nationalism influenced him, then obtained a doctorate in economics from the University of Bonn. This combination of nationalism and economic erudition impressed Brüning's colleagues, but it led to a disastrous economic policy and the fall of the Republic. After the trauma of December 1929, the Müller Cabinet and the SPD were in torpor and Brüning's views became decisive.[1]

The fiscal policy of Heinrich Brüning remains controversial mainly because Brüning himself was so unwilling to admit mistakes. Years later, he still insisted that deflationary policy and balancing the budget had been proper. Since the 1970s, a group of economic analysts has claimed that Brüning had no choice. He could not raise domestic capital from investors, foreign countries had shut off their loans, business needed to cut the wages of workers because they were not productive enough, and Germany needed a depression to become more competitive. In short: Dr. Brüning's operation was necessary and successful, though the patient died as a result. Balderston finds that deflation was the only option because of the severe deficits of the localities and the lack of a majority to raise taxes for reparations. A weak market ruled out loans because long-term investors were cautious after the recent inflation.[2]

A close examination of the Cabinet files of the fateful spring and summer of 1930 reveals a very different story. Simple arithmetic suggested only two ways for Brüning to gain a majority in the Reichstag: the enthusiastic support of the Nationalists or the tolerance of the Social Democrats who had just left office. Brüning pursued neither tactic. He spent so much time trying to deal with six parties with a few dozen members apiece that he lost all sight of the real situation. With SPD tolerance, he would not have to worry about Bavarian opposition to the beer tax. Yet there were no serious negotiations. As the divisions within the DNVP caused that party to fracture, winning its enthusiastic support for anything was difficult, but there was no real effort besides the recruitment of Martin Schiele as Agriculture Minister. By July, his political and economic ineptitude had landed him in trouble: there was no legal budget, investor confidence was ebbing, and the deficit was growing. Instead of resigning as a failure, Brüning forced the budget through with Article 48. When the Reichstag rejected that, he called immediate elections without ever

1. Ellen Lovell Evans, *The German Center Party, 1870-1933: A Study in Political Catholicism* (Carbondale, IL, 1981), pp. 348-356. Heinrich Brüning, *Memoiren, 1918-1934* (Stuttgart, 1970), p. 687.

2. Galbraith, p. 165. Balderston, *Financial Crisis*, pp. 330-331.

considering the consequences.  From September 1930 until his ouster in May 1932, Brüning piled on the errors as he served at the pleasure of President Hindenburg.  Brüning also failed to realize the changing situation of foreign capital by 1930.  While American firms had ceased extending long-term credits and were not renewing short-term credits, the French had become significant players in supporting the German economy.  Brüning never missed an opportunity in 1930 and 1931 to offend the French.  When those credits were lost, there was no way out.  An economic crisis had broken out in 1929 and required an economic solution.  Since the initial center of the crisis was in agriculture, it would make sense to deal with this first.  Paul Silverberg had proposed a central credit institute for agriculture that would extend low-interest loans to reforming farmers to improve their land, not to repay debt.[3]  Instead, the economic crisis developed into a political crisis.

The resignations of Hilferding and Popitz in December 1929 cleared the air for several months.  The new Finance Minister was Paul Moldenhauer of the People's party, a professor at Köln who brought an academic approach to the budget.  He had taken over the Economics Ministry in October 1929 when Curtius replaced Stresemann.  The Finance Ministry needed a new State Secretary, and the Ministerial Directors were too inexperienced or politically suspect.  The choice fell on Hans Schäffer, a young business lawyer from Breslau who was a left-wing member of the DDP.  He had risen through the ranks of the Economics Ministry after making a fortune and now moved over with Moldenhauer.  Müller believed that Moldenhauer and Curtius had forced Hilferding out and now had a moral responsibility to get the government out of trouble.[4]

The government dealt simultaneously with a supplementary budget for FY29 and the regular 1930 budget.  From October 1929 to January 1930, it had not realized RM44 million in income and spent an additional RM187 million.[5]  The reduction in reparations covered most of this, but left RM65 million uncovered.  An uncovered deficit could exist legally for two years, and the government thought the economic situation would be better by March 1931.  It pushed the deficit into the next fiscal year.  The Reichstag considered the supplementary budget for a month and passed it on March 28.

The supplemental was a technicality because it postponed the hard decisions into the 1930 fiscal year.  The government had to take prompt and decisive action on the 1930 budget.  Germany had faced and failed this test in 1921.  The new revenues had to take effect by April 1 to relieve the budget shortfalls.  Debate swirled around three main issues: (1) unemployment

---

3. Abraham, p. 198.
4. Krosigk, p. 58. Blaich, *Wirtschaftskrise*, p. 91. *Kabinett Muller II*, Doc. #399, p. 1304.
5. *Kabinett Müller II*, Doc. #405, p. 1329.

insurance, (2) a tax-cut program based on the Hilferding/Popitz program that had crashed when its authors resigned, (3) the 1930 budget deficit. Without counting on any tax cuts or further subsidies to the Unemployment Office, the Finance Ministry initially estimated a deficit of RM108 million in the ordinary budget. The reality was far worse. The 1928 budget had left a RM154 million deficit. The Reich's loan of RM372 million to the unemployment-insurance fund thus far in the 1929 Fiscal Year was matched only by a raise of RM130 million in premium payments; it needed cuts or rate hikes to balance these figures. Crisis relief had also risen for those who had exhausted their insurance. Moldenhauer felt that the estimate of tax revenue should be decreased based on the 1929 example. This meant a possible deficit of RM657 million. He proposed barring further credits to the insurance fund and passing a package of tax increases featuring the politically dangerous beer tax. This would clear much of the deficit, and a few budget cuts could deal with the rest.[6]

Each party made proposals odious to other parties in the coalition: the SPD wanted to raise the unemployment-insurance premium, Moldenhauer wanted to raise the wine and beer tax, the Catholic Center wanted a tax surcharge on those with annual income exceeding 5,000 Marks. Moldenhauer now proposed another solution: cap the FY30 budget subsidy to the unemployment office at RM150 million and the FY31 subsidy at RM100 million and cover this with the sale of Reichsbahn preferred stock. The directorate of the office would raise additional funds as needed: it could raise the premium, make administrative cuts, or make benefit cuts. This was a very clever solution that should have solved that particular problem because it removed the political onus of raising taxes from the DVP. Moldenhauer also had a clever way to reduce the remainder of the deficit. The government had promised Schacht that it would add RM450 million to the sinking fund. The law mandated the covering of the 1928 deficit. But the government *could* cover that deficit with the addition to the sinking fund. These proposals would leave the gap at RM222 million. A solution seemed on the horizon.[7]

Further declines in income and another RM49 million in spending added by the Cabinet raised the deficit again to RM305 million. To cover this, Moldenhauer now proposed: (1) raising the beer tax and the coffee and tea tariff, (2) an oil-import fee, (3) a mineral water tax, (4) adjusting the due dates of the tobacco and sugar taxes, and (5) delaying reduction of industrial burdens. This plan would also bring RM170 million to the hard-pressed states. The SPD objected to this because it did not contain any direct taxes nor did it tax property. Müller suggested that perhaps the surcharge on the income tax could suffice. Joseph Wirth, Minister for the Occupied Regions, revived his old idea

6. Ibid., Docs. #405, p. 1330; #432, pp. 1422-1426.
7. Ibid., Docs. #434, pp. 1429-1432; #444, pp. 1456-1457; #447, pp. 1461-1462.

of the forced loan. This revived bad memories of the drawn-out debates of the Wirth Cabinet over this loan and its disappointing results. The Cabinet should not have ignored Wirth. The crisis of 1930 was very different from the crisis of 1921 and prompt action would make all the difference. The Cabinet rejected the idea of an income-tax surcharge, which the SPD and the Bavarian Schätzel supported. It trimmed administrative salaries in the unemployment office as a form of shared sacrifice and accepted the rest of Moldenhauer's proposals except the mineral water tax. Winning most of the Cabinet did not mean the majority of the Reichstag. Neither the SPD nor the BVP accepted this package. Severing believed that the Communists would gain a potent issue for agitation if there were no direct taxes included in the package. The Chancellor was beginning to fear that this deadlock would lead to the dissolution of the Reichstag and new elections with a radical result.[8]

By the beginning of March, it was clear to the two liberal parties that the hoped-for tax cuts would have to put off for a year. Both the DDP and DVP opposed civil-service cuts and direct taxes and called for tax cuts in FY31. The delay in the budget had been very costly. Had the Reichstag passed the Hilferding financial program in some form, the tax cuts coming into effect April 1, 1930, would have stimulated the economy and slowed the free fall into the Depression. The actual revenue shortfalls of 1930-32 would dwarf the various plans for tax cuts. The government had decided to sell railroad shares to cover some of the 1930 unemployment-insurance fund, but 1931 funding was still undecided. The Cabinet now resorted to tough talk. Some believed that if there was no agreement, the government should call for new elections and enact the measures in the interim using Article 48. This would mean the assent of Hindenburg. Trying to assuage the SPD, Moldenhauer discovered that the Young Plan could release about RM50 million from the Bank for Industrial Obligations that the government could use as a reserve fund for unemployment insurance. This could satisfy the SPD's demand for a shared sacrifice of property. Maintenance of this reserve, the RM150 million already committed, a permanent ¼% raise in the premium, and a temporary ¼% raise could provide RM305 million. Schäffer was discussing a foreign loan with the Schröder banking house. Even if the DVP found this impossible, maybe it would support the budget if the 1930 budget included tax cuts for 1931. The 1931 cuts or tax increases could wait, but Moldenhauer was eyeing the contribution to the sinking fund. No one had ever promised Schacht that the contribution had to go beyond 1930. The Finance Minister thought this would do the trick and anticipated passage through the Reichsrat by March 15 and through the Reichstag by the end of March. On March 5, the Cabinet endorsed the entire plan. But Moldenhauer and the Cabinet constantly underestimated the

---

8. Ibid., Docs. #454, pp. 1497-1498; #455, pp. 1502-1509; #457, pp. 1513-1514.

depth of opposition of the People's party to raising the unemployment premiums. Scholz condemned the gimmickry on the industrial loads. The Bavarians stated their absolute opposition to the beer tax. The Bavarians and SPD also opposed cutting the income tax in 1931 while the financial picture was unclear. It should have been obvious that if the government were to survive, it would have to choose between the Bavarians and the DVP.[9]

Many in the Reichstag already understood this. The leaders on the Budget Committee, including Thomas Esser, Reinhold, Leicht, and Wilhelm Keil, decided to draft their own alternative without speaking to Moldenhauer or the DVP. On March 11, they presented their plan to Müller. It eliminated the beer tax increase to win Bavarian support. The states could raise their own beer taxes if they desired. There would also be an immediate capital gains tax cut. This created a gap of RM195 million. Adjustments in the government's proposed taxes and increases in the champagne and turnover taxes would plug the gap. This would still leave RM23 million, a paltry figure. The tax cut of 1931 would depend on floating RM500 million of long-term debt. The Catholic Center had endorsed this plan, and Keil believed the SPD could support it though the military budget was too large and there was no direct tax on property. The need to avert a government crisis outweighed the DDP's doubts. Müller agreed that this plan could probably win a majority, even without the DVP.[10]

It seemed on March 11 that the crisis had been solved. The main players of 1926 had come together again and come up with a plan like the Reinhold budget of that year. Fiscal policy and coalition building had worked together to maintain stability. The most dubious part of the plan was the long-term credit. After Hilferding's abysmal failure in 1929, a new credit seemed almost impossible. If the parties had instead put Moldenhauer's cut in the sinking fund together with RM250 million in short-term credits marketed to the public, it would have been perfectly fine. Simply passing any budget for 1930 would save them since they would not have to deal with the uncovered deficits for two years.

But it did not work out. Müller promised a review, but as far as I can tell, never submitted it formally to the Cabinet. He thought the Cabinet's plan was better and that the only virtue of the Budget Committee plan was making tax cuts unlikely. Had the more political animal Otto Braun chosen to be Chancellor, would he have made a different decision? Had Ebert still been President, could he have brought the parties to their senses? It is impossible to say. Müller put blind faith in the DVP, a faith that had never been justified. The adoption of the committee's plan would have led to Moldenhauer's

---

9. Ibid., Docs. #458, pp. 1516-1523; #460-461, pp. 1527-1535; #462, p. 1539; #469, pp. 1554-1559. *Vorwärts*, February 28, 1930.

10. Ibid., Doc. #471, pp. 1561-1565.

resignation and the likely exit of the People's party from the coalition. The government would still hold the majority and would have another three to six months until the next cash crisis. Schacht resigned from the Reichsbank on March 7 and the way was open again for new credit authorizations and treasury transfers from the Bank. The DVP would have been out in the cold for the first time since 1922. This would dash its dreams of entering the Prussian Cabinet. Would it have really thrown all that away for a futile gesture on unemployment premiums? In 1926, Hermann Müller was the first one to congratulate Reinhold after the passage of the budget. He should have done the same thing in 1930. For want of a handshake, 50 million people died.

Two weeks later came the end. While Brüning and Reinhold urged that business confidence and economic peace through an orderly budget were the top priority, Scholz said relieving the tax load on business was most important. Müller framed the choice: if the Cabinet could not achieve unity, it should resign. All but Labor Minister Wissell agreed with this. The use of Article 48 only seemed possible if all the ministers stayed in the Cabinet, but the DVP ministers would resign if the decree contained or allowed rises in the unemployment premium without mandating cuts. Oskar Meyer (DDP) and Brüning offered a last-minute compromise: the government would cover the immediate gap in the insurance fund, but it would not raise the premium and would cap the subsidy to the fund at RM150 million. The government would propose cuts later. Müller, Severing, Economics Minister Robert Schmidt, and Hilferding all supported the compromise, but Wissel, looking like an Old Testament prophet with his white beard, thundered against it. The unions put heavy pressure on the SPD, and it quit the government rather than vote for the compromise. It seemed to feel that postponing the issue would make it easier to vote for benefit cuts in the future. However, the Prussian SPD Landtag representatives passed a resolution critical of their national cousins for leaving the government. The Reichstag had ratified the Young Plan on March 13 and removed the last link holding the coalition together. A majority government could have survived under the Reinhold/Budget Committee Plan without the DVP, or if the SPD had accepted the Meyer/Brüning compromise. Severing urged the government to keep pushing its own plan even at the risk of alienating the BVP and the DVP. He did not believe the parties would bring down the government in the end. The three Weimar parties had 240 votes, six short of a majority. They could have limped along with a minority government. A minority of six should not have been insuperable, although the problems with the Catholic Center made it unlikely that this coalition could have lasted until May 1932. Given what happened, anything would have been preferable.[11]

---

11. Ibid., Docs. #484, p. 1594; #487, p. 1602; #489, pp. 1608-1610. E. L. Evans, p. 361. Krosigk, p. 44. Ilse Maurer, Udo Wengst, and Gerhard Schulz, eds., *Politik und Wirtschaft: Quellen zur Ära Brüning, 1930-1932* (Düsseldorf, 1980), Doc.

The conservative and reactionary groups had been expecting a government crisis since January. Scholz had talked to Brüning, Schiele, and Gottfried Reinhold Treviranus of the DNVP about the next government. Hans Luther, now a member of the DVP, was most often mentioned as the replacement for Müller. This campaign came to naught when Luther succeeded Schacht as Reichsbank President. Luther told Scholz that he was not leaving political life. He believed that Brüning's ambition would soon carry him to the Chancellorship, but that would only lead to a series of short-lived governments. Luther would wait them out until the parties were ready to form a "battle Cabinet" to enact the needed reforms. Brüning put together a Cabinet with unseemly haste. Paul Moldenhauer returned to the Finance Ministry. The Brüning Cabinet inherited his last proposal on financial reform, which included hikes in the beer, mineral-water, and mineral-oil taxes. The Meyer/Brüning compromise on unemployment insurance passed the Reichstag on April 14, but the budget remained open. Schätzel again warned that the BVP would not support the beer tax. The Economics party recommended a smaller beer-tax hike and an increase in the turnover tax. None of the government's proposals asked for additional loan authority from the Reichsbank. This is a key point. The government was proposing taxes worth about RM500 million; additional loan authority of an equal amount would have made all the negotiations easier and perhaps could have won the toleration of the SPD.[12]

Brüning's situation was similar to that of Luther and Reinhold four years earlier. Germany was in a bad recession, and the Reichsbank was pursuing a tight monetary policy. The difference was that the Reich had generated large surpluses in 1924 and 1925 and had not been in a cash crisis. Luther and Reinhold had not only promoted a tax cut program aimed at business but negotiated with the SPD to win its support and quadrupled the Reichsbank loan authorization. Had Brüning proposed a doubling of that authorization in the spring of 1930, the Reichstag would have accepted it. It might have allowed for a quick passage of the budget, provided a safeguard for additional revenue shortfalls, and reassured investors.

Things should have been looking up for the Germans because of the successful conclusion of the Young Plan. They had paid the first full Dawes year of RM2.5 billion in 1928 complaining all the way. The Young Plan ended occupation of the Rhineland, reduced annual payments by RM500 million, and released the Reichsbank and Reichsbahn to full German control. Stresemann had charged during negotiations that Gilbert was a French pawn, and a provision eliminated the post of Agent-General. The Plan also provided a new loan of

#43, p. 99. Brüning, p. 156. Breitman, p. 159.

    12. *Politik und Wirtschaft*, Docs. #7, pp. 15-18; #14, pp. 41-43; #29, pp. 74-76; #31, pp. 78-82; #43, pp. 98-102; #55, pp. 121-124. Tilman Koops, ed., *Akten der Reichskanzlei. Die Kabinette Brüning I/II* (Boppard, 1985, 1989), Doc. #9, pp. 18-21.

RM1.2 billion. Germany should have welcomed the easing of the budget burden of reparations and occupation costs, but it did not. The negotiations had brought France and Germany closer together. Their mutual interests far outweighed their relations to Britain and the United States. France had returned to the gold standard, and its reserves grew rapidly. Both France and the United States had a surfeit of gold and should have used policies to export the gold to other parts of the world. Since the middle of 1928 France had exported short-term credits to Germany as a way of redistributing capital and taking advantage of the higher German rates. Germany's vulnerability was clear during a key moment of the negotiations in 1929, when the French suddenly began to recall their loans in response to German intransigence. The Reichsbank had then raised its discount rate to protect reserves, an unwise move in a time of recession. The Germans no doubt remembered all the concessions they had tried to win from the French at the time of Thoiry, when they held the upper hand, and must have feared the French demands. An ardent nationalist such as Brüning would not stand for this.[13]

Parker Gilbert's business with Germany ended on May 17, 1930. He balanced his books and turned over the balance of cash and investments to the Bank for International Settlements created under the Young Plan. The *New York Times* praised him for handling "in a supremely successful manner one of the biggest and most complicated financial tasks in world history."[14] The Reparation Commission ceremonially burned the certificates of the 1921 London Ultimatum. Gilbert left Berlin on May 23 and traveled to Paris, where the French Finance Minister awarded him a plaque of the grand officer of the Legion of Honor. At the dinner, the Minister compared Gilbert's efforts on the French behalf to those of General Pershing. He returned to New York on June 16 and received an honorary degree at Harvard's commencement. He would spend the next few months enjoying the honeymoon he had postponed six years before. Gilbert's final report expressed confidence in the basic strength of the German economy and saw no need for tax increases. He saw the major problem as the ongoing transfer of revenue to the states. The Dawes loan as a private loan was still in effect, but the bonds had lost their protector.[15]

By the end of May, the unresolved budget looked worse still, and the government wanted to consider the usual means of job creation such as the railroad and housing construction. These subsidies would bring the budget gap near a billion Marks. The Chancellor fell ill with a 104° fever. The only piece of good news was that Fiscal Year 1929 had come in RM35 million better than

---

13. Kent, pp. 278-304. James, *Reichsbank*, p. 62. Schacht, *Old Wizard*, pp. 221-230. McNeil, pp. 225-229. Eichengreen, pp. 183, 216-223, 243.

14. *New York Times*, May 19, 1930, 7:1.

15. Ibid., May 18, 1930, 27:3; May 19, 1930, 7:1; May 24, 1930, 6:8; May 25, 1930, 13:1; May 28, 1930, 8:5; June 16, 1930, 1:5; June 17, 1930, 8:1.

expected. Moldenhauer again presented the usual program: sell Reichsbahn preferred stock, raise rents to pay for the construction program, increase the cigarette tax by RM50 million, and gain another RM150 million either from a 25% beer-tax increase or a higher turnover tax. Given the earlier troubles, Moldenhauer suggested an Enabling Act similar to that of 1923. After the Cabinet refused to raise the rent tax, Moldenhauer proposed that the civil service absorb a pay cut. Depending on the percentage of the cut, this "Reichshilfe" could raise between 150 million and 265 million Marks. Brüning supported this proposal: it could scale back the hated raise package of 1927. Since they were servants of the government, was it not fair for them to head the line of sacrifice for the budget? Schätzel squealed again at the mention of a beer tax. When RM40 million remained uncovered, the Cabinet agreed to levy an income tax surcharge on unmarried persons. After a frustrating three months, Moldenhauer shouldered the blame for the failure of the government; he resigned after underestimating the deficits and the Reichsrat rejected his covering proposals. Economics Minister Hermann Dietrich of the Democrats now moved over to take Finance. Dietrich came from Baden, had been Mayor of Konstanz during the war, and represented the smaller farmers of western Germany, who had different needs from the large-scale East Elbian agrarian interests. Müller had appointed him as Minister of Agriculture. Southwestern farmers formed an early base of the Democratic party, but it was not able to build on early success. In 1928, the DDP had won about as many votes in Baden and Württemberg as in 1920, but its percentage had fallen. As Finance Minister, he was prepared to execute his party's official program to reform the tax structure and cut government spending deeply.[16]

As the months slipped by, the yields of the proposed taxes grew smaller and smaller. The government was in a position similar to that of the Wirth Cabinets during the inflation: delays were making proposals moot. The Cabinet adjusted the proposal to omit the beer tax and insert RM100 million in unspecified savings. The total package would raise taxes and cut spending by RM755 million (see Table 7.2). The Reichsrat received the Chancellor's program skeptically but passed Brüning's plan on July 3. The Saxon Minister President urged consideration of a new plan by Peter Reinhold to suspend payments on the pre-1924 debt. As the budget came to the Reichstag, Esser posed the obvious question: how was a majority possible when both the Socialists and Nationalists stood firmly opposed? The DVP's poll tax was obnoxious to the Center party and it was questionable whether the workers' wing of the Center would support unemployment-insurance cuts. There was no

---

16. *Politik und Wirtschaft*, Docs. #77, p. 188; #85, pp. 205-212; #92, p. 246. *Kabinette Brüning*, Docs. #31, pp. 165-168; #45, pp. 178-184; #47, pp. 193-200; #52, 216-217. Brüning, p. 118. James, *Slump*, pp. 62-63. L. E. Jones, *German Liberalism*, p. 343.

**Table 7.2**
**Brüning's Budget Changes of June 1930 (millions of RM)**

| | |
|---|---|
| Smaller deficit from FY29 | 35 |
| 2½% surcharge on taxable income over RM2,000 | 135 |
| 5% surcharge on taxable incomes over RM8,000 | 58 |
| Tax on single persons | 110 |
| Tobacco tax | 48 |
| 1% increase in insurance premium and cuts in unemployment support | 269 |
| Budget cuts in FY30 | 100 |
| TOTAL | 755 |

Source: *Berliner Morgenpost*, June 29, 1930.

enthusiasm among the government parties; members were not even showing up for the Reichstag sessions and some feared that a sudden move by the SPD and KPD could scuttle the government.[17]

There were alternatives to the exhausted Müller and Brüning governments. The Hansa-Bund of Reinhold's mentor Hermann Fischer had proposed a bold plan to take action against the Depression. It called for RM700-800 million in savings coupled with a tax cut of RM1 billion. The savings would come from a spending freeze at 1929 levels in post offices and telegraphs, maintenance of government office buildings, and moving expenses. The Fischer plan would pay the sinking fund in debt, not cash, and revalue property. It also called for a new relationship between the budget and the insurance offices. Several members of the DDP supported this plan. Reinhold suggested that the government repeat the job-creation schemes of 1926. The Cabinet was not prepared to think so dramatically. The government did propose some mild business stimulus from reductions of the capital-transfer and land acquisition taxes. Dietrich wanted to delay the tax increases because there might be confusion over the government reducing some taxes while complaining about deficits and raising other taxes. Trendelenburg pleaded for greater business stimulus without success.[18]

The Social Democrats recoiled at a poll tax and even a vague promise to cut the guaranteed loans to insurance. The compromise alienated the SPD, but there was no indication that the Nationalists would support this package. Stegerwald angrily put his foot down against his one-time protégé. Stegerwald and the Catholic unions had paid a political price for supporting the government

---

17. *Politik und Wirtschaft*, Doc. #102, pp. 264-270. *Kabinette Brüning*, Docs. #42, p. 169; #56, pp. 235-239; #59, p. 246; #63, pp. 255-258.

18. *Kabinette Brüning*, Docs. #63, pp. 255-258; #64, p. 260; #67, pp. 275-279. James, *Reichsbank*, p. 319.

"reforms" of welfare, unemployment insurance, and sickness insurance. The end of the guarantee to unemployment insurance would deal a terrible blow to the Catholic unions. As long as the Reichstag remained in session, he could remain a Cabinet minister since it could vote down the government's unwise proposals. Once the Reichstag adjourned, the Cabinet would have more latitude and Stegerwald thought he would have to resign. Over his vote, the Cabinet nevertheless ended the guarantee. The poll tax and license tax would support the needs of localities in crisis relief.[19]

The compromise collapsed within a week. The Economics party opposed the licensing tax while the Bavarians opposed the poll tax. No other party was very supportive. A group of Nationalists led by Wilhelm Bazille and Westarp tried to win DNVP support for the budget. The Tax Committee rejected the Reichshilfe as the DNVP, SPD, and KPD joined forces. The Reichstag would not pass an Enabling Act, but rumor suggested that the DNVP would not vote against an Emergency Decree. Hugenberg and Hergt made the DNVP's support conditional on the dissolution of the Prussian coalition. Interior Minister Wirth urged negotiations with the SPD, but Brüning and the others opposed feared their demands would be too costly. Dietrich believed that stressing the debt and threatening new elections would convince the Reichstag.[20]

Nowhere in this debate was there any estimate of what the results of the election might be. Before each of the previous elections, the Cabinet had accurately predicted the results. The rising vote of the Nazis was apparent since October 1929, when it more than doubled its percentage in Baden from 1928's Reichstag elections. A month later, it tripled its support in Thuringia. On June 22, it quadrupled its 1928 vote in the Saxon state elections while the DNVP lost 60% of its support from 1926. There was no indication that budget conditions would be better after elections, but Brüning and the others would not deal with the SPD, nor did they possess enough imagination to promote a sweeping reform program that would cover the deficit, stimulate the economy, and win a majority in the Reichstag. The Hansa-Bund program was the best prospect of this. The uncertainty over the budget, rather than any specific concerns, led investors to withdraw deposits in the summer of 1930.[21]

---

19. *Kabinette Brüning*, Docs. #67, p. 239; #69, pp. 284-286; #70, p. 286. *Politik und Wirtschaft*, Doc. #82, p. 200. Heinrich August Winkler, *Der Weg in die Katastrophe: Arbeiter und Arbeiterbewegung in der Weimarer Republik* (Bonn, 1990), p. 161.

20. *Politik und Wirtschaft*, Docs. #107, pp. 277-281; #112, pp. 296-297. *Kabinette Brüning*, Doc. #71, pp. 289-293; #77, pp. 311-318. *Märkischer Zeitung*, July 18, 1930, in BAP R 8034 II/4676.

21. E. J. Feuchtwanger, *From Weimar to Hitler: Germany, 1918-1933*, Second Edition (New York, 1993), p. 327. L. E. Jones, *German Liberalism*, p. 364. Balderston, *Economic Crisis*, pp. 170-171.

As the crisis broke out in mid-July, Hans Luther was in Basel. The Reichsbank President had seemed quite fond of using Emergency Decrees and Enabling Acts during his time as Finance Minister, but now he begged Brüning not to use Article 48. The failure of Reichstag negotiations would badly damage Germany's reputation and ability to get foreign credit for productive purposes. Luther had given Brüning a confidential American cable to this effect. The Americans expected the normal budget process to work its will. The upturn in the New York Stock Exchange after the crash of 1929 raised hopes that American money would soon be flowing again. Luther in a telegram stressed that the conditions in no way resembled those of December 1923. On the evening of July 14, Luther spoke with Brüning on the telephone. The government should only use Article 48 when there were no parliamentary possibilities. Luther was right; only Brüning's stubbornness and his bad relations with the SPD precluded a budget agreement.[22]

But Brüning's ego could not accept such a judgment. He may have feared that Luther was staging a power play and preparing to oust him. He would rub the SPD's nose in this foul arrangement. He expected the SPD to protest but take no action just as in 1923-24. Not only did Brüning issue the decree, but he crammed all of his proposals into the decree: the Reichshilfe; the income tax surcharges; the tobacco tax; the poll tax; the licensing tax, cuts in unemployment insurance, sickness insurance, and welfare; measures against price-fixing of cartels, and money for subsidies to the East to appeal to the DNVP. He asked for RM322 million in additional credit authorization to make the budget balance. When the SPD brought its motion to strike down the decree, the government could have postponed the Reichstag vote, but Brüning leapt ahead. He said that postponing the vote would leave too much doubt about German finances. He remained confident until the night of July 17, when Hugenberg announced that the DNVP would support the Socialist/Communist motion. Westarp refused to support the motion, and several Nationalists followed him out of the party. The Nationalists were finished as a political force. The Reichstag struck down the decree 236 to 221. Having made the threat of new elections, Brüning felt honor-bound to carry out the threat. His only hope was that the Reichstag might give him an Enabling Act after elections. While the Reichstag was dissolved, Brüning reissued the decree; Dietrich gave it the Orwellian title of "the measure to correct unemployment insurance and enable employment of the jobless." It would be a good election slogan. Dietrich's belief that a false title could disguise a noxious bill symbolized the decay of the Democratic party. With the split of the DNVP, Brüning's program

---

22. Feuchtwanger, p. 223. *Kabinette Brüning*, Doc. #77, pp. 315-316.

had fourteen of the twenty-eight votes on the Reichstag oversight committee and could sustain the decree until the elections.[23]

The Brüning program of 1930 was an unmitigated catastrophe and completely unnecessary. Some have recently tried to defend Brüning. Knut Borchardt argues that wages were too high relative to productivity and deflation was healthy. As seen before, corporate profits were high enough to justify high wages, and productivity gains of the mid- to late 1920s probably justified them as well. Another argument has taken the nature of "what choice did he have?" The attempts by Reinhold in 1927 and Hilferding in 1929 to sell long-term bonds on the German market had failed. The foreign credit market was very restricted. Balderston spends a long chapter examining the options of Brüning and finds the key in a crucial flaw: the Germans simply had no cash reserves unlike most nations with a well-developed debt structure. This is true, but let us examine the causes: Germany should have had ample time to develop some structuring of debt between 1926 and 1930. Luther and Reinhold had created some breathing room by quadrupling the authorization of Reichsbank credits from 100 million to 400 million Marks. Reinhold had erred by trying to redevelop the domestic market at a single stroke. Instead of a long-term bond, Reinhold should have begun the development of debt structure by offering three-month and six-month bills on the open market.[24] Parker Gilbert pointed this out in his June 1927 report. After the inflation, it would take time to rebuild the trust and confidence of investors in the "full faith and credit" of the German government. Balderston finds that the inflation and revaluation process left the German debt market at only 55-60% of the prewar size. Given the state of the short-term credit market in 1926, it should have been easy to sell these bills and then roll them over at the appropriate intervals. By 1927 and 1928, the government should have marketed substantial sums of one-year notes, and by 1929, investor confidence should have allowed the marketing of notes with maturities ranging between five and seven years. It is possible that with greater confidence a twenty-year bond could have marketed, but this is probably too much of an assumption.[25]

Borchardt saw no way out for Brüning. Foreign credits, especially from France, would bring political demands. Domestic credits would clash with

---

23. *Politik und Wirtschaft*, Docs. #112-114, pp. 286-301; #127, pp. 360-361. *Kabinette Brüning*, Docs. #82-83, pp. 328-330; #86, pp. 333-334; #92, p. 354; #107, p. 399.

24. In the most technical sense, the government started to offer short-term bills on the "open market" in March 1928. However, the smallest denomination of these bills was RM10,000, far above what an upper-middle-class investor could buy. I therefore prefer to designate these as "Treasury transfers," mostly sold to institutional investors. I would expect a "Treasury Bill" as we currently understand it to have a denomination as low as RM100, roughly 10% of the German per capita income in the late 1920s.

25. Balderston, *Financial Crisis*, p. 275; "Economic Instability," p. 508.

the Reichsbank law. The Young Plan forbade devaluation of the Mark and controlled bank credits. Finally there was a public fear of inflation. Let us demolish each of these in turn. French investors had put money into Germany for two years with no political demands. To the contrary, the Young Plan's revisions had all been in Germany's favor. Marketing debt did not involve the Reichsbank at all; only changing the credit authorization would involve amending the law, as had been done in 1926. There was no need to devalue until after August 1931. The "fear of inflation" played no role in the 1930 events but was significant in the 1931 bank crisis. The irony is that Germany had gotten hold of government spending. Before the war, German Reich, state, and local governments had spent 17% of the Net National Product. This rose to 38% during the time of inflation, but fell after 1925 and averaged 30% of NNP, a figure comparable to Great Britain's. Borchardt also suggests that policy-makers believed the crisis would be short, that they hoped for recovery in spring of 1931, and that by summer of 1931 when the banking crisis was in full swing, it was too late to do anything for the winter. But Schäffer in September 1930, more than a year into the Depression, said the economy had not yet hit the bottom. By the time Brüning became Chancellor it was clear this was no "short and sharp" crisis. Even if true, Luther and Reinhold had begun to fight the recession of 1925-26 within six months of the onset.[26]

The lack of investor confidence and a debt structure still did not foreclose choices to Heinrich Brüning. Given the party alignment in the Reichstag, Brüning should have found a majority that would support another increase in the Reichsbank credit authorization. Instead of quadrupling it, as Reinhold and Luther had done, a mere doubling to RM800 million would have been a good start, with most of that money going to subsidize the unemployment fund. Borchardt objects that reparations treaties governed the Bank Law, but treaties can be amended. Brüning also could have tried to market a small quantity (RM50 to 100 million) of Treasury Bills to the public, just to test the market. Even if this bill sale failed, it would have provided some income. The rest of the debt could remain uncovered for the moment. The impact of borrowing the money rather than trying to cut purchasing power of the German people by reducing spending and raising taxes would have been enormous. As we shall see, Brüning pushed through a much larger authorization of Treasury transfers through a much more hostile Reichstag two years later. Brüning set off a vicious circle with his policies of raising taxes and cutting spending. Raising unemployment premiums sky-high gave workers less money to buy goods and forced employers to lay off workers because their premiums were too costly. This further burdened the unemployment insurance fund. Rising unemployment meant that tax revenues would not reach their anticipated levels

---

26. Holtfrerich in Kershaw, pp. 62-63. McNeil, p. 241. Borchardt, pp. 145-147. *Politik und Wirtschaft*, Doc. #134, p. 380.

and the resulting deficits would confront the government with one budget crisis after another.

To understand the real impact of these austerity programs, we turn again to Cohn's "high-employment budgets." As seen in the last chapter, Cohn uses employment peaks in 1927 and 1937 to create a projected Gross Domestic Product and tax revenue. This has the effect of factoring out unemployment and the enormous sums that would be spent on unemployment relief and insurance. Cohn justifies factoring this out because it represents a natural balancing effect in the business cycle. The theory behind the "high-employment budget" is that modern welfare states provide a natural corrective mechanism to economic downturns: as more people are thrown out of work and incomes fall, a budget will slip into deficit and provide money to the unemployed in benefits and to others in relative tax cuts. Cohn's projections show that Fiscal Year 1929 had a surplus of between 2% and 3% of Full Employment Net National Product, while FY30, governed by Brüning's decrees, would show a surplus of between 3% and 4% of NNP. Cohn proves that fiscal policy was becoming increasingly restrictive when it should have been less restrictive. Brüning pushed the brakes on a stalled economy and wondered why it was not moving.[27]

I am not suggesting that taking more Reichsbank credit authority and selling a small amount of Treasury Bills would have headed off the entire experience of the Depression in Germany. It would not. Global conditions, especially falling agricultural prices, dictated an economic downturn. Problems specific to Germany included the lost assets of the war and a large age cohort entering the workforce. The proposal outlined above could have commanded a majority in the Reichstag. Had Brüning continued to meet further budget crises with further credit authorizations (up to about two billion Marks) and some modest spending cuts and tax increases, the Reichstag could have held out until elections in April 1932. These results probably would have been similar to the actual results of 1930 or May 1924. There would have been about ten months of trouble, but by 1933 the German economy would be recovering. The Nazi and Communist tide would have receded, as in December 1924, and the government could have gone on, providing economic stimulus where necessary and repaying the credit to the Reichsbank while creating a well-structured national debt.

Brüning had Hindenburg call for new elections in September 1930. There was no discussion in the Cabinet about what the new elections would bring, just that they would somehow make things easier. In contrast, the Cabinets in 1920, 1924, and 1928 had always discussed the election results in advance, usually with a fair degree of accuracy. The best contemporary indication we have is a letter written by Hans Schäffer to Max Warburg. The State Secretary believed that the Nationalist splinters would outpoll the

---

27. Cohn in Komlos and Eddie, pp. 261-283.

Hugenberg party and that the Nazis would triple their 1928 vote and gain forty seats.  In 1944, Brüning wrote to Arnold Brecht and told him that he had fully expected the 1930 result.  He claimed that he had predicted that the Nazis would win 140 seats rather than the 107 that they did win.  In his memoirs, Brüning made no such claim.  One must always debate whether Brüning was foolish or malicious, but even if one takes him at his word, the calling of new elections was an act of gross irresponsibility.  Even if Brüning's goal was to establish a dictatorship, as some charge, there could be no certainty that the Social Democrats would not overturn every decree and force Brüning out of office.  The Chancellor pinned his hopes on the DNVP splinters defeating Hugenberg's faction.  While Reusch and other industrialists offered financial help, there was insufficient time for the ex-Nationalists to build a proper framework for a new party.[28]

The Nazi party arrived on the political scene with the 1930 elections.  It far outstripped its showing in the May 1924 elections and became the second-largest party behind the SPD.  The foreign reaction to the rise of the Nazis was catastrophic.  The problems of Wall Street and the German budget had already led to a tepid reception of the Young Plan loan.  After the elections, gold and foreign exchange began to flow out of Germany.   The price of German bonds plunged in the New York and London markets.  Brüning complained that the German press was making this worse by spreading false rumors about impending putsches against the government.  The Reichsbank reserves fell RM650 million in the four weeks following the elections.  With a 40% covering ratio, this loss in effect meant RM1.6 billion in stimulus was unavailable.   The foreign underwriters would extend no more long-term foreign loans to Germany.[29]

The election had taught the Brüning Cabinet nothing.  It resumed its work on the austerity package.  The Decree of July 26 was only the beginning.  Schäffer tried to place RM230 million in Treasury transfers with German banks, but they gave him a cold shoulder.  Worsening unemployment created a RM400 million gap in the insurance fund and strained the crisis-relief fund for those who had exhausted their insurance.  Dietrich proposed using RM200 million from general revenue and a hike in the unemployment premium from 4½% to 6½%.  A projected RM600 million shortfall in tax revenue meant that RM900 million needed covering.  Dietrich and Luther were negotiating a short-term foreign loan of $125 million from Lee, Higginson to cover half of this shortfall.[30]

28. James in Kershaw, p. 33.  *Politik und Wirtschaft*, Doc. #126, p. 356. Brecht, p. 503.  E. L. Evans, p. 364.  L. E. Jones, *German Liberalism*, p. 365.

29. Kent, pp. 326-331.  *Kabinette Brüning*, Docs. #107, pp. 398-399; #116, p. 434.  Brüning, p.  198. *Politik und Wirtschaft*, Doc. #141, pp. 397-400.  James, *Slump*, p. 135.

30. James, *Slump*, p. 64.  *Kabinette Brüning*, Doc #116, pp. 434-440.

The Cabinet also had to face the 1931 budget. Dietrich estimated that this would have a deficit of RM618 million, most of which was lower revenue from taxes and tariffs. The Cabinet decided to cut the budget, limit unemployment-insurance payments, and reduce the salaries of civil servants even more. Guérard and Stegerwald wanted to explore new ways of fighting unemployment. Dietrich opposed employment measures. He felt that these should be left to the private sector. Stegerwald warned that the winter of 1930-31 would be a very difficult one if the government did not provide employment opportunities. Dietrich wanted reductions in the ground tax and the business tax, supported by RM400 million from rent tax revenues. The Cabinet made a 6% cut in administrative personnel and cut the salaries of the rest by 5%. There would be a 5% income-tax surcharge and an increased tobacco tax. It raised the unemployment premium to 6½%. It also cut RM163 million in transfers to states and localities. Luther raised the question of unifying all the budgets of the Reich, states, and localities. The states and especially the cities were slipping into chronic deficit. According to their respective mayors, Frankfurt am Main had a deficit of RM8 million, Leipzig RM5.5 million, and Duisburg RM11 million.[31]

In his memoirs, Brüning claimed he had a plan. He felt falling prices already reflected his success. He told Luther that he would stage a second round of wage and price deflation and use Germany's distress to end reparations. Once the Young Plan no longer bound Germany, he would devalue the currency by 20%. Brüning noted that Luther was "somewhat shocked" but went along with the spirit of the scheme.[32] If this conversation ever took place, Luther's shock was well founded. Brüning was pursuing completely contradictory goals. Devaluing the currency would undo the effect of the deflation while raising the real value of Germany's foreign debt. This was madness unless the Chancellor intended to repudiate the debt, which would open a new series of problems. According to Max Habermann, Brüning planned to build a budget surplus and deflate wages and prices to build a large trade surplus that would in turn put pressure on Allied leaders to end reparations.[33] Brüning's "risk theory" was pure fantasy. Days before Müller's resignation, the United States Senate had passed the Hawley-Smoot Tariff, igniting a general trade war and assuring that any trade surplus Germany ran would be a small one. By the end of 1930, French creditors dominated Germany's short-term debt. If Brüning threatened France, the counterstroke would be devastating. The Chancellor showed no awareness of the short-term credit structure and preferred to try to

---

31. *Kabinette Brüning*, Docs. #107, pp. 398-402; #116, pp. 434-440; #117, pp. 440-445; #121, p. 459; #123, pp. 461-466; #126, pp. 477-479. *Politik und Wirtschaft*, Doc. #177, pp. 508-512.
32. Brüning, p. 221.
33. Patch, p. 157.

tap the dwindling credit of the United States.  Brüning felt that the austerity program would build confidence for a new American loan.  In defending the regime's refusal to draw additional credit from the post office, railroad, and Reichsbank, Borchardt says: "Governments which did not wish to pursue an adventurist course in foreign policy were not in a position to disregard these international constraints."[34] But on so many fronts, Brüning had already passed from "adventurism" to hallucinatory fantasy.  He supposedly told Hitler that once reparations were abolished, he would move to restore the monarchy.[35]

In November 1930, Dietrich and the Reichsbank concluded negotiations with Lee, Higginson and a pair of Dutch banking houses for a two-year loan worth $125 million.  As part of these negotiations, the Cabinet had to guarantee balanced budgets for Fiscal Years 1930 and 1931.  The regime remained below its credit allowance: it had RM400 million in loan authorization from the Reichsbank dating back to 1926, and the Reichsbahn and Post had another RM225 million in authority.  Of this potential RM625 million, the government was only using RM420 million.  The Cabinet also responded that it was working on fulfilling Gilbert's demands from his final report of May 1930: it was scaling back the 1927 civil-service raises and working to unify the budget under Reich control.  Unlike the 1930 budget, Brüning wanted to pass the 1931 budget in proper parliamentary fashion to appease the foreign bankers.[36]

The states, especially Baden, Bavaria, Württemberg, and Hesse, protested the draft budget for FY31.  The different compositions of the state economies doomed any attempt to make their budgets conform.  Baden was entitled to RM12 million as part of a loan authority to spur construction, but the tax reductions would take over RM13 million.  Both the Mecklenburgs had exhausted their funds by November 1930 and needed bailouts from the Reich.  By the next spring, all of the states were facing staggering deficits.  Prussia estimated a gap of RM200-210 million for FY31.  The states had cut their budgets to the bone, and the localities were at the limit of their short-term credit.[37]

The Social Democrats were in a quandary after the September 1930 elections.  The party could again vote to overthrow the decree.  When it demanded the removal of the offensive poll tax, Brüning threatened to pull the Catholic Center party out of the Prussian coalition.  The SPD feared that new elections would strengthen the power of the Nazis and Communists.  It would abstain on votes to overturn the decrees.  The Nazis introduced a sweeping bank bill that would ban many bank transactions on securities.  The bill would

34.  Borchardt, p. 148.

35.  Brüning, p. 193.

36.  *Kabinette Brüning*, Docs. #127, pp. 480-484; #130, p. 489; #131, pp. 502-503; #148, pp. 553-554. James, *Slump*, p. 70.

37.  *Kabinette Brüning*, Docs. #138-139, pp. 517-530; #145, pp. 540-546; #160, p. 597; #261, p. 945.

expropriate all capital of banks and stocks involved with "eastern Jews and various foreign races" or profiting from war, inflation, and deflation. The government did not dare to bring any banking legislation, even an increased authorization from Reichsbank credit, to the Reichstag because the Nazis would seize the opportunity to attach their bill and unleash a bitter debate. Attempts to sell Treasury transfers to banks failed. Even reducing their term did not help. Only the Bank for International Settlements and the Golddiskontbank would buy them. Brüning had boxed himself in with the elections. All that remained was a program of austerity or flagrant violation of the credit laws. Not until March 1931 was there a bit of bright light as the Reich renewed RM53 million in Treasury Bills and sold an additional RM72 million to banks.[38]

The Reichstag passed the 1931 budget, but it was an exercise in futility. The revenue for the first quarter of 1931 fell short of the estimate by RM410 million, while the spending for unemployment insurance and crisis-relief had risen by RM120 million. Despite the 6½% premium, which was ruining employers and employees alike, the unemployment-insurance fund projected a RM262 million deficit for FY31. To secure a bridging credit from the Reichsbank, the insurance fund had to accept bank controls over its transfers. By May 1931, Dietrich was projecting another shortfall of RM782 million and proposed new taxes and budget cuts. The Reich abandoned the states to their own devices. Prussia by this time was estimating a deficit of RM760 million, and Bavaria's estimate was RM70 million. On a per capita basis, Prussia's short and medium-term debt was one-third of that for Bavaria, Saxony, and Thuringia. Brüning believed that if the states wanted more, they should cut their officials' salaries. As the Cabinet deliberated, German bonds continued to fall on foreign markets. The Young loan had been issued at 90% but fell to 68.75% on June 2, 1931.[39]

Brüning issued a sweeping decree on June 5, 1931, to close yet another deficit. He sought to cover the current deficit and any possible shortfall that might occur before April 1, 1932. It also would dedicate funds for job creation. Budget cuts, an additional 7% cut in the salaries of civil servants, and increases in the oil tariff and the sugar and turnover taxes would close the Reich's budget gap. A similar cut for officials of the states and cities would reduce their deficits as well. A special crisis tax would cover the shortfalls in unemployment insurance, crisis relief, and welfare. The government forced commercial banks to swallow RM250 million in renewed treasury bills. There would be RM100 million for job creation and RM34 million kept for the winter. The Chancellor wanted to combine the decree with a call to revise the Young Plan to head off

38. Ibid., Doc. #183, pp. 663-679. *Politik und Wirtschaft*, Doc. #186, p. 534. James, *Slump*, p. 73.

39. *Kabinette Brüning*, Docs. #255, Note 1, p. 925; #261, p. 945; #269, p. 979; #290, p. 1053; #320, pp. 1164-1166. James, *Slump*, p. 80.

domestic opposition.   Luther was aghast.   He thought the Chancellor had promised not to reopen reparations in 1931.   This move could cause a massive capital flight.   Dietrich disagreed: a high discount rate would keep that capital in Germany.[40]

Brüning thought that this decree, his visit to Chequers to consult with the Allies on possible reparations revisions, and Luther's trip to the Bank for International Settlements (BIS) would give a boost to German credit.   After all, had he not balanced the budget and opened the prospect for elimination or reduction of the reparations payments?   He also hoped to get a foreign loan from the BIS.   Brüning could not have been more wrong.   Investors had hoped that Germany would take positive measures to pull out of the Depression instead of yet more austerity.   We should note that in Brüning's term up to June 1931 his main accomplishments had been to nullify what he considered the great errors of recent fiscal policy: Reinhold's tax reduction program of 1926 and Köhler's civil-service raises of 1927.   Brüning had studiously ignored all other options in his obsession to erase these acts.   The feckless government publicly announced that Germany was in "a precarious economic and financial situation."   Authorities would now interpret Luther's trip to Switzerland as desperation.   The prudent investor would conclude that further investment in Germany or even holding the current German portfolio was a losing proposition as long as Brüning was Chancellor.   There was little prospect that alternative governments would be an improvement: the Socialists were still supporting austerity, while the social revolutions preached by the Nazis and Communists were unacceptable to the investment community.   It therefore made perfect sense for the investors to pull their capital out of Germany.[41]

The collapse of the Austrian Creditanstalt on May 11, reports of business difficulties, the decree, and the loss of confidence in Brüning by the investment community led to an exodus of capital.   Between May 26 and June 15, 1931, the Reichsbank lost a billion Marks in currency reserves.   RM386 million was lost on just three days: June 12, June 13, and June 15.   Bank runs soon followed, but the banks did not have enough cash.   The ghost of inflation now haunted Hans Luther.   The Reichsbank raised its discount rate to 7% to increase Germany's attractiveness to foreign investors and keep enough gold and foreign currency to cover the money in circulation.   Given the deflationary situation, this meant that real interest rates in Germany were hovering in the 15% range, a completely impossible situation (see Figure 7.1).   The high interest rate policy was especially harsh on farmers.   Their interest rate payment as a percentage of sales would rise from 10.7% to 13.8% in 1931-32.   The loss of foreign confidence was so severe that the discount rate could never be high

40. *Kabinette Brüning*, Docs. #300, pp. 1089-1091; #307, pp. 1114-1118. *Politik und Wirtschaft*, Doc. #210, pp. 620-621.  James, *Slump*, p. 73.

41. Kent, p. 341.

**Figure 7.1**
**Real Interest Rates, 1929-1932 (Discount Rates Minus Price Change)**

*Sources*: **Balderston,p.148; Winkler,p.83.**

enough to compensate.   Brüning proposed a simultaneous reduction of the covering percentage combined with higher interest rates.   Cutting the covering rate from 40% to 17% would mean a 13% discount rate, he said.   Brüning seems to have gotten these numbers off the top of his head, a very dubious place for economic theory.   The Chancellor had lost all trust in Luther during the bank runs.  Meanwhile Dietrich was fighting with Schäffer after the Finance Minister had fulminated against the actions of "Jewish bankers" and offended Schäffer.[42]

The banking crisis caused a panic of investment capital.   Germany had lost RM1.5 billion in gold and foreign currency reserves from May 30 to July 1.   Luther received an emergency covering of $100 million from the Bank of England, the Bank of France, the Federal Reserve, and the Bank for International Settlements.   Bankers Trust cut its credit line to the Deutsche Bank.    The Guaranty Bank began withdrawals.    The bankruptcy of the Nordwolle concern and withdrawal of RM800 million since September 1930 led to the collapse of the Darmstädter- und National Bank (Danat) on July 13. President Hoover called on Germany to pass a decree against the flight of

42. *Kabinette Brüning* Doc. #332, pp. 1198-1204. James, *Slump*, pp. 267, 303. *Politik und Wirtschaft*, Doc. #223, p. 654. Krosigk, p. 62.

capital. This had not worked during the early 1920s, and there was no reason to believe it would work now. Nevertheless, Brüning issued another decree. On July 15, the Reich raised the discount rate to 10% and the lombard rate to 15%. In real terms, interest rates were in the 15-20% range. This would snuff out any attempts at raising capital domestically while the ineptitude of the Brüning regime made it doubtful that foreigners would invest. When rumors swept the markets that Crédit Lyonnais would be part of a consortium to bail out Germany, that bank's reserves tumbled. Luther desperately raised the discount rate to 15%. The government declared a bank holiday and closed the markets. It imposed a limit of one hundred Marks in payment of cash to customers per day. Luther even contemplated pulling the old Rentenmarks out of the vaults and adding them to the money supply for banks to issue. Brüning recoiled in horror because that would remind people of the Inflation days. The Reich set a limit of thirty Marks in interest payments on savings accounts.[43]

The Reich budget deficit grew as another RM230 million shortfall had occurred in July income. The cities were running a cumulative deficit of RM800 million. Dietrich said the cities should conform to the civil-service and wage cuts made by the federal government. At the beginning of August, Dietrich proposed a doubling of the turnover tax to close the deficit.[44] While Hilferding warned of the danger of inflation, former Finance Minister Dernburg replied in exasperation: "I am no inflationist! We are in a wide deflation. A certain inflation to combat deflation, as proposed in England, would not be a mistake."[45] When Melchior proposed a RM3.5 billion credit to stimulate business, Dietrich flatly opposed any short-term credit.[46]

The solution to the crisis would have to lie abroad. Luther planned for foreign credits to the Golddiskontbank, which had lain dormant with an unused $50 million foreign credit, and a public/private partnership to guarantee loans to restore confidence. The United States, Britain, France, and the BIS rolled over the $100 million rediscount credit. The Reichsbank did not repay it until April 1933. For new credits, France was the only possible source. The United States and Britain were mired in the financial miseries of the Depression, the BIS was limited, and the French had vetoed Norman's proposal of an international corporation to lend money to troubled countries. The French did not want an international board deciding where French capital should be spent. France had been piling up gold reserves since it stabilized in 1927, but it continued to insist on deflation because prices were still above 1913 levels. The

---

43. *Kabinette Brüning*, Docs. #361, p. 1288; #377, p. 1334; #387, p. 1361; #396, 1383-1387; #424, pp. 1483-1497. James, *Slump*, pp. 284, 303. *Politik und Wirtschaft*, Doc. #258, pp. 749-750; #261, pp. 758-759; #266, p. 778.

44. *Kabinette Brüning*, Docs. #424, pp. 1483-1497; #446, p. 1575.

45. Ibid., Doc. #427, p. 1506.

46. Ibid., Doc. #436, pp. 1534-1539.

French did not lower their interest rates or expand their money supply or promote foreign loans. For Germany, France was the only game in town and had been the main source of short-term credit since 1928.[47]

The wheel had come full circle since Thoiry, and the Germans trembled at the possible demands the French might make. After all, the Germans had demanded territorial concessions from France and Belgium at Thoiry. Might the French demand the Saarland or renewed military occupation? The French demands turned out to be trifling: the Germans should cease construction of a new battleship, promise not to ask for revision of the Young Plan, and maintain the status quo with Austria. In return the French would extend a ten-year $500 million loan. These demands were extremely reasonable: the Germans should honor their previous promises and stop wasting their limited resources on the military. Had the Germans accepted the deal, it would have finally stabilized the budget, ended the credit crisis, and begun economic recovery. Brüning dismissed all these suggestions and tried to portray it as a general problem that Germany could solve if the Allies rescheduled all outstanding credits, offered new loans, and delayed reparations indefinitely. For Borchardt, this is potentially fatal to his theory of a Brüning forced against his will. He cites a 1966 letter from Hans Schäffer asserting that Hindenburg would have resigned had Germany taken credits from France. Schäffer said the evidence of this is in his own diary, the Pünder papers, and the Cabinet minutes. To my knowledge, this information has never appeared in the published versions of these documents, nor have I seen it asserted in other secondary sources. Hindenburg was sitting in Neudeck for the entire bank crisis and was not active.[48]

We should pause at this point to consider whether there was a danger of "stagflation." Was it possible that Germany could have suffered a bout of rising prices and inflation while having high unemployment and a stagnant or shrinking economy? The answer is no. The two keys in the stagflation of the 1970s were rising commodity prices, directly or indirectly caused by the increased price of oil from $1.25 to $40 between 1967 and 1980, and the power of corporations and unions to maintain steady or rising prices to secure profits and wages.[49] Neither factor was present in Germany in 1931. Commodity prices were uniformly falling, not rising. Union power had never really recovered from the Inflation, and the slump had broken it. The destruction of consumer purchasing power by the Brüning regime had cut back corporate profit

---

47. *Politik und Wirtschaft*, Docs. #253, pp. 733-734; #254b, pp. 757-758; #268, p. 784. Edward W. Bennett, *Germany and the Diplomacy of the Financial Crisis, 1931* (Cambridge, MA, 1962), p. 223. Kent, p. 340. Eichengreen, p. 254.

48. André François-Poncet, *The Fateful Years: Memoirs of a French Ambassador in Berlin, 1931-1938* (New York, 1949), p. 7. Eichengreen, p. 268. *Politik und Wirtschaft*, Doc. #279c, p. 832. Brüning, pp. 321-330. Borchardt, p. 248.

49. Galbraith, pp. 280-281.

sharply.   An attempt to maintain prices would only drive a company into bankruptcy.

The states also ran into ever more serious cash problems after the Reich reduced their transfers.   Prussia, Baden, the Hanseatic cities, and Lippe now joined the primarily agricultural states on the critical list.   The debt problem was different for each state, but the Reich prescribed heavier budget cuts for each. In a real sense, the states had lost control of their budgets.   The southern, more Catholic states saw this as a deliberate plan.   They particularly suspected that Luther, "a Protestant zealot," wanted to subordinate the southern states to the Reich.   This is going a bit far.   Luther believed that if the Reich bailed out some of the smaller states, Prussia would be encouraged to either appeal for help or else print money through its own state bank, which could lead to inflation. Prussia held RM451 million in floating debt.   While Köln had done its utmost to economize, the city could receive additional aid from the Reich only if it turned over its profits from its gas, electric, and water works.   A decree of fall 1931 also forbade savings banks from extending credit to local institutions.   Paul Thomes has interpreted this as a way to force the savings banks to invest in the Reich.   Another decree authorized state governments to force local budgets into balance.   Sixty years after the proclamation of the German empire at Versailles, the Reich had finally united financial policy brutally.   The first programs to come to the chopping block were often those that promoted job creation, so that unemployment and the income shortfall fed on themselves.   Brüning's decrees clearly violated state and local rights, but the Constitutional Court generally supported their legality.[50]

The financial crisis of the summer of 1931 also crippled the mechanism of the open markets.   From July 13 to September 3, 1931, and again from October 3, 1931, to April 12, 1932, the stock and bond markets were closed. Those who say that a Keynesian solution could not work because there was insufficient investor confidence to buy public debt have put the cart before the horse.   Appeal to public investors was not used properly in 1929-30.   The Nazi breakthrough began a steady assault on confidence, but by July 1931 the markets were not even open to test investor confidence.   Short-term national debt actually fell from December 1930 to July 1931 by RM3 billion as the Reich redeemed all of its short-term treasury transfers taken from 1927 to 1930.[51]

While the Reich slashed social spending, especially unemployment payments, it had no problem bailing out the great banks as they failed.   The

---

50.  *Kabinette Brüning*, Docs. #389, pp. 1368-1370; #471, pp. 1690-1693; #492, p. 1755. James, *Slump*, pp. 80-81. *Politik und Wirtschaft*, Doc. #266, p. 777. Krosigk, p. 88. Thomes in Cassis, Feldman, and Olsson, p. 155. Feuchtwanger, p. 237. Mommsen, *Rise and Fall*, p. 362.

51.  James in Kershaw, p. 44. *Politik und Wirtschaft*, Docs. #288, p. 897; #328, p. 1002.

Reich propped up both the Danat and the Dresdner Banks with massive purchase of stock on condition that the boards of directors would resign on demand of the government. The government-sponsored Golddiskontbank held over 50% of the stock, and the Reich held another 14% directly. The Reich also sponsored a new institution, the Akzeptbank, capitalized it at RM1.5 billion, and used it mostly to support the savings banks. It heavily subsidized other banks such as the Deutsche Bank with stock purchases. The takeover of the banks afforded the Reich an opportunity for even more financial room to maneuver if it were willing to indulge in some fiduciary irresponsibility. With the resources of the banks at its command, the Reich could have forced the banks to accept large amounts of Treasury Bills. Depositors anxious for their money could have reassurance with plentiful cash supplies after the Reich purchased bank bonds or stock. Obviously this is a version of a "shell game," but it is precisely these sorts of creative solutions that eluded the Brüning regime during the Depression. The Nazi regime would use them to help Germany recover from the Depression. Looting the banks was undesirable, but again the alternatives were worse. An awful lot of modern finance is simply a fancy shell game. After the recovery, the government privatized the Deutsche Bank in 1936 and the Dresdner Bank in 1937.[52]

The situation became more dire after England devalued its currency on September 20, 1931. This would make English exports more competitive with German exports and worsen the German trade balance. Other nations now abandoned gold and cut their currency coverage percentages. When depositors in Denmark made a run on the banks, the government provided unlimited cash to end the run. Most governments, however, raised their interest rates to protect their currencies and did not engage in open-market operations to pump cash into the economy. Germany did not devalue the mark for fear that it would lead to an uncontrollable slide in the currency. Instead the Cabinet now resorted to a 20% reduction in the rent tax and tried to push wages down even more. The devaluation of the pound at last prompted the government to loosen monetary policy. Even Dietrich now conceded that a continued deflationary policy would lead to terrible results. The Reichsbank must lower interest rates. Now Luther took the hard line. He continued to look at the weak reserves and believe that inflation was around the corner. The covering of notes from reserves had again fallen below 40%. Trendelenburg replied that since he estimated all current debt to be RM17 billion, a 1% cut in the discount rate would save RM170 million. Even more effective would be raising agricultural prices because Germany had not reached the bottom of the business cycle. Luther said that he would not cut interest rates until wages and rents fell another 20%. The Reichsbank President warned that reducing rates alone would not

---

52. *Politik und Wirtschaft*, Doc. #279c, p. 837. Brüning, p. 349. Krosigk, pp. 84-86.

help: the United States had reduced its rate to 1½% with no appreciable effect. Before its devaluation, England had covered 100% of its currency with gold or foreign reserve, Germany only covered 40%.[53]

Some have argued that the easing of monetary policy that began at the end of 1931 was the key to bringing Germany out of the Depression. James has downplayed the role of fiscal policy in the recovery from the Depression. He prefers to look at the reduction of interest rates after the summer crisis and an acceleration of the purchase of noncommercial bills by the Reichsbank to pump cash into the economy. However, J. K. Galbraith points out that the attempt by the United States to rely on a purely monetary solution to the Depression was a total failure. Part of the problem is that to have effective monetary policy in a Depression of that magnitude, one must employ negative interest rates. Since the human mind rebels at a loan of $100 repaid at $95, normal financial markets and assumptions break down.    Germany had suffered great monetary contraction. In November 1929, currency and deposits equaled RM24 billion; in February 1932 RM19 billion.    As Hans-Joachim Voth notes, had the Reichsbank maintained the money supply at its 1929 level, the gold/currency cover would have fallen to 13.4%. Only in late 1931 did Luther  allow the cover to fall below the 40% limit; by October 1932 the cover fell to 15%. This was not monetary expansion, merely monetary recovery.[54]

The October 1931 decree extended the fiscal year to July 1932 because of uncertainty in the budget and reparation plans.  Brüning had finally realized that he had a burgeoning political crisis on his hands and that another call for wage reductions would lead to open revolt unless coupled with a larger job-creation program.  The Nazis had scored more victories.  In December yet another hole of RM600 million had opened in the budget. The Chancellor came up with another rationalization for the balanced budget.  He would need it for the next round of negotiations with the Allies to show Germany's stability. Stresemann had said otherwise at the beginning of 1926.  The late Foreign Minister had warned that if Germany was flush with cash, the Allies would believe it had a high capacity to pay.  Far better to run deficits, Stresemann had told Luther and Reinhold.  With other nations raising their discount rates in the wake of devaluation, Luther refused Brüning's request to incorporate a discount rate cut into the new decree to give some hope.  The government raised the turnover tax to a staggering 3½%.  Brüning was neatly reversing everything he had hated about Reinhold's fiscal policy.  This proposal sent the People's party and the Economics party into opposition, but this was not significant since the

---

53.  Eichengreen, pp. 291-304.  *Kabinette Brüning*, Docs. #502, pp. 1782-1784; #503, p. 1790; #523, p. 1850; #524, p. 1852; #592, pp. 2074-2076. Brüning, p. 367.

54.  James, *Slump*, pp. 237, 296.  Galbraith, pp. 218-219.  Hans-Joachim Voth, "Wages, Investment, and the Fate of the Weimar Republic," *German History* 11, no. 3 (1993), pp. 290-291.

Reichstag had become a mere afterthought.    Economics Minister Hermann
Warmbold protested vigorously. The turnover tax increase would take about a
billion Marks out of the economy and make things much worse. He proposed
a forced loan similar to Wirth's attempt of 1921-22, but the rest of the Cabinet
opposed this. Warmbold refused to sign the decree raising the tax and offered
to resign. Balderston sees this decree as the key policy error of the Brüning
government. Although unemployment had skyrocketed, real wages for those
who still had jobs had either remained steady or risen. From the first quarter
of 1931 to the fourth quarter of 1932, German wages adjusted for deflation fell
7.6% while British wages over the comparable period rose 4%. By the end of
1931, German civil servants had lost almost one-quarter of their salaries since
Brüning took office. It is small wonder that many of them became sympathetic
to Nazism.[55]

By the end of 1931, many were openly denouncing the policies of the
Brüning government and proposing alternatives. A group of young economists,
raised in the traditions of Adolf Wagner and Karl August Dietzel, called for
expansionary fiscal and monetary policy. The Economics Ministry became the
home of the "German Keynesians" such as Ernst Wagemann and Wilhelm
Lautenbach. Wagemann, the head of the statistical bureau, had put together
much of the program of 1926. In January 1932, he outlined a plan for
economic recovery. Its centerpiece would be the issuing of RM3 billion of
interest-bearing debt in small denominations. A more elastic credit policy would
create more flexibility to react to business cycles. Wagemann was Warmbold's
brother-in-law and some suspected collusion. Brüning believed that this would
endanger the entire government policy. How could he cut social programs if
workers believed they would soon get two billion Marks in credit? Luther and
Dietrich decried the inflationary aspects of this plan. When asked to write a
formal rebuttal, Warmbold said he would need at least four weeks. The
government was petrified that the Nazis might adopt the Wagemann Plan as their
economic platform.[56]

The socialist unions had grown weary of Hilferding's conservative
economics. At the end of 1931, Wladimir Woytinsky, Fritz Tarnow, and Fritz
Baade devised the "WTB Plan," which called for credits of RM2 billion to
spend on housing and roads. It would employ one million workers and save
RM600 million in unemployment costs and thus relieve the budget. Hilferding
and Paul Hertz attacked this plan, but in April 1932, the ADGB endorsed the
WTB Plan and abandoned Hilferding's orthodox policy. The SPD refused to

---

55. *Kabinette Brüning*, Docs. #545, pp. 1928-1930; #589, pp. 2061-2068;
#591, pp. 2069-2074; #596, p. 2087. Balderston, *Financial Crisis*, pp. 45-47. James,
*Slump*, p. 69.
    56. Krosigk, p. 65.   Curtius, p. 27.   *Kabinette Brüning*, Docs. #651, pp.
2241-2242; #653, pp. 2246-2248.

endorse it after Hilferding condemned it for questioning the labor theory of value and not attributing the Depression to "capitalist anarchy." He thought that the SPD's role in the Depression should be to defend sound currency and Marxism.[57]

By the beginning of 1932, the government estimated that 5.6 million Germans were out of work and that 800,000 of them had exhausted all of their support. The Cabinet remained deadlocked. Dietrich called for yet more cuts in unemployment support; Stegerwald said that was politically impossible. Brüning again wanted to link job creation to spending cuts. Dietrich ranted on that the budget must be balanced. With Hitler running strongly for the presidency and Prussian state elections looming, another government decree as disastrous as the previous ones would tip the balance to the extremists.[58]

The decree of December 1931 did not solve the budget miseries. In February the Rentenbank issued RM500 million in bonds to consolidate agricultural debt. Repayment of the bonds would come from the Industrieobligationbank. On March 17, Brüning told the Cabinet to prepare for the worst. Despite even more draconian cuts, Schäffer estimated that the Reich would be completely out of cash in August. There had been hope that Ivar Kreuger could provide another loan, but he had killed himself in Paris that day. The 1930 and 1931 budgets had come in with large deficits despite (and because of) all the cuts and tax increases. This was a breach in the Reich's loan contract with Lee, Higginson. The government prepared a decree to raise the debt authorization by RM1.1 billion. This unmasked Brüning's fiscal policy as a fraud. All of the pious talk of balanced budgets and the need to sacrifice had been empty. Had Brüning authorized this amount of credit at the beginning of his tenure, the Reichstag would have passed it, it would have taken care of the initial budget and unemployment office problems of 1930, and the Depression would not have been so deep. Brüning would have had no need to call early elections in September 1930; the Nazis would still have only twelve seats, and there would have been short-term foreign loans available. He could have continued to use the fractious but democratic Reichstag to pass budgets until at least May of 1932. The states would not have fallen into bankruptcy.

With Germany's finances a wreck and his infinite illusions shattered at last, Brüning wanted to put this debt authorization into a decree, but the debt administration flatly refused because it was unconstitutional. Now he had to turn to the Reichstag. It raised the authorization to RM1.3 billion and passed

---

57. *Kabinette Brüning*, Doc. #664, pp. 2276-2278. George Garvy, "Keynes and the Economic Activists of Pre-Hitler Germany," *Journal of Political Economy* 83 (1975), p. 397. Robert A. Gates, "German Socialism and the Crisis of 1929-33," *Central European History* 7 (1974), pp. 337-350. James, *Slump*, p. 239. Smaldone, pp. 120-121.

58. *Kabinette Brüning*, Doc. #682, pp. 2318-2320.

it 287 to 260. It was only in the last desperate six weeks that the Brüning government finally began to get matters in hand. With a balanced budget so much nonsense, it began to manipulate debt freely. In an even more hopeful development, Lee, Higginson agreed to extend and reschedule the debt that was due, despite the deficits. Perhaps this could lead to a trickle of short-term foreign loans if a small measure of confidence in Germany returned. The Cabinet also put the finishing touches on the long-overdue job-creation program. Brüning still did not understand the fundamental problems. Shortly before he was forced from office, Brüning blamed the Depression on two factors. The first was cyclical: with the end of the war, living standards simply had to fall. The second was the political uncertainty centered on reparations. He felt that once Germany finally settled reparations, it would reach the deep point of the Depression. There is another explanation for Brüning's destructive fiscal policy: he deliberately drove the German economy into a ditch so that he could get out of solemn treaty commitments on reparations. Again the historical record does not support this. Not until the very end of his term did Brüning raise this as a key issue and it smacks more of excuse-making than an actual policy.[59]

Balderston concluded that the only real alternative to deflation was a loss of fiscal discipline. He agreed with Borchardt and James that there were strong constraints on budget policies and that Germany had to build confidence in the currency.[60] However, the measure of investor confidence seems to suggest that the consequences of the deflation were the Nazi victory of 1930 and the financial crisis of the summer of 1931. Brüning's successors did not inspire much more confidence, but their flexibility on budget policies allowed recovery to begin. Even in 1935, investor confidence was not that strong, and the Hitler government had difficulty selling bonds. By that time, the government had grown so skillful in manipulating existing debt and creating new debt that it hardly mattered. Brüning in his memoirs claimed that his secret goal was to build up executive power and pave the way for the return of the monarchy. Dieter Hertz-Eichenrode found the real solution to the Brüning puzzle. The Chancellor had deeply ingrained beliefs about the economy. The Reinhold and Köhler years had been deep affronts. Once given a chance to run policy, Brüning's policy aimed at reversing these "errors." He kept referring for years to the mistakes of 1926-27: the job-creation program, the tax cuts, the civil-service raises. Even in his memoirs, Brüning was obsessed with these policies. What he never acknowledged was that Reinhold was right and he was wrong.

Brüning had limited options, but most of the constraints were self-imposed. The failure of the Hilferding loan showed the weakness of the long-

---

59. James, *Slump*, p. 274. *Kabinette Brüning*, Doc. #697, pp. 2377-2379; #732, pp. 2482-2483; #743, pp. 2508-2510; #759, pp. 2544-2550. Krosigk, pp. 100-102.

60. Balderston, *Financial Crisis*, pp. 405-406.

term bond market.  The short-term market and the foreign market, especially France, were still viable options.  Between April, when Schacht left the Reichsbank, and the Nazi victory in September 1930, Brüning could have had the Reichstag boost the short-term credit allowance from the Reichsbank.  Instead of paying off the treasury transfers, the regime could have rolled them over and tried harder to sell new transfers to banks.  The disastrous events of June 1931 also opened new possibilities with the effective nationalization of Deutsche Bank and Dresdner Bank.  The Reich had the option of selling transfers to these "captive buyers."  With Brüning and Dietrich gone, the government turned to more creative solutions.  Germany could and should have solved its problems with planned deficit spending.  It would have saved democracy and averted Hitler.

# Chapter 8

# The Hard Dictatorship

The Dawes bonds languished forgotten in drawers and vaults far from Germany. Although the Reich had pledged to redeem them, hope diminished with each passing month. Brüning's catastrophic policies and his admission of failure to balance the budget discredited the orthodox fiscal policy. While that policy lingered through the summer of 1932, a growing chorus demanded strong action and credits to finance job creation. These credits would not be retroactive attempts to cover past spending, but would be carefully planned with a multiyear impact. The view that Germany could and should make countercyclical policy and fund it with credit now became dominant. When Hitler took power and demanded even more spending, the leaders of the Finance Ministry were ready and knew how to fund the spending.

"Who is Papen?" asked Ambassador to France Leopold von Hoesch in May 1932.[1] Von Hoesch was not alone in his ignorance. Franz von Papen was the most reactionary member of the Catholic Center and had sought an alliance with the Nazis. Behind the scenes, General Kurt von Schleicher had undermined Hindenburg's confidence in Brüning and produced Papen as a Chancellor who would lead a right-wing Cabinet. Schleicher told Papen that Brüning's purely negative economic policies had caused radicalism to grow and that only job creation could defuse it. The general said he could trust Papen to be a moderate conservative without dictatorial tendencies. In his memoirs, Papen said that he protested the implied betrayal of his party's leader, but then he met with Hindenburg. The President put his hands on Papen's shoulders and said "You cannot possibly leave an old man like me in the lurch. . . . You have

---

1. Krosigk, p. 106.

been a soldier and did your duty in the war.  When the Fatherland calls, Prussia knows only one response--obedience."[2]

Germany had suffered a complex crisis  from 1912 to 1924 with entangled political, international, monetary, and fiscal problems.  The crisis of 1929-33 stemmed simply from an economic downturn.  Brüning's attempts to emulate Luther and run a "soft dictatorship" had been a disaster because of mistaken policies.  Now Germany turned to a hard dictatorship under Papen, Schleicher, and Hitler.  Under this regime, the trends in fiscal policy reached their logical conclusion.  The Reich centralized budget policy, learned how to run large-scale budget deficits, and began a new job-creation program.  Gisela Upmeier has rightly called this an extension of the Reinhold program of 1926.[3]

The Papen Cabinet was essentially a Nationalist Cabinet, though that party did not support it officially.  Most ministers were members of that party or were Junkers associated with the DNVP.  Pünder was forced out as Chancery State Secretary and replaced by Erwin Planck, a close associate of Schleicher. Konstantin von Neurath, a veteran diplomat and former Rhodes Scholar, became Foreign Minister.  Warmbold returned as Economics Minister from the Brüning government.  For Finance Minister, the regime sought an expert from business or the civil service.   The State Secretary, Hans Schäffer, was obviously unsuitable.  Krosigk, the budget chief, was suggested.  Krosigk went to the Chancery, saw Planck settling in, and told him that his meeting with Papen would be short and that he would not accept a Cabinet position.   Planck laughed, "That is what Neurath said, too."[4]  As they talked, Papen picked up the phone and called Otto Meissner in the President's office.  Meissner then told Krosigk that Hindenburg hoped that as an officer and nobleman, he would not leave his old field marshal in the lurch.  Krosigk, like Papen, found this appeal irresistible.  Krosigk had risen through the ranks of the Finance Ministry and served on the 1926 Job-Creation Committee.  Popitz had called him "the Red Baron" because of his democratic leanings, yet he belonged to the DNVP and lied about his affiliation to Hilferding when the socialist appointed him budget chief in November 1928.  Hugo Schäffer, a former member of the board of directors of Krupp and the head of the Reich Insurance Office since 1924, became Labor Minister.  Since neither Papen nor Schleicher had any economic expertise or real interest, Warmbold, Krosigk, and Schäffer took control of policy.[5]

The departures of Brüning and Dietrich lifted a heavy weight from the policy-making apparatus.  The government had mostly ignored the job-creation

2.  Franz von Papen, *Memoirs* (New York, 1953), pp. 151-158.

3.  Upmeier in Hansmeyer, p. 124.

4.  Krosigk, p. 43.

5.  Ibid., pp. 107-110.  Köhler, p. 197.  Karl-Heinz Minuth, ed., *Akten der Reichskanzlei. Das Kabinett von Papen* (Boppard, 1989), pp. XIX-XXII.  Papen devotes almost no attention to his government's economic policy in his memoirs.

programs of the labor unions and the Economics Ministry. Now it allowed a thousand job-creation schemes to bloom. Faced with the same problems as Brüning, the Papen government took radically different actions. Even more than Brüning, Papen ignored the Reichstag and kept it out of session through most of his six-month term. There was a thorough purge of the civil service. Papen and his "Cabinet of barons" were determined to have their own people who would carry out the decrees without question.

The first financial challenge was the completion of the 1932 budget. Brüning had extended the fiscal year by decree to June 1932. Brüning and Dietrich had prepared one of their typical budgets, studded with deep cuts in social spending and tax increases. Even with these cuts, there was still a projected deficit of almost RM200 million. Krosigk noted that income collections were already RM100 million short of the projection. The revenue estimate anticipated selling RM100 million of railroad preferred stock, but Krosigk doubted it would yield this much. RM78 million in Treasury transfers were coming due. Both Belgium and the United States had treaty claims upon Germany that would amount to RM61 million. Income projections were dubious. The unemployment fund was as shaky as ever. Its total income equaled RM2.7 billion and expenses totaled RM3.6 billion. Each month the invalid-insurance program was running a deficit of RM28 million and the miners' pension a deficit of RM2.5 million. When these were added up, the worst-case scenario showed a deficit of RM1.62 billion. Krosigk's plan to cover the official deficit featured the reintroduction of the unpopular salt tax and a RM100 million cut in the Reich's contribution to unemployment relief. He would compensate for these unemployment cuts by introducing means testing to unemployment-insurance and crisis-relief and by cutting the support levels while raising the premium again on employees only until March 1933. It was up to the Labor Minister to put the invalids' and miners' programs in order. The Papen regime still had not made a decisive break with Brüning's deflationary policy.[6]

Real changes began when a RM125 million gap in the cash position appeared in July 1932. Instead of the usual round of cuts and taxes that had marked the Brüning and Dietrich years, Luther assembled a consortium of banks to extend short-term credit: 20% would fall due January 4, 1933, and 40% each on February 15 and March 15. This was a turning point. The government had finally done what it should have done three years or more before. While it is true that there was no attempt to market this debt to the public, it marked a decisive break with the last two regimes. When the leaders of the RdI met with the Cabinet leaders, Papen said that further deflation would lead to the collapse

---

6. *Kabinett Papen*, Docs. #9, pp. 17-22; #12, pp. 27-30; #17, pp. 42-51; #42, p. 155.

of the currency.  Germany did not improve under Papen, but at least it did not get any worse.  The ruinous cycle of deflation was broken at last.[7]

After dealing with the budget and cash problems, the Papen government won a victory at the Lausanne Conference, which effectively ended reparations. The regime turned to a massive job-creation program in late July 1932.  The Labor and Finance Ministries clashed on the scope.  Hugo Schäffer wanted RM318 million besides the RM135 million appropriated under Brüning for job creation.  He believed that the government could draw on credits from the railroad and post.  Krosigk threw a damper on these plans.  He preferred to wait for a natural turn of the business cycle.  Job creation should be part of a broader plan of administrative and program cuts and easier credit.  The Decree of October 1930 had mandated that the government put RM420 million each year into the sinking-fund budget.  He would reduce this to the RM100 million needed to repay the Lee, Higginson credit.  There could be a tax shortfall up to RM320 million, and there was still RM75 million in unknown items such as settlements and the Belgian Mark Treaty.  Krosigk also thought unemployment-related matters might require RM100 million in additional spending.  Thus the regime might need RM500 million, and the FY33 budget was no better because it had committed RM1,500 million for various projects.  Krosigk would only raise job-creation money to RM200 million, which Luther was willing to fund with a fifteen-month credit.  In short, the Papen government was initially prepared to raise job-creation funds by a mere RM65 million from Brüning's program.  The government devoted much more attention to bailing out the great agricultural magnates of the east than the urban unemployed.  It provided credit, put import quotas on dairy and beef cattle, banned the auction of foreclosed property, gave a 40% land-tax remission, and reduced interest payments by 2%.[8]

James argues that the fiscal policy did not provide enough stimulus to get the economy going.  He believes that the looser credit policy that began in mid-1932 and then the onset of rearmament in 1935 spurred the economic recovery.  Only rearmament really provided enough fiscal stimulus.  As we have seen, the deflation of the 1929-32 period meant that exorbitant real interest rates completely choked off any opportunity for mortgages or for capital investment. I have shown how and why monetary policy is ineffective in times of deflation. Only negative nominal interest rates can be seen as easy credit, but this theoretical idea is almost impossible to execute.  The Reichsbank lowered its discount rate to 5% in April and then to 4% in September.  A cut from 6% to

---

7.  Ibid., Docs. #42,  p. 159; #46, p. 174; #111, p. 438.

8.  Ibid., Doc. #77, pp. 286-289; #89, p. 333; #164, pp. 745-750. Abraham, p. 98.  James, *Slump*, p. 275.

4% sounds like a lot, but when it is a cut in real rates from 17% to 15%, it loses its luster.[9]

There is little doubt that Hans Luther embarked on a secret policy of credit expansion besides the job-creation credit offered in July 1932. His hysteria over inflation during the summer of 1931 seemed to have subsided, although he kept urging the public and his Cabinet colleagues to avoid inflationary habits. He had also not waited for the end of reparations, contrary to public statements. In the fall of 1931, Luther issued the "Russian discounts" to spur trade with the Soviet Union, just as his Cabinet had issued credits to trade with that nation in 1926. James calls this process "the secret (or private) reflation," as the Reichsbank combined lower discount rates with the purchase of noncommercial bills. We should not exaggerate this development too much. While the nominal discount rate fell steadily to 4% by September 1932, the real rate dipped below 15% briefly in January 1932 then shot above that level again until November 1932. Part of this was due to a fall in international rates. After devaluing the pound, the Bank of England reduced its key rate to 2% in June 1932. The British also converted their 5% War Loan to a rate of 3.5%. If one supports a monetary explanation for the economic turn of late 1932, one must emphasize the supply of cash. Krosigk called this Luther's turn from Saul to Paul. New credit institutions such as the Finanzierungsinstitut and the Tilgungskasse für gewerbliche Kredite joined the Akzept- und Garantiebank. The money supply hit its low point in February 1932. The "secret reflation" would therefore seem to have started before the Lausanne Conference, though the Young Plan (requiring a 40% cover of gold and currency) was still in effect. By the end of October 1932 the cover had fallen to 15% and Luther reported that he saw no signs of panic. From July 1931 to December 1932 the nominal value of the money supply fell 12.4%, while in real terms it rose 1.5%, hardly the "steep rise" James refers to. This rise helped end the ruinous deflationary cycle, but one cannot attribute any measure of growth to monetary policy and this is in harmony with the explanation in the previous chapter.[10]

The Papen government, after its cautious start, moved to an expansive fiscal policy. On August 26, the Cabinet met to sketch its economic plan. It supported the plan of Labor Minister Schäffer and Reichsbank Vice-President Fritz Dreyse. The Reich would issue vouchers to businesses according to how many new workers they hired. Businesses could use these vouchers for tax payments, trade them openly, and discount them at the Reichsbank. Luther, fending off Warmbold's suggestion of RM1.5 billion in immediate credit, said that the Reich could buy back the vouchers using Treasury transfers. The

9. James, *Slump*, pp. 379-380. *Kabinett Papen*, Doc. #107, pp. 411-414.

10. Krosigk, pp. 66, 140. James, *Reichsbank*, p. 296; *Slump*, pp. 321-322. Dan P. Silverman, *Hitler's Economy: Nazi Work Creation Programs, 1933-1936* (Cambridge, MA, 1998), p. 228. Voth, pp. 290-291.

vouchers could also serve as collateral for loans, so there would be a multiplier effect. The plan would raise several social insurance taxes and premiums to cover some of the cost. The government would issue vouchers, which businesses could pay instead of the turnover, business, property, and transport taxes due between October 1932 and September 1933. The total amount was RM1.5 billion. Another RM700 million would be set aside to reward those businesses that had hired in the past year and for the future year. At RM400 per worker, this would be enough to cover 1.75 million workers. Companies could cash in the RM2.2 billion in vouchers starting April 1, 1934, for one-fifth of the face value of the voucher. For each year that passed, the value would increase until it reached 100% value after April 1938. This would add RM434 million to the annual budget if the Reich distributed all the vouchers. The vouchers would be negotiable securities and their trade would be exempt from the stock-turnover tax. This all boiled down to an interest-free loan to businesses from the banking consortium organized by the Reichsbank, guaranteed by the Reich with the main condition being that these businesses hire workers. The Social Democrats complained that this was a credit that required the approval of the Reichstag, but Papen brushed off such constitutional niceties.[11]

Papen accelerated the breakdown of the independence of the states and cities. Most famously, he overthrew the Braun government of Prussia. Brüning's budget cuts had forced Prussia to scale back its police force and reduce salaries, leading to a reduction in quality. The budget of the Prussian Justice Ministry fell from RM250 million in 1930 to RM145 million in 1932. Not surprisingly, the reduced police force could not deal with Nazi and Communist thuggery. Papen used this as an excuse to invoke the emergency decree and took control on July 20. The Reich was free to plunder Prussia's resources and to coordinate its budget with that of Prussia. The states wanted restoration of greater shares of revenue and railroad preference shares worth RM70 million as compensation for the state railroads taken in 1918. Krosigk's talk with the state Finance Ministers was very different from Schlieben's all-day affair of 1925. For the most part, Krosigk dictated and they listened with few questions and little argument.[12]

The position of the cities and states had steadily worsened. Köln finished its fiscal year in July 1932 with an uncovered deficit of nearly RM25 million and had put no money into the sinking fund to retire earlier debt. It had RM40 million in Treasury transfers falling due on October 1. Frankfurt had RM30 million falling due, and Saxony also faced default on October 1. One

---

11. *Kabinett Papen*, Docs. #112-113, pp. 445-450; #116-117, pp. 455-459; #120, p. 474; #123, p. 501. Krosigk, p. 141.

12. *Kabinett Papen*, Docs. #138, p. 572; #149-150, pp. 612-619; #168, p. 767.

estimate suggested that the uncovered deficit of all the localities in the Reich totaled over a billion Marks, of which RM700 million were in Prussia. Papen was not ready to use the debt issue against the cities. The Reich demanded that states and cities bring their civil service salaries down to the 1914 levels and restore the old imperial categories of pay. When the unemployment funds began to run surpluses, the cities begged for relief, but to little avail. Finally, at the beginning of November the Cabinet agreed to raise the subsidy from RM35 million to RM65 million a month. The states did not want to rely on the kindness of the Reich and demanded a regular share on the income-tax surcharge. They also felt that the Reich should take the lead in cutting civil-service officials. Krosigk rejected these demands.[13]

At the end of October, Papen reorganized the Prussian government. He had named Franz Bracht, the former mayor of Essen and Reichskanzlei State Secretary, Prussian Interior Minister in July. Bracht now added the title of Minister without Portfolio in the Reich Cabinet. Joining him was Johannes Popitz as Prussian Finance Minister. Popitz' return changed the balance in the Cabinet. He had been Krosigk's superior in the Finance Ministry and the junior man still held him in awe, even years later when he called Popitz "*the* great expert and mastermind in his field, practitioner and scholar at the same time, a liberal with inclinations for authoritarian leadership, an intellectual who used his life for his ideals, a cynic who was deeply religious; he regarded tax measures as an art, the budget as a handicraft."[14] Popitz had gained a reputation for Machiavellian intrigue during the Luther and Marx Cabinets. Heinrich Köhler described the good and bad sides of Popitz:

[Popitz] was an extraordinarily highly qualified laborer, a man of sweepingly humanistic nature, interested in natural science and the formation of cultures. This valuable man had the character of a leader, which drove him to cynicism, slyness, arrogance, and finally his almost pathological ambition led to a sometimes quite ridiculous vanity. In my life I have never encountered such a sinister man--a true Fouché of the twentieth century! Pulling the strings behind the scenes had become a necessity of life to him, and he even conspired against his own minister [Reinhold] with the prospective successor or his party. . . .  I unfortunately learned later that the ministry officials feared him so much that they were instructed to inform him immediately of any order from the minister, no matter how inconsequential.[15]

One may say that Krosigk and Popitz served as co-Finance Ministers until Popitz' execution in 1944.

---

13. Ibid., Docs. #100, pp. 386-389; #121, pp. 486-489; #138, p. 571; #155, p. 639; #185, pp. 837-841; #187, pp. 843-846; #216, pp. 966-967.

14. Krosigk, pp. 29, 111.

15. Köhler, pp. 195-196.

Not only was the Reich taking more power from the states because of the financial crisis, it was augmenting its considerable power in the private sector. The Reich had acquired control over several major banks during the 1931 crisis and now bought a controlling interest in the Vereinigte Stahlwerke from Friedrich Flick in July.[16] Interest groups of labor and industry jostling for power and influence had built a framework of societal corporatism during the heyday of Weimar. Now Germany was turning to state corporatism as more financial and industrial power fell into its hands, and this gave the state more power over labor. Krosigk's cuts in unemployment relief had been draconian, but they had the virtue of getting the government off the crisis treadmill that Müller and Brüning had faced every few months. In mid-October, Krosigk reported that the unemployment-insurance fund had run a surplus. He projected that the three funds together (unemployment-insurance, crisis relief, and welfare) would run a surplus of RM276 million for the rest of the year. The Cabinet agreed to apply the funds to aid families with children and subsidize other insurance funds and announced that it would remove no one from the crisis-relief rolls during the coming winter.[17]

It is difficult to assess Papen's regime because it only lasted for six months. The turnaround on deflation had an immediate effect. Unemployment had averaged 5.5 million persons in Germany for the first part of 1932. It improved in the summer of 1932 and then worsened as the winter approached. Papen was still facing his greatest challenges when he resigned. Not all of Krosigk's fears had come true, but he was projecting an RM840 million deficit when FY32 ended in March 1933. About half of the shortfall came from income reduction, the other half from spending increases. The Reich had not sold about two-thirds of its railroad preferred stock, and it owed RM21 million under the Belgian Mark Treaty. In November 1932, Krosigk had a long talk with Reinhold on political and financial matters. Reinhold felt that the "Papen Plan" had many healthy aspects. There would be another serious cash crisis in March 1933. Borrowing from the turn of phrase that Reinhold had once used to dazzle the Reichstag, Krosigk noted that one must "go to the brink of illegality to return to legality." Reinhold suggested that the best solution might be a Schleicher Cabinet containing Nazis to give it a firm footing in the Reichstag.[18]

Papen's fall came a month later for political reasons. Two elections in July and November of 1932 had not changed the political landscape appreciably, and Papen had no chance of ruling with a parliamentary majority. In September

---

16. Patch, p. 186.

17. *Kabinett Papen*, Docs. #167, pp. 765-767; #168, p. 775; #187, pp. 847-850. Anton Golecki, ed., *Akten der Reichskanzlei. Das Kabinett von Schleicher* (Boppard, 1986), Docs. #24, pp. 93-99; #33, p. 141.

18. *Kabinett Papen*, Doc. #187, pp. 843-847. Krosigk, pp. 144-148.

he had lost a vote of confidence by a crushing 513 to 32. Only the People's party and Nationalists had supported him, but they held only 74 of 584 Reichstag seats after the November elections. If the Papen government were to continue, it would have to be as a naked dictatorship. Most of his ministers feared that such a development would lead to full economic collapse. Schleicher, who had created the Cabinet, decided it was time to end it. Neurath and Krosigk, the Rhodes Scholars who had joined the Cabinet only on Hindenburg's request, supported Schleicher. Tears came to Papen's eyes as he realized his own handpicked ministers were deserting him. "I see that a majority of the Cabinet no longer stands behind me."[19] Labor Minister Schäffer resigned along with Papen, but Krosigk, Popitz, and Warmbold stayed on, and were joined by Friedrich Syrup, the head of the Unemployment-Insurance Office, as Labor Minister. Schleicher persuaded Günther Gereke, former President of the German Congress of State Communities, to join the Cabinet as Commissar for Job Creation. Gereke, a member of the Nationalist party, had come up with an expensive job-creation program that the Papen government had discussed in the weeks before its fall. The original Gereke plan, supported by the Nazis, required RM650 million to employ 500,000 from the welfare rolls. Gereke wanted the scheme financed by a thirty-year credit, but the Reichsbank refused. The Papen government had decided this was too costly and uncertain. Just two weeks before, Krosigk and Warmbold had publicly denounced the Gereke program; now they would have to work with it.[20]

The Gereke appointment symbolized the shift in policy under the Schleicher government. Papen had emphasized the recovery of the private sector as the key to ending the Depression. Schleicher's team was prepared to launch massive government intervention to put Germany back to work. This fit Schleicher's improbable political goal of forging a Socialist-Catholic-Nazi majority in the Reichstag. If anything motivated Schleicher's fiscal policy, it was no more than his old mentor Wilhelm Groener's view that economic health and military preparedness were inseparable. Feldman has called Schleicher's bid the last gasp of the Groener-style approach dating back to the First World War of trying to create a corporatist government from the left and right. Societal corporatism was an exhausted force and it is easy to see why Schleicher's government failed. German citizens blamed both business and labor for the Depression. Krosigk suggested that the real author of the Gereke Plan was Walter von Etzdorf, the director in the Defense Ministry on questions of economic mobilization. The Cabinet established a Commissariat of Job-Creation

---

19. Institut für Zeitgeschichte (IfZ), Munich, NL Krosigk, ZS 145, vol. 1, p. 21.

20. Mommsen, *Rise and Fall*, pp. 484-487. Friedrich-Karl von Plehwe, *Reichskanzler Kurt von Schleicher: Weimars letzte Chance gegen Hitler* (Frankfurt, 1983), p. 259. *Kabinett Papen*, Docs. #161, pp. 725-727; #187, p. 851; #216, p. 969.

as a small coordinating body, and a job-creation committee of Cabinet-level officers would meet regularly. Gereke wanted a vast expansion of job-creation, financed by a twenty-year interest-free credit. He was encouraged by Luther's December 3 speech in Munich where the Reichsbank President had cautiously renounced the restrictive credit policy. Warmbold doubted that Luther meant he would provide long-term loans without security or interest, because business was already alarmed at this new tone.[21]

Popitz now broke from his former conservative position and supported Gereke while adding his own modifications. The Reich would extend the no-interest loan to its public corporations. It would take an interest-bearing loan from the Reichsbank that would be free of payments for a year or two. Krosigk argued that the government should announce this as a consolidation of the short-term Treasury transfers that had been piling up over the past year. The Reichsbank still would never agree unless the government sold this debt to the public. Popitz, recalling the fate of the 1927 and 1929 bond issues, replied that the credits would be backed by the Reichsbank and private banks, which could rediscount the credits at the Reichsbank if they wanted. Popitz wanted to reassure the banks that the sinking fund would receive its legally mandated payments and would have the first call on Reich income.

Until the Reichsbank provided the loan, the government could raise more money by having the Deutsche Gesellschaft für öffentliche Arbeiten (Öffa) issue short-term bills valued against the job-creation loans it had given out. The Brüning decree of July 1930 had established the Öffa. Its original assets consisted of some RM750 million in Reich credit, which it had given to public and private institutions. The Öffa could only grant a paltry RM50 million for job creation in its first eight months, based mostly on the yield from its assets. Luther had opposed plans for the Öffa to seek a foreign loan in July 1930, and after the Nazi victory in September 1930, it was impossible. As debt payments became harder for all during the Depression, the Öffa languished. Brüning's fall rescued it from obscurity. Popitz proposed a division of credits: job-creation loans to revenue-producing ventures such as gas, water, and electricity, would bear interest; loans to other works would not carry interest. It is always hard to say with Popitz whether this was a genuine conversion or whether he just saw how the wind was blowing and was eager to please the new Chancellor. It is true that he had worked well with Hilferding, but that was because Popitz had reinforced the socialist's training in classical economics. It seemed that

---

21. Richard J. Overy, *War and Economy in the Third Reich* (Oxford, 1994), p. 178. Feldman, *Army*, p. 532. Krosigk, p. 153. *Kabinett Schleicher*, Docs. #3, pp. 10-14; #8, pp. 28-33; #15, pp. 54-56.

Popitz had finally come around to the doctrine he had belittled in 1926: the use of massive deficit spending to revive the economy.[22]

At the meeting of the Job-Creation Committee, Gereke set a price of RM2.7 billion on his job-creation plan and requested that the government spend RM600 million immediately. If the Reichsbank believed such a loan would endanger currency stability, the Rentenbank could extend the funds. Krosigk strongly opposed this. If the Reich set a precedent by taking long-term interest-free loans, no government would ever take an interest-bearing loan again, and the credit facilities would retaliate by trying to hinder any use of their money.[23] Luther gave a scathing critique of the Gereke plan as "voodoo financing" (finanzierung ins Blaue). Warmbold asked Luther about his Munich speech and the Reichsbank President stiffly replied that the remarks had been misreported: he had merely said that the Reichsbank had given RM3.5 billion in credit, not that it would give that credit.[24]

Gereke finally squeezed RM500 million from the Reichsbank. This would finance most of his "Immediate Program," and he hoped for more, despite the misgivings of Warmbold and Krosigk. The Finance Minister was now reporting the uncovered deficit at RM800 million. There would be a reckoning on this, and the government would then need the Reichsbank. Gereke delivered a radio address to the nation to sum up the progress on job creation during the past nine months. The September program of Papen had dedicated RM60 million to the post office, RM280 million to the Reichsbahn, and RM342 million to projects such as streets, canals, and agricultural improvements. Voluntary work service had created another 285,000 positions. Another RM73 million went to build suburban settlements and small gardens. This totaled RM750 million. Now would come the "Immediate-Program" with another RM500 million. Those employed under the program would help pay it back while revenue-producing industries would have normal terms and conditions for their loans. The RM500 million consisted of RM300 million from the Öffa and RM200 million from the Rentenbank. A bank consortium would assume the debt, but it would be rediscountable at the Reichsbank. The Schleicher government also endorsed an old-fashioned debasement of the currency by minting one-mark pieces from nickel (rather than silver) and shrinking the size of the silver five-mark coins. Inflation was no longer seen as a worry. In response to political demands, the government repealed Papen's wage freeze under the September 5 decree.[25]

---

22. Silverman, *Hitler*, pp. 36-38. *Kabinette Brüning*, Doc. #91, p. 351. *Kabinett Schleicher*, Doc. #13, pp. 45-49.

23. *Kabinett Schleicher*, Doc. #30, pp. 131-133.

24. Ibid., Doc. #32, pp. 138-141.

25. Ibid., Docs. #24, pp. 99-101; #34, pp. 152-153; #36, pp. 156-162; #59, p. 261; #67, p. 293.

Was a dictatorship necessary?     Some might argue that only a dictatorship could have put together these plans, but I believe that in the emergency even the Reichstag elected in 1930 could have passed the measures in a reasonable period. Institutions such as the Öffa did not require Reichstag approval to seek credit. All that was required was a less cautious attitude toward property. After the elections of July and November 1932, democratic solutions became impossible as the Nazis and Communists controlled more than half of the seats in the Reichstag. Schleicher believed that he could persuade many Nazis to cooperate in a parliamentary government and program based on job creation and economic recovery. When this gambit failed, Schleicher had to resign. It is ironic that when Hindenburg signed the decree for the Schleicher/Gereke "Immediate Program," Adolf Hitler was Chancellor. Schacht claimed in 1949 that only dictatorial governments could have instituted the job-creation programs of the 1930s. Silverman suggests that business cooperated much more with the Hitler government because of a common interest against labor, fear of the Nazis, and an improving economy.[26] This would imply that business had sabotaged the earlier democratic governments, which is not true. There was no plot by the investing class to bring down democracy. Businesses were only seeking profit. When their profits collapsed in the Brüning years, it is small wonder that many turned against the system.     Had a democratic government simply shown more imagination and used existing credit devices, then exploited new opportunities to expand credit, the Republic could have continued. There was never a need for a dictator. It implies that the disrespect for law and property shown by the Nazis in their unilateral credit adjustments was necessary, and that is also not true.

Discussion of Nazi economic ideology has ranged from Rainer Zitelmann's description of Hitler as "a farsighted and rational revolutionary who intentionally planned and pursued a modernization of both economy and society" to Alan Bullock's view of Hitler as an ignoramus.[27] Avraham Barkai notes that the Nazi leaders and "experts" contributed little to economic policy, yet this led to a "unique combination of short-term anticyclical intervention and ideologically preconceived guidelines to establish a new social and economic order."[28] James sees Nazi economics as driven by four simple premises: (1) the need for individual initiative, though that became overshadowed by political collectivism, (2) a wealthy and technological future, (3) a determination to put Germans back to work, and (4) avoidance of inflation. I would add a fifth premise: the belief, taken from popular psychology, that very visible programs would move the collective psyche of the German people out of its rut, get them spending again, and pull the nation out of the Depression. This is hardly unique to Hitler; it

---

26. Silverman, *Hitler*, p. 8.
27. Quoted in Barkai, p. x.
28. Ibid., p. vii.

bears much relation to Roosevelt's statement "the only thing we have to fear is fear itself." Hitler constantly referred in meetings to "psychological moves." This also fits in with Dan Silverman's view that as he got closer to power, Hitler's economic policy became vaguer. Krosigk first met Hitler in Hindenburg's office the day the government was sworn in. Hitler gave him some simple guidelines: there should be a balanced budget, all promises should be kept, and there should be no currency experiments. When Krosigk pressed for details, Hitler referred him to Göring, who displayed appalling ignorance of the Reich's fiscal mechanisms. James and Barkai both discuss the influence of the Jewish economist Robert Friedländer-Prechtl, who had written in 1926 that changes in the capitalist system had led to chronic unemployment and then in 1931 called for countercyclical spending. This supposedly influenced Strasser, who had taken the lead on job creation for the Nazis. As we have seen, these ideas and policies had been around for a long time and Keynes said in his introduction to the *General Theory* that classical economic theory had never been very strong in Germany. There being no direct evidence, it makes far more sense to attribute specific policies to the veterans of the 1920s such as Krosigk, Popitz, and Schacht.[29]

The Hitler Cabinet sworn in on January 30, 1933, did not differ much from the Schleicher Cabinet. Papen returned as Vice-Chancellor, but had to face many of the same men--Neurath, Krosigk, Franz Gürtner, and Paul von Eltz-Rübenach--who had ousted him in November. Hugenberg came in as Agriculture Minister and Economics Minister. He intended to play the role that Neuhaus and Schiele had played in the first Luther Cabinet to force tariffs higher. Franz Seldte, leader of the Stahlhelm, replaced Syrup as Labor Minister. The Cabinet quickly agreed to retain Popitz in its meetings.[30] Gereke remained as Commissar of Job Creation and believed he could revive the broader job-creation plan that the Nazis had endorsed in 1932.

The Cabinet quickly asserted authoritarian powers by dissolving the Reichstag, setting new elections, and dissolving the Reichstag committees that had proved nettlesome in the past. After the banning of the small parties and a crackdown on the Communists, the Nazi/Nationalist coalition eked out a majority of 52% in the March 1933 election. The Nazis then demanded and received an Enabling Act from the Reichstag. While this Act had some superficial similarities to the one used by Marx and Luther, there were major differences: it could run up to four years or until the government resigned and gave all the powers of the Reichstag to the Cabinet without even a supervisory "Council of Reichstag elders." Only the Reichsrat could serve as a theoretical

29. Ibid., pp. 48-55, 69-70. Silverman, p. 49. James, *Slump*, pp. 341-353. Krosigk, p. 169.

30. Karl-Heinz Minuth, ed., *Akten der Reichskanzlei. Die Regierung Hitler* (Boppard, 1983), Doc. #9, pp. 31-32.

check, but with the Prussian government destroyed, that was not a serious threat.[31]

Gereke tried to expand his program by RM300 million. This would include money for the Reichsbahn, for the Labor Ministry to turn shantytowns into suburban settlements, and for the Defense Ministry's rearmament program. Krosigk opposed this and felt that the Reichsbank had reached the limit of funding. The budget would soon have to provide the money for the earlier Papen and Gereke plans. The Reichsbahn should borrow against its own funds, not general revenue, and he did not think the Defense Ministry could spend more than RM50 million. He allowed only RM40 million more for Reich spending, but only if it came from the amount allocated to the cities and states. Military spending would take about half of that share. Krosigk's attempt to play the fiscal watchdog failed. The Cabinet added RM50 million for rural housing in February. Gereke then persuaded his colleagues to add another RM100 million to the budget and give it to the Defense Ministry. Hitler replaced the cautious Luther as Reichsbank President with Schacht.[32]

Germany still had a mountain of foreign debt looming over its head, including the Dawes bonds. Depending on the estimate, short-term foreign debt ranged between RM8 billion and RM12 billion. During the financial crisis of the summer of 1931, Germany had signed a temporary "standstill" treaty with its creditors. This had been due to expire in spring 1932, but political divisions in the United States led to an extension of the "great" standstill treaty to February 28, 1933, and of the "little" standstill treaty to March 15. After the American elections, there would be talks for a long-term solution. The Hitler Cabinet estimated that Germany owed RM10.27 billion in long-term foreign debt and RM8.7 billion in short-term foreign debt. Before leaving the Reichsbank, Luther concluded a treaty with foreign bankers to reschedule the short-term debt at an interest rate lower by half a percentage point and make a nominal payment. The government repaid the remainder of the loan from the Bank for International Settlements from June 1931 and the Lee, Higginson loan of 1930.[33]

The tax revenues had again fallen far short in 1932, and by October the Finance Minister was reporting an income shortfall of RM783 million. The Reich's share of this grew from RM500 million to RM600 million by the beginning of December. As the new Hitler Cabinet showed signs within its first three weeks of breaking all budget constraints, Krosigk laid down the law. He reported that there was still an uncovered deficit from FY31 of RM1,270 million. There had been a catastrophic fall in the collection of tariff revenues since the beginning of the year. The total income shortfall for FY32 was now RM880 million, comprising RM500 million for the Reich and RM380 million

---

31. Ibid., Docs. #2 and #3, pp. 5-10.
32. Ibid., Docs. #19, pp. 58-64; #22, pp. 70-71; #67, pp. 237-238.
33. Ibid., Doc. #22, pp. 70-74. Kent, pp. 353-357.

for the states. The unanticipated spending on job creation added RM400 million to that total. The Reich was therefore looking at a two-year shortfall of RM2.2 billion.[34]

The picture for 1933 was no brighter. Krosigk had penciled in revenue of RM6.6 billion and could perhaps pad this with another RM500 million in "special income," including another attempt to sell the railroad stock. The Reich would transfer RM1.6 billion to the states, and Reich spending requests totaled RM6.5 billion. The projected deficit was RM945 million. Hitler and Krosigk used the same device used by Brüning and Dietrich the year before: a three-month emergency budget and then a nine-month budget. Krosigk worked some budget magic: he called for unspecified cuts of RM100 million, and a reform in unemployment relief that would save RM400 million. Under a 1925 law governing revaluation, the Reich was supposed to contribute RM314 million to a sinking fund to redeem debt from the preinflation days. Krosigk proposed to put Treasury transfers instead of cash into the fund, which had been Peter Reinhold's proposal back in 1930. Krosigk would not consider raising new taxes and extended the law banning any new taxes for another year.[35]

The states and localities were in even worse shape. At the close of FY32, the states would have an uncovered deficit of RM350 million, the localities RM1,100 million. The localities were also short on their cash payments. Prussia alone had a RM100 million cash shortfall. Popitz proposed grabbing this from cities because they had not paid their share of taxes owed to Prussia. FY30-32 had a total uncovered deficit of RM300 million, and the Prussian commissars anticipated another RM100 million deficit for FY33. Hitler could not enact this loan authorization by decree. The Prussian Landtag would have to pass it and the government would have to confront the illegal deposition of the Braun government the previous July. The commissars waited a month until Hitler's *Gleichshaltung* did away with such inconveniences. With Göring now Commissar for Prussia, Popitz said the loan authorization should be presented to the Landtag, but not debated.[36]

The evolution in the Reich's politics matched the change in Prussia. The first couple of months saw debates take place as they had in the Brüning, Papen, and Schleicher Cabinets with little reference to the Reichstag. With the parliament out of the way, the Cabinet authorized RM850 million of credit to cover the FY32 deficit. Krosigk and Schacht also dispensed with Schacht's earlier scruples and put only RM100 million into the general sinking fund to retire debt instead of the RM420 million mandated by law. The additional spending was straining the Reich's reserves. On April 7, Schacht delivered his first report on the state of the currency since February 1929. To Schacht, his

---

34. *Kabinett Schleicher*, Doc. #2, p. 6. *Regierung Hitler*, Doc. #26, p. 103.
35. *Regierung Hitler*, Docs. #26, p. 104; #60, pp. 219-220.
36. Ibid., Docs. #26, pp. 105; #48, pp. 172-179; #104, pp. 366-368.

absence had been a time of woe for the currency.  The reserves had been RM3.3 billion when he left; now they were RM450 million.  The reserves were well below the 40% level to cover the notes in circulation.  By the end of May, the reserves were down to RM280 million.   The Reich would have to discriminate among its foreign creditors, including the Dawes and Young loans, the Lee, Higginson credit, and the Ivar Kreuger loan.  Schacht also noted that Germany's trade balance was worsening.  When Hugenberg introduced a plan to increase tariffs by 10%, Schacht objected so strongly that the Cabinet never raised the matter again.[37]

Schacht continued to deal with the devil.  To him, it mattered little what the Nazis did as long as his power and the institutional power of the Reichsbank increased.  He was willing to swallow any financial scruples about the weak covering of the currency.  The Cabinet amended the Bank Law in October so that the government could hire and fire the  Reichsbank President.  It also allowed the Reichsbank to carry out open market operations, its final step in becoming a true central bank.  The discount rate was a blunt instrument in controlling monetary policy.  The Reichsbank now could buy and sell bonds, notes, and bills of the Reich, states, and private companies for cash.   That would affect the interest rates by adding or removing liquidity.  Among others, the central banks of Sweden, England, and the United States already had this power.  The Reichsbank could apply this debt to cover the notes in circulation.  In many ways, this was a return to the old pre-1923 system when debt covering debt had gotten Germany into inflationary trouble.[38]

Meanwhile, Hitler had fallen in love with yet another big spending project.  There had been discussion of building superhighways since the days of Marx and Luther.  The Finance Ministry had always opposed it bitterly.  In 1928, negotiations opened on building a road from the Hanseatic cities to Frankfurt and down to Basel (HAFRABA).  The costs were ferocious: about RM250,000 per kilometer.  The Economics Ministry opposed it as well and struck it from Schleicher's job-creation package.  In an April 6 meeting with HAFRABA Executive Director Willy Hof, Hitler declared that the development of motorization was very important and that the Reich would guarantee loans for the entire highway net of 4,827 kilometers.  Hitler found a parallel with Italy, which had begun building highways in 1922.  Would it not be better to spend RM250 million on highways than RM180 million on unemployment relief?  Hitler identified the road problem as a critical issue.  The autobahn project

---

37.  Ibid., Docs. #77, p. 268; #93, pp. 318-320; #156, pp. 547-550.

38.  Ibid., Docs. #212, pp. 747-748; #232, pp. 909-910.  Silverman, *Hitler*, p. 32.

would cost RM1.2 billion, but the Reich would guarantee the loan for ten years.[39]

By the end of April 1933, the Papen and Gereke (*Sofort*) programs were kicking in. The stimulus and the coming of spring reduced unemployment to 5.5 million. Seldte centralized job creation in the Labor Ministry and eliminated Gereke's position. Seldte was particularly keen on pushing women out of the workplace. Hitler's newfound autobahn project now stimulated another job-creation program. Fritz Reinhardt, a Nazi politician who was now State Secretary of the Finance Ministry, prepared a program with four main sections. First was direct job creation: the Reich would distribute one billion Marks in "Job-Treasury-Transfers." These would be repayable in five equal installments from FY34 to FY38. They would pay for repair work, suburban and rural settlements, flood regulation, and gas, electricity, and water works. These three-month bills were renewable for up to five years and would be distributed to the Öffa, the Rentenbank, the Siedlungsbank, the Reichs-Kredit-Gesellschaft, and the Bau- und Bodenbank. Second would be tax exemptions for firms that hired substitutes. Third would be direct spending from the budget. Fourth would be tax incentives for marriage and childbearing aimed at getting women to stay out of wage-paying jobs. He estimated that his plan would create about 750,000 jobs. Krosigk sighed that this would add RM200-250 million a year to his overburdened budget.[40]

Schacht was appalled at the profligacy of the Nazi regime. He would support Reinhardt's program, but refused to create any money that was at the heart of the plan. The "Job-Treasury-Transfers" would become cash. One might as well print up a billion Marks' worth of paper bills and pump them into the economy. The same day Reinhardt presented his program, Schacht told Seldte he would oppose any further expansion of credit and urged a return to Brüning's policy. Seldte disagreed. He believed that a sharp stimulus backed by short-term credits could jolt Germany out of the Depression. Special bills could pay wages if the workers immediately deposited them in bank accounts. Despite the protests, Hitler signed the plan into law on June 1.[41]

The additional spending and the failure to enact reform in unemployment relief left Krosigk's budget for 1933 a sad joke. His call for cuts in unemployment relief were ignored. To the contrary, Hitler and Seldte wanted an expansion of paramilitary youth training, which would cost an additional RM375 million. The Finance Minister simply left the money for unemployment relief out of the budget. He reduced the money transferred to the states. For

---

39. *Kabinett Papen*, Doc. #154, pp. 636-637. *Kabinett Schleicher*, Doc. #13, p. 45. *Regierung Hitler*, Docs. #91, p. 305; #92, pp. 309-311; #147, pp. 508-510.

40. *Regierung Hitler*, Docs. #114, pp. 401-412; #149, pp. 530-534; #166, p. 589.

41. Ibid., Doc. #149, pp. 530-534. Silverman, *Hitler*, p. 29.

the RM1,880 million of previous years' deficits, he provided a RM100 million fig leaf. No money at all was dedicated to cover the Treasury transfers that had covered repayment of the Lee, Higginson loan. He put RM100 million more on the income side to anticipate the unlikely sale of the remaining railroad stock. Krosigk noted that the government had previously pledged this stock as collateral for a variety of debts that it had marketed. Disposal of stock would leave this debt uncovered. He estimated an average of 4.8 million unemployed through the course of the year and thought even that too optimistic.[42]

Seldte, Krosigk, and Eltz-Rübenach did not share Hitler's enthusiasm for the road building and did not appropriate any Reinhardt funds for the autobahns, but Hitler took a personal hand and appointed Fritz Todt as Commissar for Streets. Todt announced on September 18 that construction on the Frankfurt to Heidelberg and Munich to Bad Reichenhall autobahns would begin in eight days. They would cost RM100 million together. The Reichsbahn had provided RM50 million, but he needed the rest. The government had eliminated the automobile tax for new cars in April to stimulate that industry, and it had worked like a charm. Auto sales in May and June had doubled from the previous year. The Chancellor found autobahns to be a good investment. The Reich would recoup its money from tolls and increased income from the gasoline tax. RM400 million in autobahn construction could employ 300,000 to 350,000 a year. Krosigk pleaded that the FY34 budget could not pay for continued construction, but Hitler brushed aside his objections. Hitler constantly harped on psychological effects. If the private sector saw the Reich taking vigorous action on job creation, it would follow. The Cabinet decided to build a thousand kilometers of autobahn a year until it met a goal of 6,500 km, which was more than enough to complete Hof's highway net. In December, the government chartered the autobahn company as a public corporation with sweeping powers, including the authority to confiscate property.[43]

Hitler's devotion to strong psychological impacts and fear of trouble during his regime's first full winter led him to endorse yet another job-creation measure in September 1933, known as the "Second Reinhardt Program." The government linked it with a plan to cut the rent tax 30% across the board, reduce the turnover tax for agriculture, and exempt newly built homes from some taxes. The Reich would subsidize 20% of housing repairs and 50% of housing expansions. The plan added at least RM500 million to spending in the budget. Again the funding would involve a significant amount of short-term credit. The banks said that they did not have the liquidity to fund such credit. Schacht agreed to provide RM500 million in credit for the autobahns and the Reinhardt programs. (See Table 8.1 for a summary of repayments.) Todt also

---

42. *Regierung Hitler*, Docs. #85, p. 287; #169, pp. 596-600.
43. Ibid., Docs. #211, pp. 740-743; #274, pp. 1037-1039. Silverman, *Hitler*, p. 66.

received continual loans from the Unemployment-Insurance Office, supposedly based on security from future road tolls and fees.[44]

The Nazis forced out the state and local governments not under their control. In Köln, the Nazi Gauleiter seized city hall and ordered the district president to dismiss Adenauer. As in Prussia, the line between Reich and state was becoming unclear. Only when the vestiges of democratic government had been forced out did the Nazis consider restructuring communal debt. Under a September 1933 decree, the Reich required the localities to form associations under the oversight of the Reich Finance Minister. These associations (*Umschuldungsverband*) would issue long-term bonds at 4%, payable after October 1936. If creditors refused to accept these new bonds in exchange for the old debts, the government would put them on a five-year repayment schedule, which stretched out payments for short-term debt at effectively lower interest rates. The Reich guaranteed this debt: if an association missed a payment, the creditor would receive money taken from the transfer revenue to the localities. The Reich had established yet another debt-issuing public corporation. A decree from Popitz in December 1933 centralized all urban finance in Prussia.[45]

Even as the centralizing forces reached their peak, decentralizing forces set to work. While Berlin was the center of the political structure, the supremacy of the Nazi party after July 1933 increased the power of local Gauleiters. No matter what the official decisions of the Cabinet and the ministries, the Nazi party apparatus found ways of diverting funds. An aggressive Gauleiter such as Erich Koch in East Prussia could use his ties to Göring to tap enormous resources and drive down unemployment. Duisburg and Frankfurt also had success stories, but other Gauleiters clashed with each other and the remnants of state authorities over the use of funds.[46]

In December 1933, Hitler's economic adviser Gottfried Feder noted that most of the job-creation money had still not been spent. Only 77% of the Papen program's RM182 million, 55% of the Gereke program's RM600 million, and 4% of the Reinhardt program's RM1 billion had been spent. That still amounts to RM510 million, far more than anything spent in the Brüning years and comparable to the Luther/Reinhold program of 1926. From January 1933 to January 1934, the unemployment rolls decreased by 2.25 million. Depending on how one measures unemployment, that is a reduction of between one-quarter and one-half of the Depression's losses. Angus Maddison suggests that the

---

44. *Regierung Hitler*, Doc. #212, p. 746. Silverman, *Hitler*, pp. 154-156.

45. Hans-Peter Schwarz, *Konrad Adenauer: A German Politician and Statesman in a Period of War, Revolution, and Reconstruction* (Providence, RI, 1995), vol. 1, p. 236. *Regierung Hitler*, Docs. #212, p. 745; #213, p. 761. James, *Slump*, p. 107.

46. Silverman, *Hitler*, pp. 70-76, 131-132.

economy grew by 10.45% in real terms in 1933 and made up one-third of its losses since 1929.  The British devaluation and cut in interest rates gave the Germans greater freedom to lower their rates.  The end of a deliberate policy of deflation brought real interest rates to their lowest level since early 1929. One may attribute the upswing to a natural cycle, positive monetary and fiscal policies, and the psychological boost of a stable government willing to stimulate the economy.[47]

As FY33 ended, the usual end-of-budget-year crisis was absent.  Tax revenue had kept pace with estimates.  Since most of the second Reinhardt program would be spent in FY34, there was little to worry about.  The 1933 deficit looked like it would come in at RM350 million, a mere drop in the bucket after the previous years.  There would be a separate deficit for the unemployment programs of RM150 to 200 million.  It would leave a total running deficit of RM2,100 million, not too different from the year before.  The Nazi regime had used extraordinary measures to keep the deficit under control and cheat its creditors.  It capped interest rates on regular loans at 6%, and on agricultural loans at 4.5%.  It converted RM2.8 billion in short-term debt to a 4% five-year loan in September 1933.[48]

As the unemployment picture steadily brightened, discussion began on further job-creation programs.  The officials of several departments and debt-ridden public corporations were eager to see the job creation end.  Even Labor Minister Seldte conceded by January 1934 that the job market no longer justified a major construction program, but he tried to argue that the Reich still needed suburban developments, single-family houses, and urban renewal.  Some called for a program similar to the Brauns/Reinhold housing plan of 1926, fueled by another RM200 million temporary credit.  Krosigk's first draft of the FY34 budget kept the income estimate identical to 1933.  However, he estimated there would be RM2,240 million more in spending, including RM450 million for the second Reinhardt program, RM470 million for the army and navy, and RM10 million for the Luftwaffe.  These figures did not include RM600 million for "special" military spending or RM500 million for apartment construction.  The Finance Minister proposed capping spending for the Sturmabteilung (SA), paramilitary training, and the job service, and reclassified housing repair to take it out of the ordinary budget.  To savings of RM1,140 million, he added RM790 million more in revenue.  These measures would leave an official deficit of RM300 million.  Warming to the art of budget gimmickry, the Finance Minister decided to cover this by raising the estimates of tax revenue again.  He

47.  Ibid., p. 221-228.  Overy, pp. 52-54.  Maddison, pp. 180-181.

48. *Regierung Hitler*, Doc. #304, pp. 1136-1140. Barkai, p. 204. Silverman, *Hitler*, p. 122.  James, *Slump*, p. 107.

estimated that the unemployment office would have a surplus of RM150 million as unemployment would fall to 2.2 million on average.[49]

Various offices and Nazi party organizations were now writing the budget, rather than open Cabinet meetings.  They ignored many proposed savings of the Finance Minister, and the military demanded more money.  When the Cabinet met to discuss the 1934 budget, the Labor Ministry had lost.  It could only build temporary apartments for the most desperate states.  The Labor Ministry protested that in 1933, there had been 320,000 new households created, many out of divorces.  Only 180,000 new dwellings had been built to meet that demand and the demand from the Brüning years.  Krosigk said the Ministry would have to try its luck at issuing bonds if it wanted additional funds because the official deficit had risen to RM900 million.  Along with the budget came a variety of changes in debt management.  A 1909 law required retirement of some national debt each year.  The government amended this to match the scheduled redemption of Treasury transfers by the budget and sinking fund payments.  It further reduced transfers to the states.  The Finance Ministry would guarantee all loans to the autobahns.  The law also compelled the investment of dividends into Reich bonds.[50]

The budget of 1934 marked a turning point.  The regular functions of government became increasingly less important.  Hitler, his cronies, and the Reich commissars made decisions.  The idea of a government-controlled central budget that gave an accurate account of revenue and spending became an illusion.  The actual 1934 budget for the army and navy ended up reaching RM1,310.5 million while the Luftwaffe consumed RM643 million.  The "military budget" ended up being whatever Krosigk and Schacht negotiated with the leaders of the military, without reference to the rest of the budget, tax revenue, or fiscal policy.  The idea of a "budget" had become superfluous.  All that remained was devising the credit to fund the spending.  The Reinhold policy had taught officials how deficit spending could serve the budget.  Now the budget was a mere cover for the credit policies.  Credit could have saved democracy, but now it served a dictatorship.[51]

It was clear by mid-1934 that the economic crisis had been resolved. Unfortunately, Germany had stabilized its political system with homicidal maniacs at the helm.

---

49. *Regierung Hitler*, Docs. #279, pp. 1054-1060; #293, pp. 1095-1099; #304, pp. 1136-1142.

50. Ibid., Docs. #312, pp. 1171-1174; #321, pp. 1203-1207. Barkai, p. 196.

51. *Regierung Hitler*, Doc. #304, p. 1139. Krosigk, p. 261.

**Table 8.1**

**Repayment of the Job-Creation Programs (in millions of Reichsmarks)**

|  | FY34 | FY35 | FY36 | FY37 | FY38 | TOTAL |
|---|---|---|---|---|---|---|
| 1.Papen Program | 190 | 55 |  |  |  | 245 |
| 2.Gereke(Immediate) Program |  |  |  |  |  |  |
| A.Discount Redemption | 53 | 137 | 137 | 137 | 137 | 601 |
| B.Associated Costs | 28 | 25 | 17 | 8 | 1 | 79 |
| 3.Reinhardt Program |  |  |  |  |  |  |
| A.Discount Redemption | 28 | 243 | 243 | 243 | 243 | 1,000 |
| B.Associated Costs | 35 | 40 | 25 | 15 | 15 | 130 |
| 4.Building Repair Law (Second Reinhardt Program) |  |  |  |  |  |  |
| A.Subsidies | 475 |  |  |  |  | 475 |
| B.Interest-Rate Compensation Notes | 58 | 58 | 58 | 58 | 58 | 290 |
| Sub-Total | 867 | 558 | 480 | 461 | 454 | 2,820 |
| Tax Vouchers | 312 | 324 | 336 | 348 | 360 | 1,680 |
| GRAND TOTAL | 1,179 | 882 | 816 | 809 | 814 | 4,500 |

*Source*: *Regierung Hitler*, Doc. #351, p. 1292.

# Aftermath and Assessment

By the middle of 1934, the Nazis had established their financial structure. The once-mighty Dawes bonds were now worthless, classed with the debts of the Russian tsar and the Egyptian khedive. Their best use might be as wallpaper to warn future investors. The regime had dispensed with the parliament, the political parties, and the states of the Reich. Rule by decree was firmly in place. The Cabinet met ever less frequently, and had its last formal meeting in February 1938. The Reich would also rely on borrowing directly or indirectly through institutions. With every Reich financial institution being used as a device for attracting credit, it was a simple step for Schacht to set up the famous Metallurgische Forschungsgesellschaft (Mefo) and issue Mefo bills, which would not mature for five years, to finance rearmament. The Mefo issued RM12 billion in bills between 1934 and 1937. According to Krosigk, Schacht never intended to redeem these bills, but during the war, the Reich did repay almost RM4 billion.[1]

By mid-1934, the economic crisis was abating as unemployment fell by half. The vicious cycle of the Brüning years was now reversed as more Germans had jobs and money to pay taxes and spend on consumer items. Had Hitler kept restraints on spending, the budget soon would have balanced itself. But there would be no restraints. The tripling of the military budget in 1934 was a sign of things to come, and Germany would have to seek ever more credit and juggle its mounting debt in increasingly elaborate contortions. To close the gap, the regime raised the corporate tax rate in October 1934. In 1935, it

---

1. *Regierung Hitler*, p. VIII. IfZ, NL Krosigk, ZS A-20, vol. 3, pp. 50-53, 173; ZS 145, vol. 2, p. 14.

capped the yield on bonds at 4.5%, a modification of the Papen cap that further cheated creditors. The sustained policy of budget deficits would have led to serious trade deficits over time, but the Nazi regime blocked that development temporarily with the introduction of the "New Plan" in September 1934 to restrict imports and regulate trade with other nations.[2]

## AFTERMATH

The government had to finance the deficits. It could not borrow abroad after it defaulted on foreign loans in June 1934, so it initiated a coordinated strategy to place a new domestic loan of RM500 million. A law of December 1934 capped corporate dividends at 6%. This cap, the increased corporate taxes, and the compulsion on business to buy public bonds discouraged enterprises from placing new issues of stocks and bonds on the market. This gave the government a clear shot when it floated a bond issue in 1935. Unlike 1927 and 1929, the sale was a success. Some might say this proved the inclination of the investing class to the NSDAP, but without fair competition, it is not possible to draw any parallels. The military budget would triple between 1934 and 1937, then triple again in the two years before World War II. By 1939, Germany was spending 23% of its NNP on the military. Economic growth averaging 8.2% annually helped balance some of this spending. By 1935, the NNP had exceeded its 1928 peak. According to Krosigk, the government borrowed RM4.1 billion in FY34, RM5.5 billion in 1935, RM10.3 billion in 1936, RM11 billion in 1937, RM17.2 billion in 1938, and RM11.9 billion in 1939. A total of RM60 billion was added to the national debt. James reckons that the Reich had extraordinary spending of RM80 billion. Taxes and revenue from public businesses covered 56%, long-term loans 24%, short-term borrowing 12%, and floating debt at the end of the 1930s covered the rest. Only in 1939 did the private purchase of government debt begin to fall. Then the Reich had to use inflationary methods and print money.[3]

This was the same device that had gotten Germany into trouble during the First World War. Inflationary pressures were mounting. The policy of autarky affected the quality of German goods and limited the ability of consumers to buy goods. German reserves, which had been of such great concern in 1931, plummeted below RM395 million in 1933 and below RM100 million by the summer of 1934, leading to the effective default on the Dawes bonds. James estimates that only a 50-70% devaluation of the currency could

2. Barkai, pp. 185, 204. James, *Slump*, p. 416.

3. James, *Slump*, pp. 372-377, 416. Jackson Spielvogel, *Hitler and Nazi Germany: A History* (Englewood Cliffs, NJ: Prentice Hall, 1988), p. 92. Maier, *Stability*, pp. 102-105. Cohn in Komlos and Eddie, p. 263. IfZ, NL Krosigk, ZS 145, vol. 2, p. 14.

have led to a return of free exchange. After 1934, the government stopped the flow by using aggressive trade policy. Many states of southeastern Europe had repudiated all or part of their debts and suffered trade sanctions on top of the protectionism of the industrial powers. Germany signed bilateral agreements with these states and served as an export outlet. The price was steep as they were forced to accept a large volume of German goods. Trade volume remained well below its 1929 peak. The government was slowly preparing for the future by repurchasing the defaulted bonds, which now were worth only one-third of their face value. By 1936, 35% of the dollar-denominated bonds were back in German hands.[4]

The "New Plan" had difficulties within a year, and Göring replaced it with his "Four-Year Plan" of August 1936. The Nazis claimed their program would solve the food and fuel problems within eighteen months, called for full mobilization of economic strength, and threatened nationalization. By 1938, it was clear the Plan was failing. James sees the Nazi recovery as limited only to employment. The Nazis merely transferred distributional conflicts and structural problems to other areas. One might see the shift from state power to Gauleiter power as symptomatic. In his view, there was no solution until Allied bombers reduced German society to rubble. It is very difficult to ascertain whether there was a brewing political crisis or not in Germany in the year before the outbreak of war. The euphoria over economic recovery and the repudiation of Versailles was fading, and there were complaints as hidden inflationary pressures began to affect the quality of life. There were no cheering throngs as there had been in August of 1914. The war did sweep doubts under the rug for a few years; had war not come, perhaps the Nazi regime would have faced a serious economic and political crisis in 1940 and 1941.

This thesis needs much more research, but it could help explain a paradox that has long puzzled historians. The Four-Year Plan and other schemes of military preparation would not fully rearm Germany until the early or mid-1940s. Yet Hitler, knowing this, was clearly spoiling for war in September 1938 and bitterly disappointed when it did not come. Did economics, rather than international politics or Hitler's medical problems, account for the timing of the war? Tim Mason drew a parallel between 1914 and 1939. He suggested that the annexations of 1938-39 brought temporary relief to an overheating economy by adding more resources, but Hitler's diplomatic miscalculations led to war in 1939. Mason also denied that the Nazi regime had popular support. He felt that only repression kept the public will down, and as discontent grew in 1938-39, it would have been impossible to maintain that

---

4. James, *Slump*, pp. 394-396. Philip Friedman, "The Welfare Costs of Bilateralism: German-Hungarian Trade, 1933-1938," in Komlos and Eddie, pp. 287-294. Overy, p. 216. Adam Klug, "The Economics of Buying Back German Debt in the 1930s," in Komlos and Eddie, pp. 299-305.

much repression until 1943.  Mason finally concluded that this crisis was a factor, but not the main cause of the war.  Richard Overy found no sense of "crisis" in the government in 1938-39.  Only exiles, the British, and some German conservatives described a crisis at the time and their descriptions were imprecise.  The British and French were suffering more of an economic crisis that might have spurred them to war, not the Germans.  Germany faced hard choices over foreign currency and wage inflation, but there are always hard choices.  Overy's points are well taken.  If there is a parallel to the time before 1914, then 1939 was a point where some problems were just setting in.  It is as if war had broken out in 1906, done almost entirely from diplomatic and military motives.[5]

The war enabled Hitler, Todt, and Albert Speer to demand extraordinary measures, but in 1944, the wheels came off the Nazi economy.  Krosigk proposed raising taxes to pay for the expenses of the war on three occasions, but did not succeed.  As the old bonds came due, they were rolled over at a 3% interest rate.  Once the war broke out, the Reich declared an "interest moratorium" and avoided payment.  Unlike World War I, there was no point where the Reich just gave up and ran the war on printed money.  Krosigk estimated that the first year of the war was 40% covered by taxes and the last year was 30% covered.  The cumulative effect was staggering: the Finance Minister estimated that by May 1945, the long-term debt of the Reich was RM150 billion with another RM150 billion of short-term Treasury bills and RM100 billion in Reich-Treasury Exchange bills outstanding.  The government pumped RM200-300 million more notes into circulation each month.  The economic collapse witnessed by the occupation troops did not begin with the Reich's surrender; barter and the use of cigarettes as currency had become common practice months before.[6]

Schacht had failed to support Krosigk on holding the fiscal line against the autobahns but continued to warn against excessive spending.  Göring soon overshadowed him.  He resigned as Economics Minister at the end of 1937 and left the Reichsbank in 1939.  His carefully cultivated reputation as the "old wizard" backfired on him.  Many believed (and a few still believe) that he was the "architect" of the Nazi economy.  He was brought before the War Crimes Tribunal on the charge that he had financed the Nazi war machine.  To Krosigk's astonishment, Schacht explained that he had only ever supported peaceful and defensive rearmament and did not have a clue that offensive action might be in the cards.[7]  The tribunal acquitted him and he went on to have a career advising dictators in Indonesia, Egypt, and the Philippines.

---

5.  James, *Slump*, pp. 418-419.  Tim Mason, *Nazism, Fascism, and the Working Class* (Cambridge, 1995), pp. 104-128.  Overy, pp. 205-232.

6.  IfZ, NL Krosigk, ZS A-20, vol. 2, pp. 198-211.

7.  Weitz, pp. 315-318.

Schwerin von Krosigk was left holding the bag. He remained Finance Minister until the end of the war. Krosigk could make a case that he had thought Hitler's financial schemes dangerous and ruinous, but he had stayed until the end. He was tried in the "Wilhelmstrasse" phase of the war crimes trials. The tribunal convicted him of war crimes, crimes against humanity, plunder, and spoliation. He was sentenced to ten years in prison, but the sentence was reduced to time served and he left prison in January 1951.[8]

Popitz, the eternal schemer, did not fare as well as Krosigk and Schacht. He worked closely with a group that warned that Hitler's reckless diplomacy would lead to a world war whose costs would dwarf those of the first war. Germany could not possibly support such a burden. Popitz helped draft plans for a new unitary regime to replace Hitler and dissolve the Nazi party. He continually talked about leaving the government, but stayed until he was arrested in 1944. On February 2, 1945, Popitz was executed.[9]

Heinrich Brüning, after ruining the economy, caving in to the Nazis, and voting for the Enabling Act, fled the country in 1934. He received a job teaching at Harvard University, but yearned to return to Germany and resume his leadership. He returned after the war with these goals in mind, but Adenauer and others informed him that memories of the "Hunger Chancellor" still lingered and his services would not be required.[10]

Parker Gilbert had tried to move German finance into a modern structure of publicly held debt. His role as overlord of the Dawes Plan blinded many Germans to his good intentions and vital protection he had afforded Germany in the 1920s. Stresemann succeeded in eliminating the position of Agent-General for Reparation Payments from the Young Plan, and Gilbert had gone home in 1930, just before the fiscal apocalypse. He joined the Morgan concern in 1931 and died in February 1938 of heart and kidney failure, aged forty-five. Many said he had worked himself to death.[11]

Peter Reinhold had blazed the way with deficit financing in 1926, imitated by some and blamed by others in the years thereafter. Had Müller accepted the plan of Reinhold and the Budget Committee on March 11, 1930, much horror might have been averted. After Hitler's takeover, he went to Austria and continued to run a business. He took up his old profession as historian and wrote an admiring biography of Maria Theresa of Austria. After

---

8. U.S. Government Printing Office. *Trials of War Criminals before the Nuremberg Military Tribunals under Control Council Law #10* (Washington, DC, 1949), vol. XIV, p. 1004.

9. Theodore S. Hamerow, *On the Road to the Wolf's Lair* (Cambridge, MA, 1997), p. 254. Peter Hoffmann, *German Resistance to Hitler* (Cambridge, MA, 1988), pp. 68-69.

10. Schwarz, pp. 452-453.

11. Chernow, pp. 420-421.

the war, he used some of his old Weimar contacts to secure transit for himself and his son to try to resurrect the businesses.[12]  He died on Capri in 1955.

## ASSESSMENT

This work has focused on three recurrent themes in budget politics from 1912 to 1934.  The first theme was the centralization of the budget.  The Reich did not overcome the resistance of the states until after 1918.  They fought Erzberger's plan to shift most tax revenue to the Reich, and the states and the Reich did not reach a shaky financial compromise until 1925.  In the Depression, Brüning used decree powers to cut back the transfers to the states with catastrophic results.  Not only were the states and localities now burdened by a mountain of debt, but his move pushed states that would have remained financially healthy, such as Prussia, over the edge.  Prussia had to respond by cutting its police budget, among other things, which enabled the Nazis and Communists to run riot through the streets.  The Reich took over Prussia in July 1932, and the other states succumbed by degrees until there was no independence from the Reich.  The Reich ordered states and cities to avoid loans.[13]

The second theme was the control of deficit spending.  Germany did not have the financial instruments in 1914 to finance a peacetime or wartime budget.  For two years, it kept the war going by selling bonds and other credits, but it gave up in the middle of 1916 and funded the rest of the war with printed money.  The new Republic never had a chance to get over this legacy.  Had the Reichstag taken firm and timely action before Wirth resigned in November 1922, perhaps the inflation could have been tamed.  The maladroit administration of Cuno caused the final meltdown.  In contrast, the Luther/Reinhold deficit policy of 1926 was done in a measured and cautious manner.  It relied primarily on two forms of debt: the increased credit authorization from the Reichsbank and the issue of RM500 million in long-term bonds.  However, Germany missed an opportunity from 1925 to 1929.  The government should have begun by selling short-term debt to the public that it could easily repay and then gradually work its way up to long-term debt.  After the inflation, the investing community in Germany was understandably wary.  Reinhold and Köhler did not get into serious fiscal trouble, though one can question the spending on the civil service.  Hilferding panicked when deficits appeared.  Rather than explore a full range of short- and long-term credit, the Socialist supported deep spending cuts and sharp tax increases, repeated Reinhold's error on the long-term bond, then built a mountain of short-term debt from private institutions.

Brüning stumbled through two years of illusions, believing that a balanced budget could end the Depression, and insisted that ever more sacrifice

---

12.  BAK NL Dietrich, vol. 581, p. 62.
13.  James, *Slump*, p. 372.

was necessary. The economic crisis turned into a political one. Brüning chose a path to balancing the budget he knew did not command a majority, then forced it through by decree despite Reichsbank President Luther's pleas not to take that action. When the Reichstag overrode the decree, he compounded his foolishness by calling for new elections without thinking through the ramifications. Brüning and Dietrich met the Depression with deflation and dictatorship. Stingy fiscal policy combined with real interest rates well over 15% made the Depression into a cataclysm. In the spring of 1932, to complete the fiasco, Brüning had to admit that he had run up RM1.3 billion in debt anyway. The Papen regime recognized that fighting unemployment had to take top priority. Papen financed his job creation largely though vouchers and loans from the Öffa. Schleicher accelerated this policy, and Hitler squeezed every institution even more and created a new one, the Mefo, to finance his expansion. The Nazi regime drew on capital by threats and terror. In the Four-Year Plan, there was the explicit threat of possible nationalization in the future. The 1934 Credit Law placed savings banks under central control. In that year, mortgages, individuals, and local authorities constituted 63% of savings banks' credits. By 1939, this had fallen to 45%, and by 1944 it was down to 10% as the regime looted assets to buy bonds. The idea that investors and businesses welcomed Hitler and provided him with capital they would not give previous regimes is probably misguided: Hitler simply took the money or terrified them into handing money over. Germany had problems selling its bonds domestically all the way back to 1906. Only during the euphoria of the first twenty months of World War I did those bonds sell well. It is still remarkable that Germany financed rapid expansion of spending and then World War II without giving in to the printing press, as the Kaiser had. By Krosigk's estimate, only 25% of the total debt was in Treasury transfers at the national banks. The rest was debt that someone had accepted for cash.[14]

   The third theme I have stressed in this work is that the mid-1920s was a period of genuine stability between two distinct crises. The Twelve-Year Crisis began with the confluence of the international, monetary, and fiscal crises. The political crisis of 1912 served as a catalyst. Each of these four crises continued to interact with one another until 1924. The currency reform solved the monetary crisis, the tax decrees solved the fiscal crisis, the Dawes Plan solved the international crisis, and the passage of the Dawes Plan and the grudging moderation of the DNVP solved the political crisis. The second crisis began around 1927 with a fall in farm prices, which had not been a significant factor in the Twelve-Year Crisis at all. It soon spread to the industrial sector in 1928-29 as a deflationary crisis. This was the exact opposite of the fiscal and monetary crisis of the first round. The only relationship between the two is that

---

   14. Thomes in Cassis et al., p. 155. IfZ, NL Krosigk, ZS A-20, vol. 2, pp. 198-211.

some people who remembered the first crisis were slow to act against deflation, but the record shows very little of that fear at the highest levels in the first part of the Depression. The inflation fear did not set in until mid-1931, when the banking crisis and the withdrawal of foreign credits stirred memories of 1923. Heinrich Brüning almost singlehandedly turned this economic crisis into a full-blown political crisis with his foolish insistence on deflation and his dissolution of the Reichstag when he did not get his way. As Hertz-Eichenrode demonstrated conclusively, Brüning's economic view had nothing to do with forced circumstances of 1930-32; he had always believed in deflation and had bitterly attacked Reinhold's stimulus program of 1926. It was never expedience, it was fanatical belief. Without the Depression, none of Germany's lingering problems, from religion and class to the revaluation issue, would have brought democracy down.

Ten weeks after Germany's surrender in 1945, Krosigk asked another former Nationalist what had gone wrong. In the mid-1920s, it seemed that the DNVP was poised to take over leadership of the rightist groups as a conservative social party. Had the better elements in the party prevailed, the Nationalists might have achieved this, shaken off Versailles, and perhaps even restored a Hohenzollern. However, many voters turned against Westarp for his failure to win full revaluation, as he had promised during the December 1924 campaign. Krosigk noted that the revaluation movement weakened the DNVP and destroyed the last hope of the monarchists.[15] The Nationalists also failed to deliver sufficiently high agricultural tariffs and then turned to Alfred Hugenberg, who was completely unsuitable as leader. A strong Nationalist party would always block the advance of the Nazi party. When Hugenberg destroyed the DNVP, the Nazis could appropriate its message of conservative social policy and high tariffs and ride that message to victory.

There have been close examinations and counterfactual arguments presented in Germany's case during the Depression. Clearly one key development occurred in late 1927 when the system of long-term foreign credits cracked. This had been a bountiful and easy source of capital in the wake of the Dawes Plan and had helped stabilize the Weimar system. Heinrich Köhler did his utmost to alienate Parker Gilbert, the keystone to the credit flow. The second Prussian loan of 1927 and Köhler's mulish determination to bloat the salaries of the civil servants turned the American into an enemy and the long-term foreign credits trickled to a halt. This would make things extremely difficult for the Germans, but it did not doom them.

I have argued that from 1929 to 1932, several viable alternatives existed that the Weimar leaders knew about and should have used to avert the dictatorship that fell upon Germany and the horror that followed. First, one must understand the true picture of fiscal policy from year to year in the last

---

15. IfZ, NL Krosigk, ZS 145, vol. 4, p. 4.

part of Weimar.  Cohn has calculated a full employment budget to examine the effect of fiscal policy, and the results are startling.  As a percentage of Net National Product, the budget of 1927 ranged from a deficit of 0.2% to a surplus of 1.8%, depending on whose budget data you follow.  FY28 ranged from a 0.3% deficit to a 1% surplus.  Starting in 1929, all the figures move into surplus: from 2.1% to 3.1% in FY29, from 3% to 4% in FY30, from 4.9% to 8.1% in FY31, and 6.1% to 8.3% in FY32.  Using this analysis of a full-employment budget, there was not a budget deficit pumping money into the economy until 1933 or 1936.[16]  The advantage of this method is that it shows how much money was being taken out of the economy during the Brüning years in particular.  When one adds to this real interest rates above 20%, it is small wonder millions were thrown out of work, further worsening the budget.  The move into surplus occurred before Brüning's Chancellorship.  The socialist government, guided by obsolete economic principles, supported heavy budget cuts and tax increases that alienated its base of support.  It is no surprise that the Communists gained quickly with such a failure of leftist leadership.

Had Reinhold and Köhler established a tradition of rotating short-term bills marketed to the public, as Parker Gilbert urged in his reports, it would have been easy to get the government through the periodic cash crises that racked it.  Without a tradition, it would have been more difficult, but Müller probably had a majority to gain authority from the Reichstag for treasury transfers and an issue of bills sufficient to cover the short-term cash flow.  This alone might have given him, Hilferding, and Popitz the breathing room to enact the tax-cut package that would have been a decent stimulus for the German economy in 1930.  When things worsened in March 1930 and a new budget was due, the SPD did not face a stark choice between raising the unemployment premium or cutting working-class benefits, as has often been depicted.  The People's party probably would have bolted the coalition anyway, but the Bavarians were willing to remain as long as there was no talk of the beer tax.  The package proposed by Reinhold and other members of the Budget Committee was critical in this regard: it would command Social Democratic, Democratic, Catholic, and Bavarian support, and get the government over the hump.  There is no explanation about why Müller did not forward this proposal to the Cabinet.  Had it and the Reichstag adopted this budget, the DVP would have resigned, but the government would have held on for at least another six months.

Many raise the issue of reparations at this point.  They argue that no German government wanted to borrow much because it would serve the politically unpopular end of keeping the flow of reparations going.  But there was little or no outcry at the Reinhold or Hilferding loans.  The Müller government held a majority of the seats elected in 1928 on an explicit policy of fulfillment, whatever the leaders felt in private.  Furthermore, the government

---

16.  Cohn in Komlos and Eddie, pp. 280-281.

did not have to face the voters again until 1932.  It is probably too much to hope that people would credit the Müller government for its success in the Hague Conference in reducing the level of reparations, but the Reichstag did not bring the government down in May 1929 when it asked for long-term loans.  It would not have brought the Cabinet down then or in March 1930 for requesting short-term credit authorizations.  The bigger problem was Schacht, but had the government survived to April, it could have worked with the more accommodating Hans Luther.

A budget passed by the Müller government and the democratic Reichstag in March 1930 would mean no uncertainty, delay, and raising of interest rates; no Brüning and his deflationary budget; no decree; and, most important, no elections of September 1930.  It is almost certain that Müller would have faced another cash crisis in September, but without the Nazi gain at the polls, it could have arranged a short-term foreign credit, probably on superior terms to the actual Lee, Higginson loan.  The 1931 budget debate would have been very difficult as the Depression worsened, but solid fiscal policy would have made it less severe than the one Brüning faced.  To counteract the effects of the Depression, the government would have needed some RM4 billion of credit authority to counteract the Depression's effects.  To make matters worse, Müller died in early 1931, so a new Chancellor would have to be found.  Brüning was obviously temperamentally unsuitable: a good leader like Otto Braun would have been preferable.  If the Weimar Coalition plus the Bavarians could have survived this far as a government, perhaps it could have gained another billion in short-term foreign credits (some feelers were extended to Brüning at this time), another billion in domestic credits, and the other two billion would simply have to be uncovered.  Under law the Reich could leave a budget deficit uncovered for two years.  The continued presence of the Bavarians would probably have warded off more draconian measures such as compelling banks to accept Reich bills and bonds.

The main objection for this course would be its effect on the German balance of payments.  I would not dispute that an effective deficit of RM4 billion added to the debt would have a very deleterious effect.  The budget of 1926 sent the trade balance into deficit, and this would probably have happened again.  Capital would have flowed out of Germany.  However, I refuse to believe that the exodus of capital from this model would have been worse than the catastrophe of 1931 when Nazi agitation, foreign policy bungling by Brüning and Curtius, and currency uncertainty led to a massive withdrawal of foreign credits.  A stronger Prussian police force not suffering from budget cuts would have kept the Nazis on a tighter leash.  Even if Brüning had taken power in March 1931 and instituted austerity, it would have been one year less of the "Hunger Chancellor," and Germany would never have reached the terrible depths it did reach nor would it have resorted to the terrible political choice.

Cohn's estimates for the 1932 budget show that Germany would need another RM3-4 billion deficit to counteract the Depression's effects, but had the government stimulated the economy in 1931, that figure would be much smaller. If the government of 1928 had made four full years, nursing itself along as the Braun government did in Prussia, it would have to face the voters in May 1932. It is likely that the results would have been not too different from the September 1930 or May 1924 Reichstag elections: a sharp rise in the Nazi and Communist votes making governing difficult if not impossible. The time lapse between September 1930 and May 1932 would have made all the difference in the world. The economy was bottoming out, and another two years of stumbling through by any democratic regime would have led to better times and a stable election in 1934 that could have cemented democracy.

The final objection that critics of the above scenario might lodge is that the German government officials lacked the economic sophistication to carry out the above program. Of all the charges, this one is the most false. As I have explained, continental economic theory, especially German economic theory, had always moved along different paths than Anglo-American economic theory. In particular, the English and American economists accepted the paramountcy of Say's Law, stating (roughly) that supply creates its own demand. The conservatives argued during the Depression that stimulus would simply be swallowed up and would not increase marginal demand that could spur the economy. The Germans operated under no restraints and under the guidance of Luther and Reinhold in 1926 had perfectly executed a countercyclical economic policy. Many Germans knew precisely how to end the Depression. It was simply a matter of getting the right people into the right positions.

This counterfactual exercise and the actual recovery of 1933-34 beg another question: what underlay the recovery? The figures calculated by Cohn show that in FY33, the fiscal policy improved, but was still on the surplus side, still taking money out of the economy instead of providing a stimulus. Harold James is probably correct in attributing recovery at this point to changes in monetary policy, but that change really amounted to ending the deliberate deflation of Brüning, which caused real interest rates to fall from 20% to about 10%. In FY34, the Reich applied far more stimulus. While Cohn's calculations are not in agreement, the balance of the figures suggests that some real fiscal stimulus took place for the first time since Heinrich Köhler's last budget.[17]

None of this answers questions that have bothered many scholars: Why could Papen and then the Nazis embark on a policy of fiscal stimulus funded by credit, while Müller and Brüning could not? When the Nazis continued to apply stimulus after recovery began, why was there no significant inflation beyond the hidden costs covered by price controls? Conservative classical economics that rules out fiscal stimulus in 1929-32 would rule it out for the 1934-39 period as well. I believe that the solution lies in the old historiographical argument about productivity in the Weimar era. On the surface, it is hard to doubt that the

---

17.  Ibid., p. 281.

crucible of the inflation and the rationalization that followed made Germany more productive. I follow Holtfrerich's belief that productivity increases during the Weimar Republic justified rising wages, especially when there is now considerable evidence that the businesses were making very tidy profits. Whether one accepts a growth or stagnation in the productivity of the workforce, it seems indisputable that the productivity of the population grew. In 1910, 63.3% of the total population was of working age. This peaked at 71.1% in 1925 and dipped to 70.5% by 1933. Fewer children and senior citizens generally connote higher productivity. In the working-age cohort, the workforce grew, largely because of greater use of female labor. Employment plus unemployment was 86.3% of the age group in 1895, 90.5% in 1925, and 93.1% in 1933.[18] Thus, the full employment of the Nazi regime was appreciably fuller than that of the Kaiserreich.

Productivity changes often take a long time to filter into the economy. I would theorize that this is exactly what happened in the German case. There was enough productivity gain that inflation averaged about 2% a year from 1925 to 1929.[19] Significant productivity gains did not keep pace with the enormous fiscal stimulus that the Nazis poured in, but it ran close enough that the government could keep the lid on with price controls. World War II brought more crash productivity gains, but not enough to keep the economy from melting down in 1943-44 leading to the cigarette economy described by Krosigk.

The fall of Weimar also demonstrates the problem of corporatism. Charles Maier argued that Italy, France, and Germany all showed degrees of corporatism in the 1920s: industry, labor, and government all coming together. In Italy's case, the government/industry axis became completely dominant. As an alternative to the messiness of democracy, corporatism can be attractive, at least in theory. The German case shows its shortcomings. The combination of the imperial government with the rye and iron alliance was ruptured in the crisis of World War I, when industry and labor found it mutually profitable to work together. After the revolution, industry supported moderate socialist elements for fear of the alternatives. After 1920, the balance shifted back and forth. Industry seemed to regain the upper hand in the period of inflation, but the Reinhold policy showed that there was enough money to go around to satisfy business with tax cuts and labor with modern housing and extended unemployment benefits. Just as it seemed that there could be some rough agreement from the Nationalists to the Social Democrats on the form of government and some of its policies, a group of anticorporatist rebels rose. Many of them were in small groups left behind by prosperity such as farmers' groups and revaluation diehards, but the most prominent was the NSDAP. Even as the Nationalists moved to accept the Republic and various social insurance measures and

---

18. Detlev Peukert, "The Lost Generation," in Evans and Geary, pp. 173-174.
19. Michalka and Niedhart, p. 297.

continue the ban on the Kaiser's return, key elements of their disparate coalition deserted them in the 1928 elections, leading to an internal upheaval and the destruction of the Nationalists. Without DNVP support, the corporate model could not survive.    Industrialists became increasingly hostile and labor increasingly meek during the Depression.    One might say that Papen and Schleicher represent a more Italian model of corporatism.    None of it succeeded. Hitler and his anticorporatist group, opposed to the interests of business and labor, were victorious.

Maier has suggested that the failed corporatism of the 1920s set the stage for the post-1945 paradigm.    Unfortunately, the fading of the memories of the Nazi era has led to the development of a new group of anticorporatist rebels.    In France, the far right National Front threatens the old order of moderate socially minded conservatives and social democrats.    Jörg Haider's Freedom party has influenced the Austrian government.    Even Denmark's equanimity between business and labor has been shaken by the anti-immigrant People's party.    In Germany itself, the far right is stirring from its pits to discomfit the SPD and Christian Democratic Union (CDU).    Corporatism may seem attractive but has limited durability in a democratic system and modern economy.

The story of German fiscal policy from 1912 to 1934 can provide some lessons for today's global economy because it has grown directly out of the experience of the 1920s and 1930s.    Many institutions that undergird the global financial system are either remnants of that time (such as the Bank for International Settlements) or are reactions against the trade and budget policies of the time.    The first lesson is that in a deflationary situation, monetary policy is almost useless.    One must try to lower real interest rates as much as possible. Much of the global turmoil of 1997 and 1998 had its roots in the abnormally high real interest rates maintained by the U.S. Federal Reserve in its hunt for the phantom of inflation.    When one sees prices falling or unemployment growing, one should lower real interest rates (the nominal rate minus inflation) to the lowest point possible without endangering the currency.    This is also wise policy when other countries face that difficulty so you do not get into a beggar-thy-neighbor situation.    All this being said, it is impossible to lower nominal rates below 1% because a negative rate is too difficult to swallow.    If a deflationary spiral sets in, a government or bank is helpless to stop real interest rates from climbing.    The key to avoiding deflation is fiscal policy.    Nations must use fiscal policy to break any hint of a deflationary spiral from setting in, just as governments must use monetary policy when there is a danger of an inflation getting out of control.    The device of "full-employment fiscal policy" is good for setting a real benchmark.    A regime that recommends austerity in the middle of a deflationary spiral is asking for terrible trouble.    Austerity can cause millions of people to suffer and can destabilize the government and allow extremist factions to take control.    They will do far more damage than any free-spending policy.

In emerging democracies especially, one often faces an unpalatable choice among two or more evils. If a lesser evil is in charge, it makes a great deal of sense just to continue aid and assistance, no matter the circumstance. Lenders grew terribly picky about whether Germany was using foreign credits for "productive" or "nonproductive" purposes. When the Nazi regime took over and froze all payment on loans, the creditors lost their money. It would have been far better to shove credits at Müller and Brüning just to keep them afloat even with Brüning's rearmament and nefarious plans to restore the monarchy. Giving aid does not mean one should refrain from criticism. One wants reforms made in countries to help their long-term growth by encouraging productivity. A protectionist trade policy is nearly always counterproductive.

One would hope that the famous case of the fall of Weimar is lesson enough. There are plenty of advisers out there now who are clever about marketing debt, even at very short terms and very small denominations. Most countries now do not have figures of both the stature and the peculiarities of Hjalmar Schacht. There has been a superior international system for extending debt, so that it is not left to the whim of individual countries and bankers. Political leaders may be no smarter than in 1930, so we may soon see the spectacle of a leader reject a budget that can command majority support and plunge the country into chaos. I would remind these leaders, the people who advise them, and the bankers who hesitate to lend, of the slagheap that was Germany in 1945.

On January 4, 1995, the financial papers announced that the Deutsche Bank would exchange the interest-bearing portions of the 1924 and 1930 national loans and the 1926 and 1927 Prussian loans for new German government bonds. These bonds will mature on October 3, 2010, exactly eighty-one years after Stresemann's death.

The Dawes bonds had come home at last.

# Selected Bibliography

## ARCHIVAL SOURCES

### Bundesarchiv Koblenz (BAK)

R 2 (Finance Ministry)
R 43 I (Reichskanzlei)
R 45 II (Deutsche Volkspartei)
R 45 III (Deutsche Demokratische Partei)
NL Hermann Dietrich
NL Otto Gessler
NL Erich Koch-Weser
NL Hans Luther
NL Hermann Pünder
NL Max von Stockhausen

### Bundesarchiv Potsdam (BAP)

R 101 (Reichstag)
R 401 (Vorläufiger Reichswirtschaftsrat)
R 601 (Büro des Reichspräsidents)
R 8034 I (Reichslandbund)
R 8034 II (Reichslandbund-Press-Archiv)
R 8048 (Alldeutscher Verband)

### Historisches Stadtsarchiv (HSA), Köln

NL Wilhelm Marx

### Institut für Zeitgeschichte (IfZ), Munich

NL Lutz Schwerin von Krosigk

### Politisches Archiv (PA), Auswärtiges Amt, Bonn

NL Gustav Stresemann
Büro Reichsminister
Büro des Staatsekretär
Sonderreferat Wirtschaft
Wirtschaft Reparationen

### Preußische Geheime Staatsarchiv (PrStA), Berlin-Dahlem

Rep. 77, Prussian Interior Ministry
Rep. 90, Staatsministrium
Rep. 151, Prussian Finance Ministry

## NEWSPAPERS

*Berliner Tageblatt*
*Germania*
*Kreuzzeitung*
*New York Times*
*Vorwärts*

## DOCUMENT COLLECTIONS

*Akten zur deutschen Auswärtigen Politik (ADAP)* Series B: 1925-33. Göttingen: Vandenhoeck and Rupprecht, 1966-93.
*Documents on British Foreign Policy (DBFP)* 1919-1939, Series IA, vol. 2. London: HMSO, 1968.
Erdmann, Karl-Dietrich and Hans Booms, eds., *Akten der Reichskanzlei. Weimarer Republic.*
    *Das Kabinett Scheidemann. 13. Februar bis 20. Juni 1919.* Edited by Hagen Schulze. Boppard: Harold Boldt Verlag, 1971.
    *Das Kabinett Bauer. 21. Juni 1919 bis 27. März 1920.* Edited by Anton Golecki. Boppard: Harold Boldt Verlag, 1980.
    *Das Kabinett Müller I. 27. März bis 21. Juni 1920.* Edited by Martin Vogt. Boppard: Harold Boldt Verlag, 1971.
    *Das Kabinett Fehrenbach. 25. Juni 1920 bis 4. Mai 1921.* Edited by Peter Wulf. Boppard: Harold Boldt Verlag, 1972.

*Die Kabinette Wirth I und II. 10. Mai bis 26. Oktober 1921. 26. Oktober 1921 bis 22. November 1922.* Edited by Ingrid Schulze-Bidlingmeier. 2 vols. Boppard: Harold Boldt Verlag, 1973.

*Das Kabinett Cuno. 22. November 1922 bis 12. August 1923.* Edited by Karl-Heinz Harbeck. Boppard: Harold Boldt Verlag, 1978.

*Die Kabinette Stresemann I und II. 13. August bis 6. Oktober 1923. 6. Oktober bis 30. November 1923.* Edited by Karl-Dietrich Erdmann and Martin Vogt. 2 vols. Boppard: Harold Boldt Verlag, 1978.

*Die Kabinette Marx I und II. 30. November 1923 bis 3. Juni 1924. 3. Juni 1924 bis 15. Januar 1925.* Edited by Günter Abramowski. 2 vols. Boppard: Harold Boldt Verlag, 1973.

*Die Kabinette Luther I und II. 15. Januar 1925 bis 20. Januar 1926. 20 Januar bis 17. Mai 1926.* Edited by Karl-Heinz Minuth. Boppard: Harold Boldt Verlag, 1977.

*Die Kabinette Marx III und IV. 17. Mai 1926 bis 29. Januar 1927. 29. Januar 1927 bis 28. Juni 1928.* Edited by Günter Abramowski. Boppard: Harold Boldt Verlag, 1987.

*Das Kabinett Müller II. 28. Juni 1928 bis 27. März 1930.* Edited by Martin Vogt. Boppard: Harold Boldt Verlag, 1970.

*Die Kabinette Brüning I und II. 30. März 1930 bis 10. Oktober 1931. 10. Oktober 1931 bis 1. Juni 1932.* Edited by Tilman Koops. Boppard: Harold Boldt Verlag, 1985, 1989.

*Das Kabinett von Papen. 1. Juni bis 3. Dezember 1932.* Edited by Karl-Heinz Minuth. 2 vols. Boppard: Harold Boldt Verlag, 1989.

*Das Kabinett von Schleicher. 3. Dezember 1932 bis 30. Januar 1933.* Edited by Anton Golecki. Boppard: Harold Boldt Verlag, 1986.

*Die Regierung Hitler. 30. Januar 1933 bis 31. August 1934.* Edited by Karl-Heinz Minuth. 2 vols. Boppard: Harold Boldt Verlag, 1983.

Maurer, Ilse, Udo Wengst, and Gerhard Schulz, eds. *Politik und Wirtschaft: Quellen zur Ära Brüning, 1930-1932.* Düsseldorf: Droste, 1980.

Michalka, Wolfgang, and Gottfried Niedhart, eds. *Deutsche Geschichte 1918-1933: Dokumente zur Innen- und Außenpolitik.* Frankfurt: Fischer, 1992.

Morsey, Rudolf, ed. *Die Protokolle der Reichstagsfraktion und des Fraktionsvorstands der deutschen Zentrum Partei, 1926-33.* Mainz: Matthias-Grünewald, 1969.

## PRIMARY SOURCES

Braun, Otto. *Von Weimar zu Hitler.* Hamburg: Hammonia Nord-deutsch Verlagsanstalt, 1949.

Brecht, Arnold. *The Political Education of Arnold Brecht: An Autobiography, 1884-1970.* Princeton: Princeton University Press, 1970.

Brüning, Heinrich. *Memoiren, 1918-1934.* Stuttgart: Deutsche Verlags Anstalt, 1970

Bülow, Bernhard von. *Memoirs of Prince von Bülow.* 3 vols. Translated by Geoffrey Dunlop. Boston: Little, Brown, 1931.

Curtius, Julius. *Sechs Jahre Minister der deutschen Republik.* Heidelberg: Carl Winters Universität, 1948.

Dawes, Charles G. *A Journal of Reparations.* London: Macmillan, 1939.

Feder, Ernst. *Heute sprach ich mit . . . Tagebücher eines Berliner Publizisten 1926-32.* Stuttgart: Deutsche Verlags Anstalt, 1971.

Köhler, Heinrich. *Lebenserinnerungen des Politikers und Staatsmannes, 1878-1949.* Edited by Josef Becker. Stuttgart: Kohlhammer, 1964.

Krosigk, Lutz Schwerin von. *Staatsbankrott. Die Geschichte Finanzpolitik des deutschen Reiches 1920-45.* Göttingen: Musterschmidt, 1974.

Luther, Hans. *Politiker ohne Partei.* Stuttgart: Deutsche Verlags Anstalt, 1960.

Office of the United States Chief on Counsel for Prosecution of Axis Criminality. *Nazi Conspiracy and Aggression.* Washington, DC, 1946.

Papen, Franz von. *Memoirs.* New York: E. P. Dutton, 1953.

Schacht, Hjalmar Horace Greeley. *Confessions of "the Old Wizard."* Boston: Houghton Mifflin, 1956.

Statistischen Reichsamt. *Finanzen und Steuern im In- und Ausland: Ein statistisches Handbuch.* Berlin: Reimar Hobbing, 1930.

Stresemann, Gustav, *Vermächtnis.* 3 vols. Edited by Henry Bernhard. Berlin: Ullstein, 1932.

US Printing Office. *Trials of War Criminals before the Nuremberg Military Tribunals under Control Council Law #10,* vol. XIV. Washington, DC: US Government Printing Office, 1949.

*Verhandlungen des deutsches Reichstags (VdR). Stenographische Berichte* and *Drucksache,* vols. 262-409. Berlin, 1912-28.

*Verhandlungen deutsches Reichrats,* 1926-1930. Berlin, 1926-30.

## SECONDARY SOURCES

Abelshauser, Werner, Anselm Faust, and Dietmar Petzina, eds. *Deutsche Sozialgeschichte: ein historische Lesebuch.* Munich: C. H. Beck, 1985.

Balderston, Theodore. *The Origins and Course of the German Financial Crisis, November 1923 to May 1932.* Berlin: Haude and Spener, 1993.

_____. "The Origins of Economic Instability in Germany 1924-1930: Market Forces versus Economic Policy." *Vierteljahrschrift für Sozial- und Wirtschaftsgeschichte,* 69. Band, Heft 4 (1982), pp. 488-511.

Barkai, Avraham. *Nazi Economics: Ideology, Theory, and Policy.* New Haven: Yale University Press, 1990.

Barkin, Kenneth D. *The Controversy over German Industrialization.* Chicago: University of Chicago, 1970.

Becker, Josef.   "Josef Wirth und die Krise des Zentrum während des IV. Kabinette Marx, Darstellung und Dokumente." *Zeitschrift für die Geschichte des Oberrheins* 109 (1961), pp. 361-482.

Bennett, Edward W.  *Germany and the Diplomacy of the Financial Crisis, 1931*. Cambridge, MA: Harvard University Press, 1962.

Berger-Thimme, Dorothea.  *Wohnungsfrage und Sozialstaat. Untersuchungen zu den Anfängen staatlicher Wohnungspolitik in Deutschland (1873-1918)*. Frankfurt: Peter Lang, 1976.

Bessel, Richard, and E. J. Feuchtwanger, eds.  *Social Change and Political Development in the Weimar Republic*. London: Croon Helm, 1981.

Blaich, Fritz.  *Die Wirtschaftskrise 1925/1926 und die Reichsregierung*. Kallmünz: Michael Lassleben, 1977.

_____ .  *Der Schwarze Freitag: Inflation und Wirtschaftskrise*. Munich: Deutscher Taschenbuch Verlag, 1985.

Borchardt, Knut.  *Perspectives on Modern German Economic History and Policy*. Cambridge: Cambridge University Press, 1991.

Boyle, Andrew.  *Montagu Norman*. London: Cassell, 1967.

Brady, Robert A.  *The Rationalization Movement in German Industry*. New York: Fertig, 1933.

Brandes, Joseph.  *Herbert Hoover and Economic Diplomacy: Department of Commerce Policy, 1921-28*. Pittsburgh: University of Pittsburgh Press, 1962.

Breitman, Richard.  *German Socialism and Weimar Democracy*. Chapel Hill: University of North Carolina Press, 1981.

Bry, Gerhard.  *Wages in Germany*. Ann Arbor: University of Michigan Press, 1960.

Cassis, Youssef, Gerald D. Feldman, and Ulf Olsson, eds.  *The Evolution of Financial Institutions in Twentieth-Century Europe*. Aldershot, UK: Scolar Press, 1995.

Chanady, Atilla.  "The Disintegration of the German National People's Party 1924-1930." *Journal of Modern History* 39 (1967), pp. 65-91.

Chandler, Lester V.  *Benjamin Strong, Central Banker*. Washington, DC: Brookings Institution, 1958.

Chernow, Ron.  *The House of Morgan: An American Banking Dynasty and the Rise of Modern Finance*. New York: Atlantic Monthly Press, 1990.

Childers, Thomas.  *The Nazi Voter: The Social Foundations of Fascism in Germany, 1919-1933*. Chapel Hill: University of North Carolina Press, 1983.

Clay, Henry.  *Lord Norman*. New York: St. Martin's, 1957.

Dieckmann, Hildmarie.  *Johannes Popitz. Entwicklung und Wirksamkeit in der Zeit der Weimarer Republik*. Berlin-Dahlem: Colloquium Verlag, 1960.

Eichengreen, Barry.  *Golden Fetters: The Gold Standard and the Great Depression, 1919-1939*. Oxford: Oxford University Press, 1992.

Erkelenz, Anton, ed. *Zehn Jahre deutsche Republik: Ein Handbuch für republikanische Politik.* Berlin: Zehlendorf Sieben, 1928.

Evans, Ellen Lovell. *The German Center Party, 1870-1933: A Study in Political Catholicism.* Carbondale: Southern Illinois University, 1981.

Evans, Richard and Dick Geary, eds. *The German Unemployed: Experiences and Consequences of Mass Unemployment from the Weimar Republic to the Third Reich.* New York: St. Martin's, 1987.

Eyck, Erich. *A History of the Weimar Republic.* 2 vols. Cambridge, MA: Harvard University Press, 1962-1963.

Falter, Jürgen, Thomas Lindberger, and Siegfried Schumann, eds. *Wahlen und Abstimmungen in der Weimarer Republik, Materialen und Wahlverhalten 1919-1933.* Munich: C. H. Beck, 1986.

Feldman, Gerald D. *Industry, Army, and Labor, 1914-1918.* Princeton: Princeton University Press, 1966.

_____. "Industrialists, Bankers, and the Problem of Unemployment in the Weimar Republic." *Central European History* 25 (1992), no. 1, pp. 75-96.

_____. *The Great Disorder: Politics, Economics, and Society in the German Inflation, 1914-1924.* Oxford: Oxford University Press, 1993.

Feldman, Gerald D., Carl-Ludwig Holtfrerich, Gerhard A. Ritter, and Peter-Christian Witt, eds. *Die Erfahrung der Inflation/The Experience of Inflation.* Berlin: de Gruyter, 1984.

_____, eds. *The Consequences of Inflation/Konsquenzen der Inflation.* Berlin: de Gruyter, 1989.

Feuchtwanger, E. J. *From Weimar to Hitler: Germany, 1918-1933.* Second Edition. New York: St. Martin's, 1993.

Fischer, Fritz. *War of Illusions: German Policies from 1911 to 1914.* New York: Norton, 1975.

François-Poncet, André. *The Fateful Years: Memoirs of a French Ambassador in Berlin, 1931-1938.* New York: Harcourt, Brace, 1949.

Frye, Bruce. *Liberal Democrats in the Weimar Republic.* Carbondale: Southern Illinois University Press, 1985.

Galbraith, John Kenneth. *Money: Whence It Came, Where It Went.* Revised edition. New York: Houghton Mifflin, 1995.

Gates, Robert A. "German Socialism and the Crisis of 1929-33." *Central European History* 7 (1974), pp. 337-350.

Garvy, George. "Keynes and the Economic Activists of Pre-Hitler Germany." *Journal of Political Economy* 83 (1975), pp. 393-398.

Grathwol, Robert. *Stresemann and the DNVP: Reconciliation or Revenge in German Foreign Policy, 1924-1928.* Lawrence: University of Kansas Press, 1980.

Habermas, Jürgen. *The Structural Transformation of the Public Sphere: An Inquiry into a Category of Bourgeois Society.* Reprint edition. Cambridge: Massachusetts Institute of Technology, 1989.

Hallgarten, George, and Joachim Radkow. *Deutsche Industrie und Politik von Bismarck bis in die Gegenwart*. Frankfurt: Europäische Verlagsanstalt, 1974.

Halperin, S. William. *Germany Tried Democracy: A Political History of the Reich from 1918 to 1933*. New York: Norton, 1946.

Hamerow, Theodore S. *On the Road to the Wolf's Lair*. Cambridge, MA: Harvard University Press, 1997.

Hansmeyer, Karl-Heinrich, ed. *Kommunale Finanzpolitik in der Weimarer Republik*. Stuttgart: Kohlhammer, 1973.

Hardach, Gerd. *Weltmarktorientierung und relative Stagnation: Währungspolitik in Deutschland 1924-31*. Berlin: Dunker and Homblot, 1976.

Haungs, Peter. *Reichspräsident und parlamentarische Kabinettsregierung: eine Studie zum Regierungssystem der Weimarer Republik in den Jahren 1924 bis 1929*. Köln: Westdeuscher Verlag, 1968.

Heckart, Beverly. *From Bassermann to Bebel: The Grand Bloc's Quest for Reform in the Kaiserreich, 1900-1914*. New Haven: Yale University Press, 1974.

Hehl, Ulrich von. *Wilhelm Marx 1883-1946. Eine politische Biographie*. Bonn: Matthias-Grünewald, 1987.

Henning, Friedrich-Wilhelm. *Landwirtschaft und ländliche Gesellschaft in Deutschland, vol. 2 1750 bis 1986*. Second edition. Paderborn: Schönigh, 1988.

Hertz-Eichenrode, Dieter. *Wirtschaftskrise und Arbeitsbeschaffen: Konjunkturpolitik 1925/26 und die Grundlagen der Krisenpolitik Brünings*. Frankfurt: Campus Verlag, 1982.

Hoffmann, Peter. *German Resistance to Hitler*. Cambridge, MA: Harvard University Press, 1988.

Hughes, Michael L. *Paying for the German Inflation*. Chapel Hill: University of North Carolina Press, 1988.

James, Harold. *The Reichsbank and Public Finance in Germany 1924-1933: A Study of the Politics of Economics during the Great Depression*. Frankfurt: Fritz Knapp, 1985.

_____. *The German Slump: Politics and Economics 1924-1936*. Oxford: Clarendon Press, 1986.

Jarausch, Konrad H. "The Crisis of German Professionals, 1918-33." *Journal of Contemporary History*, 20 (1985), pp. 379-393.

Jones, Kenneth Paul. "Discord and Collaboration: Choosing an Agent-General for Reparations." *Diplomatic History* 1 (1977), pp. 118-139.

Jones, Larry Eugene. "Inflation, Revaluation, and the Crisis of Middle-Class Parties: A Study in the Dissolution of the German Party System, 1923-28." *Central European History* 12 (1979), pp. 43-68.

_____. *German Liberalism and the Dissolution of the Weimar Party System 1918-1933*. Chapel Hill: University of North Carolina Press, 1988.

Jones, Larry Eugene, and James Retallack, eds. *Elections, Mass Politics, and Social Change in Modern Germany: New Perspectives*. Cambridge: Cambridge University Press, 1992.

Kent, Bruce. *The Spoils of War: The Politics, Economics, and Diplomacy of Reparations, 1918-1932*. Oxford: Clarendon Press, 1989.

Kershaw, Ian, ed. *Weimar: Why Did Democracy Fail?* New York: Weidenfeld and Nicholson, 1990.

Kindleberger, Charles P. *Germany's Persistent Balance-of-Payments Disequilibrium Revisited*. Bloomington: Institute of German Studies, Indiana University, 1976.

_____. *Manias, Panics, and Crashes: A History of Financial Crises*. Revised edition. New York: Basic Books, 1989.

Kohler, Eric Dave. "Otto Braun." Ph.D. diss., Stanford University, 1971.

Komlos, John and Scott Eddie, eds. *Selected Cliometric Studies on German Economic History*. Stuttgart: Franz Steiner Verlag, 1997.

Kroboth, Rudolf. *Die Finanzpolitik des Deutschen Reiches während der Reichskanzlerschaft Bethmann-Hollwegs und die Geld- und Kapitalmarktverhältnisse (1909-1913/14)*. Frankfurt: Peter Lang, 1986.

Krohn, Claus-Dieter. *Stabilisierung und ökonomische Interessen: Die Finanzpolitik des deutschen Reiches, 1923-1927*. Düsseldorf: Bertelsmann, 1974.

Leopold, John. *Alfred Hugenberg. The Radical Nationalist Campaign against the Weimar Republic* (New Haven: Yale University Press, 1977)

Lewis, Cleona. *America's Stake in International Investment*. Washington, DC: Brookings Institution, 1938.

Link, Werner. *Die amerikanische Stabilisierungspolitik in Deutschland*. Düsseldorf: Droste, 1970.

Machlup, Fritz. *International Payments, Debts, and Gold: Collected Essays*. New York: Scribner's, 1964.

Maddison, Angus. *Monitoring the World Economy, 1820-1992*. Paris: OECD, 1995.

Maier, Charles S. *Recasting Bourgeois Europe: Stabilization in France, Germany, and Italy after World War I*. Princeton: Princeton University Press, 1975.

_____. *In Search of Stability: Explorations in Historical Political Economy*. Cambridge: Cambridge University Press, 1987.

Mason, Tim. *Nazism, Fascism, and the Working Class*. Cambridge: Cambridge University Press, 1995.

McKibbon, Ross. "The Myth of the Unemployed: Who did Vote for Hitler?" *The Australian Journal of Politics and History* 15, no.2 (1969), pp. 25-40.

McNeil, William C. *American Money and the Weimar Republic: Economics and Politics on the Eve of the Great Depression*. New York: Columbia University Press, 1985.

Mommsen, Hans. *The Rise and Fall of Weimar Democracy*. Translated by Larry Eugene Jones and Elborg Forster. Chapel Hill: University of North Carolina Press, 1996.

Mommsen, Hans, Dietmar Petzina, Bernd Weisbrod, and Dirk Stegmann, eds. *Industrielles System und politische Entwicklung in der Weimarer Republik*. Düsseldorf: Droste, 1974.

Overy, Richard J. *War and Economy in the Third Reich*. Oxford: Clarendon Press, 1994.

Patch, William L. *Christian Trade Unions in the Weimar Republic*. New Haven: Yale University Press, 1985.

Pease, Neal. *Poland, the United States, and the Stabilization of Europe, 1919-1933*. Oxford: Oxford University Press, 1986.

Peterson, Edward N. *Hjalmar Schacht: For and Against Hitler: A Political-Economic Study of Germany, 1923-1945*. Boston: Christopher Publishing House, 1954.

Plehwe, Friedrich-Karl von. *Reichskanzler Kurt von Schleicher: Weimars letzte Chance gegen Hitler*. Frankfurt: Ullstein, 1983.

Pohl, Karl Heinrich. *Weimars Wirtschaft und die Aussenpolitik der Republik 1924-1926: vom Dawes Plan zum internationalen Eisenpakt*. Düsseldorf: Droste, 1979.

Pruessen, Ronald W. *John Foster Dulles: The Road to Power*. New York: Free Press, 1982.

Schuker, Stephen A. *The End of French Predominance in Europe: The Financial Crisis of 1924 and the Adoption of the Dawes Plan*. Chapel Hill: University of North Carolina Press, 1976.

_____. *American "Reparations" to Germany, 1919-33: Implications for the Third-World Debt Crisis*. Princeton: Department of Economics, Princeton University, 1988.

Schwarz, Hans-Peter. *Konrad Adenauer: A German Politician and Statesman in a Period of War, Revolution, and Reconstruction*. Vol. 1. Providence, RI: Berghahn Books, 1995.

Silverman, Dan P. "A Pledge Unredeemed: The Housing Crisis in Weimar Germany." *Central European History*, vol. 3 (1970), pp. 112-139.

_____. *Reconstructing Europe after the Great War*. Cambridge: Harvard University Press, 1982.

_____. *Hitler's Economy: Nazi Work Creation Programs, 1933-1936*. Cambridge: Harvard University Press, 1998.

Smaldone, William. *Rudolf Hilferding: The Tragedy of a German Social Democrat*. DeKalb: Northern Illinois University Press, 1998.

Spoerer, Mark. *Von Scheingewinnen zum Rüstungsboom: Die Eigenkapitalrentabilität der deutschen Industrieaktiengesellschaften 1925-1941*. Stuttgart: Franz Steiner Verlag, 1996.

Stürmer, Michael. *Koalition und Opposition in der Weimarer Republik, 1924-28*. Düsseldorf: Droste, 1967.

Ten Cate, Johannes Houwink . "Hjalmar Schacht als Reparationspolitiker 1926-1930." *Vierteljahrschrift für Sozial- und Wirtschaftsgeschichte*, 74, no. 2, (1987), pp. 186-228.

Voth, Hans-Joachim.   "Wages, Investment, and the Fate of the Weimar Republic." *German History* 11 (1993), No. 3, pp. 265-292.

Wandel, Eckhard. *Die Bedeutung der Vereinigten Staaten von Amerika für das deutsche Reparationsproblem 1924-1929.* Tübingen: Mohr, 1971.

Wehler, Hans-Ulrich, ed.   *Sozialgeschichte Heute: Festschrift für Hans Rosenberg zum 70. Geburtstag.* Göttingen: Vandenhoeck und Rupprecht, 1974.

Weisbrod, Bernd.   "Economic Power and Political Stability Reconsidered: Heavy Industry in Weimar Germany." *Social History* (May 1979), pp. 242-258.

Weitz, John. *Hitler's Banker: Hjalmar Horace Greeley Schacht.* Boston: Little, Brown, 1997.

Williamson, John G.   *Karl Helfferich: Economist, Financier, Politician.* Princeton: Princeton University Press, 1971.

Winkler, Heinrich August.   *Der Weg in die Katastrophe: Arbeiter und Arbeiterbewegung in der Weimarer Republik 1930 bis 1933.* Bonn: J. H. W. Dietz, 1990.

Witt, Peter-Christian. *Finanzpolitik des deutschen Reiches von 1903 bis 1913: Eine Studie zur Innenpolitik des wilhelminischen Deutschland.* Lübeck: Matthieson, 1970.

Wolfe, Martin. *The French Franc between the Wars, 1919-1939.* New York: Columbia University Press, 1951.

# Index